# Development Among Africa's Migratory Pastoralists

**Frontispiece. Dinka herdsman removing ticks and grooming common white cattle with cattle dung ash.** (Source: Sarah Errington © 1982 Time-Life Books[Nederlands] B.V., from *Peoples of the Wild--Warriors of the White Nile*.)

# DEVELOPMENT AMONG AFRICA'S MIGRATORY PASTORALISTS

*Aggrey Ayuen Majok*
*Calvin W. Schwabe*

GN
645
.M28
1996

**BERGIN & GARVEY**
Westport, Connecticut • London

**Library of Congress Cataloging-in-Publication Data**

Majok, Aggrey Ayuen.
  Development among Africa's migratory pastoralists / Aggrey Ayuen
Majok, Calvin W. Schwabe.
    p.    cm.
  Includes bibliographical references (p.     ) and index.
  ISBN 0–89789–477–4 (alk. paper)
    1. Nomads—Africa.  2. Herders—Africa.  3. Rural development—
Africa.  4. Veterinary services—Africa.  I. Schwabe, Calvin W.
II. Title.
  GN645.M28      1996
  305.8′00954—dc20           96–10374

British Library Cataloguing in Publication Data is available.

Library of Congress Catalog Card Number: 96–10374
ISBN: 0–89789–477–4

First published in 1996

Bergin & Garvey, 88 Post Road West, Westport, CT 06881
An imprint of Greenwood Publishing Group, Inc.


Printed in the United States of America

The paper used in this book complies with the
Permanent Paper Standard issued by the National
Information Standards Organization (Z39.48–1984).

10 9 8 7 6 5 4 3 2 1

To our wives Yar and Tippy and our

children Adior, Majok, Cathy and Christopher

# CONTENTS

# FIGURES AND TABLES

Figure

Table

# PREFACE

Beginning with the Sahelian drought of the 1970s, plights of Africa's migratory pastoralists have received occasional saturation-type television and other press coverage. But resulting short-term outpourings of global concern and emergency aid have done almost nothing to help better their ordinarily difficult lots in life. Development within pastoral Africa remains essentially a "non-starter." Should outside pressures upon these tens of millions of people, especially ones new to their experiences, continue unabated, their fates might well resemble those of Native Americans and Australia's aborigines.

We believe that their lives could be improved--and the welfare of nations of which they are at least nominally parts could also benefit--without large-scale initiatives that African (and donor) nations seem unable to afford. We think practical measures must begin where things are *locally* and then proceed in whatever modest ways appear most evident. That approach requires ascertaining first who is doing anything useful right now. That applies not only to existing branches of government and resident nongovernmental organizations (NGOs), but especially to traditional pastoralist institutions. In our view, an extreme paucity of available resources requires the maximum flexibility locally if the aim is to achieve meaningful results. The steps we propose are based on our joint perceptions of present realities and the opportunities they suggest for sustainable improvements in pastoralists' circumstances.

In many respects our "bottom up" approach inverts the "top down" approach taken in many planning documents, including the valuable continent-wide overview of animal agriculture in Africa provided recently by a Winrock International advisory committee chaired by William R. Pritchard. Their appraisal concentrates mostly upon mixed plant-animal smallholder systems, devoting relatively less attention to extensive pastoralists. But that assessment does identify a number of problems overall that are most critical in the arid and semiarid zones of Africa that most migratory peoples now inhabit. We believe our "finer brush" approach and closer to the ground "how to" suggestions will usefully complement the Winrock overview and other prior appraisals of resources and needs.

However, many of those past assessments--and resulting efforts--too commonly reflected the usually unstated notions that, first, pastoralists' resources are not their own to use and exploit as *they* wish and, second, that others who "know better" should have control over them. In contrast, we believe that any desirable development within pastoral Africa must grow out of the expressed needs of pastoralists themselves. New measures and technologies, in order not to prove otherwise destructive, must be adapted to or utilize existing institutions and services as fully as possible and, especially, long-established indigenous institutions. Moreover, beyond concerted national efforts for more equitable distribution of resources--of distributive justice--and some "jump-starting" of particular efforts through external sources of funding, we believe that pastoral development must become self-financing to a practical degree--that is, that results generate capital as well as contribute to what is locally understood to be a better life.

We are interested in helping to build functional bridges among the several principals contributing to the development process among pastoral peoples in Africa. Since our proposals are directed to that broad audience of concerned individuals representing diverse national, professional, disciplinary and other experiential backgrounds, we have tried to provide enough common ground to develop our main points. Though we recognize that we lack the specific knowledge that optimal development possibilities in particular local circumstances might well require, we nonetheless believe we offer practical beginnings to local realization of many development goals. Some of our more novel proposals have been at least tentatively tested in the field. Others have been reviewed by persons experienced in working within the economic, social and political realities of Africa.

Our interests in development among Africa's migratory pastoralists are long-standing. The first author, born and reared within a pastoral family in the southern Sudan, still owns a cattle herd there. His perspective on development possibilities in such situations was extended during a year as a Parvin Fellow in the Woodrow Wilson School of Public and International Affairs at Princeton University and subsequently at the University of California, Davis. The second author's interests originated in efforts begun in the 1950s to investigate and control hydatid disease, the principal global plague of pastoralists, plus broader involvement in intersectoral cooperation in public health and agriculture.

We both express our gratitude to the several agencies which supported our separate and joint efforts through fellowships, consultantships, grants or logistic aid: the Rockefeller and Ford Foundations, the Fulbright Fellowship Board, the World Health Organization, the African Medical and Research Foundation, the Deutsche Gesellschaft für technische Zusammenarbeit, the United Nations Childrens Fund and the United Nations Environmental Programme. Substantial progress on this book was made during our appointments in 1993 as Scholars-in-Residence at the Rockefeller Foundation's  Study and Conference Center in Bellagio, Italy.  The first author is particularly indebted to Vice Chancellor Professor G.L. Chavunduka and to Dean of Veterinary Science Professor C.B. Nyathi, of the University of Zimbabwe, for supporting a leave-of-absence for that period. The second author takes special pleasure in thanking his son, Dr. Christopher L. Schwabe, who worked for six years with UNICEF in the southern Sudan and since then as program financing consultant, health economist and team leader in other African development efforts.  He not only brought Elinor Ostrom's seminal work to our attention but gave permission to extract from some of his own unpublished reports.

We also want to thank Professors Donald Rothchild of the Department of Political Science of the University of California, Davis (UCD) and David Leonard of the Department of Political Science of the University of California, Berkeley for their valuable suggestions. We are grateful, too, for help from Professor Thomas Farver and Dr. Thomas Carlton of the Department of Epidemiology and Preventive Medicine of UCD's veterinary school and Professor Karl-Hans Zessin and Dr. M.P.O. Baumann of the Department of Tropical Veterinary Medicine and Epidemiology, Free University of Berlin.

# Development Among Africa's Migratory Pastoralists

# 1

---

# PASTORALISM IN AFRICA

Over two-thirds of the [African] continent is unsuited to growing crops, consequently ruminant animals constitute the only practical way such land can be utilized for food production.

W. R. Pritchard (1988)

In our view, African pastoralism represents an ultimate development challenge. In this introductory chapter we construct a platform from which to consider some proposals for facing it. These include that (1) pastoral development be based upon full consideration of the intricacies of man-animal-environment relationships in each case, including the customs and institutions these spawn; (2) it involve at all stages full participation of pastoralists themselves; and (3) programs be decentralized as much as possible. To those notions, with which increasing numbers of concerned individuals would agree, we add a critical implementing proposal, namely (4) that veterinary science provide the *facilitating* vehicle for mobile outreach to, two-way communications with and practical service interventions among migratory pastoralists. That is, a range of cost-attractive efforts could be grafted upon existing veterinary programs to capitalize more fully upon their already achieved acceptance by, experience of and systems of outreach to pastoralists.

One of our main premises is that much of pastoral Africa already has resources to do more than is being done. Sticking points, therefore, are barriers which make it difficult to employ them to maximum advantage. We believe these barriers are higher the farther one goes within government above the local level.

## PASTORALISM: ECOSYSTEM AND SOCIAL SYSTEM

Some believe that in ancient times profound ecological determinants within natural Eurasian and African grasslands gave rise to remarkably similar social patterns which have defined pastoralism since (Lincoln, 1981). To understand pastoralists' mentality is to understand the complexity of such relationships (see Chapter 3). Pastoralism now most characterizes areas that are ecologically marginal and economically poor; most least developed countries (LDCs) are pastoralist to considerable extents. Therefore, a tendency in the North is to believe that this "Third World's Third World" is "un-developed" economically--is poor--*because* it is pastoralist (with the implication that such peoples could have some choice in the matter). This perception would have to come to grips with, as one polar instance of relative prosperity, a country such as New Zealand, whose economy also rests in large measure upon a pastoral base.

Most present-day students of animals' domestication believe that, while sheep and goats more or less domesticated themselves sometime prior to 8,000 BC (Clutton-Brock, 1981: 55), domestication of the larger, more powerful *Bos primigenius*, the ancestor of most domestic cattle, not only occurred later but was more complexly motivated. Man's initial "keeping of cattle" appears to have been closely associated with his grasping the significance of such ideas as territoriality, dominion, social hierarchies and human relationships to a visualized cosmos (Frankfort, 1948; von Lengerken and von Lengerken, 1955; Conrad, 1957; Mellaart, 1967; Schwabe, 1994). Such cattle-man comparisons and emulations, widely represented in ancient times, survive more or less among many of today's African pastoralists (Schwabe, 1978a: 29-40; Robertshaw, 1989). Thus, African pastoralism is distinguishable in very important respects from other social systems.[1]

Two main forms of pastoralism currently exist: *extensive* systems in which herbivorous livestock are herded upon open range, and newer, more *intensive* systems in which they are grazed within fenced areas. In colder climes temporarily confined animals are fed harvested forages seasonally in the forms of silage and hay. Extensive pastoralism is usually migratory and of either the *transhumant* or *nomadic* type. Transhumance implies that herders (and often their nuclear families) accompany their herds' grazing over a more or less remote area, then seasonally return for a period to grazing around a home base.[2] In nomadism animals and herders' families are continually transient. African migratory pastoralism is of both types. In either case, more or less prescribed grazing routes are often followed and extended families, clans or larger social groupings almost always have grazing territories recognized by them as their own. Only in very recent years have those variants of pastoralism been at all complemented by confinement feeding of herbivores throughout long periods of their lives as a way to produce food. As yet, that has occurred on a large scale (Figure 1.1) in only a few places, first in parts of the United

**Figure 1.1. Intensive feeding system for beef cattle dependent upon availability of high-energy feed concentrates. Aerial view of cattle feedlot in Colorado** (Source: Dr. Roger Ruppanner.)

States where cheap grains (and other nutritional concentrates) became at least temporarily available.

Nomadism and transhumance are the features of pastoralism that have the most readily recognized ecological determinants: seasonal phenomena relative to the survival and prosperity of their adherents which *require* them and their animals to move (see Chapter 2). The most striking phenomenon in Africa is rainfall. It affects not only available grazing, but also, indirectly, other things that may cause pastoralists to move, such as the densities of biting flies, incidences of major livestock diseases (see Chapter 4), crop-raising possibilities for some transhumants (see Chapter 2) and the like.

### Human Modifications of Grasslands Ecology

Most of the formerly extensive grassland plains of North America and to a lesser extent the pampas of South America, as well as, more recently, portions of the Asian steppes, have been put under plow during the past 150 years. Some of this conversion, in North America especially, has resulted in vastly increased production of grains with an associated substitution in some areas of intensive confinement systems for feeding livestock for formerly prevalent hunter-wildlife and/or pastoral economies. Strong cases have been made for half a century for similar conversions of African savannas, and some development projects have had those primary goals. A concomitant has been the settling of the continent's numerous pastoralists, often with the notion that they adopt sedentary agriculture as a way of life. Where this is clearly impossible, many Northerners--particularly North American and Australian rangelands and beef cattle specialists--have advocated more intensive livestock production systems following their own models or a very conservative stocking strategy based upon a variety of negative presumptions about African husbandry.

A virtually universal feature of almost all efforts to transform traditional African pastoralism is that their motivation comes from the North and finds support mostly among settled African agriculturists who are far more frequently educated in the Northern tradition than are pastoralists. Such proposals have also been driven by widely held Darwinian beliefs originating in 19th-century Europe alleging a natural social evolution from hunter-gatherer to pastoral to sedentary agricultural to industrial. Coupled with a rise in romantic European ethnocentrisms ("tribalism" carried to often disastrously fatal outcomes) and of rapid colonialist expansions in Africa--followed by global competition between two alternative political and economic conceptions of progress and ultimate ends, the capitalist and socialist--such popular beliefs in the North were used not only to justify paternalistic aspects of colonialism but underlie some post-colonial concepts of the desired ends of "development."

However, recent years have seen some newer Northern livestock and crop production systems opened more and more to questions of their sustainability (NRC/NAS, 1975). For example, at the western margins of North American grasslands (and in ecologically similar parts of central Asia) it is now realized that climatic constraints to grain production require that, once introduced, grain farming be regularly subsidized because of almost predictable crop failures every few years. Arguably, some of these marginal areas might better have remained, or should be restored to, grasslands which could sustainably support varying degrees of pastoralism.

### Pastoral Africa Defined

Pastoral Africa extends from some coastal areas and mountains of the Mediterranean North, to seasonally grazable areas north and south of the Sahara desert, including the Sahelian zone and the more favorable trans-African Sudanic (savanna) zone, thence down the eastern side of the continent into South Africa. Over this vast area, keepers of cattle and other herbivores speak a myriad of tongues representative of all four phyla of African languages. Since the onset of colonial times, some of these pastoralists have been displaced from their best grazing lands (Jarvis and Erickson, 1986) to the extent that, within sub-Saharan Africa, its arid and semiarid zones now possess 51% of cattle, 57% of sheep, 65% of goats and 100% of camels (ILCA, 1987, after

Jahnke, 1982).  Characteristic of those areas are highly seasonal plant communities within biotopes which lack potential for alternative uses supportive of similarly sized human populations.  These inhospitable territories comprise 74% of West Africa, 70% of East Africa and 54% of southern Africa (ILCA, 1987, after Jahnke, 1982).  Besides permanently dry areas and those few at very high altitudes, absence of livestock dependence in Africa is defined largely by distribution of the tsetse fly.

Not unexpectedly, pastoralist populations are poorly enumerated, their total numbers in sub-Saharan Africa being estimated by some at more than 50 million (Coughenour et al., 1985).  According to Pritchard et al. (1992: 22), about 10% of the population of sub-Saharan Africa inhabit its arid zone alone. But, to put even a conservative estimate of 30 million into perspective, Africa's migratory pastoralists today are at least half as numerous as the French and twice as numerous as Australians.

Of Africa's land area of 3.03 billion hectares, 5.2% was being cultivated in 1975 of the 23.5% regarded then as potentially arable (Buringh et al., 1975). A portion of the area supporting pastoralism could be converted to crop production at varying short-term and long-term costs, including important ecological costs in some instances.  Those areas could support possible lifestyle alternatives for some pastoral peoples.  But for large portions of Africa still available to pastoralists, the climate is too dry, the growing season is too short and/or the soils are too deficient for alternative food-producing uses.  That is, ecology is an even more important determinant of pastoralism's extent today than in the past and many pastoral peoples have no practical choice. Explanations for why pastoralism and poverty are now so highly correlated in Africa are that pastoralism has been more and more restricted to areas that otherwise could not support any human economy, much less a materially prosperous one.

## "TRAGEDY OF THE COMMONS"

A few comments need be directed to the seductively catchy notion of "tragedy of the commons," since its "proponents . . . appear to assume that pastoralist societies . . . cannot devise or impose appropriate rules of behavior on individual members" (S. Sandford, 1983: 120).  This theoretical proposition, which predicts destruction of grasslands shared in common, has greatly influenced Northern developers' thinking about the future of extensive pastoralism in Africa. As stated by its modern formulator:

The tragedy of the commons develops in this way.  Picture a pasture open to all. . . . As a rational human being each herdsman seeks to maximize his gain.  Explicitly or implicitly, more or less consciously he asks "What is the utility *to me* of adding one more animal to my herd?"  This utility has one negative and one positive component.

1. The positive component is a function of the increment of one animal. Since the herdsman receives all the proceeds from the sale of the additional animal the positive utility is nearly +1.

2. The negative component is a function of the additional overgrazing by one more animal. Since, however, the effects of overgrazing are shared by all the herdsmen the negative utility for any particular decision-making herdsman is only a fraction of -1.

Adding together the component partial utilities the rational herdsman concludes that the only sensible course for him to pursue is to add another animal to the herd. And another. . . . But this is the conclusion reached by each and every rational herdsman sharing a commons.

Therein is the tragedy. Each man is locked into a system that compels him to increase his herd without limit--in a world that is limited. Ruin is the destination to which all men rush, each pursuing his own best interest in a society that believes in the freedom of the commons. Freedom in a commons brings ruin to all (Hardin, 1968).

Our own experiences caused us to concur years ago with S. Sandford (1983: 118ff) that this "type situation" used by Hardin derives from *prior assumptions* about pastoralists' behavior, not inductively from the results of actual field observations on the behavior of particular groups. Moreover, as Ostrom (1990: 8, 12) has noted, those who have most accepted as immutable fact these dire outcomes have usually been strong advocates of an "only one possible solution" (private ownership of both animals and land, as Hardin preferred) *or* another "only possible solution" for communal ownership of both (usually state ownership). *Both* of those advocacies have been based on economic theories intertwined with opposing political ideologies.

"What makes [this and like models] so dangerous--when they are used metaphorically as the foundation for policy--is that the constraints that are assumed to be fixed for the purpose of analysis are taken on faith as being fixed in empirical settings, unless external authorities change them" (Ostrom, 1990: 6). She then adds that "not all users of natural resources are similarly incapable of changing their constraints. As long as [they are believed to be], policy prescriptions will address the metaphor." As natural scientists, and epidemiologists especially, we also draw back reflexively from any purportedly scientific theory derived by Hardin's approach. We know especially that in no natural science would the results of such a process ever serve as the basis for widely consequential actions. At the least, these a priori assumptions must be verified, in this case among African pastoralists whose indigenous institutions have, in fact, successfully resisted Hardin's predicted inevitable ruin for many more centuries than civilization has existed. Pastoral peoples of Africa, who have lived in the closest relations to their lands for millennia, must be given some benefit of the doubt and it must be considered seriously that they know a lot about what they are doing and are not hell-bent on their own destruction. At the least, we believe that a new openness in approach to pastoral development, including meaningful North-South dialogue, is badly in need of trial.

We think it also important to note that most Northern experiences of pastoralists in Africa date only from the late 19th century. That was a very atypical period in African pastoral history, representing the immediate aftermath of the great pandemic of rinderpest, a cattle disease whose historic consequences globally have been matched only by plague and malaria (see Chapter 4). Kjekshus (1977: 126-160) was one of the first to point out the significance of rinderpest in shaping Northern views of pastoralist Africa up to the present time, especially that Africans have all-consuming interests in cattle numbers, but no interest in cattle quality, and that their management of cattle and grazing areas is irrational. With respect to pre- and postrinderpest situations in Tanzania specifically, one of Kjekshus' main points is conveyed in observations (pp. 66-67, 162) by three early European travelers:

1. In earlier times the mountains of Ushingo and parts of the lowlands . . . were cattle districts, the cattle having died from rinderpest some time before European administration. The loss of stock caused the people to move, the one-time cattle areas became re-forested, and the tsetse returned. . . . [W]ithin the memory of natives still living, an open grassy plain dotted with cattle, sheep, and goats is today a vast deep papyrus swamp. . . (from Grant).

2. Prior to the Rinderpest, . . . [the Watusi, also called Tutsi] used to import half-breed cattle [crossings of Uha and Ussukama stock] from the western parts of the district . . . with the aim of improving the milk yield of their own cattle (from Wölfel, a German veterinarian).

3. It is this practice [keeping of many inferior bulls] which primarily accounts for the uneven nature of the herds. But this practice is not the result of lack of understanding [of breeding], but stems from the present economic situation [in rinderpest's aftermath] (from another German, Lichtenheld).

Thus, at the time when many of the most persistent and consequential Northern prejudices about African pastoralism arose, a very atypical situation existed vis-à-vis cattle and man: namely, *there were abnormally depressed cattle numbers from which many pastoralist populations were desperately attempting to recover as quickly as possible.*

Ten years ago the prevalent Northern view was still "that most of the world's rangelands are suffering from desertification and that . . . in most cases the cause of desertification is overgrazing by domestic animals" (Sollod, 1991). However, as Sollod pointed out, the "literature contains very little discussion of what human-assisted desertification might be [and c]omments on the creeping Sahara have been more often than not anecdotal [and] biased toward dry years." He added that, while "'common knowledge' of ecological ruin has been invoked to save nomadic people from themselves, it is unconfirmed by scientific empirical research." Dodd (1994) concluded similarly and Jarvis and Erickson (1986) found no support from 90 years' records in Zimbabwe.

Recent studies in different parts of Africa (Behnke et al., 1993; Baumann et al., 1993) support a counterbelief that while herbivores do modify range plant productivity and plant community structures in arid lands, sometimes considerably, both remain largely under climatic control and traditional pastoral systems are concerned almost entirely with responding effectively to such often disequilibrial conditions rather than to influencing them. Drawing upon a range of sources, a Winrock International Committee assessing animal agriculture on the African continent (Pritchard et al., 1992: 124) concluded that "it remains arguable . . . the degree to which arid rangelands can be destroyed from grazing pressure (except around water points)."

While some Northern agents of development (and large segments of the public) continue to lay blame for pastoralists' problems solely upon them, an alternative (but growing) assessment for any worsening environmental situation in Africa shifts blame from pastoralists to outside officials, including range and livestock specialists, who have attempted to force changes among them. That argument is essentially that "migratory pastoralists [in Africa] have tradition-ally lived with their cattle in balance with the vegetation. This balance was disrupted in the 1950s and 1960s by (i) the settlement of pastoralists around wells, and (ii) the cash crops coincident with increasing human and cattle populations" (Sinclair and Fryxell, 1985). Others stress predominant effects of long-term secular trends in climatic patterns upon the quality of the physical environment over broad areas of Africa (e.g., citing the geological and paleontological evidence for more than one cycle of dryness and wetness in the Sahara's past). Sen (1981) attempted to explain periodic famines in pastoral Africa more in terms of economic entitlement factors, of various interacting mechanisms underlying food acquisition and deprivation. Better documented than most of the above are short-term recurrent drought cycles and instances of cattle epidemics (Zessin, 1991) as important causes of a general correlation of relative poverty with pastoralism in much of Africa today.[3] And beyond all such considerations, recent instances of warfare with modern weapons are having disastrous effects not only upon many traditional pastoral societies, but upon many efforts toward pastoral development (Sivard, 1990-1994).

We make no attempt to apportion blame for evident failures to adequately cope with social needs in pastoralist Africa in the present or past. Recent events suggest more than enough to go around and that the causes of almost no success in improving the lot of pastoral peoples or to integrate them into national economies are multiple. Rather, we shall attempt to visualize practical minimally disruptive ways to proceed modestly but steadily with available resources in moving the status quo to more favorable situations not only for the persons most intimately involved, but also for the mostly new nations within which pastoralists now find themselves. That is, we accept current realities throughout  pastoralist Africa as starting points and concern ourselves solely with, given these, can we nevertheless move ahead?

Another controversial point about pastoralism requiring mention is a growing misunderstanding among prosperous Northerners (of this increasingly urban generation) about the roles animals do and should play in feeding people *anywhere*. Extremists question whether animal domestication itself was not an historic mistake that needs rectifying through their "emancipation" (Rifkin, 1992). In championing simplistically emotional notions such as "by consuming meat, which wastes the grain that could have saved them, last year we [the North] ate the children of the Sahel, Ethiopia and Bangladesh" (Dumont, 1975), animal rights zealots are actively forming alliances with philosophic vegetarians, antivivisectionists and other persons concerned, as are we, with anticruelty and animal welfare. Such alliances have begun to generate political consequences in the North that could put Africa's pastoralists at greater risk than they might otherwise be and reinforce already established beliefs that pastoralists can and should be settled.  Such deep misunderstandings about animals and people would have been inconceivable in any prior generation.

Here we refer mostly to misinformation about the conversion efficiencies for plant energy and protein by ruminants--that is, to mistaken inferences that some Northerners with little knowledge of livestock production have made from correct or partially correct data.  One reason that large portions of the earth's surface are suitable only to support grazing and browsing animals is that most of the world's potential food is in the form of cellulose, which cannot be digested by people. Only herbivores can convert this immense store of plant roughage and scattered vegetation into human food. Were it not for ruminants especially, people would derive no food value at all from these enormous food stores in naturally occurring plant communities (plus other major sources of cellulose convertible by animals from wastes following harvesting and processing of food crops--for example, the stalks, leaves and cobs of maize/corn).

The rates at which *gross* energy and protein conversions of vegetation take place vary with the species and animal product, but for American cattle they are, for milk, 23.1% for energy and 28.8% for protein and, for beef, 5.2% for energy and 5.3% for protein (Bywater and Baldwin, 1980).  While such gross conversion efficiencies have absolutely nothing to do with pastoralism as a way of life or with pastoral development, they are causing more and more Northerners to believe that livestock raising is a bad thing, *a negative factor in efforts to feed the world's human population*.  In one of its most repeated forms, "the average steer is able to reduce 21 pounds of protein in feed to 1 pound of protein in the expensive steak or roasts on our plates" (Lappé, 1975),[4] implying that meat production from cattle necessarily wastes enormous quantities of plant feedstuffs directly consumable by people.  This is not only patently untrue, but is a needlessly inflammatory statement in that, if believed, can help lead to totally misguided policy decisions globally, including those affecting the future of Africa's pastoralists.

The conversion rates needed for the purposes intended are not gross conversion rates for energy or protein, but *human-edible* conversion rates--that is, what human-edible inputs (feedstuffs) are fed livestock versus human-edible outputs produced by them.   Even under the extreme case of typical U.S. commercial conditions, human-edible energy conversion by cattle is 101.1% for milk and  57.1% for beef, while their protein conversion is 181.4% for milk and 108.8% for beef (Bywater and Baldwin, 1980)--in worst case scenarios against cattle, more human-edible food often comes out than goes in.  This is the only direct area where herbivores and people are in competition other than with respect to alternative uses of potentially arable lands.  The most vital thing to understand here is that, *in extensive pastoral systems, such as in Africa, the human-edible conversion efficiencies for cattle and other ruminants are infinite.* Almost no human-utilizable plants are eaten by them and meat and milk are produced.  Thus the livestock of African pastoralists, like wild herbivores, consume highly scattered vegetation not utilizable directly by people (not edible, not digestible or not harvestable) and convert it to human-utilizable energy and protein (milk and meat) of high nutritional quality.

Beyond such considerations, another important point for nonanimal scientists to understand about extensive pastoralism is that livestock harvest this very scattered vegetation under their own power and store it.  Only a few countries in the world still are major grain producers and/or net food exporters, and the number of these most fortunate countries seems to continually decrease. Most of the world's stored food reserves in the form of grains are poorly distributed, therefore most subject to political manipulation and entitlement relationships.  Much more equitably distributed among and within countries is productive capacity of foods through livestock, hence also food storage in those forms.  That is partly because most of this storage is on the hoof (Clutton-Brock, 1989) and its "harvest" is usually much less seasonally determined than for foods of plant origin.

A further general question of man-animal relationships is the additional draft and other energy contributions animals make to crop production, the traditional complementary relationships between animal and plant production. Unlike countries like the United States and Canada where tractors replaced animal power very rapidly, but for poorly studied reasons (Schwabe, 1984b: 80-85),[5] much of Africa still has these choices to make.

## THE IDEA OF DEVELOPMENT

For our purposes, development is a social process of change involving a set of value judgments about what constitutes the good society (Barkan, 1984: 13) and the means of achieving that good society.  But the value judgements we consider are more those of African pastoralists than of various outsiders, no matter how well motivated.

Until the end of World War II and subsequent pressures to end colonialism, the notion that "more fortunate" peoples should help others less "well off" were either so complicated by ulterior motives like missionary zeal or were otherwise so intertwined with principal thrusts of colonialism that their altruistic motives were suspect or compromised. There are many who still see (and, of course, sometimes correctly) only selfish motives for proffered assistance from one national government to another. The idea of bilateral governmental assistance on any scale to other independent nations originated among U.S. President Harry Truman's advisors as the Marshall Plan for war-torn Europe, a related approach to defeated Japan and "Point 4" (of his presidential message to Congress) with respect to what began more and more to be referred to as the Third World. Confusion over motives for such bilaterally based governmental aid was partially removed in theory with the creation of multilateral technical assistance programs through the United Nations, although some would argue that these too have become increasingly subject to interests of major contributors to those few international agencies (e.g., the World Bank) which finance many of the aid projects run technically by UN or other agencies.

We believe that, unless substantial nonmaterial aspects of development also occur in the North, its richer peoples, whatever they may say, will continue simply to outbid poor peoples not only for nonrenewable materials like petroleum, but also for the foods poorer peoples can or could produce for themselves (Sen, 1981). For example, a country like India, which may now in some years export grain, does so *not* because its own people's food needs are being adequately met internally by this augmented production, but because much of this grain is being produced at costs which large segments of the Indian population cannot afford to pay (but which other people can and do). Similarly, "modern beef-production operations [in Central America] have expanded greatly in recent years in response to a strong U.S. [import] demand; not surprisingly the local price of meat has climbed steeply, further reducing the consumption of the [local] poor" (Scrimshaw and Taylor, 1980). Such realities underline our belief that development is an apropos concept for *all* peoples and more than purely material considerations are involved.

Germane to this is what Kusum Nair (1961) pointed out years ago for India, namely, that "planners and economists tend to overlook . . . lack of consensus on economic values. It is assumed . . . that given equal opportunity, financial incentive and resources, all communities will respond . . . similarly in their productive efforts. . . . From what I have seen," she added, "it would seem that a great majority of rural communities [in India] do not share in this concept of an ever-rising standard of living." "Most economists have ignored [such] criticisms [of past development efforts and] . . . are convinced that the great majority of people are far more interested in the economic goods whose production economists have encouraged than in any psychological or environmental losses" (Daly and Cobb, 1989). As an economist and a theologian, respectively, Daly and Cobb expound in this context (pp. 25ff) Alfred North Whitehead's "fallacy of misplaced concreteness,"[6] a problem we believe not just of economists, but which all of us confined within highly abstracted disciplines have in perceiving real-world situations in their actual complexities. We believe that development efforts must better attempt to encompass such elusive realities and that the North, as well as the South, must come to appreciate more realistically the global consequences of limited supplies and rising demands of ever-larger populations (Barney, 1980; Worldwatch Institute, 1990-1995; Brown et al., 1995). More balanced perceptions of development process and ends may motivate programs of some development-related NGOs, and that often broader, locally oriented motivation (Boulding, 1988: 35ff, 118ff) also drives our own general approach to development. More historical and ecological perspectives, therefore, could help Northern developers appreciate that appropriate development--practically achievable, minimally disruptive change--might better be sought among many African pastoralists through "fine-tuning" present systems than attempting to transform them radically. Newer thinking is vital if Africa's pastoralists are to benefit from any practical improvements in their lot and not slide irreversibly into an imposed morass from which their time-tested traditional mechanisms can no longer extricate them.

As African governments struggle to make appropriate choices, they make bargains with specially influential groups. Some groups are excluded and pastoral people have always been among these, in large measure because they have lagged behind their settled counterparts in education within almost every African state. For such reasons, the real intentions of pastoral development programs have not often been made known to those most affected. For instance, government may tell pastoralists that "these boreholes will be dug so that your cattle will have water and grazing within your communal areas and therefore in the future you will not need to trek them long distances as you now do in search of these vital needs." But what they often do not say is "government is interested in changing your traditional mode of life and why these boreholes are being dug is really so that you settle permanently." Thus, we are most concerned with better recognition and enlistment of existing civil society, indigenous institutions of governance and cooperation among pastoralists, in the development process. Our proposals are mostly grassroots ones concerned with the design and especially the implementation of local development efforts more than with problems which arise at levels removed from the peoples most intimately affected by development (or from those Northerners who may be involved in the real processes on the ground). Pastoralist empowerment will probably be a slow process.

## Development of Pastoralist Africa

It is unfortunate that development of African pastoralist *communities,* versus development of pastoralist *areas* (see Chapter 5), seems to be a subject in virtual limbo, bereft of ideas. While some segments of the development literature pay lip service to ascertaining pastoralists' desires, rarely has this expressed concern been fully translated into process.[7]  In concentrating so exclusively on land (crop production, range management, water resources and animal production), little attention is directed to, for example, meeting educational and human health desires of pastoralists (see Chapters 5 and 7). Much of what has been proposed fails in visualizing affordable ways to reach migrating pastoral peoples with any social services. We believe that is largely because of ineffective communications or cooperation among concerned outsiders themselves, and especially across the "development technician"-anthropologist chasm.  On the other hand, some anthropologists eschew altogether the *idea* of development among such peoples.

Beside ecological influences, and forces represented by the motives or perceptions of foreign donors to and participants in the development process, many African pastoralists are subjected to other influences over which some have little if any control.  These latter may be prominent in African states which contain *both* pastoral and settled agricultural populations. Often the two are of different ethnic stock, represent different linguistic affinities, adhere to different religious systems or a combination of these. In some they have been traditional enemies. Usually the settled peoples have been more exposed to and influenced by Northern education and are in control politically. The animosity between the sedentary Hutu and the pastoral Tutsi of Rwanda and Burundi is but one of many cases in point. "Differences [in general] between those who have and those who have not extricated themselves from commons dilemmas may . . . have to do with factors *outside* the[ir] domain . . . [and] there is the possibility that external changes may sweep rapidly over a group, giving them insufficient time to adjust their internal structures to avoid the suboptimal responses" (Ostrom, 1990: 21).  Especially consequential, therefore, is that some development funders so believe that doom is inevitable and *near at hand* among African pastoralists that they actually resist efforts to associate local research with specific development proposals (Zessin and Farah, 1993).

S. Sandford (1983: 123) has pointed out some other biases that outsiders, whether persons concerned directly with development, or influential bystanders, espouse which can have major impacts upon African pastoralists.  For example, work of some Northern economists has tended to overlook, sometimes completely, subsistence returns of traditional pastoralism (Jarvis and Erickson, 1986).  In considering pastoralists' productivity, Sandford noted specifically that "the numbers of animals marketed expressed as offtake rates in relation to the number in the herds, are not a proper assessment of the relative productivity of different pastoral systems" in that, for one thing, they reflect a beef bias which does not consider other subsistence returns, including milk, which African pastoralists view as of prime importance.  Nor do they consider the larger human population employed by the traditional sector or otherwise supported in traditional extensive systems versus more intensive systems. However, Sandford added, when "capitalist and traditional systems are compared by other indices of efficiency, for example, in terms of dietary calories which they produce for human consumption or the economic value of all their products, . . . the results tend to favor the traditional rather than the capitalist systems."  Unfortunately, there have been few comparative studies considering the magnitude of the consequences that ride on such assumptions.

Another major problem in African pastoral development efforts remains intercultural communications more generally, to which we now turn.

### Intercultural Communications Across the Development Gap

In 1957 a social scientist named Frederick Riggs identified some of the kinds of problems in communications and program effectiveness encountered when outsiders from one type of society, which he called "industrian" (and we call Northern), attempt to apply their expertise to solving problems of governmental services delivery within another type social system, which he called "agrarian."  Later Riggs (1973) broadened his discussions to include a third type of social setting, which he called "folk" (pastoralist plus hunter-gatherer) and elaborated an optical analogy for comparing these three situations in development-related particulars.  Thus, a "fused" social system (*folk*) was analogous to a beam of white light, a "prismatic" system (*agrarian*) to the spectrum produced when such a beam enters a prism and a "diffracted" social system (*industrian*) to completely separated colors which are projected from the other surface of the prism.  Adding the additional category of "animal roles" to Riggs' classification, we have the taxonomy and characteristics summarized in Table 1.1.  Successful attempts at development among pastoralists must not only recognize such general, but also local, characteristics of "fused" systems. For example, activities which may, to the eye of the "diffracted" system outsider, appear totally distinct, may be to persons within the fused system inextricably and multiply merged. Tampering with one, may seriously effect others in ways not readily foreseen by the outsider, but which may prove highly disruptive to pastoralists, both culturally and socially.[8] For those reasons our approach to pastoral development is as "fused" as the societies we wish to benefit.

So much for introductory information intended to provide enough of a common platform to individuals of very different disciplines to consider African pastoralism in terms of those spheres we believe require special emphasis. Now a few words about our approaches to these.

| Societal Types (Riggs) | I. Folk | II. Agrarian | III. Industrian |
|---|---|---|---|
| "Optical Analogs" (Riggs) | "Fused" | "Prismatic" | "Diffracted" |
| Modern Equival-ents | Economically undeveloped | Economically developing | Economically developed |
| Type-Economy | Pastoral | Village-based, mixed plant-animal agriculture | Industrial with increasingly intensive monocultural agriculture |
| Social Charact-eristics | Slight division of labor (age, sex, priests, warrior-herders); no differentia-tion among institutions (e.g. religion, healing, animal husbandry); close linkages among values, loyalties, functions with respect to families & larger social structures | Considerable division of labor & differentiation of institutions; slightly separated conceptions of values, loyalties, functions at the different levels of social structure | Extreme division of labor & differentiation of institutions (e.g. "disciplines" like sociology, political science, religion, philosophy); compart-mentalization/fragmentation of values & loyalties in individual lives at different levels of social structures |
| Animal Roles | Species and individual animals completely integrated culturally & economically within social fabric | Individual animals fulfill multiple utilitarian purposes central to the family & wider economy | Species & individual animals with highly specialized functions & relations as direct food providers, close personal companions, providers of esthetic & recreational pleasure |

**Table 1.1. Different social systems and the roles of animals.** (Source: Adapted from Schwabe [1984b], employing concepts and terms of Riggs [1957, 1973].)

## SELECTED PASTORAL SITUATIONS

To assure sufficient specificity to appreciate the practicality of our proposals, we will concentrate significant portions of most discussions upon circumstances and possibilities within one principal pastoral situation, that of the Dinka, from which the first of us originates, and, secondarily, upon three comparative situations representative of other pastoral peoples among whom we both also have had practical experiences. These four "models" are intended not only to illustrate a range of circumstances, but indicate the types of information outsiders involved in development within pastoralist Africa should possess about each situation and people.

### Primary Dinka Situation

The Sudan is the largest country in Africa in area and one often cited by observers as possessing enormous unrealized potential. Like several other countries which include both semidesert Sahelian and grasslands Sudanic zones, it is populated by diverse peoples, those in the north of mixed African and Mediterranean-Asian origins and those in the south of purer African stock. Together they comprise 56 ethnic groups speaking 26 major languages. The Sudan has the largest number of pastoralists of any country in the world and its more than 2 million Nilotic Dinka are the most numerous pastoral group. In more familiar context, there are as many Dinka or more, than people in Wales or in each of about 26 of the 50 states of the United States of America.

### Comparative Situations

Because important differences exist among diverse African peoples who embrace pastoralism, the environments they inhabit, their beliefs, practices and future potentials, we have illustrated some of these through less detailed reference to three other pastoral peoples. Two are from Kenya, a country much favored until recently by some donors as an example of "development successes." Of these, the better known Maasai illustrate one important characteristic of African pastoralists in that their traditional territory extends into a neighboring country, in this case Tanzania, which since independence has followed a very different developmental path than its northern neighbor. The Kenyan Maasai have been subjected to major political and cultural stresses both before and since independence, with considerable alienation of the extensive lands, including most of the better portions, they considered their own before British rule.

Our second comparative situation is that of the Nilotic Turkana, who inhabit the semidesert to desert extreme northwest of Kenya and have, until recently, been a pastoral group very little influenced by outside forces.[9] Their territory is the most fragile ecologically of the three Nilotic peoples considered and is comparable to those of many West African pastoralists living under similarly extreme environmental conditions.

Last, we will refer to the Somalis, a pastoral people who speak a language unrelated to these others and who, although they are the only people among this model group who have a country of their own, are also a people whose traditional area extends considerably beyond Somalia's political borders into Ethiopia and Kenya. Most of their territory is also severe but, of these four groups, the Somalis have been influenced far more by the outside world, with many of their traditional beliefs and folkways appreciably overlain by an Islamic veneer of many years' duration.

The uses we make of these model situations reflect an eclectic array of approaches, but we hope these accounts will help provide common meeting ground for development economists, political scientists, cultural anthropologists, range specialists, ecologists, veterinarians, epidemiologists, public health officials, educators and others interested in the present and future of Africa's pastoral peoples.

## A PRACTICAL DEVELOPMENT PARADIGM FOR LOCAL ACTIONS

In the next few chapters we will develop bases for future thinking about pastoral Africa given prevailing circumstances, especially the constraints of very limited governmental and external resources. First, we shall consider the kinds of man-animal-environment knowledge about *each* pastoral society which outside development agents should possess. Chapter 5 then illustrates development mistakes which become almost inevitable where this and other local "people information" is lacking or ignored, as it largely has been in Africa in the past. These examples indicate how vital is our proposals' point two on pastoralist participation, leading us to the need to investigate, understand and work through traditional governance institutions whenever possible. Chapters 4 and 6 provide nonveterinarians the background information required for understanding our proposals' key point four, the unique facilitating role veterinary services could provide to immediately better the lot of many African pastoralists. Chapter 7 illustrates beginning implementation of such local intersectoral initiatives with current resources. Chapter 8 proposes augmenting two-way communications with pastoralists, improving environmental monitoring possibilities and practical decentralization of planning and intervention initiatives through full implementation within Africa of a currently global movement to base governmental veterinary services upon systematic epidemiological intelligence.

## NOTES

1. It has been our personal experience that Northern developers and African pastoralists can realize mutually enjoyable camaraderie from understanding that the forebears of most persons of European descent were themselves pastoralists. For example, the second author's family name designates one such tribe, the Swabians (called by the Romans Suevi or Suebi) who entered Europe from the east with other pastoral peoples like the Franks and Alemanis and advanced as far as Galicia and Asturias in Spain before concentrating mostly within the southwestern corner of present Germany. Pastoral Celts had been in Europe long before these newer cattle-keeping invaders. An historian of the highland Scots (Prebble, 1966: 30-31) had this to say about life among their clans up until the dawn of the 18th century: "[Their] economy . . . was cattle, short, black animals with shaggy hair, melancholy eyes and fearsome horns. [They] determined the people's lives and enriched their oral culture. The herding of cattle or the stealing of cattle kept the young men alert and healthy, training them for war and nurturing endurance and guile. . . . [C]attle were an indication of a Highlander's power and influence. . . . In winter [they] were closeherded near the townships. . . . In the summer . . . [they] were . . . driven . . . eastward out of the glen to the slopes. . . . Summer began with the Feast of Beltane. . . . There the women made the Beltane Bannnock which was . . . offered to the wild beasts [for protection of their animals against misfortune]. . . . 'This we give to thee, o Fox,' cried the people, 'spare thou our lambs . . . and this to thee, o Eagle.' [The men and women who drove them to the slopes then] lived in the shielings, huts which their ancestors had built and which were repaired each summer. . . . Shieling life was the happiest time of the year for the [clan]. Women and girls sat before the turf huts making butter and cheese, . . . while the men watched the cattle. . . . Younger men hunted and fished and went on forays [in search of cattle]. . . . Young boys waited impatiently for such days of manhood to begin." Compare this with Chapters 2 and 3.

2. As examples, transhumant pastoralism is practiced in the United States not only by Navajo and Zuni Indians in New Mexico and Arizona, but by Mormon sheepraisers in Utah and people of Basque descent throughout other parts of the American West (Araujo et al., 1975; Pappaioanou et al., 1977).

3. One must note at the same time that these are precisely the forces against which African pastoralists have demonstrated often amazing resilience within the historic past (Zessin, 1991: 1-31).

4. Lappé is a concerned food activist, many of whose other ideas are well founded and important. Her inferences in this instance are very misleading and incorrect *even* under American-type intensive feeding regimes where grazing is complemented by, or substituted by, feeding concentrates during portions of the life of food-producing cattle. She assumes that all cattle are fed concentrates *only* and that all concentrates fed to cattle are human-edible grains (for fuller discussion of this and related issues see Schwabe, 1984b: 58-67).

5. Loomis (1976) was one of the first agronomists to caution against peoples becoming too dependent upon crop-enhancing inputs (like fossil fuels), which will then support population increases which could not be sustained were that input to become no longer available (because it had become too expensive locally). Given extreme difficulties in obtaining any spare parts, fuel and servicing for machinery right now in the southern Sudan, plus the ever-increasing costs of petroleum, the idea of many individual pastoralists there owning their own tractors seems hardly feasible. Moreover, a tractor rental program would be, among the Dinka, for example, a highly seasonal demand, leaving the question of their use during the dry season a significant one.

Although animal traction would appear to be a possibility because Dinka already possess this historically important source of energy in abundance, they are reluctant to discuss with outsiders any altering of their covenant with cattle (see Chapter 3)--one through which each species has its prescribed obligations to the other, and benefits equitably from the partnership. Such questions are delicate ones. The few attempts at introducing use of oxen to till land have produced mixed results in the southern Sudan. Thus, a Harvard-coordinated development project among Dinka Abyei ran into problems when the American field manager threatened to terminate the project if they did not accept plowing and other uses of cattle he suggested (Deng, 1985). They did not acquiesce and the manager was replaced. Another project in Lakes province, an ox-plow training program among the Dinka Agar (Duncan, 1978), was approached more knowledgably and sensitively and showed signs of a breakthrough when renewed war intervened.

We believe that an informed approach to this important issue might be to visualize some proposed *quid pro quo* for working oxen that would compensate *them* equitably for this new draft role and thus not violate the spirit of the overall Dinka-cattle covenant. If properly planned and discussed with full participation of pastoralists themselves and with demonstrated benefits as in the case of the Rumbek ox-plow project, we believe some Dinka might be induced to put some castrated oxen to this added power use. But such would need to be promoted in terms of being *mutually* advantageous, such as feed supplements for these particular work cattle (e.g., some of the increased grain produced by their work, something cattle elsewhere enjoy) so that, as another benefit, they need not trek long distances for feed and water as must ordinary cattle Thus, if the availability of more grain is guaranteed through the use of a local energy source such as animal traction, which the Dinka could afford and operate themselves, then they might interpret that use of oxen for tilling the land as a reasonable change.

6. That is, a Northern "industrian" compartmentalization of knowledge spheres (see Table 1.1) resulting in too little communication among compartments (disciplines, sectors) and such a degree of abstraction within compartments that many practitioners "apply their conclusions to the real-world without recognizing the degree of abstraction involved" (Daly and Cobb, 1989: 25). From different backgrounds and perspectives than our own, those authors argue for a "paradigm shift" within economics, a new

openness to such real world circumstances. We aim to help correct that fallacy which has been so operative heretofore vis-à-vis pastoral development in Africa.

7. As one indication of how little input pastoralists have had in development plans for the resources they have traditionally managed, fewer than 15 authors cited by S. Sandford (1983) for more than 300 sources on pastoral development worldwide bear possibly Third World names (and some of those probably are not of pastoralists).

8. While the South African film *The Gods Must be Crazy* was a mix of slapstick satire and sensitive treatment of the Bushmen, the opening episode of the Coca-Cola bottle tossed from an airplane overflying Bushmen territory and its myriad consequences as a "foreign element" in the midst of their "fused society" should make that film required viewing for all Northern developers.

9. In 1961, one of us (Schwabe, 1964: 211) determined that the Turkana were experiencing the world's highest known rate of infection with hydatid cysts (a usually fatal infection of pastoralists if untreated, see Chapter 4). He attempted then with George Nelson (a researcher in Kenya's colonial medical service) to obtain government permission to investigate this tragic situation among a  people who were without any access to health services. The colonial government categorically refused on the grounds that it could raise Turkana's expectations that some health services might be provided to them in the future.

# 2

---

# CLIMATE, LAND USE AND MIGRATIONS

It appears that the negative effects of [African] drought . . . could be
lessened if development policies . . . recognized the appropriateness
of pastoral ecosystems in these [arid to semiarid] environments.

M.B. Coughenour et al. (1985)

Ecologically restrictive environments more and more define distributions of
most of Africa's pastoralists so that today, in many areas, they occupy only very
marginal lands. Among our model populations, alienation of former territories
has been most apparent among Kenya's Maasai. In any rational consideration
of pastoralists' remaining options, the obvious place to start is with the ecology
of each area and how the pastoral occupation adapts to and becomes part of its
environment.

The overriding problem African pastoralists face is low, highly seasonal
and unpredictable rainfall. During the approximately 100-year period of Northern observations, most have adapted well to a continuing desiccating trend, plus
in many areas recurrent single-year periods of drought. Under conditions of
high risk, they employ a variety of opportunistic mechanisms to protect their
livestock, hence their livelihoods. Many reduce or apportion risks by dividing
their herd in separate places, including through elaborate systems of social
obligations in which animals are lent or exchanged. Some also keep multiple
species of animals. In drought years they temporarily deplete particular species
or keep to known drought-resistant habitats. But attention of the world has been
directed to unusually acute multiyear periods of drought in some parts of Africa
in which these traditional coping mechanisms, subjected in many places to in-

**Figure 2.1. Insufficient and unpredictable rainfall is an overriding hazard in many areas to which Africa's large populations of extensive pastoralists are now confined. Nomads in Mali moved unusual distances in attempts to find pasturage during the severe multiyear drought of the 1970s.** (Source: WHO.)

creasing external constraints, have partially failed (see Figure 2.1).[1]

This chapter begins with a sketch of our main model area in order to consider the migration strategy Dinka transhumants use to cope with more predictable exigencies. That will be compared with our other three model populations. Studies exploring different pastoralists' strategies for accomodating to these ecological realities are of comparatively recent origin (Behnke et al., 1993). Near the end of this chapter we shall consider long-term monitoring approaches being recommended by some observers as ways to help deal with emergencies or facilitate particular aspects of development.

## PRIMARY SITUATION: THE SOUTHERN SUDAN

The Sudan is Africa's largest country, with varied topography and climate. Pastoralists in its south (see Figure 2.2) must adjust not only to inadequate rainfall during a long period each year, but serious flooding in another season. Generally speaking the southern Sudan is a large basin gently sloping northward, through which flow the Bahr el Jebel (White Nile) from the

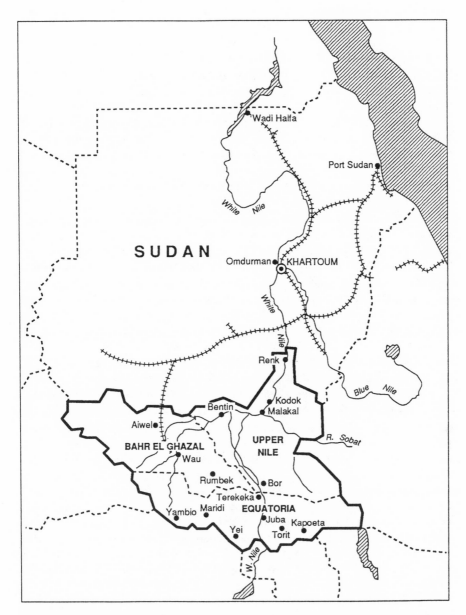

**Figure 2.2. The Sudan, Africa's largest country, showing principal towns, rivers and rail links. The Southern Region is outlined in solid black; its former Upper Nile province is now divided into Upper Nile and Jonglei provinces, former Bahr el Ghazal is now Bahr el Ghazal and Lakes, former Equatoria now Eastern Equatoria and Western Equatoria.**

south, the Bahr el Ghazal and its tributaries from the west, and the Sobat from the east, all merging into a vast barrier swamp, the *Sudd*, from which the White Nile continues northward. The region may be divided into five subzones: (1) the Floodplain, (2) the Ironstone Plateau, (3) the Green Belt, (4) the Eastern Hills and Plains and (5) the Central Rainlands (GOS, 1954; Democratic Republic of the Sudan, 1977). Subzones 1 and 5 contain about 90% of the livestock. Dinkaland is by far the largest ethnic territory within those two subzones. Subzones 2, 3 and 4 correspond approximately to the distribution of the tsetse fly, which precludes cattle-raising except for herds kept by the Toposa and Didinga tribes (subzone 4), and Dinka around the town of Wau (subzone 2).

We shall concentrate upon the Floodplain which supports several migratory peoples, the better known to outsiders being, beside the most numerous Dinka (Lienhardt, 1961; Deng, 1971, 1972, 1978), the Nuer (Evans-Pritchard, 1940, 1951, 1956), Atuot (Burton, 1987), Mandari (Buxton, 1973), Shilluk (Seligman and Seligman, 1932; Evans-Pritchard, 1948) and Murle (B. A. Lewis, 1972). Here seasonal migration of the Dinka illustrates an effective method of land use under circumstances of unfavorable environment. Its sociocultural, as well as economic, importance will be amplified by an account of the activities attached to each season. In many cases such activities, and their importance, have been unknown to outside interests promoting development of pastoral areas, and in no instance of which we are aware have they been taken into account seriously enough (even though they may provide the cement which holds these dispersed communities together).

This Floodplain, divided into four land classes--highlands, intermediate lands, the *toich*[2] and the *Sudd*--covers Jonglei province, some of Upper Nile province, large areas of Lakes province, plus parts of northern Bahr el Ghazal and Eastern Equatoria provinces. It is flat land with heavy, impermeable soils and rainfall of between 750 to 1,000 mm during a season of six to seven months (Howell et al., 1988: 147-197). The highlands are higher than the surrounding plains by only a few centimeters but remain comparatively flood-free. These are the sites for permanent transhumant settlements. Vegetation consists of open thorn woodland and/or open mixed woodland with both perennial and annual grasses. The intermediate lands lie below the level of the highlands and slightly above the *toich*. This is the area where "creeping flow" of river water (as a result of heavy rainfall in the Ethiopian and East African highlands) is a common feature. Vegetation is predominantly open perennial grassland with some areas of acacia woodland and other sparsely distributed trees (*Balanites aegyptiaca*). The *toich* is associated with the main rivers and inland water-courses. These lands are seasonally inundated or saturated. They retain sufficient moisture throughout the dry season to support grazing for livestock. The *Sudd* consists of land which is below the level of the *toich* and, therefore, permanent swampland. It covers a substantial part of the Floodplain, the dominant vegetation being *Vossia cuspidata, Cyperus papyrus* and *Typha*

**Figure 2.3. Dinka herdsmen catching fish as a major seasonal occupation when flood waters recede into the *Sudd* during the annual dry season migration.** (Source: Sarah Errington © 1982 Time-Life Books [Nederlands] B.V., from *Peoples of the Wild--Warriors of the White Nile.)*

*domingensis.* This is not available for livestock, but this area provides good fishing (Figure 2.3) in places where the vegetation thins out into isolated ponds.

### Suitability for Plant Agriculture

Soils of the southern Sudan are alluvial clays, which are found mainly in the Central Rainlands and Floodplain subzones, and lateritic soils elsewhere. Of the alluvial clay type, alkaline clays and heavy loams predominate. Here, soil quality is not a limiting factor for agriculture and erosion is practically absent. However, full crop potential cannot be realized because of seasonal lack of moisture. Sandy soils which occur in isolated patches on the plains are less fertile, but are often more intensively cultivated because, although plants suffer more from drought, their tillage is easier and they are less liable to water-logging. In areas where lateritic soils occur, their moisture content is more fav-

**Figure 2.4. Dinka transhumant homesteads.  Family huts, with tobacco cultivation in the foreground.** (Source: Sarah Errington © Time-Life Books [Nederlands] B.V., from *Peoples of the Wild--Warriors of the White Nile.*)

orable for crops, but nutrient status is definitely inferior.  Nutrients tend to accumulate under the natural vegetation in the surface soil and are quickly lost to leaching and erosion.

In the central Rainlands and Floodplain, production of dura (sorghum), sesame, beans, peanuts and, in some areas, maize (corn) and tobacco is practiced around transhumant homesteads in the "highlands" (Figure 2.4). This is mostly at subsistence level. Planting and weeding employ hoes and digging sticks and are largely jobs of married men and women.

### Dinka Transhumant Homesteads

The typical Dinka transhumant homestead contains a large conical cattle byre (*luak*) and one or more huts.  The *luak*, with a circular base 4 to 6 meters in diameter, consists of a pole frame thatched with *Hyperenia* grass.  Its entrance is wide enough to admit cattle with long horns.  Near it is a fireplace about which men and cattle sleep.  Huts are smaller and are mainly for women and children. These may be ground-based or built on a raised platform. They also are cone shaped and covered with thatch. The entrance is much smaller than that of the *luak* and persons have to crawl to enter. Construction of both is the collective responsibility of a lineage group for which the host family provides food. A weaner bull is usually given to the person entrusted with directing the thatching and, upon completion, a bull is sacrificed to a general or local spirit as a form of blessing. During the dry season migration Dinka's only shelter is a simple one of papyrus supported by a few poles or bundles of reeds. These are abandoned upon the homeward journey.

*Possessions.* One characteristic of Dinka is their lack of enthusiasm for accumulating possessions. That is not solely absence of opportunity or lack of knowledge that other possessions exist, for theirs is a society is which individual behavior and societal relations count far more than material goods. Besides cattle, all a herder wants are the few objects (leather tethering cords, spears, clubs and of late, firearms) used for their protection and management. Beyond those, the household possesses fishing spears; utensils for milking cows, production of ghee and eating food (of baked clay, gourds or sometimes manufactured); a wooden mortar and pestle for pounding grain; wooden head rests, woven matting and skins. Outside are pegs for tethering cattle and branched tree trunks stuck in the ground as shrines (Figure 2.5).

Traditionally, Dinka men wore no clothing and women wore only skins of goats and sheep made into soft leather aprons. After independence, wearing of clothes became more commonplace and almost never nowadays would a young man enter a town without a robe (Arabic *jalabiya*) or less often a shirt and slacks. Women, whether in the cattle camp or at the transhumant settlement, now often wear dresses of different kinds.

*Food.* Food of the Dinka is both animal-based (milk, cattle, goats and sheep, game and, seasonally, fish) and crop-based (sorghum, sesame, beans, peanuts, maize). Everyone drinks milk fresh, fermented into curds or shaken to separate butter. Whey is drunk separately or mixed with water for making dura flour porridge. Dinka do not slaughter cattle simply for the sake of meat, but cattle flesh enters the food chain in indirect ways through animal sacrifices and celebration of important visitors. It is either boiled or roasted. Offal are boiled and fish are boiled or roasted. Blood is not normally a food as such, but blood from an animal sacrificed is boiled with its offal.

Making dura flour is an exciting activity for women who enjoy singing praises to their husbands or young men (if unmarried) to the rhythmic beat of the pestle. Sesame is fried and ground into an oily paste eaten as such or added to porridge. Boiled beans may be eaten as is or ground into a paste with sesame butter. Peanuts are usually fried and mixed with cooked whole dura grains. The only "sweet" is the mildly sweet dura stalk. It is thinly cut, dried, soaked in water and eaten as such or boiled and added to other food. Today some Dinka purchase and use salt.

The main opportunistic strategy employed by Africa's pastoralists is migration. While, of our four examples, the Dinka, Maasai and southern Somalis are transhumants with a home base, the Turkana and northern Somalis are nomads. Transhumant migrations are seasonal responses for which pastoralists usually are well prepared and into which they incorporate important aspects of social intercourse and cultural identity.

**Figure 2.5. Agar Dinka cattle camp. Branched shrines (*ghoro*) bear cattle-tethering cords. Cattle dung fires help ward off biting flies and mosquitoes.**

### The Dinka Seasonal Migration Cycle

Dinka, who comprise 25 subtribes or sections, graze their herds over about a tenth of the Sudan's total area. Most are concentrated close to the Nile and its tributaries within the four provinces of Bahr el Ghazal, Lakes, Jonglei and Upper Nile. They keep sheep and goats as well as cattle, and women may also maintain small flocks of chickens. Livestock distribution and their general patterns of management are determined by environmental factors: scarcity of dryseason grazing and water supplies, the degree of flooding during rains and the prevalence of tsetse and other biting flies.

While Dinka are at their homesteads in the "highlands," cattle are kept on the intermediate lands, which, at that time of year, have very good grazing. They become fat and milking animals give comparatively high yields. These are a resting area for cattle between migrations in which minor movements (determined by grazing quality or directives from a general spirit--Chapter 3) may occur over distances of not more than 15 miles.

The most important determinant of seasonal migration is availability during the dry season of *toich* grazing. Movement there from the permanent homesteads starts in December-January at the beginning of the dry season, *mei*.

The return journey to the permanent homebase usually starts in May-June, the early part of the rainy season, *keer*. These major migrations are planned by the clan or larger lineage group; individual decision is not acceptable in such matters that greatly determine the survivability of cattle. Each lineage group has specific delineated *toich*, intermediate and highlands grazing areas through tribal inheritance (but without formal titles in the Northern sense). Dinka as a whole usually demonstrate a high degree of cooperation, especially at times of localized natural disasters (e.g., flooding or drought) which severely affect grazing in a particular area. Under those circumstances, elders of the affected areas approach those of areas not affected to allow their cattle access to their grazing lands, and this is usually granted.

This migration strategy is aimed at maximizing use of land and water and, additionally, to provide the opportunity for Dinka to undertake social functions which, by deeply rooted customs, are attended to in specific seasons of the year. During the early part of the rainy season when cattle leave the *toich* for the highlands, cultivation of dura and other edible crops begins there. In June-August (*ruer*), when rains are heavy, harvest of crops begins and initiation of boys into manhood is undertaken. People eat more in this season in order to be physically fit for the hard times of the dry season.

During *rur* (September-November) rains gradually become scanty and usually stop by early December. During that season, harvest of crops is completed and cattle are turned onto the dura fields to graze the stalks. There is still enough food and the main community and family activities are settlement of marriages plus sacrifices to general and/or local spirits for protection against cattle diseases and crocodiles. Depending on the condition of grazing and the level of water in pools in the highlands, cattle are driven to the *toich* in the middle or end of *rur*. *Mei*, the *toich* season, is when people drink lots of milk and eat fish from the shallow flooded areas. Young men and girls interact intensively, and future couples identify themselves and marriages are planned. Thus, the most important seasons are *rur* and *mei* when the most vital family and community activities take place.

Beyond such sociocultural events, going to the *toich* is like going to a summer resort for a Northerner, and more. This is a period of fun, especially for Dinka youth. Activities like fishing, swimming and sacrifices to spirits--in addition to courting--provide much of this excitement. These relationships between migration cycle and social organization and functioning are basic to Dinka life in ways not readily apparent to outsiders. They exemplify the types of things that it is vital to learn about particular pastoral peoples if development proposals are to enjoy their support. It is not necessarily true, therefore, as many outside development agents, planners and/or external government officials have believed, that if provided with alternative sources of water and grazing, transhumant pastoralists like the Dinka might voluntarily give up their seasonal migration. What might more realistically happen is an increase in the proportion of milking cows left at the homesteads to provide milk for children and the elderly who do not travel to the *toich*.


## TURKANA MIGRATIONS

The Turkana are nomads occupying the northwest corner of Kenya where they share borders with traditional enemies, the Toposa of the southern Sudan and the Karamojong of Uganda.   Cattle raiding among them is frequent, especially in years of severe drought and/or cattle epidemics.  Turkana have three subtribes which, though homogeneous in culture, traditions and language, show differences in preferences for livestock species. Thus, the Kuatela around Lokichogio keep cattle, sheep and goats and camels in that order; for the Kamatak of Lake Turkana the order is camels, goats and sheep and cattle; while within the Yapakuno subtribe in the north it is goats and sheep, camels and cattle.

The physical topography of Turkanaland divides it into two areas, the lowlands with clay soils and the mountainous area of ironstone soil types.  In contrast to Dinkaland, this whole area is semiarid to arid with sparse vegetational cover: "Turkanaland appears from the surrounding escarpment as a vast sandy plain far below, where the flat scenery is relieved by isolated mountain blocks, and where dust devils rise in high columns for most of the day. . . . On descending . . . , it seems at first glance impossible for men or animals to live there" (Gulliver and Gulliver, 1953).  Vegetation is mainly acacia shrubs with occasional thorny bushes.

The average annual rainfall in the plains is 300 to 400 mm, falling to less than 150 mm in the central desert region (Gulliver, 1955: 21).  Thus, some Turkana receive about the same amount of rainfall as the West African Sahel (Sollod, 1991; McCabe, 1987).  Turkana divide the year into two seasons: the dry, *akumu* and the wet, *agiporo*.  The dry season extends from September to March while the wet season covers the months of April to August.

The sources of water are seasonal rivers draining from the escarpment which, although they flow irregularly, enable retentive rock pools to be filled and underground supplies to be refurbished.  There are several types of water-points, (1) rock pools, *ebur*, filled during the rains; (2) springs, *ecuar*, which are scarce and confined chiefly to the mountains where they are used extensively during the dry season, and (3) wells, *akar* (Figure 2.6), which are the usual type in the plains (Gulliver and Gulliver, 1953: 55-56).  In recent years, the government has drilled boreholes in some of the small towns which have sprung up.

Wells in dry riverbeds are dug after the rains.  This process is well organized, each household watering its animals in turn while other families patiently wait (Figure 2.7).  Young women stand one above the other on steps cut into the well's sides,  pass water  up in wooden  containers and pour it into a

**Figure 2.6. Young Turkana women at a well dug in a seasonal river bed.** Some wells require as many as six women standing one above the other to pass water to the surface. (Source: Dr. Igor Mann.)

larger wooden trough from which animals drink singly.  In this well-digging and watering process, we see a traditional mechanism for cooperation in sharing a common resource.

Physical circumstances dictate two main seasonal movements: from the lowlands to the mountains for dry season grazing and back again for rainy season grazing. While still basically a "cattle culture" with respect to traditional institutions and priorities, many Turkana keep multiple species; their specific grazing-browsing abilities, in addition to vegetational sources available, determine migration patterns.  Cattle spend most of the time on grasslands in mountain areas and banks of watercourses, but in a comparatively good wet season they are driven down to the plains and are taken back when grazing deteriorates at the beginning of the dry season.  Camel-keeping is a recent feature of Turkana life and this species continues to grow in popularity. Camels are able to browse trees and bushes while sheep and goats are capable

**Figure 2.7. Turkana families and herds awaiting their turns to be watered at a hand-dug well in the mountains.**

of both grazing and browsing. Thus those species may be kept on different vegetation cover from cattle. During a two year drought period in 1979-1981, sheep and cattle declined to 24% and 37% of prior numbers, as compared to 52% and 55% for more drought-tolerant goats and camels, but recovery of all to predrought populations took only three years (Wienpahl, 1984; McCabe, 1987). As Dinkaland and Turkanaland exemplify, ecological conditions and harshness of environment may differ markedly from one pastoral region of Africa to another. While Dinkaland offers possibilities for increased production of both crops and livestock, Turkanaland offers no such opportunities. The cause of Turkana nomadism, unlike that for transhumance among the Dinka, is an extreme poverty of vegetation which is a product of rainfall that is not only small, but highly irregular both in quantity and effectiveness. Also, unlike the Dinka, there apparently are no specific grazing land rights among the far less numerous Turkana for any particular group. All members of the tribe have equal rights and privileges for the use of any available pasture. Where wet and dry season areas are contiguous, and browsing stock tend to follow more or less the same migratory patterns as cattle, more than one homestead belonging to the same nuclear family (i.e., a man, his wives, sons and their wives and children, and unmarried daughters) may remain in contact and cooperate in the total effort. But, when wet season grazing is geographically remote from the cattle pastures of the dry season, different subfamilies (a wife with her children and their animals) remain apart for much of the year (Gulliver, 1955). In such instances, a temporary matriarchal pattern in family decision-making exists.

Thus, the migration patterns of the Turkana are more differentiated, being more animal species-oriented and a function of the vegetation type suitable to a particular species of livestock, particularly in years of greatest environmental stress (Wienpahl, 1984). Unlike the communal cooperation manifested in watering their stock, animal movements do not involve consensuses of larger than the single family group. These are important differences in decision-making and governance from those of the Dinka, where the subtribe or clan makes a collective decision to which everyone must adhere.

The Turkana had been little disturbed until recently. With increasing international attention, and a road transecting their territory, their fragile ecosystem is now being subjected to very rapid outside influences. Especially disruptive have been large concentrations near towns, usually without their animals, for implementation of outside food aid. This may be encouraging a generation of young people less experienced in ways to cope.


## MAASAI MIGRATIONS

The Maasai occupy the area south of Kenya's Lake Baringo extending into central Tanzania. Their land is part of the East African Plateau which varies between 2,000 and 6,000 feet. The western portion is better watered and provides better grazing than the eastern areas which are hot and windy and receive a maximum of 350 mm of rain per year (Berntsen, 1977). Runoff is rapid with the result that little water is absorbed by the soil. There are few rivers and lakes and many streams go underground after short distances. Banks of permanent rivers provide breeding habitats for tsetse flies and thus are unavailable for maximum use.

Organizationally each Maasai subtribe (*ol-osho*) consists of a number of localities or *enkutot* with their own permanent water resources and grazing areas upon which cattle camps depend during the dry season. Each subtribe has its own pastures for wet season grazing and individual male heads of compound polygamous families share rights to communal grazing and water within these subtribal boundaries (Huntingford, 1969: 108). Transhumant movements of herds and families are from dry season pastures based on permanent river, well or spring water supplies (Figure 2.8) to temporary, outlying wet season grazing areas based on rain ponds and other temporary surface water supplies (Branagan, 1962: 23). Thus, tribal organization and patterns of land use for the Maasai are similar to those of the Dinka, the Maasai locality or *enkutot* corresponding to the Dinka *dom* or *bai*.

But, in striking contrast to the Turkana and the bulk of the Dinka, the Maasai have had a great deal of contact with, and manipulation by, first, colonialists, then outside development agents and planners. In this 100-year process, they have lost some of their best lands and much of their original transhumant capacity to optimally adapt to ecological circumstances. Some

**Figure 2.8.** Part of a Maasai family before the thornbush corral of its transhumant homestead (*manyatta*).

have been forced to settle permanently in low-potential formerly wet season grazing areas after having lost their high-potential dry season reserves (Tepilit, 1978). For example, in the Narok district of Kenya, most family settlements (*manyattas*, Figure 2.9) are permanently located near a natural spring and their

**Figure 2.9.** Maasai transhumant homestead of mud and wattle huts within dry season pasture reserves.

traditional transhumance has ceased.  During the dry season when this spring fails, *daily* trekking of cattle for long distances must take place.  The first author was told that because they can no longer carry out their transhumant migration, total grazing time for cattle is reduced (since they need extra time to reach water).  Maasai are being forced into such new ways.  That is, they are a pastoral people who clearly have passed the point of any rational optimization of tradition and "modernization."  Other important changes in Kenya have been introduction of individual and group ranches (see Chapter 5).  Those changes reflected the ideological thrusts of one of the two main groups of development competitors in Africa between 1960 and 1990, that communal grazing lands be converted to private ownership (abolition of commons) or to more formalized patterns of traditional group ownership and management.

A net result of these efforts among the Maasai which few would now dispute is that, through them, Maasai already are losing much of their traditional pastoralist culture, probably irretrievably.  Much control is out of their hands and the results already have been highly disruptive both socially (e.g., alcoholism is a growing problem) and culturally.  Their plight resembles more and more that of Native Americans and Australia's aborigines.[3]

## SOMALI MIGRATIONS

"If geography is the progenitor of history, it could be said that Somali ecology gave birth to Somali pastoralism.  Much of the Somali peninsula is an arid semidesert unfit for reliable cultivation and only precariously suited for raising livestock. . . . In this land of hardy vegetation, steaming sand dunes, and sun-baked coastal plains, the Somalis have evolved during the centuries a way of life peculiarly suited to their demanding environment: on the one hand, . . . pastoralism designed to maximize the meager resources of water wells and pasturelands for the pastoralists and their herds and, on the other, a social organization that encourages collective action and mutual aid" (Laitin and Samatar, 1987: 21-27).

Rainfall in Somalia is irregular and unreliable, but environmental conditions are much harsher in the north than in the south (which has two rivers, the Shebelle and Juba).  Much of the north receives as little as 50 to 150 mm annually (Kaplan, 1982: 68).  Thus, emphasis is upon camel, sheep and goat husbandry.  The south offers better conditions for animal hubandry and some crop production.  There are two wet and two dry seasons.  In *jilal* (December-March), the weather is dry and hot.  *Gu* (April-May) has the heaviest rainfall but is still hot.  *Haga* (June-September), though the hottest period of the year in the north along the Gulf of Aden, is slightly cooler elsewhere with occasional showers occurring on the southeast coast, though dry inland.  *Der*, the second wet season (October-November) is again hot with some intermittent rains (Kaplan, 1982: 68).

Unlike Dinka, Turkana and Maasai, Somali pastoralists practice both nomadism and transhumance, the former in the north. There, migration is unstructured and is under the control of individual herders. There are only two sources of water, wells and *berkeeds*, hand- or machine-dug ponds, for temporary storage of rain water (Figure 2.10). In their general vicinities families concentrate during *haga* and *der* and from which, after the *gu* rains, they move out to much more dispersed pastures. Those movements are to anywhere pasturage and/or water is believed available (I. M. Lewis, 1969: 92-93). This takes place within a traditional clan/tribal grazing area, the *degaan*, some of which are as large as 2,500 square kilometers. During times of drought, movements into less drought-stricken neighboring *degaans* also may occur (Bouzarat et al., 1988: 72) and are usually tolerated. In the south, in contrast, each tribe's and section's pastureland is defined by settled villages. Transhumance consists of two annual movements, one away from these base

**Figure 2.10. Somalis watering cattle from a shallow well dug in a seasonal stream bed.** (Source: Jorg Janzen in Baumann et al., 1993.)

villages into the grazing areas when the new season's rains are expected, and then back again when the dry season begins.

Nomadic movements in the north resemble those of the Turkana, while transhumance practiced in the south has a lot in common with the Dinka, in that it is more time-specific. Both of the latter have grazing areas defined by traditional clan ownership rights and cooperation in sharing pasture and water during bad times is exercised similarly and to almost the same degree. However, the two differ in that while movement decisions among Dinka are collective, in the case of south Somalis it is an individual decision, thus resembling that of Turkana.

There are two other main senses in which Somali pastoralists, who are non-Nilotes, differ from Nilotic pastoralists such as the Maasai, Turkana and Dinka: (1) they cherish the camel as the most important beast,[4] followed by cattle, sheep and goats; and (2) Somalis have been much more exposed to the outside world for centuries, and consequently to commercial trade. Hence, to a much greater extent than most Nilotes, they view their livestock in terms of money within a modern economic context.

## MONITORING AS A PASTORAL DEVELOPMENT TOOL

Studies on the ecology of traditional African pastoral areas are of comparatively recent origin and, in most areas, remain to be done. As in the case of the southern Sudan's Jonglei canal project, some were stimulated for reasons other than local pastoralists' welfare (see Chapter 5). Moreover, it has been mostly in the last decade that any have incorporated study of traditional husbandry practices and, thus, begun to influence prior Northern assumptions about these and their effectiveness. Not only have these more recent studies (e.g., Behnke et al., 1993) fueled a growing belief that "with traditional grazing practices, the productivity of the grassland of . . . [sub-Saharan Africa's arid] zone [is] at least comparable to productivity of comparable rangelands in North America and Australia" (Pritchard et al., 1992: 23), but some workers have suggested that monitoring water and range resources will be vital for coping with emergencies and realistic development planning (Sollod, 1991; de Leeuw et al., 1993). They see such as ways to possibly "fine tune" pastoralists' current practices for greater productivity (Behnke et al., 1993). Some have suggested monitoring livestock productivity, mortality and morbidity in connection with measurements of variables such as those (Schwabe, 1980; Sollod, 1991), or in relation to soil erosion (Bartels et al., 1993).

Sollod (1991) urged more specifically that monitoring activities in the Sahel comprise part of an early drought emergency warning and response system. This would identify "red flag rainfall years," conditions which, if repeated an additional year, would result in an emergency situation. While de Leeuw and his associates (1993) considered that remote sensing systems from satellites might provide means to monitor primary production of rangelands, as well, perhaps, as rainfall and evapotranspiration, such high technology approaches would require not only large infusions of external funds and a coordinated multicountry infrastructure, but costly on-the-ground delivery systems for interventions based on their findings. More immediately possible, at least in theory, would be systems for periodic on-the-ground monitoring, as well as response, but those too would be costly in terms of manpower and transport required, prohibitively expensive, in our view, *were such systems independent of other services delivery.*

Sollod (1991) provided an important clue to more immediately realizable monitoring possibilities under current conditions of minimal resources in that he would associate rainfall and some other monitoring tasks with veterinary services delivery. We stress importance of much closer future attention to all such matters, since the system of pastoral management long advocated by most Northern outsiders (i.e., a stocking rate based on the carrying capacity of the *poorest* rainfall years) is steadily losing favor. We agree with Sollod (1991) and others (Zessin, 1991; Ellis et al., 1993; Bartels et al., 1993) that, generally speaking, it is "impractical and unnecessary to apply conservative stocking strategies under [African] pastoral conditions." That is, African pastoralists' highly opportunistic systems of livestock management, of rapidly adjusting to environmental and other changes, are becoming better appreciated for their merits by observers in closest touch with these people and their practices. At this point, some interim conclusions may be drawn.


**CONCLUSIONS**

Comparatively speaking, the Turkana and northern Somalis are the most necessarily pastoral of the four peoples considered in this chapter by virtue of the harshness of their environments. The Dinka, southern Somalis and some Maasai have cultivating options. The first two have partially exploited these alternatives of their own volition. While the main body of the Maasai have resisted this option, they already have been forced from some of their lands which most readily provided those possibilities. The Somalis have maintained until now the stability of a traditional African pastoral society, although subjected years before to major external disturbances. The Turkana's fragile balance for survival can be jeopardized by almost any external force, including the long-term concentration of many of their numbers for the convenience of those providing emergency aid. The Dinka are a highly adapted, numerous people in an environment with potential options, but who also are very rapidly being subjected to externally initiated forces which could disrupt their cherished way of life irrevocably with incommensurate compensation.

A first general conclusion is that African pastoralism must be recognized as an efficient form of economic order achieved through adjustments dictated by the changeable nature of the pastoralists' niche, which generally remains marginal to highly unfavorable. This rationalism (from pastoralists' perspective) has not been recognized in most past development efforts (see Chapter 5) nor have its bases been widely enough understood by Northern economists, politicians and others of nonpastoral origin. A second conclusion follows-- namely, that pastoralists must be taken seriously as judges of their own situation.[5] Surely, useful information can be provided them by some outsiders, which, as in the case of increasing popularity of camels among Turkana, may initiate significant changes. We believe that pastoralists' perceptions of their own needs, particularly in facing new outside pressures, might well change with additional information that sensitive outsiders could supply them. Yet, in Somalia, Islam and an introduced monetary economy still have not replaced many elements of traditional pastoralism, though they have eliminated some incompatible elements. It would appear that these changes among a people like the Somali, still in process, *have been gradual enough* until recently to be adjusted to by the traditional institutions of their society without destroying much of its valued bases and the people's ability to cope under major environmental stresses.

For the Dinka, at least, a third general conclusion is also apparent: that migration to the seasonal floodplain grazing areas is a unique occasion which provides them, far beyond the pursuit of water and pasture, opportunities to perform other culturally important social functions and similar reasons have been or probably could be identified with a little effort for many other African pastoralists. These associations probably all have rational origins and these may, at least in some instances, be ascertained. For example, some may reflect the seasonality of absolutely essential labor demands and the periods when these demands are minimal.

Thus, an overall conclusion that can be reached at this point about traditional African pastoral societies is that in the past they have adapted well to the realities of their physical environments. As a result, pastoralism has supported sizable human populations under often severe environmental stress. In fact, when uninfluenced by human forces from the outside, pastoral societies usually have constituted portions of natural ecosystems. The necessary corollary with respect to outside development agents is that the ecology of the local area must be understood by them, and considered both for its historical effects as a rational determinant of prevailing cultural and social patterns and practices and, more important, for its current status vis-à-vis important manifestations of the culture intimately entwined with pastoral migrations and other aspects of life. The qualifier, of course, is whether pastoralists *totally on their own* can continue to effectively adapt when faced by the external influences so many now increasingly face. Such will unquestionably change their needs for certain types of outside information both in terms of quantity and complexity. Likely too is that this total process will continually compress the timeframe within which pastoralists would be allowed to assimilate or react rationally to new information.

Finally, we would stress the future importance in pastoral development of being able to effectively monitor over the long term various conditions and phenomena, a need being repeatedly emphasized by recent observers, but without practically affordable suggestions for implementation. We shall propose in Chapter 8 a realizable route to accomplish intersectorally essential aspects of ecological and other monitoring as key parts of a locally based but more broadly coordinated program of pastoral development.

## NOTES

1. Lack of availability today for some groups of other coping strategies from the past (e.g., cattle-raiding, locally collected "taxes," slavery) makes them more vulnerable to climatic changes and more dependent upon purely husbandry measures. In areas with a more commercial basis for livestock raising and more alternative occupations within families and other social groupings (e.g., parts of Somalia and West Africa), other means of risk reduction more familiar to Northerners may also be employed.

2. *Toich*, the Dinka word for dry season Floodplain grazing areas, will be used henceforth.

3. When, in 1987, Professor Geoffrey Maloiy, a noted Maasai animal physiologist, arranged for the second author to conduct interviews with leading tribal elders about aspects of their traditional religion, there were then only three surviving Kenyan Maasai whom he believed were still competent repositories for many Maasai beliefs and bases for traditional practices.

4. With only an estimated 0.83% of Africa's population, Somali pastoralists own 43% of the continent's camels (MLFR/GTZ, 1990:3).

5. It is the height of arrogance to assume, as many Northerners have been prone to, that policy making based largely upon uninvestigated metaphors and often supported by little more than transient "safari consultantships" by total aliens (or upon equally patronizing beliefs of local outsiders to their cultures), has much to recommend it. It completely defies logic not to centrally and meaningfully involve pastoralists themselves in every process which intends to alter or impinge upon their evolved way of life.

# 3

---

# CATTLE, OTHER LIVESTOCK AND PASTORAL LIFE

Planners, administrators and veterinary experts usually have insufficient knowledge about the social and cultural conditions in nomadic societies.

G. Dahl and A. Hjort, 1976

Of Libya's shepherds why the tale pursue? Why sing their pastures and the scattered huts they house in? Oft their cattle day and night graze the whole month together, and go forth into far deserts where no shelter is, so flat the plain and boundless. All his goods the Afric swain bears with him. . . . All his tender care is to the calves transferred.

Virgil, *Georgics*, 30 BC

I believe a leaf of grass is no less than the journey work of the stars,
. . . and the cow crunching with depress'd head surpasses any statue.

Walt Whitman, *Leaves of Grass*

Rare among pre-World War II studies of African pastoralists were ones which focused upon their subsistence economies (Evans-Pritchard, 1937, 1940). Later, some anthropologists (e.g., Schneider, 1957; Dyson-Hudson and Dyson-Hudson, 1969) linked such inquiries to findings resulting from heightened pursuit of ecology as an investigative discipline and a few made attempts to relate some of this to efforts intended to provide services or amenities to pastoralists (Cunnison, 1960; Dahl and Hjort, 1976). But, by and large, these different avenues of activity and their literatures remained separated, with one seldom appreciably influencing the other. Most anthropologists continued to pursue themes more remote to subsistence or development like kinship relationships and indigenous religions, and virtually no efforts were made to convince persons interested in pastoral development that those too might be relevant.

In the meantime, development economists tended to overlook or credited insufficiently important aspects of pastoral subsistence or to use a suitable range of output measurements to compare those systems to Northern alternatives (S. Sandford, 1983; Jarvis and Erickson, 1986). A result was that politicians and development funders came to view traditional African pastoralism as a near "basket case" and encouraged Northern range management and veterinary/animal science specialists to recast indigenous husbandry systems in North American or Australian molds. While there have been growing reasons to question such viewpoints and decisions (see Chapter 2), meaningful communications and cooperation among anthropologists, economists and representatives of these several other concerned disciplines remained infrequent and, overall, pastoral development has reached an impasse reflecting an almost total poverty of workable ideas.

Our development proposals depend partly upon the unrealized potential for juxtaposing information and insights from such diverse sources. In this chapter we shall attempt to narrow the gaps between still far too disparate thrusts of anthropologists, developers and natural scientists like ourselves largely by illustrating how, despite growing importance among some African pastoralists of small ruminants and camels, relationships between the human and bovine species have an importance in Africa that transcends even the most realistic recognition of their subsistence value. While subsistence-type husbandry systems supportive of relatively large human populations on marginal rangelands are unfamiliar enough to diverse Northern disciplinarians with some interest in Africa's future, additional cultural relationships between pastoralists and cattle are so remote to be nearly incomprehensible even to sensitive individuals without intimate first-hand knowledge. Such cultural factors undergird, yet go far beyond, already considered social functions associated with pastoralists' seasonal migration strategies and often constitute the very fabric of a particular pastoralist culture.

Even among some African pastoralists for whom other animal species now are important economically there is a tenacious clinging to this more exclusively cattle-centered past. This is vital to understand when considering seemingly desirable changes within any particular situation. That is, ecology apparently influenced how, centuries ago, cattle became central to the connectedness of many things now so seemingly unrelated when viewed through Northern eyes. Cattle remain the "cement" which enables millions of Africans within such "fused" societies (see Table 1.1) to visualize their own positions and roles vis-à-vis their environment and cosmos much more fully than present-day Northerners do within theirs. From this, many African pastoralists derive a sense of security and well-being which compensates for absence of material things most Northerners may consider paramount.

Cattle are still by far the most economically important livestock in Africa. Within sub-Saharan Africa alone they number about 163 million, as compared to 145 million goats, 124 million sheep and 13 million camels (Pritchard et al., 1992: 23).[1] In terms of more comparable tropical livestock units (TLU), which take into account weight differences among species, cattle represent 114 million TLU, as compared to 15 million for goats, 12 million for sheep and 13 million for camels.    Because some peoples like the Dinka will not volunteer cattle numbers because of fear that that might appear boastful (while others may underestimate numbers to avoid taxes), estimates for particular countries may be reasonably accurate or not.    In sub-Saharan Africa overall, animal husbandry contributes an estimated 35-50% of the agricultural domestic product (de Haan and Bekure, 1989; Pritchard et al., 1993; Leonard, 1993: 229) depending upon whether their draft and other energy contributions are taken into account.   In the Sudan, Lesotho, Somalia, Namibia, Mauritania and Botswana they contribute 58 to 88% (USDA, 1990), even without full credit for subsistence.    These animal sources of food are more widely distributed than plant sources and can be drawn upon in emergencies by most of the population.

## CATTLE-KEEPING IN AFRICA

Figure 3.1 shows the approximate geographical range of *Bos primigenius*, the now-extinct wild aurochs ancestor of domestic cattle (except those of southeastern Asia) in relation to areas of the world where people have traditionally drunk cow's milk. It can be seen that the range of the cow milk drinking habit is broader than the range of cattle's wild ancestor, especially in Africa. While earliest known sites of domesticated cattle remains are in Greece, Anatolia and Iran, "there is [also] a definite possibility that [cattle] may have been domesticated locally within the northern Sahara region, albeit about 1,000 years later than in western Asia [that is, by about 5000 BC]" (Clutton-Brock, 1989: 204).    Thus, if cattle were independently domesticated in Africa in ancient times, it was surely in the continent's north which was part of the range of the aurochs.    Or the possibility exists, as formerly believed, that all of Africa's domesticated cattle entered that continent from Asia. Domestic cattle remains from the Fayum area and Badari sites in Middle Egypt date from well before dynastic times (c. 4000 BC), although some scholars think that the introduction of cattle-keeping on a larger scale from Upper Egypt into the lower

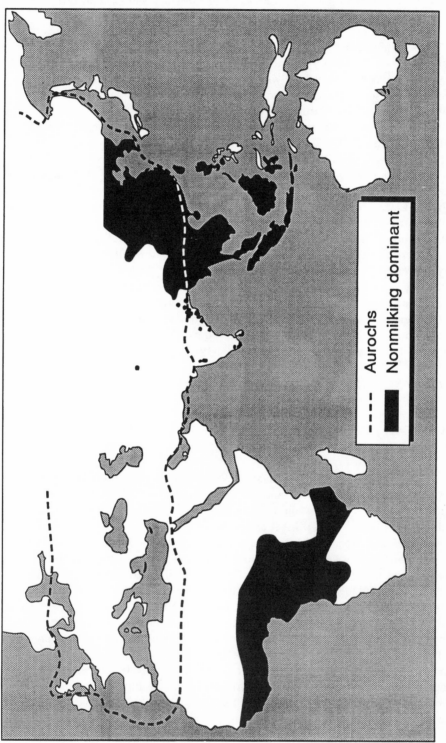

**Figure 3.1. Ranges in Africa, Europe and Asia of the now extinct wild aurochs ancestor of domestic cattle,** *Bos primigenius* **(broken line), and areas where people have not traditionally drunk cows' milk (solid black). (Redrawn after Simoons, 1979 and Clutton-Brock, 1981.)**

Aurochs

Nonmilking dominant

reaches of the Nile and its fertile delta (among peoples then practicing digging-stick agriculture)--that is, prior to or concurrent with the creation of a united kingdom under the first pharaoh Menes-Narmer--may have been an important precursor to the rapid flowering of Egyptian civilization.[2]

Early cattle-keeping in Africa is documented not only for the Nile Valley but across much of the Sahara, which the geologic record indicates has had two wet periods, separated by a dry period, prior to the present. The Sahara commenced its present cycle of drying only in about 2,500 BC and by about 1,300 BC its cattle-keeping peoples had been forced out of ever more arid areas into savannas to the south (Clutton-Brock, 1989: 205). Earliest archeological evidence of an extension of cattle-keeping into East Africa is about 2,000 BC. Oldest known sites are from the area around Lake Turkana, but about a thousand years later this practice extended as far south as the Rift Valley and highlands of Kenya and Tanzania (Robertshaw, 1989: 207).

Let us now examine briefly one of the most interesting features of pastoral societies past and present.

### Milk Drinking

One central feature of cattle cultures historically has been cow milk drinking (Simoons, 1970, 1971), a custom so well-entrenched in the societies of pastoral Africa *and Europe* as to be regarded in both areas as totally normal human behavior. But, just as prejudices are easy to recognize (and condemn or ridicule) in others and difficult to recognize (or acknowledge) in ourselves, the oddity of some of our most commonplace and taken-for-granted beliefs and practices may similarly elude us and surely never be brought into question as to whether they may be "normal" or not. For example, this idea of nurturing from the teat of another species of animal has always been totally foreign, in fact disgusting, to large groups of the world's peoples, including the Chinese and other southeast Asians (Simoons, 1970).

No mammal, man included, continues to receive the sustenance and support of its own mother's teat beyond early life. Despite such biological consistencies, at some time in man's not so distant past, between 8,000 and 5,000 years ago when the cultural and other precursors of civilization began to emerge and coalesce in several parts of the world, adult man, of his own volition, did the culturally strange, we might even say unnatural, thing of deliberately adopting for his foster-mother the female of a totally different species of mammal, the cow. Not only did adult man in some parts of the world do this generally at some point, but it was especially their kings and priests who first began to publicly kneel beside and drink from the teats of a cow (Figure 3.2), with all of the profound psychological and biological overtones of that act freely entered into and accepted (Schwabe, 1984a).

That startling act was not merely some local or transient aberration confined to a single people in antiquity, but by the dawn of history this deep

**Figure 3.2. Egyptian pharaoh depicted drinking directly from the teat of their ancient cowmother goddess Hathor** (Courtesy of the Egyptian Museum, Cairo.)

interspecific bond already had extended among the speakers of several major phyla of languages on three continents. That is to say it had become the practice not only among speakers of some now extinct Afro-Asiatic languages (ancient Egyptian, Babylonian, Canaanite-Phoenician), and of Nilo-Saharan languages that were/are spoken in Africa to the south and west of Egypt, but also among the speakers of Indo-European languages who then or soon thereafter inhabited a vast area of the Eurasian landmass as far as Spain and Portugal in the west to Iran and India in the east.    Probably at some later point this practice of man's adopting the cow as foster mother also spread among speakers of other phyla of African languages (Simoons, 1971).    While cow milk drinking has lost for Europeans all of its originally profound psychological significance, such ideas still survive not only among many African pastoralists (hence their many ritual uses of milk), but also in India.

Evidence from ancient records suggests that man's suckling from the cow originated from wild bull emulation (early man's envy of certain characteristics of the male aurochs *Bos primigenius*; Figure 3.3) and the beliefs, practices and institutions to which that led (Schwabe, 1994). For example, the earlier Egyptian pharoahs' pitting of themselves against the wild bull in highly organized hunts was an important feature of their demonstrating kingship. As we shall see, cattle eating may have for some African pastoralists a similarly deep significance. There is, therefore, no question that the universe of a number of African peoples is one in which cattle assumed a profound cultural utility.

### "Cattle Culture"

This pervasive importance of cattle is pastoral Africa's one feature which most struck Northern observers after the opening of Africa. But it is to an early 20th-century American anthropologist, Melville Herskovits, that outsiders most owe recognition of the generality of these associations which seemed so strange to them.    Upon him also rests much of the blame for any distorted understanding of African pastoralism by Northerners.    Although we think those are partially misreadings of Herskovits, he gave little attention to (1) the subsistence role of cattle; (2) environmental determinants of particular beliefs and practices; (3) an historical perspective, especially vis-à-vis cattle acquisition in the aftermath of rinderpest; and (4) any comparative time-place search for possible parallels or precedents to the people-cattle situation he considered unique to (East) Africa.

Thus Herskovits' (1926) emphasis upon cattle acquisition provided what many intent upon African development felt went hand in glove with what Hardin (1968) was to describe as the "tragedy of the commons." Yet, as we have seen, both with respect to consensus-determined decisions about grazing grounds and cattle movements by the Dinka and orderly cooperative use of water holes by the Turkana, some African pastoralists have indeed developed

**Figure 3.3. Egyptian slate palette depicting the first Egyptian pharaoh Menes-Narmer as a bull goring his enemies** (Redrawn from Petrie, 1953.)

rules for commons governance. And, as Ostrom (1990: 50ff) argues, such "rules in use" are essential components of institutions. Because Herskovits left this overall impression upon many Northerners of African pastoralists as irrational peoples intent only upon maximizing their numbers of cattle, we should attempt to understand what he did and did not set out to do.

Herskovits was intent upon exploring differences in the theoretical bases of competing cultural diffusion theories championed by German and American schools of ethnology. His was purportedly the first testing of the American theory in a non-American situation. That is, Herskovits had a very specific focus and intent with respect to what he sought and recorded. While he recognized (p. 248) that "the distribution of cattle in Africa covers by far the larger portion of the continent," he was intent upon identifying a special "culture-area" which he called the East African Cattle Area in which prevailed the East African Cattle Complex, a cultural entity in which cattle are of prime importance and are essential in connection with (1) marriage (pp. 361-388), (2) birth (pp. 494-499), (3) death (pp. 499-506) and (4) inheritance (pp. 506-516). Moreover, within this area are to be observed a great number of taboos with respect to milk, cattle care and sometimes grass (pp. 516-524) and that among such peoples cattle are the only things that constitute wealth.

Herskovits' work was based largely upon an analysis of literature which then consisted in large part of accounts of initial observations on African peoples by European explorers, travelers, missionaries, military men and colonial administrators. Many of these early sources tended to emphasize the exotic. Most important, the vast bulk of these accounts reflected conditions prevailing in the decades immediately following the great rinderpest pandemic at the turn of the 20th century, an event of major importance in African history in that it decimated its cattle population (see Chapter 4) and following which the majority of African pastoral peoples were totally intent upon a desperate attempt to rebuild their cattle wealth to its prepandemic levels. It was a long time before Northern scholars began to appreciate the enormous importance of that catastrophe, or the atypical circumstances it created. So, throughout Herskovits' work appear statements like this about the Sudanese Dinka: "here, too, every thought was how to get more cattle." While nowhere in Herskovits' papers have we found any statements to the effect that African pastoralists are not interested in the quality as well as the quantity of the animals they possess, that idea prevails in much Northern thinking about a presumed tragedy of the commons. Thus, much of the concentration of development agents upon supposedly irrational features of African pastoralism has been superficially based (with too little apparent understanding of its variations and inter-relationships to other aspects of life) and almost totally unexplored from either historical or comparative points of view.

These central roles of cattle today will be demonstrated by considering some of the functions they serve among the Dinka and their interconnectedness and bases.

## CURRENT LIVESTOCK RESOURCES IN THE SOUTHERN SUDAN

Within Africa, the Sudan ranks second in its numbers of cattle and sheep and third in its goat population. Estimated livestock numbers for the entire Sudan are 20 million cattle, 18 million sheep, 13 million goats and 2.7 million camels (MAR, 1987). This wealth is in the hands of 80% of the Sudan's 21 million people who live in rural areas (Nelson, 1983: 146). About 7 million (35%) of this cattle population, 3.7 million (20.6%) of sheep and 2.5 million (19.2%) of goats are estimated to be in the south, most of whose population are migratory pastoralists. Besides the Dinka, Nuer and Shilluk peoples, tribes that own many cattle include the Murle (Beir), Toposa and Mandari. Southern Sudanese cattle are classifiable on morphological grounds into three types: Nilotic, kept by Dinka, Nuer and Shilluk; Murle-Toposa, kept by those tribes and Boya; and zebu kept by Didinga, the Latuka-Lango group, Kuku, Bari and Mandari. Each is well-adapted to its environment (GOS, 1954); that is, the Nilotic type, found throughout the Floodplain, can endure flooding and insect worry, the Murle-Toposa type tolerates semi-arid conditions and zebu effectively utilize sparse hillside vegetation and may have some resistance to trypanosomiasis (Luxmore, 1950).

To southern Sudanese pastoralists, cattle's main product is milk, though, indirectly through rituals of sacrifice, virtually every bovine animal is eventually eaten. In addition to these food uses, cattle provide hides, dung for fuel (otherwise scarce in savannas and semiarid lands) and dung ash (*arop*). The latter, a very fine sterile powder believed to ward off biting flies and mosquitoes, is used to groom animals and people. Cattle urine is used for bathing, washing milking utensils, dressing wounds (as from spears, thorn bushes, goring animals, as well as incisions made on the foreheads of boys at manhood initiation) and it is added to milk to promote curdling for ghee production. Urine and dung both provide fertilizer when dropped on cultivated fields. Dinka do not use cattle for draft or transport as in some other pastoral areas of Africa (see Figure 2.1). Sheep and goats also are providers of milk and meat.

Despite their large numbers and broad distribution, the recorded annual contribution of livestock to the Sudan's gross domestic roduct (GDP) is only about 10% (Beshai, 1976; Lees and Brooks, 1977). Such GDP and livestock statistics can be reconciled only by realizing that, besides a large amount of livestock production for family subsistence, most by far of the exchange of (trade in) livestock in the southern Sudan (and to only a lesser degree in much of the north) is not in money transactions and therefore does not usually enter into such GDP, gross national product (GNP) and similar calculations. Livestock's real value in the Sudan has been grossly underestimated in economic analyses as a result and such monetary data are misleading in assessing the actual or potential values of the Sudanese livestock sector. The mean percentage value of animal resource exports to total Sudanese exports from 1966 to 1985 was 8.35%, with an annual range of 3.80%-23.50% (MAR, 1987), and were only 2.50% and 5.40% in 1989 and 1990, respectively (Economist Intelligence Unit, 1989; 1990), the latter out of a total export value of £S 42.9 million. Separate data for the southern Sudan are unavailable, but the percentage of households engaged in any commercial livestock trading there is only 3.9% (Duncan, 1978), whereas pastoralists comprise about 66% of the population (Regional Ministry of Finance, 1977). Such figures indicate that the Sudan's livestock industry, which employs and sustains such large segments of the population, is not highly commercialized domestically nor does it often contribute very much to foreign earnings.

Critics of GDP and GNP (especially of their growth) as measures of a population's income (or overall well-being) believe that not only are they poor measures,[3] but emphasize "how high the cost of growth of GNP has been in psychological, social and ecological terms" (Daly and Cobb, 1989: 62ff). While Daly and Cobb do not address special circumstances of pastoralism, they do discuss subsistance agriculture more generally (pp. 162-163, 268ff) in terms of improved states of human well-being.

The pastoral subsistence situation in Africa is centered upon the nuclear family but also involves in important ways extended families, sections, clans, subtribes or other lineage groups. Therefore, our consideration of cattle use by the Dinka will be prefaced by a description of the family, some of whose migration-related activities individually (and collectively with larger lineage groups) were considered in Chapter 2.

## THE DINKA FAMILY

Among the Dinka a nuclear family consists of a husband, his wife or wives and their children. Sometimes a man also takes over wives of a deceased brother or paternal uncle in order for them to bear additional children (but these are named for the dead man and considered his issue). Each wife with her children may have their own cattle hearth, depending on the number of cattle owned. In addition to his wives, matters of family interest are discussed by the husband not only with his own grown sons, but also with his brothers and his paternal uncles and their grown sons. Agreement within this extended family is usually by consensus, but in case of disputes, other elders in blood relationship may also be consulted. In any event, the husband's authority within the nuclear family itself is final and and he may override others in case of disagreement. While decisions about cattle movement and the like are made at the higher level of the total community,[4] matters decided within the extended family include accepting or rejecting the partner a son or daughter wishes to marry. Group decisions must also be made about each nuclear family's contributions of cattle toward the bride price in marriages of brothers, half brothers and cousins. The extended family also decides on the types and numbers of livestock to be sold to meet nontraditional needs (such as education or poll tax). Other decisions at this level include the number of milking cows to be left at the transhumant home base to nourish the young and elderly during the migration to the *toich* for dry season grazing.

However, most Dinka would agree that the primary importance of their extended families is security. A Dinka man's desire for more wives and more children is predicated upon knowledge that many children will not reach adulthood, so a large number are required to assure perpetuation of the family line (a major concern based partially on beliefs that it is possible to communicate with spirits of their ancestors). Also, since grown children are expected to take care of the parents in old age, children are the only "pension scheme" available. In the interval children ensure the labor force essential to care for the cattle and other livestock.

Thus, decisions involving obtaining or giving cattle are made on the basis of nuclear and extended families. However, the need to marry more wives, and this sharing in the paying of bride prices, eventually leads to cooperation among wider networks of families in relation to one another, ultimately to whole sections and clans. Beside the continuity of the human line itself, more wives and thus more children also ensure that the man-cattle cycle is uninterrupted. Girls marry and bring more cattle into the family. When boys marry, the family loses cattle, but these sons' wives will eventually have more girls who will bring more cattle into the family again. But beyond security and all aspects of the man-cattle cycle, family size within Dinka society is a symbol of prestige, since the more wives a person has, the more cattle--thus wealth--it is assumed he also has.

## CATTLE AND SUBSISTENCE

Kenyon and Kenyon (1991) have estimated that six or more head of cattle per person are required for subsistence purposes under conditions commonly experienced among migratory pastoralists in Africa, but variations among closely related peoples have been noted.  This depends partially upon the proportions of other species also kept and whether plant agriculture is practiced.  For example, among nomadic Turkana animals provide their sole means of livelihood.  Their Ngisonyoka subclan, which in 1984 grazed 85,200 sheep and goats, 9,800 cattle, 9,800 camels and 5,300 donkeys over 7,540 square kilometers of territory, derived 61% of their food energy from these animals' milk, 14% from their meat and blood, 16% from other foodstuffs obtained by trading some animals and the remainder from game and wild plants (Coughenour et al., 1985).  In contrast, a mixed economy, pastoralism and agriculture, is practiced by closely related transhumant Jie in their less severe terrain. But even among them "scarcely any ceremony, and no important one, can occur without the slaughter of a beast--e.g., rain-making, marriage, initiation, the prevention or alleviation of disease and disaster" (Gulliver, 1955).

Our main intent in this chapter is to provide sufficient understanding of "cattle culture" or "cattle complex" to indicate why its details must be investigated *locally* in each situation in which development options are being considered. Since other cattle functions are inextricably interwoven into the subsistence economy of the Dinka, they constitute essential points of departure for considering any nontraditional ideas like cattle for export (or as other means of capital generation) to pay for locally desired imports or non-traditional services.

Folktales heard repeatedly by the first author from childhood had cattle as their main subjects. In the words of a Ngok elder, "when we came out of the cattle-byre [*luak*] of Creation, we came with a white cow. We also had a bull of our own--our pied bull" (Deng, 1978: 41, 72; and see Figure 3.4). Or, as an Agar subtribe *bany bith* priest told us: "God gave foreigners the gun and the pen and Dinka the spear and the cow." Such statements reflect an intimacy between the Dinka and cattle which goes back in tribal memory to their beginnings.  And, in their current conception of cosmos, man and cattle exist, prosper and assure their perpetuation through an all-embracing three-way

**Figure 3.4. Specially prized Dinka black and white (pied) bulls. Young Dinka male (left), after initiation to manhood, assumes responsibility for herding the family's cattle as his main occupation. The left horn of his personal song bull (*muor cien*) is trained downward and forward by a series of operations. Dusting of the skin with cattle dung ash is to help ward off biting flies and mosquitoes.**

covenant between themselves and "Spiritual Force," which is most manifest in local spirits Dinka call *jok*.

Above and beyond such connections with their origins and the infinite, Dinka literally adore cattle.  Just the sight of them provides not only esthetic pleasure but gives a man the same sense of well-being as he feels when he stands with his arm about his wife and the hand of one of his children clutched in his.  Moreover, each male, when initiated to manhood, identifies himself henceforth with a particular bull of a specific color pattern (Figure 3.4), a song bull.  They love that individual bull (and particular cows) in the same way many Northerners love individual dogs. These relationships are of both companionship and near identification.[5]   Outside observers early recorded the readiness of Dinka to die for their cattle (Titherington, 1927; Seligman, 1932).

## CATTLE AS WEALTH AND PRESTIGE SYMBOLS

Pastoral ancestors of many Northerners who would play a development role in Africa shared with these present-day pastoralists an historic concept of cattle as wealth.   Thus not only does the Northern word "capital"" (literally "head") derive originally from "head of cattle," but chattel is even more directly associated etymologically with the word "cattle" itself.  In explaining such ancient ideas about wealth to his own contemporaries, the 1st century BC Roman chronicler Marcus Terrentius Varro (Hooper, 1935: 317-319) noted that "up to this day a fine is assessed after the ancient fashion in oxen and sheep; the oldest copper coins were marked with cattle, . . . the very word for money [*pecus*] is derived from them, for cattle are the basis for all wealth."  And, in modern European languages, both meanings of *pecus* still survive in the English words "pecuniary" and "impecunious" for "monetary" and "poor," respectively, while, similarly, in Spanish *peculio* means "a stock of money" and *pecunia* "hard cash," although *pecuaria* still retains the original meaning  "of or pertaining to cattle."  Such associations persist also in much more recent financial terms as "stock market," "bull market" and "watered stock."  From this perspective of wealth, cattle generate more cattle just like money deposited in a bank generates interest.  Assuming that under normal conditions a cow produces an average of one female calf every two years (i.e., reproduces herself or "doubles the original investment"), and applying the "rule of 72," these returns (exclusive of the value of a bull calf also every two years) would equal 36% annual interest!  And so with people.  Cattle are used to pay the bride price for a wife who, in turn, begets daughters who, again, bring more cattle wealth to the family at their own marriages.  Because cattle are also exchanged in most other social transactions, they *constantly circulate*, a process analogous overall to the circulation of money among people in the North.

Because a Dinka must never flaunt this cattle wealth, he never says how many cattle he owns, or will even count them.  That would be bad luck. An incentive for a wealthy Dinka to behave well is the fear that evil might otherwise befall him or his cattle. Furthermore, arrogant men may not receive community help should their cattle be attacked by predators or some similar misfortune occur. Their daughters may not be competitive for marriage and that could prove a disaster for a family for generations.  Because of such harsh societal rules, Dinka attempt to earn the respect of others.  While possession of large numbers of cattle helps earn respect, that alone is insufficient.  Dinka also judge a male by the way he conducted himself during his youth, especially at his initiation to manhood and during preparations for marriage, as well as his deportment thereafter.  His hospitality, level of respect for others and lack of arrogance are all important.

Some Dinka families cultivate large fields of sorghum and "sell" any excess to other families in need.  A bull or heifer, depending on the amount of sorghum required, provides the barter basis for such transactions.  This also is the case for acquiring possessions like hunting and fishing spears, hoes, clubs and canoes, things that are made only by rare specialists (*atet*).  Some of those objects might require only "small change," a few goats or sheep.  Moreover, not only do all Dinka transactions involving property, or services, demand exchange of cattle, but so do all significant social functions, such as marriages or religiocultural events.[6]  Since animals are commonly borrowed or lent for these or other reasons, their circulation is much greater among extensive pastoralists than most Northerners might assume. And this total process is intermeshed with opportunistic strategies like dividing the herd, which Dinka employ for coping with major uncertainties of weather and disease.

Until now money has been involved in Dinka transactions on only a very small scale and that is almost always to meet nontraditional needs like paying poll taxes or school fees. While cattle sales for money are on the increase, one could scarcely perceive a trend to embrace a money economy nor is accumulation of money practiced. However, a foot is in the door for indirect money transactions where cattle will not directly suffice and, as we shall suggest in Chapter 7, outgrowths of those economic concepts might be envisaged that would begin to realize some of the advantages of a market-based monetary system without doing undue violence to traditions.

In summary, the Dinka concept of wealth is far more complexly fused with other concepts of life than it is to a Northerner. And it is courting failure not to recognize that. However, it would also be in error to believe that cattle's sole or even most important role is as wealth. For cattle are also thought of as possessing "warm" personal qualities bordering on an equivalence to people, qualities money surely lacks.

Marriage is one of two interactions among Dinka families which involve exchange of large numbers of cattle. For men, marriage is the final stage, after initiation, of attaining manhood. A married man becomes an elder in matters of mutual interest, including decisions on movements of cattle camps to new grazing areas, arrangements for and settlement of other marriages within his clan, settlement of feuds, animal sacrifice and the like. Since traditional Dinka society rests upon the democratic notion of consensus among fairly large groups, marriage is the key to social cohesion.

To outsiders, marriage among people like the Dinka may be viewed crudely as the act of buying a woman who is to beget daughters who will bring more cattle to the family when they get married. But courtship also has strong personal elements and marriages usually have the same bonding/commitment aspects as those in other societies. As indicated in Chapter 2, the annual Dinka migration to the *toich* is fun for young people partially because it gives them the chance to seek their love, their partner. As soon as a young man identifies the girl he wants to marry, he informs his parents. If they agree, they contact the bride's parents and upon acceptance they start to collect cattle from the intended groom's relatives. Thus, collection of bride wealth and its handing over to the bride's family becomes a group responsibility. This helps maintain interrelationships among lineage members. The bride price paid is strongly regarded as a reflection of the honor, beauty and righteousness of the bride, and the reputation of the family from which she comes. While the minimum acceptable number differs from one subtribe to another (in the first author's subtribe, the Bor, the current minimum is 30), the maximum could reach 100, particularly for girls who have had some formal education. This bride price also partially determines the survivability of a marriage.  Divorce is more likely to occur easily when fewer cattle were paid.  Payment of more cattle means not only that the girl had been very carefully assessed for her qualities and background, but, should a divorce be considered despite this, it would be extremely difficult for the groom's family to recover all the cattle paid.  Thus, while marriage is not wholly an individual affair, it is not a cold transaction devoid of romance and love.

Compensation for homicide is a second interaction among Dinka families that involves payment of large numbers of cattle.  This mechanism provides a central element in traditional judicial systems.  The exact number of cattle paid (i.e., a nonviolent alternative to carrying out a death sentence) is dependent upon the nature and circumstances that led to the killing.  That cattle can satisfy such blood payments for homicide indicates again the ritual equivalence that exists between cattle and people, a conceptual relationship noted by Lienhardt (1961: 25): "cattle handed over in place of the dead man or in place of the girl [in marriage], will multiply for the lineage of people who have lost a member, the continuity of generation in cattle thus being balanced against the continuity of human generation which has been broken by the loss of a member to the lineage."

## CATTLE AND RELIGION

Cattle also serve in other ways to practically anchor the covenant between Dinka and the "Spiritual Force."  Mention was made in Chapter 1 of the current belief that domestication of cattle was a deliberate human act related to beginning recognition of social concepts such as territoriality and dominion, including explanations of the cosmos (Frankfort, 1948).  Human leaders admired the bull as master of his herd.  The ancient Egyptians' conceptualization of kingship and other social organization appears to have derived from very early observations upon herds of wild cattle.  Standing two meters at the shoulder, each wild bull controlled and protected an impressive harem.  With powerful sweeping horns, he was the largest, strongest, most brave and libidinous animal that predynastic Egyptians encountered, a magnificent beast their earliest chiefs attempted in every way to emulate[7] (Schwabe, 1994).  Accordingly, the Egyptian people referred to themselves as "cattle of Re," the sun god, a heavenly bull who traversed the sky, reinseminated his mother, the cow-goddess Hathor (see Figure 3.2) each evening and was reborn in the east the following morning.  In ancient times (in places as separated as Egypt and India), surplus young adult males of religiously important cattle were sacrificed and offered to the gods (with portions of their flesh consumed in sacramental feasts of communion[8]).  Similar practices, and to varying extents the beliefs behind them, continue among many African pastoralists, a fact that suggests what outsiders may be trifling with when they propose significant changes in cattle husbandry or marketing.  Therefore, to regard the killing and eating of the flesh of steers as simply utilitarian acts of slaughter and eating of meat, is to invite misunderstanding; although pastoralists eventually consume every bovine animal, among many cattle slaughter is a central component of rituals of profound cultural importance.

### Cattle Sacrifice

Thus, among the Dinka cattle sacrifice is the central religious act (Lienhardt, 1961), a ritual to which not only all important social interactions but their covenant with the Divine relate. Like others among the small minority of Dinka who have experienced a Northern education, some of the details of his people's traditional religious beliefs were not of personal interest to the first author until fairly recently. And, because Dinka are understandably sensitive to patronizing attitudes toward their religion, they are wary about sharing this information with outsiders (Schwabe, 1987). Moreover, all Dinka know that special access to religious matters resides in certain persons who have manifested a close connection with the Divine. Two generic names among different Dinka subtribes for these "holy men"--sacrificers with special prophetic, healing and other powers--are *wendior* and *tiet*. One specific title among certain clans or subtribes is *bany bith*. They are traditional "priests" with major community influence (Ater, 1976: xvii and personal communications; Lienhardt, 1961) who possess powers to foretell the future (e.g., when it is likely to rain). In the words of one well known contemporary *bany bith*, "I am a religious leader, known as a *wendior*, like a commissioner [provincial governor]. The community considers me as a mediator. I tell *Nhialic* [God] what they want and tell them what Nhialic does not like, especially when they are disobedient. I call upon them to bring bulls and to offer sacrifice. The *bany bith* is like a small god."

Animal sacrifice is thus the Dinka's way of communicating with God (Spiritual Force), a concept variously expressed. Its paramount form is *Nhialic* ("the above") who one *bany bith* described as "not the God of an individual but of the community as a whole." However, *Nhialic* usually acts through the intermediary of some general or local "spirit" (*jok*) whom the *bany bith* described as "'God's boys' whom he sends. *Nhialic* is like a commissioner and *jok* are like police whom he sends. All are subject to God. Whenever there is a serious matter one does not call upon *jok* but upon *Nhialic*. God is a power and even the government is not so powerful. He has power to do anything. *Jok* are *atiep* [shadows]. One cannot see *jok*. God combines them all." Another *bany bith* said: "They consider me as a mediator. I do not sacrifice to *jok* [local or clan spirits] but to 'Spirit[ual Force]' or *Nhialic*. The people know this well."

Although animal sacrifice is a process that goes on all the time for many reasons, all major events such as marriage and death in the family, trekking of cattle to the *toich* as well as illnesses among themselves or their cattle require special sacrifices (see Chapter 2). Such also are made at the conclusion of payment of cattle for homicide so that peace between the parties involved prevails thereafter. Those sacrifices are referred to as "cutting a covenant" (*tem*),[9] making a peace pact.

Dinka believe any bad luck, whatever its nature, comes as a result of the anger of some *jok*. They also believe that *Nhialic* has power over every *jok* to stop him from going too far in punishing people. That is why most sacrificial invocations refer to both *jok* and *Nhialic*. According to Deng (1971: 16), "God as a unity is conceived of as too great and far removed from individuals," therefore the need for approaching Him through such lesser divinities, manifestations and personifications. Steers are the animals used for most sacrifices. Only for the most important family or community reason would a cow be sacrificed. Nor are intact bulls (*thon*) sacrificed other than for similar reasons, or upon the death of an important man. The outward manifestations of a typical sacrifice appear straightforward enough. The selected steer is tethered and milk is poured on its tethering peg as a libation. Cattle dung ash is sprinkled down its back. Invocations are pronounced. If the steer urinates during these stages it is a sign the sacrifice will be accepted. The most common method of dispatching the animal is spearing its heart. Distribution of the flesh--which follows an elaborate lore whereby specific parts go to specific individuals-- and its consumption comprise the remainder of the ritual.

### Flesh as More Than Meat

Of special relevance to development proposals regarding cattle is that *Ring* (literally "flesh") is, like *jok*, a manifestation of Spiritual Force.[10] To the Dinka, flesh has both profane and sacred significance. Holy men who are in special contact with this divine manifestation of "living flesh" are called *ran de Ring*. Possession by *Ring* is a quality that must be recognized in that individual and accepted by the community. The outward sign is involuntary trembling of his muscles, usually during the ecstatic state he works himself into during sacrifice. Thus, divine *Ring* refers to the trembling--physiologically speaking, the fasciolations--of muscle fiber bundles. Dinka similarly regard the twitching of the sacrificed steer's muscles, uncut or cut, as the actual presence of Spiritual Force. Ideas expressed include that "Spiritual Force is tugging at it" or "Spiritual Force is eating the flesh." Alternatively, "the message to Spiritual Force has been answered" or "Spiritual Force is accepting the sacrifice." Thus flesh, in its sacred meaning, is associated with animation of the body, is the animating principle of life (Schwabe, 1987).

*Ring* "is the special divinity of *bany bith*" who believe "God dwells in him as *Ring*" (Ater, 1976: 22). Dinka sacrificers may start a sacrificial invocation with expressions such as "You, *Ring* of my father," but beyond such general appeals to *Ring*, special sacrifices by *ran de Ring* are expressly to *Ring* as Spiritual Force. In such sacrifices, before the *ran de Ring* divides the steer's flesh among other participants, he cuts one piece, placing half aside for

Spiritual Force. He then eats the other half of this raw "living" *Ring* to replenish Spiritual Force within himself, an act which students of ancient religions refer to as theophagic communion. Other participants then eat their portions of flesh cooked, as is the case when they eat the flesh of any sacrifice. Since such beliefs may relate especially closely to prospects for development of export beef industries (the outside impetus for many African development schemes), it is vital for Northerners to realize that the very idea of selling cattle for meat may appear profane and thus be repugnant to certain pastoralists. Evans-Pritchard (1956: 270) warned against underestimating the "religious significance . . . [cattle] have for Nuer." He then added, most presciently, that the "Nuer are themselves reticent in speaking of their cattle in this connexion . . . tend to be reserved in discussing religious matters, . . . a certain secrecy adheres to them."

## CATTLE CARE

The total dependence of Dinka on cattle for all traditional needs means that they are anxious to provide maximum care for these animals, to insure their safety and health. This principal duty is one we take up again in Chapters 4 and 6 because it is at the core of our proposals for local development. Here we simply reiterate that the Dinka "man-cow" relationship is a reciprocal one in which man takes care of cattle and cattle take care of man. Training for this "noble job" commences in childhood. Boys stay most of the time with men in the cattle byre or in the open around cow dung fires amid tethered herds. Before age 5, they are introduced to the colors and names of cattle. Most games concern cattle: they make cattle camps, using shells as cattle or make cattle out of clay. Riddles and storytelling also all refer to cattle. From ages 5 to 10 boys herd sheep and goats, as well as suckling calves, and are trained in the art of rubbing dung ashes on the coats and horns of cattle (see Figure 3.4). Cattle are groomed morning and evening during which they are carefully examined for illnesses, ticks are removed and cows in heat are brought to stud bulls. Boys are responsible, too, for collection of cow dung, spreading it, collecting it after drying and making the many cow dung fires (see Figure 2.5). From ages 11 to 15, just before initiation, a boy is gradually assigned responsibilities for herding adult cattle, first under the supervision of adults and later alone. Thereafter, at the transhumant home base or in a cattle camp (which usually contains herds of more than one family), they organize this in turns and learn collective responsibility. In addition to knowing each animal in his own family herd, from then on a boy should know those belonging to neighbors, including their individual names, colors and origins.

The most important duties of Dinka men toward cattle are to take them to where grazing and water are assured and to protect them from predators and other dangers at all times, being ready to die for them if circumstances demand. Daily care consists of releasing them in the morning after milking, attending to them at pasture, bringing them back to the cattle camps, or home base cattle byres, in early evening and tethering them down, each animal on its own peg. This tethering is highly organized with cows arranged in a pattern representing the horns of a bull or crescent moon.  At its midpoint are positioned the most valued cows.  To the left and right, in a descending order of body and horn size, are the remaining cows. At the "tips of the horns" are young heifers.  Stud bulls and song bulls are tethered between the most valued cows and the outer perimeter of other bulls and castrates and calves.  A special fireplace is located near the stud and song bulls, affording them and the most prized cows maximum protection from flies.  When inside the byre, men sleep near the door, remaining alert for possible attacks by predators like lions.  In summary, a Dinka man will do anything within his power and at any cost for the welfare of his cattle.

Girls stay with their mothers in the huts or in the female sitting area in the open.  Milking is the job of girls and women, although boys may lend a hand.

Other food animals are also important to the Dinka and their order of importance makes one species a surrogate in sacrifice and otherwise for the next higher one. In ascending order, these are chickens, goats, sheep and cattle. But animals other than cattle do not represent elements of prestige; a person who owns only goats or sheep, no matter how many, is a poor man in Dinka society.  He cannot afford to marry because only cattle are accepted as bride price.

## CONCLUSIONS

An additional conclusion which can be reached at this point about many pastoral societies in Africa is that their bases are an internally coherent set of beliefs and values about people, cattle and the Divine in which every person understands his relationships to his community and environment to a degree difficult for the modern-day Northerner to grasp. As summarized for the Nilotic Nuer, "the only labour in which they delight is the care of cattle . . . , cattle and their kin-owners are symbiotic . . . , [these pastoralists] tend to define all social processes and relationships in terms of cattle.  Their social idiom is a bovine idiom . . . , *cherchez la vache* is the best advice that can be given to those whose duty is to understand [their] behaviour" (Evans-Pritchard 1937: 209-214; 1940: 16-19).  If short- and long-range costs of specific development efforts are not to overwhelm potential benefits, planning must take fully into account such prevailing realities.  It seems obvious, though little acted upon by outsiders, that it would be worth trying more seriously to pursue development efforts within the context of these pastoral practices and infrastructures.  This seems most important from the standpoints of identifying, or designing changes in, traditional and governmental institutions that will more effectively engage development outsiders and pastoralists in participatory dialogue and common purpose. Only the fullest participation of pastoralists themselves is likely to yield knowledge of what kinds of solutions to problems might work among them or what the implications of certain suggested changes might be. They know what they need (want?) most in terms of the information they already possess (the bounds of their rationale).

Because cattle and other livestock have made possible sustained support of sizable human populations within large ecologically marginal areas of Africa for very long periods of time, it is obvious that veterinary/livestock services occupy a uniquely pivotal position within pastoral areas. Our proposals' key point is that this could be exploited to considerably greater advantage than at present. Despite examples of past veterinary leadership within Africa (see Chapter 6), such broader veterinary inputs are conspicuously absent today at virtually all stages of overall development planning and execution. In our view, that is partly because of faulty guidance provided by some Northern advisors (including too parochially oriented veterinarians and other animal scientists). A coordinated approach among development agents representing diverse disciplines is a further *sine qua non*. Many outsiders whom we have encountered on specific development projects were insufficiently informed about the importance to Africa of the livestock sector, local pastoral realities or possibilities inherent in veterinary science's history as a rurally oriented multi-objective field. Before developing further the rationale for what we believe possible within constraints of current resources, we must provide additional background for understanding why pastoralists so appreciate veterinary efforts.

## NOTES

1. Africa now possesses about one-eigth of the world's cattle; Africans own 1.76 times as many cattle per capita as do Europeans.

2. Yoking of domestic male cattle castrates provided early man in most of his earliest civilization sites with the first sources of power for plant cultivation which exceeded that of his own muscles.

3. Increasingly recommended as a more meaningful measure for ranking countries vis-à-vis states of development is the Human Development Index of the UN Development Programme. In 1994 Canada was in first place, Switzerland second, Japan third, the United States eighth.

Riggs' (1973) optical analogy (see our Table 1.1), in contrasting the "fused" (holistic, highly integrated, communal) worldview of peoples like pastoralists with the "diffracted" (reductionistic, highly separated, individualized) worldview of peoples from the industrialized North, identifies specific academic disciplines as being characteristic of the latter. Such partially artificial compartments of knowledge with their highly abstracted perceptions of the real world are products of the diffracted societies from which most agents of development come.

Daly and Cobb (1989) consider problems inherent in differences between such abstractions from things/phenomena and the "concretenesses" of the real world. Most specifically, they identified those faced by economists (hence politicians who depend upon their analyses) whereby these abstracting processes have tended to characterize as "externalities" certain important global or local realities.

Whitehead (1925: 74-75, 85) considered that this scientific process of abstracting "logical constructions" has commonly led to a "fallacy of misplaced concreteness," a confounding of these simplified abstractions with nature itself. He (p. 43) noted further that the idea of classifications, like the prismatic agrarian worldview of Riggs, represented a "halfway house" between concretenesses of the real world and more complete abstractions from it made by scientific disciplinarians.

Kuhn, in the revised (1970) edition of his work on scientific revolutions, noted that these abstracted perceptions of the real world and their bases within disciplines are sometimes subjected to totally new approaches and/or interpretations, thus shifting their "disciplinary matrices" (i.e., theoretical bases, disciplinary infrastructures, processes preparing disciplinarians, etc.) *and* their "paradigms" (i.e., models for successfully solving problems within their purviews), a process Daly and Cobb believe economists should embark upon to internalize important externalities.

4. In work among the Karamojong, and later among the Turkana, the Dyson-Hudsons (1969) and Dyson and McCabe (1985) directed attention to differences in decision-making processes among different Nilotic pastoral tribes in that in some this involved only the individual family, while in others a consensus among a larger lineage group was required.

5. In the words of a Maasai, "One cannot separate the Maasai from their cattle and it would be true . . . to say without cattle there will be no Maasai. [We] Maasai, knowing this better than anyone else, love and care for them. [We] have developed cattle management methods which can only be matched by expert veterinarians. [Cattle are] themselves a part of the culture. . . . A family's cows are known personally and loved, the way one knows and loves one's children . . . even their sounds can be recognized when they 'moo.' Cattle-related values affect a whole range of the society structure, the role of history, folklore, pride and personal values" (Tepilit, 1978).

6. Increasingly, sheep and goats also serve minor sacrificial roles. Keeping sheep and goats has increased among East African pastoralists generally in modern times, especially in the aftermath of the great rinderpest pandemic. But in Dinka sacrifices, statements uttered indicate these are serving as surrogates for cattle.

7. In the Pyramid Texts and later religious literature, not only were the pharaoh and the sun likened to and called "bull," as were Re and other gods, but over extended periods several gods like Apis were reincarnated successions of living bulls. Apis' tombs comprise a great underground necropolis near Memphis. Similar cattle culture beliefs originated from India and Iran in the east to Crete and other Mediterranean islands in the west. Many principal gods of varied ancient civilizations were referred to as bull (Conrad, 1957; von Lengerken and von Lengerken, 1955; Schwabe, 1978a,

1994) and bull-baiting games (bull rivalry and emulation) still remain the basis for proving one's *machismo* in some lands.

An Indian scholar remarked that "in traditional Hindu mythology . . . the cow is regarded as mother. . . . The cow cannot be allowed to become merely an economic animal  because of its high ritual position in Hindu culture.  In view of the cow's being ... mother, it might even be said that no one would slaughter his mother because she was not economically important" (Malik, 1979).

8. Thus also for the Greek god Dionyssus (Dodds, 1960) who was worshipped in communion rites by "ecstatic and frenzied worshippers . . . tearing at the raw flesh of a bull that was thought to be the actual embodiment of the god.  By eating that flesh, the worshipper believed he received a little of the god's power and character" (Young, 1979: 14).

9. Interestingly, the Hebrew verb for making a covenant also is "to cut."

10. These and other manifestations, including various divine personifications (e.g., *Garang, Abuk* and *Deng*, literally "rain," and *Macardit*, literally "Great Black Bull" thunder clouds) are considered less powerful than *Nhialic*.  Thus *Nhialic*, various *jok*, *Ring* and other manifestations and personifications comprise a total interrelated conception of what we are calling "Spiritual Force." It also includes certain things or creatures in nature, totems to which a particular clan "consider themselves related, almost as if by blood" (Ater, 1976: xvii).  Moreover, a few animals like lions, elephants (in Dinka myth, the elephant and man were once one species) and some snakes are considered by all Dinka as divine.  Sometimes these are animals that are feared and need to be placated (e.g., Dinka put out milk and butter to feed snakes which they try to protect from harm).  That is, Dinka think holistically about a cosmos of which they, cattle, the rest of nature and "Spiritual Force" are multiply related parts.

# 4

---

# ANIMAL DISEASES AND THEIR
# SOCIAL CONSEQUENCES

When my wife dies I am sad, but when my cow dies I cry.

Fulani saying cited by Uma Lele, 1975

Less thick and fast the whirlwind scours the main with tempest in
its wake, than swarm the plagues of cattle; nor seize they single
lives alone, but sudden clear whole feeding grounds, the flock with
all its promise, and extirpate the breed.

Virgil, *Georgics*, 30 BC

Considering the myriad ways animals are inextricably intertwined with African
pastoralists' lives, what are some possible implications for pastoral development? First, as they perceive it, improving animal welfare automatically im-
proves their own welfare. Second, this relationship could provide an implementing key to realizing other facets of development. Third, the value they
attach to their animals could suggest ways to help pay for such new services or
amenities. To promote those possibilities within the bounds of reasonably
assured resources requires a more imaginative approach than most agents of
development have heretofore visualized, and a more local scale, which takes
fully into account important place-to-place differences.

Besides little and unpredictable rainfall, the major risks African
pastoralists have faced historically have been epidemic livestock diseases.

Therefore, the health component of animal welfare enjoys the highest priority among them.[1]  Animal health was given much attention during the colonial period, particularly in areas where Europeans came to settle.  Many of them were already sedentary pastoralists or adopted in Africa a livestock-raising occupation.  But this past attention, or to the livestock sector overall, has been poorly reflected postindependence in (1) the share of the national budget devoted in comparison to the livestock sector's total value in subsistence and money terms or (2) recognition that attempts at *any* aspect of development among pastoralist populations should take fullest advantage of this unusual importance to them of their animals' health and safety.

Moreover, serious temporal and other errors of emphasis have been commonplace in approaches to development of the African livestock sector since independence.  Foremost was premature emphasis upon improvements for production before, in most cases, economically disruptive epidemic diseases had been brought under effective control.  In conclusions already reached by Blaxter by 1973--though more generally among other nonveterinary animal husbandry specialists years later--"mistakes have been made where countries have focused major attention on improvement of large animal stocks through importation of superior animals from temperate zones without simultaneously considering questions of disease and feed supplies and results often have been disastrous."  It is now commonly recognized that, of the livestock development triad, disruptive disease control must come first, then reasonable nutritional conditions (i.e., range conditions) must exist and, *finally*, genetic upgrading through introduced germ plasm, or all that might be temporarily accomplished through the latter risks disastrous undoing.  And a wiser course overall would probably be to concentrate the breeding component of development efforts (as had original efforts in the North that yielded high producers adapted to Northern climatic and other conditions) upon selection for production (and reproductive efficiency) among *indigenous* stock already adapted in heat tolerance and disease and tick resistance, as well as to nutritional conditions prevailing in Africa.

It is not our goal to attempt to encapsulate here the very large literature on animal diseases and their control in Africa, but simply to accent for nonveterinarians interested in the well-being of pastoral peoples, their current importance and some of the types of problems and prospects these identify for the future.  Because a veterinary facilitating vehicle for pastoral development is our proposals' most unique feature, it is vital for nonveterinarians concerned with development in pastoral Africa to understand its rationale.

We shall begin with what has been commonly regarded by outsiders as the only significant way animal health is important to pastoral peoples--or to the welfare of their nations--namely, the direct *economic* effects of livestock diseases.  As seen through "modern Northern-colored glasses" this effect is reflected in the ability of animals to produce meat and milk.  Even here the outsider's eye has almost always been focused farsightedly (and optimistically) upon potentials for livestock offtake and meat export. However, animal diseases within Africa's pastoral societies also impinge critically upon all of the types of man-animal interactions and mutual dependency which we have just examined, plus other major influences beyond food supply.

## ANIMAL DISEASES AND FOOD SUPPLY: THE GREAT RINDER-PEST PANDEMIC

To most quickly visualize the possible consequences of even this most understood effect, let us consider the single most important disease event African pastoralists have yet experienced, one which dramatically shaped the modern history of much of Africa. For persons who would wish to better understand possibilities for development today within pastoral Africa, there is no better place to begin than with some comprehension of the extent and consequences of the great rinderpest pandemic of the late 1800s.

As orientation, rinderpest (cattle plague) is an epidemic, highly fatal viral infection of domestic and wild *Artiodactyla* transmitted by close contact. Globally speaking, it has ranked with plague and malaria as among mankind's great historic scourges. First recognized in Asia, rinderpest was introduced into Europe during late-8th-century migrations of the Franks and with the Mongols in the 13th century. In the early 18th century it invaded again with Swedish armies returning from Russia. The king of Brandenburg, reacting to alarming intelligence from the East about the economic desolation which followed, warned his subjects that only by stopping rinderpest's spread westward could they "prevent ruin of the[ir own] land" (Dorwart, 1959). Its advance continued, however, destroying much of Europe's cattle population. Besides devastating the milk and meat supply, rinderpest eliminated the main source of power for crop production. Economic and political consequences led directly and swiftly to establishment within almost all European countries of new schools expressly for the study of veterinary science. Important to Africa's future is recognition that these schools' initial graduates established the *first governmental programs to serve Europe's rural peoples*. Through their efforts, rinderpest and several other major livestock diseases were eventually eradicated from that continent. Rinderpest has similarly ravished much of Asia and still survives there in some areas.

Almost two centuries after dealing this severe blow to the European economy, rinderpest produced even more devastating effects in Africa. Within a few years after being introduced from Asia with an Italian army invading Ethiopia at the close of the 19th century, rinderpest swept the continent. Individual Ethiopian families lost as many as 12,000 cattle and 90% of the total cattle population perished. How this catastrophe extended far beyond the importance of lost meat and milk is reflected in a *Manchester Guardian* reporter's dispatch that one chief in the agricultural region of Koa lost 56 of his 57 plow oxen. Because virtually all draft oxen died, farmlands went unplowed.

That triggered a major famine described as "a scourge sent by God" (Pankhurst, 1966). A French missionary added that "everywhere I meet walking skeletons" and another traveler that "it seems a cemetary" with the population driven to "abandonment of children . . . , self-enslavement, suicide, murder and cannibalism." In tieing himself to a plow in place of the fallen oxen, the Emperor Menelik wept and cried "Oh! how my country has fallen in ruins! My people are finished." Estimates are that the whole of Ethiopia lost one-third of its human population to sequellae of rinderpest, with some pastoralist areas, as of the Galla, suffering up to 80% mortality. In neighboring Somalia, previously wealthy men were also reduced to penury. Similarly, an early Italian explorer reaching the borders of Dinka country at Juba on the White Nile reported seeing "enormous areas of bleached bones of cattle" (Pankhurst, 1966).

Elsewhere throughout Africa it was much the same. Spreading southward, rinderpest left a swath of desolation which, in the words of one historian, "most likely [represented] the dividing line between initiative and apathy on the part of a large number of African peoples. . . . It broke the economic backbone of many of the most prosperous and advanced communities" (Kjekshus, 1977). In particular, "the omnipotence of the East African pastoralists was broken, and the way was now clear for the ingress of European settlers and for the rapid expansion of the Bantu agriculturalist" (Branagan and Hammond, 1965). The head of British forces invading Kenya wrote then that "powerful and war-like . . . pastoral tribes [had] their pride . . . humbled and our progress [in conquest was] facilitated by this awful [rinderpest] visitation. The advent of the white man had else not been so peaceful" (Lugard, 1893: 527). Only an estimated 5% of Maasai cattle survived and some two-thirds of Maasai themselves perished. One observer noted how cattle and human carcasses were so numerous "the vultures had forgotten how to fly" (Branagan and Hammond, 1965). Whereas individual Gogo had possessed up to 10,000 cattle, all of the Mpwapwa area in the east of their territory was left with no more than that number in total (Kjekshus, 1977). Decades later a Gogo possessing over 100 cattle was considered a rich man (Rigby, 1969; also see our Chapter 5).

In southern Africa also, where rinderpest's toll was well over 3 million cattle, a British official in Zululand wrote that this "destruction of African cattle gave the colony a most favorable opportunity for delimiting African lands which had thus been vacated" (van Onselen, 1972; Mack, 1971) to the extent that in neighboring Zimbabwe such continuing expropriations had resulted by 1930 in about 1 million African pastoralists being restricted to just under 30 million acres, while 40 million acres, including the best rangelands, were in the hands of a mere 50,100 white settlers. To which another white South African added: "the ravages of rinderpest, although reducing the native to poverty, has not been without beneficial results, and the native has now learned humility to those to whom he is subordinate, and also the lesson that by work only can he live, and having learnt to work he is now a happy and contented man, instead of the discontented, idolent, lazy and besotten being he was *when the numerous cattle he possessed provided his every want*" (van Onselen, 1972, italics added). Vivid accounts of this enormous tragedy still permeate the oral histories of most African pastoral peoples. Beginning in the mid-1920s, a degree of control through vaccination had begun to be realized in some areas and major continentwide planning for rinderpest's eradication commenced in 1948.

African pastoralists have less graphic memories but equally justified fears of other epidemic livestock diseases with high case fatality rates. Some, like contagious bovine pleuropneumonia (CBPP), can also spread rapidly and directly from animal to animal. Other important cattle diseases (and similar diseases of other species)--anthrax, hemorrhagic septicemia, blackleg as examples--may be as clinically dramatic, but are *associated only with certain environments* (in which resistant stages of their agents persist for long periods) and in which cases may occur whenever susceptible herds are introduced.

Less alarming to pastoralists are other infections also readily transmissible from animal to animal, but which cause fewer or no deaths. Although animals may survive, the *collective tolls* these exact in decreased productivity (in terms of meat, milk and offspring) may be very large. Foot-and-mouth disease is one most important example. Even more insidious are widespread and frequently undramatic complexes of worm parasites which infect all livestock species. These and other chronic infections, as well as nutritional and metabolic disorders, many as yet poorly defined in Africa, severely limit the potential prosperity of Africa's livestock-owning public. Thus, while Africa has more cattle in total *and per capita* than either Europe or North America, their productivity in Northern terms of meat and milk is abysmally low (e.g., 57 kg milk per year per cow versus 487 in North America, 1,118 in Western Europe and 397 in Oceania [FAO 1972 data]). The potential exists in pastoralist Africa for improved livestock productivity (Pritchard et al., 1992: 75) and we shall suggest some possible lines of approach, but, for their success we must be prepared to employ the right anthropological as well as the right scientific knowledge. This is surely an important economic issue for the future, one vital to Africa's ultimate development, but in terms of the real utility of livestock to Africa's pastoral peoples today, including their major subsistence roles in which milk production is so important, current concerns of many Northerners almost exclusively about productivity for meat have tended only to obscure other realistic development possibilities.

Some livestock diseases may exert additional effects which are even less appreciated by the lay public. Among these are animal diseases which also infect people.

## ANIMAL DISEASES AND HUMAN HEALTH

### Zoonoses

*The great majority of human infectious diseases described anywhere until now are zoonoses,*[2] diseases for which other vertebrate animals act as reservoirs of infection.  For many of them, infection cannot spread person to person, but only from other vertebrate animals to people.  Some of these infections are transmitted directly by close animal contact or less directly through air or water.  Others, like trichinosis and salmonelloses, are exclusively or partially food-borne (through meat, milk or eggs).  Invertebrate *vectors* (flies, mosquitoes, lice, ticks and mites or, more indirectly, snails) transmit still others, including various viral encephalitides.  Zoonoses are among the most complicated human diseases from an epidemiological standpoint (Schwabe, 1984b: 194-251, 351-392, 466-500; Schwabe, 1991a), their identification and elucidation often requiring investigations which involve people, their domestic animals, the relations between them as well in some instances, wild vertebrate and invertebrate animals and their environments.  The skills required for their study and control are thus very broad and extend beyond the capacities of the usual clinically focused human health services. To protect people against important zoonoses in Africa, like rabies, veterinary efforts must be initiated against infections in the animal reservoirs.

Some zoonoses have no suitable domestic animal hosts and are transmitted directly (or indirectly through the environment) from wild animals to people.  Yellow fever is one important African example and more recently disclosed instances are Ebola infection and Lassa Fever.[3]  Particular zoonoses, as well as certain livestock diseases per se, are transmitted only in environments which are suitable for arthropod transmitters to survive and thrive.  Some of these complex transmission and maintenance cycles also involve various wildlife species. This is especially important because Africa possesses the world's most varied, best preserved and most accessible populations of large mammalian species. The global recognition that major resource receives makes it a major earner of foreign exchange in several African countries.

Although brucellosis, one form of tuberculosis, Rift Valley fever and a number of other zoonotic infections in Africa are *dually important* because they also are of economic consequence through their effects upon livestock, veterinary efforts are undertaken against others--diseases like rabies and hydatid disease, as examples--*entirely for public health reasons.*  The relationships we need to emphasize here about this important aspect of man-animal interactions are illustrated well by hydatid disease, a zoonosis especially associated with pastoral life worldwide and for which one of our "model populations," Kenya's Turkana, have the world's highest recorded level of human infection.

**Hydatid Disease, a Plague of Pastoralists**

Hydatid disease (also called hydatidosis and echinococcosis) is a globally distributed medically serious parasitic zoonosis (Figure 4.1) in which the larval stage (hydatid cyst) of a very small tapeworm found in the small intestines of dogs grows like a noninvasive "cancer" within the liver, lungs, brain or other organs of people who swallow its eggs (passed in the feces of an infected dog). Infection is perpetuated globally primarily through a dog-sheep cycle (Figure 4.2).

Hydatidosis was first disclosed among the Turkana only in 1958 (Wray, 1958).  Follow-up studies in 1961 of those first reported cases and others (Schwabe, 1964: 211) indicated that the Turkana, by presenting at least 40 surgical cases per 100,000 persons per year to the one minimal hospital at the fringe of their territory, had an infection rate at least three times that known anywhere else. Some Turkana said then that they believed this "big-belly disease" was a curse put upon them by their enemies, the Toposa of the southern Sudan. With introduction by missionaries within Turkana territory of some basic surgical facilities following the great drought of 1958-1961, this annual surgically treated human incidence was raised to 96 cases per 100,000 people (O'Leary, 1976), with that in northern Turkanaland 220 per 100,000 persons (French and Nelson, 1982).   Subsequent ultrasound scanning surveys for abdominal cysts only (Macpherson et al., 1989a) revealed the incredible infection rate of 5.6% of all people surveyed in northwestern Turkana.

Illustrative of important differences in zoonoses risks which may be encountered among even closely related pastoralists whose lifestyles may appear to be similar to the outside observer is a marked difference in importance of hydatid disease between Turkana and Maasai who experience only 11 surgical cases per 100,000 persons in the most heavily infected Wasso area of northern Tanzania, and only 1-2 cases per 100,000 throughout all of Maasailand (Macpherson et al., 1989). Reasons for such markedly different rates still are not totally clear, but observations suggest they are partly a result of differences in man:dog contacts. Since Turkana women have a much higher infection rate than men, it is interesting that they each keep a pet dog within the hut. These pets clean babies with their tongues after they defecate or vomit, as well as cleaning up the menses of the women. Though Turkana deny they eat dogs, some acknowledge having eaten jackals (which are also a definitive host of the parasite).  Both Turkana and Maasai recognized hydatid cysts within their livestock, but neither formerly associated them with the disease in themselves. While Maasai thought such cysts were harmful to animals, some Turkana regarded them as means to store water during drought. Cysts were commonly thrown by both to their dogs, thus assuring transmission.

From a veterinary standpoint, the epidemiological complexities of such environment-specific zoonoses like hydatid disease often complicate efforts, or

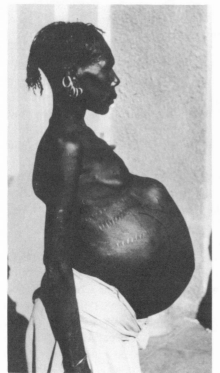

a

b

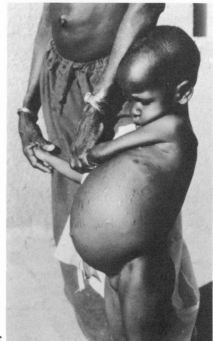

**Figure 4.1. Two Turkana women (a,b) and a child (c) infected with liver cysts of the zoonotic hydatid parasite *Echinococcus granulosus*. Scar patterns indicate that each had been treated by a traditional healer with hot iron cautery.** (Source of a and c: Dr. Eberhard Zeyle, AMREF.)

c

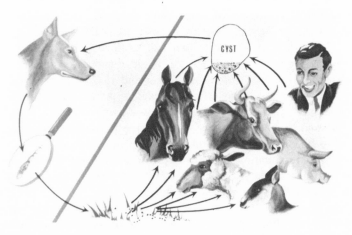

**Figure 4.2.** The life cycle of *Echinococcus granulosus*, the zoonotic parasite causing hydatid disease in people. The dog is the principal transmitter.

lessen prospects, for quick or easy successes in controlling them. Moreover, since some zoonotic and other animal diseases are unique to Africa, prior Northern control experiences (as for rinderpest and foot-and-mouth disease) may not exist and most research may be limited to what can be accomplished within African institutions. Tsetse-transmitted trypanosomiasis, some agents of which cause "African sleeping sickness" in people, is the best known instance. This zoonosis seriously hampers development efforts over major areas of Africa by preventing establishment of significant livestock populations or optimal human habitation. Most conservative estimates of its most direct economic toll in lost food alone suggest that tsetse fly eradication would result in increased production in Africa of 16% in meat and 18% in milk (Tacher et al., 1988). Pastoralists make efforts to avoid areas where such serious diseases are known to occur, thus barring them from grazing lands adjacent to traditional territories which they might otherwise utilize to advantage. Trypanosomiasis and rinderpest together illustrate also some of wider ecological consequences of some animal diseases.

## ANIMAL DISEASES AND ECOLOGICAL CONSEQUENCES

Failure by colonial medical establishments for many years to understand correctly the epidemiology of trypanosomiasis was the result of a major *ecological interaction* which had occurred at the onset of European occupation between rinderpest and trypanosomiasis. For, in addition to its livestock depredations and resultant famine, rinderpest's invasion killed game animals in unprecedented numbers. So many wild artiodactylan hosts of tsetse flies died throughout much of East Africa during the first years of the pandemic that the "game animal-tsetse fly-savanna/woodland ecosystem" which provided natural foci for maintenance of trypanosomal infections became widely separated geographically from the "man-cattle-savanna/cultivation ecosystem" in which resided most of the continent's human and cattle populations (Ford, 1971). That was because game species most susceptible to rinderpest accounted for 78-93% of the feeds of tsetse flies in East Africa and 73-75% in West Africa. The overall result was that trypanosomiasis occurred afterward over a much lesser area of Africa than it had before. That effect was only temporary, however, and, as game animal populations made a rapid postpandemic comeback, tsetse-infested areas began to expand again, in Tanzania at an estimated rate of seven miles per year.  In situations like that we can see the complexities of interactions that can occur rapidly in fragile pastoral areas through natural (or human-mediated) introductions of major new factors.

To illustrate further some of these possibilities, some microorganisms responsible for infections of wildlife produce no overt disease in these natural hosts, but may prove devastating when introduced into some domestic species. A prime example is African swine fever, a viral infection which naturally occurs asymptomatically in wild pigs.  It was first diagnosed after domestic pigs were introduced by British colonialists, resulting in a case fatality rate of 99-100%.[4]

Thus the consequences of livestock diseases are sometimes multiple, affecting not only food-producing and other economic uses to which animals are put, but more directly affecting human health as well, causing important and unpredictable ecological changes in themselves or emerging as totally new problems of livestock or human health through other ecological changes instituted by people.  Such complexities are heightened in Africa among pastoralists for whom cattle especially serve varied cultural and social roles.

## KNOWLEDGE OF CATTLE DISEASES IN THE SOUTHERN SUDAN

Mass immunization campaigns intended to *eliminate* from its large cattle population rinderpest and CBPP have constituted the major efforts of veterinary services in the Sudan.  This approach reflects aims of pan-African campaigns which assumed that those two infections more or less continually subjected all cattle to risk, and that existing veterinary resources were adequate to reach and immunize very high proportions of all cattle on an annual basis for several years, and then to maintain sufficient surveillance to quickly detect possible new introductions. Findings in the southern Sudan indicated that none of those assumptions were true (Zessin et al., 1985; Zessin and Carpenter, 1985; Majok *et al.*, 1991).

The fact was, that when these campaigns were initiated, rinderpest, CBPP, trypanosomiasis, brucellosis, tickborne hemaprotozoal infections and helminthic infections of cattle were known to exist in the southern Sudan, but scarcely more. The chief source of information for most of what had been reported before 1979 were results of unsystematically acquired data (case and outbreak reports and haphazardly submitted laboratory specimens) compiled as parts of annual administrative reports of the national veterinary services. The few actual surveys (on some protozoal and helminthic parasites, brucellosis and tuber-culosis) were mostly small ones based in main abattoirs or atypical herds. While those reports provide some historical background to *existence* of a few cattle diseases in the southern Sudan, and created some awareness of their possible consequences to the health of cattle (and human) populations of that region, such sketchy information was of little epidemiological or control value. Very little was known even about the time, place or other important distribu-tions of rinderpest or CBPP, much less other diseases of cattle or small rumi-nants.

Therefore--after it was clear that vaccination campaigns against those two major plagues could not succeed in the southern Sudan under prevailing conditions (see Chapter 6)--these and other infections were included in a German-sponsored pilot-level multiple cattle disease survey carried out in Bahr el Ghazal Province from 1979 to 1981. It was only then that Sudanese veteri-nary authorities had *any* disease intelligence basis upon which to operate effec-tively in the south.

### The Cattle Disease Survey of 1979-1981

The framework for the bilateral survey was the World Bank-financed Southern Region Agriculture Project (SRAP). According to the agreed plan of execution, there would be 400 survey days during two dry seasons. Unlike most livestock disease surveys of any size carried out within pastoral areas of Africa before then, this German Agency for Technical Cooperation (GTZ) survey was not only of *multiple* diseases, but provided some of the first comparable disease information for Africa of situations in the absence of epidemics (the most common impetus for past surveys of individual diseases in Africa often reflecting very atypical situations from which it was difficult to extrapolate epidemiologically valuable conclusions). This project proper yielded in its official report (for limited distribution) a series of frequency distribution tables and survey maps (Zessin and Baumann, 1982). Most of these data were later subjected by team members and other postgraduate students in epidemiology at the University of California-Davis to the maximum analyses they would sustain given the nature of the survey. It was believed that those analyses could form the basis for more rational planning of livestock disease control over that large area, while serving also as a pilot demonstration of the considerable need for similar efforts throughout the entire southern region. The first author was Director of Veterinary Services for the Southern Region of the Sudan at that time.

Under provisions of agreement, GTZ provided three veterinarians, two la-boratory technicians and one motor mechanic; two Unimog vehicles, four Landrovers, two Toyota Scouts and one Toyota lorry; a range of laboratory equipment and materials for fieldwork, plus drugs and diagnostic reagents. Additionally, GTZ covered operating costs, construction and equipping of a diagnostic laboratory at the provincial veterinary headquarters in Wau and a vehicle repair workshop, plus training outside the project area for two national veterinarians and two laboratory technicians. As those facilities became available, technical field and other local support personnel were trained and the testing of survey protocols carried out (Zessin et al., 1985).

Field teams consisted of one veterinary assistant/interpreter, one driver, one stockman, one assistant stockman, one camp keeper/cook and one German veterinarian as team leader. They lived and worked in easy-pitch-and-break tent camps usually for three to four days at any one survey site. While in the field, teams carried out centrifugation of blood samples and storage of sera in the refrigerator, examination of wet blood films and fecal samples, fixation of blood and lymph node smears, staining of thick drop smears and preservation of collected ticks. The team surveyed a total of 8,656 cattle. Data collected permitted calculations of prevalences of test reactions among herds and individual cattle. These were examined in relation to crude death rates, the two cattle populations surveyed (the predominat Dinka and the Fellata who migrate from the western Sudan) and individual animal characteristics like age and sex. Other variables examined among Dinka cattle only were three *toich* grazing locations and two management systems.

Sera from 77% of cattle tested were serologically positive for rinderpest even though a relatively small percentage of cattle had been vaccinated (Majok et al., 1991). That and a rise in seroprevalence with age through the five- to seven-year age group suggested a high risk of natural infection even in absence of many official case reports. Only slight differences were observed between Dinka and Fellata herds, Dinka *toich* and "milking" camps (i.e., management practices) and three *toich* grazing locations. However, models resulting from log linear analyses contained several higher order interactions between test results and other variables, suggesting a complex relationship, perhaps reflecting the local pattern of husbandry in which there are frequent exchanges of animals among herds.

In contrast, on an individual basis, only 8% of Dinka and 9% of Fellata cattle were serologically positive to CBPP, but with reactors occurring in 48% and 20% of herds, respectively (Zessin et al., 1985). Dinka cattle between three months and three years of age had significantly higher rates than those either younger or older. Both test reaction rates and crude mortality rates showed positive associations with herd size; however, none of the variability among herds in crude mortality could be accounted for by presence of CBPP infection. Since only a small percentage of cattle had been vaccinated, that study indicated that CBPP was endemic even in apparent absence of clinical cases, but with either relatively low risk of within-herd transmission or, again, a situation reflecting frequent exchanges of recovered animals among herds.

Preliminary analysis of brucellosis data indicated that, on an individual basis, 6.5% and 22.5% of Dinka and Fellata cattle, respectively, were serologically positive, with reactors in 66% and 99% of Dinka and Fellata herds (Baumann, 1983). While brucellosis is thus widespread among Dinka herds and holoendemic among Fellata herds, conditions for intraherd transmission among individual Dinka cattle were not especially favorable. There were negative test results on a limited number of human Dinka sera, but no Fellata were tested. Further analyses are possible for these data.

Three helminthic infections (*Fasciola, Paramphistomum* and mixed gastrointestinal nematodiasis) plus one tickborne protozoal infection, theileriosis, were also surveyed. Diagnostic procedures did not differentiate among *Theileria* species nor among ova of *Trichostrongylus* spp., *Cooperia* spp., *Ostertagia* spp., *Haemonchus* spp., *Nematodirus* spp. and *Oesophagostomum* spp. The highest apparent prevalence, for mixed gastrointestinal nematodiasis, was 51% (Majok et al., 1993). Multivariate regressions of herd prevalences on breed, age and sex in Dinka and Fellata herds combined indicated breed and age as significant predictors for *Fasciola*, age and sex for *Paramphistomum* and breed and sample size for *Theileria*, although the R-squared value for all predictors was only 9% for *Fasciola*, 4% for *Theileria* and 3% for *Paramphistomum*. That is, most variability observed among herds was unexplained, indicating that other possible determinants for which measurements were not recorded were more important. In similar analyses of Dinka data only (adding grazing location and herd management), location and age were significant for predicting *Fasciola* and *Paramphistomum*, location and sex for nematodiasis, sample size, location and herd management for *Theileria*. But, again, the R-squared value was only 20% for *Fasciola* and 9% for gastrointestinal nematodiasis. Although the impact of these parasitic infections on livestock productivity remains to be locally assessed, prevalences of fascioliasis and gastrointestinal nematodiasis suggest that organized programs for their control be initiated. Trypanosomiasis data have been analyzed thus far only for Fellata herds (see Chapter 8).

Beyond a critical need among most pastoralists for similar multidisease surveys under nonepidemic conditions (as part of organized epidemiological surveillance, see Chapter 8), Sollod and his colleagues (1984) suggested that, when combined with other anthropological and ecological information, "gaining an understanding of the pastoralists' own knowledge of animal health problems and their solutions" may be a complementing key not only to meaningful control interventions, but for promoting gradual social changes. In that regard, it is important to realize that many African pastoralists have one or more classes of traditional veterinary healers. While some employ methods that are not scientifically acceptable, others are reasonably skilled in some manual medical and surgical procedures or employ natural remedies worthy of serious evaluation. We shall return in Chapter 8 to possible enlistment in development of such healers, but will illustrate here some of their folk knowledge and beliefs.

### Dinka Folk Knowledge About Cattle Diseases

Vernacular names for some cattle diseases vary among Dinka subtribes. Veterinary healers (*atet*[5]) we interviewed among the Agar subtribe were asked three questions about each of several diseases they claim to recognize: (1) How do *you* recognize such and such a disease in a sick cow or bull? (2) What do you see when a bull or cow dies of this disease and you open it? (3) What other beliefs do you have about this disease? Answers given were fairly consistent and the following are illustrative (Schwabe and Kuojok, 1981).

*Anthrax.* (1) First one sees a swollen throat, muzzle and face, and bleeding from the nose and anus. Death is sudden. (2) There is a very enlarged spleen that is black when cut. Subcutaneous hemorrhages occur throughout and dark, clotted blood is found on most organs. (3) A Dinka name for anthrax is derived from *tak* (spleen). Those observations are accurate.

*Contagious Bovine Pleuropneumonia (CBPP).* (1) The affected animal stands apart from the herd, seeks the shade and faces the wind with its head lowered. It craves water, grunts and has a short dry cough. The distinctive cough associated with CBPP (*awuok*) is differentiated from other coughing (*rot*). A high proportion of animals die. (2) Lungs are inflamed, discolored and attached to the ribs. The pleural cavity smells putrid. (3) A Dinka name means "swelling of the chest." Owners of cattle with the *awuok* cough are ostracized and forced to flee the cattle camp with their animals in order that their animals' breath will not make the other cattle sick. These observations are all astute.

*Rinderpest.* (1) The animal has severe diarrhea and will not eat. Tears flow from the eyes, there are spots on the gums and lower lips and the mouth is red. A high proportion of animals die. (2) The gall bladder is much enlarged and the mucosae of the intestines are necrotic. (3) One of the Dinka words for rinderpest, *maketh*, means "gall bladder." The disease is believed to be acquired from dead giraffes and buffaloes. Dinka will immediately separate the well cattle and flee with them if rinderpest is suspected. Some thought incorrectly that rinderpest was communicable to people.

*Foot-and-Mouth Disease.* (1) There are spots then blisters on the tongue, lips, and gums and cracks between the digits. The animal pants. (2) Cattle do not die of this disease. (3) The Dinka name means "tongue disease."

*Tuberculosis.* (1) The superficial lymph nodes are enlarged, particularly in the jowls and limbs. (2) Lymph nodes are enlarged, especially in the mesenteries. They often contain pus. (3) The Dinka name given means "swollen glands." The affected parts or the whole carcass are put out for hyenas to eat.

*Fascioliasis.* (1) The hair coat of the thorax is rough; mucosae and sclerae are pale. The animal coughs. (2) Worms are found in the "vessels" of the liver. (3) It is believed by some that fascioliasis is associated with rain and "dirty water" and that the worms "crawl up on the grass," partially correct ideas.

*Trypanosomiasis.* (1) The coat is rough, hair loss occurs beneath the tail, there is a dry nose and "clear" eyes. Death occurs. (2) The flesh and fat are watery and no blood flows in the cut vessels.

*Blackleg.* (1) Swollen and hot forelegs and thorax and lameness. Death. (2) Seepage of fluid from muscles containing clotted blood. (3) The name means "disease of the shoulders."

*"Tick Disease."* (1) Fever and pale mucosae and sclerae. (3) Name means "tick disease." It is believed to result from the heads of ticks being left in the skin. Tick birds are valued, but it is realized they often leave the head.

*Diarrhea.* (3) In calves and infants diarrhea is called *alaakic, yac.* These mean "stomach." This is differentiated from dysentery, *yac riem,* "stomach of blood." Calves and infants are often quarantined.

While contagion is clearly recognized in some instances and sick animals separated, these will not be killed because it is hoped they will recover. The other most common form of intervention is invocation and sacrifice.

### Some Comparative Beliefs

Among the earliest accounts of African pastoralists' beliefs and practices about livestock diseases were those of Merker (1910) about the Tanganyikan Maasai.[6] Their *ol obani*, the equivalent of the Dinka *bany bith* (see Chapter 3), was their principal healer of animals and people. Some traditional lore, as for the Dinka, was in the form of invocations at bull sacrifices, as well as various fetishes. However, like the Dinka, Maasai differentiate many cattle diseases and have made astute epidemiological associations for some.

Soon after rinderpest's introduction into sub-Saharan Africa at the turn of the century, Maasai noted that their cattle contracted a milder form from wild eland and that recovery from it protected these cattle from exposure to more virulent forms of the disease. Much later it was confirmed that the strain of rinderpest virus found in eland is, in fact, naturally attenuated for cattle. Similarly, it has been a Maasai belief that malignant catarrh (another viral disease) of cattle is contracted from wildebeests during the latter's calving season (when cattle graze on grass contaminated by their uterine blood and placental fluids). Only post-World War II did veterinarians confirm that wildebeests are the major reservoir host for malignant catarrh virus in Kenya and that this Maasai association of risk with the wildebeest calving season was correct.

Probably the most striking of such associations concerns another noted by Merker. That is, when cattle were diagnosed as having CBPP and they died, an *ol obani* would remove a putrid lung, gash the noses of all unaffected cattle and rub a piece of the lung into these bleeding incisions. The noses of these animals swelled, ulcerated and eventually healed with formation of much scar tissue. Merker recorded with astonishment that survivors of this indigenous procedure were immune to subsequent exposures to CBPP. Maasai credited this preventive inoculation to a famed *ol obani* named Mbatyan. That attribution is interesting because this procedure is practiced by peoples across the African continent, suggesting that it may be very old (McCorkle and Mathias-Mundy, 1992; Bizimana, 1994). Such protected animals possess considerably enhanced value within pastoral communities.

The main points to note from these examples of indigenous beliefs is that, in some instances, as for the Dinka's clinical and gross pathological observations on CBPP and anthrax, and epidemiological observations by Maasai on rinderpest and malignant catarrh, they may be impressively astute. But Dinka diagnoses of "tuberculosis," "tick disease" and "diarrhea" surely embrace multiple conditions. This raises the very important additional point of difficulties in diagnosing diseases, particularly when the only available means are clinical observations plus gross pathology.

## THE POORLY UNDERSTOOD PROBLEM OF DIAGNOSING LIVESTOCK DISEASES

Therefore, in closing this chapter we shall just touch upon what is probably the single most important aspect of a wider lack of understanding about veterinary science on the part of many nonveterinarians concerned with development in pastoral areas. Laypersons commonly misunderstand what is required to identify particular livestock diseases and seem to believe that diagnoses can usually be accomplished by somewhat perfunctory examinations of sick animals and that minimally trained personnel should be able to do that satisfactorily. Such an information gap is not in our experience a rare event and is symptomatic of much of what has gone wrong in African pastoral development.[7]

Disease interventions cannot possibly succeed--and other productivity-boosting measures such as genetic and nutritional improvements which depend upon their success will fail--unless disease diagnoses are accurate. Some of the less realized reasons and one very important part of improvements in diagnostic capabilities which must be forthcoming in the future will be deferred until Chapter 8. But here we shall mention a few basic facts needed to follow the logic leading up to our proposals for local development initiatives.

**Clinical Diagnosis**

A clinical diagnosis in medicine is made on the basis of signs (i.e., *objective* symptoms) displayed by the affected individual and the observer's ability (determined by training and clinical experience) to associate particular signs with a particular illness. The diagnostician may be aided in this process by communication to him of signs recognized by a secondary observer such as a livestock owner who is very familiar with his animals. The diagnostician can elicit some of these observations and opinions by careful questioning of the secondary observer (a part of history-taking). These objective symptoms are usually detected by a trained observer in some systematic fashion. That is, they elicit sensory responses from him if he is trained to recognize them. Relatively simple instruments heighten some of these. As examples, otoscopes, ophthalmoscopes, endoscopes and the like increase the ability to recognize objective symptoms by sight; stethoscopes amplify body sounds; percussive instruments augment senses of both sound and touch.

Physicians, except when diagnosing illnesses in very young infants, have available to them in addition *subjective* symptoms which are detected (and described to them) by ill individuals. In fact, the decision of a person to seek a physician's assistance or advice results from his detecting some of these subjective symptoms (e.g., pain) in himself, generally some time before another observer would note them. These important diagnostic aids are not available to the veterinarian. A result is that illnesses in animals are often seen when they are in a more advanced stage than are those in people. While subjective symptoms can sometimes be misleading, they usually provide physicians decided advantages over veterinarians in arriving at a purely clinical diagnosis. Therefore an accurate clinical diagnosis is surely not a simpler matter in veterinary medicine than in human medicine, although it depends in both fields upon identical skills and experience.

Some diseases of animals (and people) present certain clear signs that are specific for that disease and no other (called pathognomonic signs). Many more do not, however, and therefore a clinical diagnosis usually depends upon a process of *differential* diagnosis, identification within the diagnostician's mind (in a descending order of probability) of all diseases which *might* be associated with a particular combination of symptoms. That procedure is highly dependent upon accumulated *confirmed* experience. Confirmed experience is most commonly forthcoming from various pathological and/or laboratory procedures.[8] Therefore, something more than clinical skills are frequently required for *any diagnosis upon whose accuracy much will depend*. This is true in the individual and even more true if population-level considerations also ride on the result.

### Laboratory/Pathological Diagnosis

Because some sick individuals do die no matter what is done, dissection of the dead (gross pathology) is an exceedingly valuable practice adjunct in medicine. Though it obviously does not benefit the particular patient, it confirms, or makes possible, a diagnosis in many instances where it is otherwise impossible and adds to the confirmed clinical experience of the observer in ways that increase his diagnostic acumen in the future. Necropsy (usually called autopsy in people) is *very commonly* resorted to by practicing veterinarians, but very rarely by practicing physicians. In fact, in Africa (and in many other Third World settings) human autopsy is almost never done, only partially because of strongly held cultural objections by many peoples to such operations upon the dead. Moreover, in veterinary medicine where diseases are much more often faced on a population (herd) basis than in human medicine, this diagnostic adjunct may be immediately applicable in distinguishing *in the field* between diseases that may clinically resemble one another. In addition, veterinarians frequently kill (euthanize) sick individuals within an infected herd specifically to be able to perform necropsy examinations under scientifically favorable circumstances.

Perfection of physical techniques like light microscopy and methods of chemical analysis, together with development of pure culture methods for isolating and identifying microorganisms and serological techniques for the latter, added an important clinical pathological or laboratory complement to clinical (and gross necropsy) diagnosis. Laboratory diagnosis, as a further adjunct to clinical diagnosis plus gross pathology, thus originated with inputs from three sources: (1) necropsy pathology yielding tissues from dead individuals for further microscopic (histopathological), chemical and other forms of examination; (2) clinical pathology, which extrapolated these approaches of necropsy pathology to living individuals, yielding tissues (biopsy specimens) and samples of body fluids and excretions for microscopic and chemical examinations; and (3) the developing etiologic disciplines of parasitology, bacteriology, mycology, virology, serology, toxicology and the like, for processing such specimens in order to isolate and/or otherwise identify the *specific* etiological agents responsible for particular diseases.

While procedures exist (including specific kits of reagents, etc.) for doing some of these types of tests quickly in the field rather than remotely in a laboratory, other than with certain intradermal-type immunologic tests (and a few others), many existing procedures are costly, and for many instances where field tests would be very useful to perform in the field, they do not exist at all. Therefore, laboratory-type diagnoses usually require not only special investments in housing, equipment and highly trained personnel, but a certain dependable level of general infrastructure, including transportation and communications. We shall return to those needs in Chapters 6 and 8.

In pastoral Africa, by far the highest priority veterinary interventions for the forseeable future will be those performed on a population basis (herd or larger group). Individual animal medicine either is far too costly or is justified largely on the basis of eliciting livestock owners' cooperation for other population-based programs. For practicing population medicine, the clinical and pathological/laboratory bases for diagnosis often do not answer many questions which need answering in order to intervene effectively (see Table 4.1).[9] Epidemiology provides this additional diagnostic complement.

### Epidemiological Diagnosis

Epidemiological diagnosis has been the most recent addition to this series and we shall consider it in Chapter 8 with respect to institution building in the interests of pastoral development. Here we would simply note that distinctions among these three complementary diagnostic tactics are less clear-cut in veterinary livestock (and wildlife) practice (services delivery) than in either human medical or small animal (pet) veterinary practice. Another point is that, while the mental process of making a differential diagnosis resembles the mental process of research, epidemiological diagnosis definitely is a form of ongoing *field-based* research.

## CONCLUSIONS

To this point we have shown why pastoralism as a way of life may be the only alternative for large parts of Africa and how the welfare of cattle and other livestock are so inextricably linked to almost all facets of that millennia-old lifestyle. Consequently, livestock diseases are of paramount concern to nomadic and transhumant pastoralists and impinge upon almost *every* aspect of their lives. Not only is disease a factor which importantly affects their subsistence economy (and prospects for a supplementary cash income), but a large number of livestock infections are zoonoses which are transmissible to and cause disease in pastoralists themselves. Some affect wildlife species too and these, plus other infections solely of wildlife, may influence the ecology of an area in complex ways. Because cattle especially also fulfill deep psychological functions among some pastoralists as prestige symbols and pet-equivalents, and may be esthetically stimulating in ways which some outsiders have difficulty comprehending, their diseases exert further emotive force. It is vital, therefore, for persons involved in development in Africa to understand that animal diseases, with rainfall, are the most critically and variably manifested negative forces to which pastoralists have been traditionally subjected, and *diseases are the only one which science now offers meaningful prospects of alleviating*. Therefore, in stressing particular difficulties encountered in serving at all pastoralists' needs for new information (that is, extension), the recent Winrock Committee report opined (Pritchard et al., 1992: 117) that "advice on

|  | CLINICAL DIAGNOSIS | LABORATORY DIAGNOSIS | EPIDEMIOLOGICAL DIAGNOSIS |
|---|---|---|---|
| UNIT OF CONCERN | Sick individual | Dead individual, or parts of dead or sick individuals | Population (dead, sick, well) |
| USUAL SETTING | Hospital or clinic | Laboratory | "Field" (farm, cattle camp, etc., i.e., setting in which the disease occurred) & computer facility |
| PRIMARY OBJECTIVE | $R_x$ individual | $R_x$ individual or future individual (i.e., to obtain information) | Control disease or prevent its future occurrence |
| DIAGNOSTIC PROCEDURE | Naming the disease on the basis of signs, largely an organoleptic procedure | Naming the disease on the basis of host responses or associated agents | Measurement of frequency and patterns of occurrence of diseases and their possible determinants, with analysis for probabilities of causal associations |
| QUESTIONS ASKED | What is it? How do I treat it? | What is it? What is its mechanism (pathogenesis)? What "caused" it (specific etiologic agent)? | What is it (nature & frequency of the population event)? Which individuals have it (frequency by host characteristics)? Where is it occurring? When does it occur (i.e., its place & time patterns of occurence)? What "caused" it (determinants of the event directly or indirectly associated with frequency & pattern of occurrence)? Why did it occur (required combination of circumstances)? How is it controlled or prevented? |

**Table 4.1. Complementary diagnostic tactics in veterinary medicine.** (Source: Schwabe et al., 1977.)

animal health may be the most important extension information required by pastoralists."

Those facts can be taken advantage of multiply in contemplating possible approaches to pastoral development within the constraints of a severe paucity of resources. We would hold that such approaches are clearly visualizable and could be practically implemented. We shall suggest how that fact may readily be built upon, particularly since veterinary services within pastoral Africa provide not only advice (within that single important sphere), *but also skilled services* to these large but diffusely distributed communities. But before that, we need to consider some of the problems associated with past "development" efforts among Africa's pastoralists.

## NOTES

1. For example, when University of California epidemiologist Thomas Carlton went to Somalia in 1994 on an aid team requested by a regional self-help group, the American agency facilitating that visit by experts in human health, water resources and veterinary science considered their relative importance to be in the order listed. However, the team discovered that to the Somali self-help organization and to Somali pastoralists they met, their relative importance was definitely veterinary first, water second and human health last.

2. Approximately 250, or four-fiths of all described human infectious diseases are in this animal-man category.

3. Some evidence also exists to suggest that human HIV infection may have had similar zoonotic origins in African wildlife among simian populations which harbor closely related viruses.

4. Some such "new diseases" have subsequently escaped from Africa to threaten well-established animal industries in the North. Thus, in the mid-1950s African swine fever appeared in Portugal, probably traveling from one of its colonies via airline garbage. Spread occurred into Spain, France, Italy and Malta, thence to the Caribbean and Latin America. The costs of combatting it, including its complete eradication from many areas, were enormous.

5. *Atet* is simply the Dinka word for "specialist," anyone who has special skills not possessed by most pastoralists.

6. Knowledge of livestock diseases on the part of East African pastoralists has been recounted by Schwabe (1978a: 42-49). Ohta (1984) and Dyson-Hudson and McCabe (1985) have recorded other Turkana folk beliefs and Baumann (1990) discussed aspects of this subject for the Somali. More recent reviews of traditional veterinary medicine for Africa have been provided by McCorkle and Mathias-Mundy (1992) and Bizimana (1994). A number of "case studies" are being collected and edited by McCorkle, Mathias-Mundy and Schillhorn van Veen (1996). An annotated bibliography (Mathias-Mundy and McCorkle) appeared in 1989.

7.  Part of this misunderstanding reflects popular mythologies about both human and veterinary medicine--and especially of their relationships to each other (Schwabe, 1978a, 1984b).

8. Or suggested by the patient responding positively to the treatment prescribed, an event usually complicated by not knowing whether or not the sick individual might have improved also *without treatment*.  Since many diseases cannot be definitively diagnosed clinically, any treatment or other intervention then prescribed is simply an educated guess (or in some instances merely an attempt to make a human patient or livestock owner believe that something useful has been done).

9. The three main intervention *strategies* at the population level are prevention, control or eradication of a disease (a fourth strategy is more research).  The available *tactics* within veterinary practice are summarized in Table 6.2.

# 5

---

# PASTORAL DEVELOPMENT--PAST
# EFFORTS, FUTURE OPTIONS

Pastoral development in the Sahel . . . has reached an impasse.

Albert Sollod, 1991

From Chapters 2 and 3, it should be clear that "diffracted" Northern perceptions of man-animal relationships (see Table 1.1) are not germane to development in pastoral Africa. Concerned Northerners require a new perspective (rather, an *old* perspective) to be able to communicate and function effectively. Accepting that, we can consider past aims and strategies and what these largely unsuccessful efforts at considerable cost might suggest for the future. Narrative chronologies are virtually limited to places like Kenya and Zimbabwe where Northern colonists intended to stay. Duggan's (1986) examination of that pattern within southern Africa was prefaced by the summarizing remark that "British colonial governments that ruled the region judged that sweeping aside African agriculture was cheaper and easier than changing it." Jarvis and Erickson's (1986) historical analysis for Zimbabwe provided additional perspective on colonial assumptions about African husbandry and the types of "development programs" such beliefs fostered. But, outside of small portions of the anthropological literature, there has been virtually no consideration of past events from an African herder's perspective.

## DO PASTORALISTS FEEL DEPRIVED AND POOR?

Oddly, what different peoples want most from life, believe possible and are most prepared to devote efforts to secure (or retain) have been poorly studied subjects.  Beyond such, it becomes increasingly clear to many Northerners that modern materialism, of whatever political stripe, has its profoundly negative as well as positive aspects.  One consequence will be that, if sensitive and well-motivated persons are not prepared in sufficient numbers to explore their own and other peoples' deepest longings and sources of a sense of well-being--and help direct more positively possibilities for overall improvements in life--political demogogues or other exploiters are quite prepared to play upon such situations to their own advantages.  The growth, for example, of politically active so-called religious fundamentalism in many parts of the world (within totally different traditions) suggests not only some generality of personally valued nonmaterial needs, but the real dangers their neglect by responsible persons can portend.

Therefore, if a Dinka pastoralist is told not to go to the *toich* so that he could market his animals and thereby get money to buy radios, television sets, fancy clothing for himself and his family, the first author would expect that he would simply laugh and walk away, or if he chooses to talk, would ask "but who told you we needed those things you are talking about?" As long as development agents are unwilling to try to understand, for example, why the initial reaction of many Dinka men upon first exposure to the Sudan's capital city of Khartoum is less one of jealousy than pity for its inhabitants, then development efforts to improve the situations of Africa's pastoralists will continue to fail. For, from the Dinka point of view, Khartoum's inhabitants are underprivileged people forced to live lives devoid of its really important things that bind all of life together, like rain, grass and cattle. If that Dinka perception of accessible glimpses of the more "modern world" is at all a common first reaction of other pastoralists away from home, one might legitimately ask "why is development a relevant consideration at all for traditional African pastoralists?"  Despite the material simplicity, if not sparsity, of their lives, do they not already enjoy that sense of inner peace so many Northerners now desperately seek?

## EXTERNALLY INDUCED CHANGES

Conscious or unconscious Northern beliefs in the "primitiveness" of extensive pastoralism see traditional methods of livestock husbandry as constraints to livestock sector development, as visualized mostly in terms of potential meat exports (Goldschmidt, 1980), or of overall economic progress. In the latter case, settling pastoralists became the prime objective.  Such beliefs started to feature unusually prominently in Northern development circles as independence approached for colonial Africa and found expression in statements like this: "There can be no solution of Northern Nigeria's agricultural problem so long as the cattle[-owning] population remains divorced from its soil; . . . there can be no question of their preservation as nomadic cattle owners, owing loyalty neither to the soil nor the Territory.  The aim of policy should be their absorption into the country's agriculture" (Shaw and Colville, 1950).

Virtually all attempts at forced settlement over a period of decades have failed miserably and, in recent years, appreciation has grown that the physical realities of many pastoral areas do not afford realizable alternatives. Nevertheless, this goal of mandatory settlement still lingers on to varying degrees, and 25 years after Shaw and Colville an official World Bank publication (Lele, 1975: 60) still opined that "the only long-term solution to the problem of range development in pastoral areas in Kenya may be for many of the pastoralists to be absorbed by the nonnomadic sector of the society."

When impetus and justification for development efforts in pastoral areas remain different in outsiders' and insiders' eyes, serious problems are inevitable. Thus, when the outsider's assumption is that the objective is to settle pastoralists for more intensive livestock raising, crop production or both, the primary task becomes to remove the reasons they migrate. The most obvious means has been to provide "permanent" watering points. Because such settlement goals have been paramount to many facilitating agencies, "spending money on new water supplies" became in S. Sandford's (1983: 63) words "the easiest form of pastoral development . . . [and] different aid agencies actively compete with each other for opportunities to scatter new water points . . . without any clear conception of what is there already or why they are adding to it." Attempts to settle the pastoral Peul people of northern Senegal is but one example of the failure of almost all such attempts at induced settlement (Toure, 1988). Boreholes were meant to permit Peul who formerly occupied the Ferlo area only seasonally to relocate there permanently. However, when they did concentrate around these water sites, progressive environmental degradation resulted, particularly in the dry season. Many observers now believe that most evidence of desertification caused by overgrazing is precisely that about boreholes drilled by outsiders (Pritchard et al., 1992: 124).

That largely haphazard approach has been based on outsiders' assumptions that pastoralists migrate *only* because they have to, not that they also may migrate partially because of social institutions that are vital parts of their cultural fabric and may be difficult or impossible to retain if migration ceases. Some schemes have fomented conflict between pastoralists and settled peoples, some of whom were new to formerly pastoral areas. Thus, in 1945, Sudanese authorities introduced crop production tracts to the Funj area with the assumption that nomads there would settle onto them (Ahamed, 1973). They chose not to settle, competition for land between them and sedentary agricultural producers heightened, with government planners favoring the latter.

It is ironic that the survival tactics pastoralists employ for the welfare of their cattle, and consequently for themselves--the adjustments to disequilibrial ecology they have made for millennia--have been seen as impediments to development. There are many known instances, therefore, of how attempts to rapidly and significantly change traditional pastoral practices and institutions have not achieved their instigators' goals. In Kenya some of the better Maasai lands were converted to wheat production, with tragic results because such high-potential, dry-season pastures, and associated water sources, played an indispensable role in making the yearly cycle of Maasai transhumance possible (Goldschmidt, 1980). Yet, it is precisely such lands for which competition (with outside forces) remains the highest. Other examples include the Ankole ranching scheme in Uganda and tribal grazing land policy in Botswana (Behnke, 1983).

Although numerous periodicals exist to publish information about development issues (Welsh and Butorin, 1990: 1161-1194), accounts of successes and failures within pastoral Africa are often confidential or are intended for limited distribution. Works which have attempted to marshall this record must draw heavily upon unpublished reports, many of them not verifiable by others.[1] For example, of slightly over 300 sources cited by S. Sandford (1983), 55 (including a number of the statedly most valuable) are listed as unpublished, while at least 56 more are in the very limited distribution category. So the pastoral development process remains mostly one of repeatedly "reinventing the wheel" and, far too often, a defective wheel visibly driven by the strong hand of political ideology.

We shall use the Dinka situation to begin now to look at a few past attempts at pastoral development and what might be learned from them. Quite atypically, alleged development prospects for the lands of southern Sudanese pastoralists have inspired some outsiders to such extravagant expression as: "The southern half of the Sudan is potentially one of the richest farming regions of the world, with the soil, sunlight and water resources to produce enormous quantities of food--*as much, perhaps, as the entire world now produces.* . . . To unlock the promise of the southern Sudan . . . [huge] swamps would have to be drained . . . *and the nomadic cattle raisers of the region somehow changed into sedentary farmers.* . . . Such a reserve cannot long be neglected" (Hopper, 1976, italics added).

## SOUTHERN SUDANESE "DEVELOPMENT" IN THE POST-ADDIS ABABA PERIOD

The Sudan, the largest country in Africa in land mass, is sparsely populated. According to the 1955/56, 1973 and 1983 censuses, the population was 10.3 million, 14.8 million and 20.6 million, respectively, indicating an average annual increase of 3.57%, with total growth during that 28-year period of 100%. This population is concentrated in Khartoum province and the Central Region. Within the "Three Towns" of Khartoum, Omdurman and Khartoum North (greater Khartoum), income per capita in 1956 was approximately £S120 per annum or four times the national average of £S28 (Güsten, 1966: 1-49). In areas with irrigation agriculture, income averaged £S65. In the semidesert belt and in the Nile Valley north of Khartoum, inhabited mainly by Arab nomads and seminomads, per capita income was only about three-quarters of the national average. The Floodplain and Ironstone areas which cover most of the southern Sudan had an income about half the national average and one-tenth of that in the "Three Towns" (Yongo-Bure, 1983, 1985). However, the southern Sudanese economy was far more dependent upon subsistence production than the national average (Güsten, 1966). Yongo-Bure contended that with continued emphasis of development policy on irrigation agriculture, these disparities are probably becoming considerably greater, especially in the southern Sudan where hardly any development has taken place since the beginning of the first 17-year civil war. No exports are as yet being produced from that region, nor have large domestic markets emerged. It needs to be added that the earlier colonial policy for the southern part of the Anglo-Egyptian Sudan can best be described as paternalistically benign neglect with no practical integration of the region within the overall Sudan. There is no clearer reflection than that, during the period of British rule, this immense territory possessed but a single senior secondary school.

The immediate task of the Southern Sudan Regional Government established following the Addis Ababa Agreement of 1972, which ended the first civil war, was repatriation, rehabilitation and resettlement of returnees from the "bush" and neighboring countries. Even full restoration of the physical infrastructure and public amenities to their prewar states would have been a very modest accomplishment, but that was not nearly achieved. Funds to carry out those tasks were to come from the national Five-Year Plan (1970/71-1974/75), as amended and extended to a Seven-Year Plan (1970/71-1976/77), but expenditure was far below expectation (Regional Ministry of Finance and Economic Affairs, 1984). In 1975/76, the Regional Government introduced a method for formulating a detailed annual plan, including elementary program and performance budgeting. Planning committees were set up in all ministries and parastatal organizations, but, overall, the objectives of those were not realized. The major cause of failure was lack of financial resources. Although direct transfers from the Central Government were to be the largest component, the Regional Government had difficulties in obtaining these promised subventions, which inhibited implementation of projects financed through external sources because of the importance of this counterpart component.

In July 1977 the Regional Government embarked on another Six-Year Plan for Economic and Social Development. It formed an integral part of the national Six-Year Plan for the same period which aimed at special treatment for depressed regions or those possessing unique economic characteristics or social conditions (Yongo-Bure, 1985). Planned investment was about £S286.7 million, but actual levels fell far below targeted amounts. As a consequence, since 1978/79, national and regional plans were discontinued and the government operated on the basis of "rolling plans," with the result that the southern Sudan remained in a situation of virtual nondevelopment.

The largest specific "development" effort undertaken in the South was the *Jonglei Canal Project*. It illustrates not only the external impetus for much of what has been contemplated among Africa's pastoralists, but the fact that *pastoralists have almost never been involved in planning or execution of efforts that would affect them enormously.*

The Floodplain of the southern Sudan (see Chapter 2) has remained essentially untouched until recently. Through it passes the White Nile, including for a distance of about 300 to 400 kilometers its great swampy excrescence, the *Sudd*. The idea to divert Nile waters before they enter the *Sudd* originated in the very early colonial period (Howell et al., 1988, Collins, 1990). Such an ambitious "world class" engineering project aimed to benefit agricultural peoples downstream. At first, that was exclusively for populous Egypt, but, after Sudanese independence, the project aimed also to benefit the arid northern Sudan. The plan eventually adopted involved constructing a diversionary canal about 360 km long. This Jonglei Canal Project, which cuts across the territory of the Dinka, was launched with virtually no consideration of them or other inhabitants of the area bordering the *Sudd*.

Despite warnings from the late 1960s on that that effort might have considerable environmental consequences, including adverse effects on climate over a broader area of Africa, only in retrospect were possible impacts upon local peoples examined (Lako, 1988). Following the first southern Sudanese insurrection, pastoralists were consulted for the first time and the canal project was presented as an effort that might improve their living standard. It was emphasized then that it would reduce seasonal flooding east of the *Sudd,* a sometimes disastrous event. Thus, a benefit of the canal to the area was to be reintroduction of pastoralists into lands deserted by them in the 1960s.

Because the entire Sudan has relatively few kilometers of improved roads, virtually none in the southern area, it also began to be emphasized that the parallel embankment created by digging the canal would provide an all-weather north-south road. The only existing unpaved all-weather roads in the south are between just a few district town centers, with all other roads linking such small centers closed much of each year. To put this problem in better perspective, the sole direct link of the south's capital town of Juba with the northern Sudan is via Nile steamer, which over the last few decades has changed from a dependable service to a situation of utter chaos. Moreover, the single track rail line from Khartoum to Wau in the southwest also deteriorated steadily since independence, and internal air service is, to say the least, limited and undependable. The result overall was that most experienced persons from the outside quickly identified this virtual absence of internal transport as the single most prominent feature of nondevelopment in the Sudan's south that seriously impeded virtually all other efforts. Thus the importance of an all-weather road linking Juba with the Sudan as a whole.

Contract signing in 1974 triggered both local and international reactions. However, what some foreign environmentalists seemed to fear most were consequences to wildlife of the canal's interruption of their annual seasonal migration routes. Fewer concerns were expressed for the peoples whose lands these had been for millennia. But, while those controversies made headlines abroad, most local opposition remained uncoordinated. Educated pastoralists, especially those from the most immediately effected Bor and Kongor districts, failed initially to make any felt doubts publicly known because of vividly recalled floods of the 1960s, thus any efforts that would ostensibly help prevent a repeat of that disaster were welcomed politically. Only in the regional capital were political reactions less subdued and rioting resulted in some deaths, with many arrested, including members of the Regional Assembly.

The main concerns of internal opposition were not wildlife migration, but the fate of pastoralists whose livelihood depended upon annual migrations to the *toich*. The canal was to cut across the zone of transhumant home-base settlements, with some falling west and others east of it. Of primary local concern was how cattle would cross the canal. To help counter such opposition, the national government belatedly created a National Council for Development Projects for the Jonglei Canal Area charged with insuring that the best local use would be made of the canal (Howell et al., 1988). They suggested that 10 gasoline-powered ferries and three permanent bridges be provided for its crossing. Local opinion held that these would be totally inadequate to handle the crossing of over a million cattle.

These local concerns beclouded other potential advantages the canal might bring to the area in the context of overall economic development, and only in the mid-1980s did studies begin to appear that realistically weighed its potential to the south (Mefit-Babtie, 1983, Howell et al., 1988, Collins, 1985, 1990). Positive arguments emphasized controlling flooding by varying the flow of water through the canal; improvement of access by veterinary and, potentially, other governmental services; and improved transport and communications generally. Disadvantages included reduction in grazing areas during the dry season with possibilities that less nutritious grasses would become dominant on the eastern side of the canal (where cattle spent most of their time) and that the embankment barrier could lead to flooding east of the canal.[2] But even such late projections did not take sufficient note of the issue that continued most to stir local political sentiments, namely that the canal would deny access to grazing areas on the main Nile.

Even where development projects involving pastoral areas have taken greater note of pastoralists as people, it has almost always been from the negative perspectives described, ones in which the traditional system is believed to be understood and that it badly requires drastic reorganization if not outright replacement. The first of the examples that follow considers direct efforts to convert migratory pastoralists to sedentary agriculturalists. The second is of a less disruptive attempt to increase the monetary value of cattle with the expectation of increasing pastoralist interest in selling their "surplus" for export. The third illustration is of a more complicated and imaginative attempt to change traditional husbandry practices and land use bases in order for both to conform more to Northern practices and capitalist economic theory.

## TANZANIA: ATTEMPTED WAGOGO SETTLEMENT

As already indicated, "the attitudes of national administrations towards pastoralists are, with few exceptions, negative: nomads are generally regarded as 'not yet settled'" (Dahl and Hjort, 1976). Such a settlement effort among the Wagogo of Tanzania (Mascarenhas, 1977) is illustrative of development projects in which the results have been the reverse of what planners envisioned. It was intended to persuade this transhumant tribe to increase the scope of, and intensify, the cultivation portion of their existing system of mixed livestock and crop production, in effect to become a more settled people. However, increasing areas for arable farming reduced grazing areas close to their seasonal home bases. In addition, rather than increased cash income from sales of crops going to improve their material well-being, as outside developers expected, much of it was invested in additional cattle--Wagogo tribal memory recalling prerinderpest days when they had been a much wealthier tribe (see Chapter 4). The result was a larger herd and smaller grazing area! Cattle nutrition and health deteriorated and formerly maintained stocking levels were upset, causing overgrazing with flash flooding. Bush encroachment further reduced grazing. Thus, a system "balanced" by traditional opportunistic responses was converted into a more ecologically unbalanced system with which the Wagogo no longer possessed as great ability to cope. We see here a common feature of many pastoral development efforts in Africa: inadequate anthropological inputs to understanding local bases for man-cattle interdependence and insufficient local historical inquiry.

Even when the objective is not settlement, the relative lack of cultural information required for success, or inadequate pastoralist inputs and participation during the planning and execution stages, cause projects to fail in the eyes of their Northern sponsors or create new problems where they did not formerly exist. Consider a United Nations Development Program (UNDP) project begun in 1973 in Swaziland.

## SWAZILAND: CATTLE EXPORTS FOR CASH

One of the first, and still rare, attempts to publicly identify *causes* of relative success or failure of pastoral programs was an analysis of a Swaziland effort by Doran et al. in 1979. In that program, ostensibly aimed at improving the quality and value of pastoralists' livestock (and reducing *assumed* overgrazing), emphases were given to development of cattle fattening and marketing facilities, with associated breeding improvement efforts. This project was based upon unexplored presumptions that, thereby, (1) the offtake rate for Swazi cattle would increase, (2) this sale of "meat on the hoof" would increase Swazi herders' cash income and (3) their "general prosperity" would increase as a result. From prior data, it was assumed that fattening cattle would increase their local market value per capita by about U.S.$50.

A regression analysis by Doran and colleagues of the prior 25 years' offtake rates in relation to local market price (an analysis *which should have preceded design of this project*) then showed that, instead of the Northern assumption that offtake rate would relate positively to market price (i.e., higher price, more sales), the reverse had been the case: 40% of variations in offtake rate had been accounted for by *inverse* fluctuations in market price. Because Swazi herders sell cattle only to meet specific nontraditional needs, like children's education and taxes, *they sell the fewest animals possible to obtain that specific amount of cash*. Thus, with the increase in price paid per head, sale of *fewer* cattle would meet those limited cash needs, a relationship any anthropologist acquainted with pastoralist economies might have predicted.

Adequate studies of traditional husbandry systems and their outputs were not carried out either before promotion of a large project among Kenyan Maasai beginning in the 1960s.

## KENYA: GROUP RANCHING IN MAASAILAND

The Kenya Ministry of Lands set up a group ranch registration and management authority in the 1960s with the stated aim of helping Maasai "administer their land use" (Pritchard et al., 1992: 125). Twenty five ranches averaging 18,000 hectares were established initially in 37,500 square kilometers of Kajiado district, which lineage groups of Maasai would own in common. That idea was initially popular because Maasai saw it only as a way to "legally" establish enforceable title to their remaining lands, thus stopping a process of land alienation begun with colonial rule, including continuing losses since independence to small groups of large commercial ranchers (Hedlund, 1971; Galaty, 1980) and neighboring groups of cultivators such as the Kikuyu (Behnke, 1983).

Little actually worked as the plan's instigators assumed. Maasai who better understood the overall plan considered it irrational, because one of its main bases had been the then prevalent notion among Northern animal husbandry/range management advisors that the livestock carrying capacity of African rangelands should be only that sustainable *under the worst likely weather scenario*. That approach, never understood by pastoralists, has been generally unsuccessful and is now rejected more and more by informed outsiders (Pritchard et al., 1992; Bartels et al., 1993). Other facets of the plan more acceptable to Maasai, such as improved water resources, proved only partially sustainable: surveys at the end of the 1970s showing that only 62% of drilled boreholes still functioned (S. Sandford, 1983: 63). Also, group ranch management committees with considerable power over individual ranch members (and responsible for relations to the rest of the economy, e.g., incurring loans) did not function as intended (Sandford, 1983: 139).  Since those committees were quickly dominated by the richest Maasai, an intended quota system was unenforced because committee members took no steps to reduce their own prior herd sizes nor to bring poorer families' holdings up to a basic minimum (Sandford, 1983: 160).

## SOMALIA: A LARGE-SCALE UMBRELLA APPROACH

Acting upon UNDP responses to the catastrophic African drought of the early 1970s (in which about 30% of Somali livestock were believed to have died), an extraministerial National Range Agency was created in 1980 with support of a consortium of external donors.  This new umbrella agency was intended to radically change the pastoral system over one-fifth of Somalia. From the start some donor groups had serious reservations about the rigidity of this centrally mandated project, in effect "to replace existing nomadic ways by placing grazing control on certain areas and restricting grazing in reserves" (Zessin and Farah, 1993).  In practice its varied aspects lacked overall direction and each component went its own way.  Thus, not only did that new agency partially parallel and not relate well to existing service sectors, but even its own specialized groups failed to communicate with one another or effectively mesh their own efforts.

As multinational field staff gradually realized that local data did not exist upon which to base these sweeping managerial interventions, the project was modified after four years' efforts to include accumulation of missing baseline information.  "In retrospect, it appears that [this project's] greatest strength was to have eventually followed . . . an investigative/pilot approach rather than embarking on large-scale, rigid . . . 'military' interventions" (Zessin and Farah, 1993).  The project was terminated abruptly by eruption of interclan warfare.

A postmortem by participants concluded that development programs that assume a priori that

herders' self-interests will cause them to overuse common grazing lands, rendering this form of pastoralism unproductive and ecologically damaging are not addressing the real problem.  If highly variable rainfall rather than absolute livestock numbers is the main factor which  controls the  dynamics of the ecosystem  [as in pastoral Africa], then . . . measures seeking to establish a stable stocking density through vegetation manage-ment alone will fail.  Herds which are rebuilt by traditional pastoralists as fast as possible after a drought and are inevitably knocked back again in subsequent dry years use range most efficiently in this case . . . [and] livestock numbers only temporarily reach a level that will seriously harm the range. . . . This is not to say that no over-grazing occurs . . . and it would be irresponsible to claim that no long term damage [may result but] all points of argument indicate that our knowledge of range ecology is too incomplete to justify in the name of development aid the use of unproven interventions to forcefully change . . . , perhaps to the point of no return--a system that may be more efficient and less damaging than any planned alternative (Zessin and Farah, 1993).

Such large umbrella efforts, as we have witnessed them, also have been *far too neglectful of other important human considerations.* For, not only as Sandford (1983: 87ff) pointed out, are "different aspects that fall within the broad definition [of range management itself] ... very closely intertwined, and [therefore] many difficulties have arisen in pastoral development programmes from failure to appreciate that tinkering with one aspect will have indirect consequences on other aspects," but such intertwinings of relationships--*in pastoralists' eyes*--are far more extensive.  As members of "fused societies" (see Table 1.1), pastoralists believe that areas of life *which almost no Northerners consider related at all*--animal husbandry, religion and healing as examples-- are so closely joined that tinkering with any one may, in ways uncomprehended by the outsider, affect the very fabric of pastoral life. We believe therefore that such costly undertakings are premature--are far too grandiose in conception and far too little based upon knowledge of specific local situations and institutions.

An arrogance has been manifest vis-à-vis pastoral development in Africa that, in our joint view, has had almost no precedent elsewhere.  In an as yet rare historicoeconomic study of a national pastoral situation, Jarvis and Erickson (1986) more specifically addressed in Zimbabwe some of these prior assumptions of outside agents of change.

## ZIMBABWE: REFLECTIONS ON PAST EVENTS

To preface this analysis, we should note that extensive pastoralism as considered here in terms of nomadism and transhumance no longer practically exists in Zimbabwe.  The impact of colonialism there has been substantially greater than even among Kenya's Maasai, and migratory pastoralism is a thing of the past.  However, the large Ndebele tribe of southern Zimbabwe were transhumant pastoralists with their center of authority a kingdom, as among the southern Sudan's Nilotic Shilluk.  When white settlers came, they took the Ndebele's most productive lands and cattle following bloody battles. Indigenous peoples were relocated to unproductive rocky, so-called Communal Areas. Herders within these graze common range, but seasonal migrations no longer take place.  Thus, most of Zimbabwe's pastoralists have been forced to evolve a new way of life which has substituted crop production for cattle herding as principal means of livelihood.[3]  This compulsory evolution of pastoralism in Zimbabwe reflects a less than happy course of actions.

Jarvis and Erickson's purpose, however, in examining these historical records (1890-1980) was to explore the proposition "predicted for over 50 years" that a "decline of African livestock systems due to the overgrazing of common range resources" was imminent.  It's impetus was contrary observations that "instead of [predicted] collapse, livestock herds in many areas [of

Africa] seem to have exhibited sizable increases through time and to have sustained increasing human populations." Among their findings were that "the value of livestock services and products . . . , especially draft services, milk and dung" had been poorly documented for indigenous livestock owners, a point we stress generally. As to evidence for overgrazing and range degradation during this extended period, they concluded that, despite expropriations for European settler use of large areas of the best range lands, "surprisingly, there is little or no evidence of either [overgrazing or range degradation] in the data analyzed." Possible explanations ventured for why the "tragedy of the commons" theory had not been borne out in Zimbabwe were: "1) specific rules regulating access to common range exist and are reasonably effective, so that the stocking rate is not greatly in excess of the economically optimal; or 2) livestock density was initially far below the optimal level so that even with the growth of herds the critical point has not yet been reached; or 3) the carrying capacity of the Zimbabwe range has been rising rapidly in response to output increasing investments; or 4) the data, on livestock output and livestock productivity are deceptive in failing to reflect the declines which have taken place in each of these variables in response to herd numbers."

As we have seen in Chapter 4, and Jarvis and Erickson document, the second of these possible explanations no doubt has considerable validity in what we know of the immediately prior depredations of rinderpest in Zimbabwe and blows to which livestock numbers there also were subjected by the subsequent onslaught of East Coast Fever. Those losses of an estimated 90-95% of the prior "national" herd no doubt influenced indigenous pastoralists to attempt to increase their individual herd sizes during subsequent years. But it is the suggested possibility number 1 that is most intriguing and that we believe requires follow-up everywhere in Africa. In Chapters 2 and 3 we indicated that differences in processes of decision-making, and the levels at which decisions are made, may prevail among different pastoral peoples, especially in uses of grazing and water resources. Such questions are in urgent need of exploring in each individual situation and in detail before development initiatives are undertaken.

## EMERGENCY FEEDING CAMPS

Sen (1981: 124) has addressed another political alternative voiced since the 1970s Sahelian disaster that *deliberate* depopulation of some pastoral areas in Africa might be a serious option. Suggestions of "a strategic withdrawal from areas of very low and unreliable rainfall" as policy elicited from him arguments beyond the overridingly obvious one that the pastoral inhabitants of the Sahel and other very harsh areas of Africa already have coped over extremely long periods, including that the "bulk of the population from the Sahelian north who migrated south [to less dry areas during the height of that famine] have, in fact, returned north again [to their traditional drier lands]." But, beyond such deliberate depopulation proposals, some emergency relief measures launched following worldwide TV coverage of a succession of subsequent instances of severe drought (or drought plus warfare[4] plus mismanagement by authoritarian regimes) might accomplish similar results. On first consideration, these emergency feeding and support programs represent a totally positive outpouring of sympathy by more fortunate Northerners for persons in distress. But, from the standpoints of realistic perceptions by outsiders of what life among pastoralists *normally* is like (of necessity and through custom), Northern TV news coverage provides a totally warped view of pastoral Africa and suggests very superficial cures--misplaced ideas about what really needs doing.[5]

More important, such efforts, *if sustained for considerable periods*, could, in themselves, have disastrous effects. We refer to common practices of requiring potential recipients of emergency food and other aid to congregate in makeshift camps, often without any of the livestock they may still retain. This is done to make the work of aid distribution easier for workers involved in these difficult efforts. In our experiences of such situations, these camps, beside food distributions, provide some other amenities not normally accessible to pastoralists. Thus sizable numbers of Turkana and Somali youth are growing up with the expectation that a tap to fill almost unlimited containers of water is available no more than a few hundred meters from their huts and that rudimentary health outposts and the like may also be near their doorsteps. They are no longer being trained to live unaided in harsh terrain. Their traditional social structures are deteriorating and being replaced by "temporarily" expedient ones introduced helter-skelter. These latter situations, increasingly common, do not even remotely resemble what we would regard as sustainable development approaches in pastoralist Africa, but provide only measures which will favor depopulation of productive lands and further overcrowding of already bursting cities with their attendant problems. In contrast, our approach envisages provision of realistic, high-priority services and amenities to pastoralists at the literally "grass roots" *where they normally live,* efforts which will help them live more securely in their accustomed manner.

From our experiences, even such more accessible accounts of past development failures are rarely sought out or read by new "Northern experts," too many of them now "safari consultants" recruited for relatively short-term service on particular projects in Africa. Some NGOs especially have longer term personnel on the ground but many lack sufficient expert technical backup for what they attempt with good motives.

Overall, past development efforts in pastoral Africa have been characterized by ideology-driven policies based upon Northern planners' assumptions, including such "Northern as normal" beliefs as motivations to continually augment material well-being, utility of animals and the extent and depth of man-animal interactions. Policy choices (strategies) continue to be (1) sedentarization, which attempts radical transformation of social systems, (2) modernization, which ignores social systems and, to far lesser extents, (3) cooperativization, which attempts to reinforce existing social systems (Sollod, 1991: 232). These alternatives represent more than development strategies, they have been the "ideological camps" of politicians, natural scientists and some social scientists, respectively. While either settling pastoralists or introducing totally different husbandry systems have overwhelmingly predominated over attempts to study and strengthen existing social systems, some recent efforts toward the latter still are not being honest with pastoralists. Thus, Sollod noted that the strategies of cooperation and settlement are being advocated by some funding agencies in combination, but that, although "cooperativization became the rhetorical call, . . . sedentarization [remained] the goal." As a consequence, pastoral peoples in Africa now appear to be caught in "catch-22" situations, mixes of development strategies "their governments" are ostensibly promoting to "alleviate poverty," but ones in which pastoralists themselves have had almost no say.

The fact is that, in countries worldwide where authoritarian rule prevails (as it does throughout much of Africa), the military, the intelligencia and the populace of the capital city have been the only power bases. In the eyes of demogogues, these three groups must be placated first in allocation of national resources. Evidence for these biases in resource allocation throughout Africa is appalling. The least threats to the political status quo are the rural masses and, in such hierarchies of power, *pastoralists are the group least considered*. As a result, there are countries in Africa in which the pastoral sector generates almost all of the national income, including foreign exchange, yet that sector receives a minuscule portion of the national budget. In Somalia, for instance, where nomads and transhumants own 95% of domesticated animals (Abdullahi, 1993), 80% of foreign currency earnings were from livestock exports and livestock generated just under 50% of the GNP (Janzen, 1993), development plans overlooked pastoralists' interests completely, and that sector's share in the national budget was less than 2% (Abdullahi, 1993). This virtual absence of empowerment is most conspicuous in African states where improvement of food productivity in arid and semiarid regions is seen as the only preventive to chronic food shortages *among already burgeoning populations of the capital and other mushrooming cities*--beliefs that are almost the sole preoccupations of some governments (Bates and Conant, 1980), as well as of many outside agencies. Thus, most pastoral peoples have been burdened with initiatives not of their choice, some misleadingly promoted by outside forces who have their own agendas. Dishonesty in disclosing real intentions of efforts clearly has been one major cause of past "development" failures.

No small part of this confusing vacillation in official policies vis-à-vis pastoral Africa during past decades resulted from a propensity of outside advisors to eschew enough locally pursued empirical research. Moreover, advisors representing different disciplines which obviously have something useful to contribute have almost completely gone their own ways without so much as a side glance to what the others were concluding and advising. That this may be slowly changing--and assessments of traditional husbandry and land use approaches are revolving almost 180° (Behnke et al., 1993)--cannot help but confuse pastoralists still further and increase their suspicions about what outsiders may really have to offer them. For, with recent Northern research efforts with broader inputs, expert groups on the ecology of different parts of Africa are now concluding increasingly, with Behnke and Scoones (1993), that while "international development agencies and African governments have devoted considerable effort to the suppression of pastoral techniques of land and livestock management . . . these programmes were undertaken on the presumption pastoralism was inherently unproductive and ecologically destructive and, hence, required radical reform. Current empirical research supports none of these presumptions."

However, despite such recently growing opinion that "extensive pastoralism is probably the only possible way of putting the barren pastures of these regions to economic use without an immense expenditure of capital" (Scholz, 1986: 113), "this fact is [still] frequently not adequately recognized . . . by representatives of the urban elites of these countries, nor even by development experts.  Instead, to suit the interests of the urban upper classes, priority in national development planning is usually given to costly and prestigous projects promoting irrigation, industry and infrastructure" (Janzen, 1993).  Many who control the purse strings of development still believe that, as long as traditional systems prevail, technical innovations are not possible (Toure, 1988).  At the same time pastoralists continue to struggle, often ineffectually, against these outside pressures which they only partially understand. Used to struggling against and usually coping opportunistically with their uncompromising environments, they show no intention of placidly giving up their mobility, which has been their principal strategy for managing climatic, disease and other ecological risks.

## FUTURE ALTERNATIVES

Since the primary necessity, in our opinion, is to see that, in the future, changes do not lessen pastoralists' historic abilities to cope, lead to unmanageable environmental degradation or encourage cultural disruption, pastoralists *must* be convinced that the positives of proposed changes clearly outweigh possible negatives. The jettisoning of things pastoralists know from centuries of experience to work must not continue to be unthinkingly proposed in favor of those that may not. One of the most flagrant of early instances of disrespect for pastoralists' knowledge was a wide-scale attempt to halt their seasonal burning of grasslands.  Only much later was it realized by Northern agronomists that this practice was essential in many areas to perpetuate a grasslands proclimax and prevent encroachment of a brush-tsetse climax ecosystem (see Chapter 4).

But greater respect for local values and practices in the future does not mean that optimal situations now exist for pastoralists within the bounds of forseeable resources. Possible complements to traditional practices can be exposed, the strengths *and weaknesses* of alternative practices within other societies can be examined and some new possibilities tried *on pilot scales.* We believe that desirable change is most possible by taking advantage of, and grafting any new efforts and ideas upon, traditional beliefs and institutions. For that to happen, local desires and felt needs must be much better explored and local institutional arrangements carefully examined. Meaningful communications have heretofore been virtually lacking. Even the "cattle-complex" idea (Herskovits, 1926; also see Chapter 3), which described to outsiders for the first time the centrality of cattle in many aspects of African pastoral life, was for many years misunderstood by development agents as proof of a basic irrationality of such "primitive" peoples. Ways to achieve *two-way* communications based upon mutual respect become vital.

Some changes already forced upon particular pastoralists with damaging results could still be corrected, so in that sense pastoral development in Africa surely remains relevant. Moreover, impetus for change within some pastoral communities now originates internally as well as from without. Education has been the most obvious reason. The notion that a Northern-type education is of potential value is producing pastoral "elites" with varying experiences of the outside. Tending at first to borrow uncritically perceptions and values from their mentors, formally educated pastoralists increasingly seek balances between tradition and "modernization" (Deng, 1971, 1978, 1985). In coming to view strengths of their own communities with renewed appreciation, they see aspects of traditional culture which, in comparison with the goods *and bads* of the North, are well worth preserving.

One other induced change which has been fairly widely embraced within pastoral societies like the Somali and some in West Africa is for money to complement livestock as the means to realization of a range of traditional as well as nontraditional goals (Zessin, 1991: 188ff). But far less commented upon within official development circles for its also broad portent is the fact that some forms of nonindigenous disease management and health maintenance also have been enthusiastically embraced by many pastoralists. While some NGOs, especially missionary groups, have attempted to build their programs upon such initiatives, what has almost totally escaped notice is that those changes have been accepted far more widely among pastoralists for their *animals* than themselves. Thus, possibilities for *broader* development successes from veterinary initiatives have been largely overlooked.

While, more than a decade ago, S. Sandford (1983: 6) noted that most pastoral development schemes have been "attempts to copy the [North] American or Australian models of pastoral development" and that "both . . . have been characterized during their brief existence by considerable environmental damage and economic instability," he did not suggest alternative sources of "range management" expertise. Noting (p. 4) that "any sensible development policy will strive not only to provide better material standards of living for the pastoralists and to ensure that the pastoral areas supply some of the commodities of the nation as a whole, but also to conserve . . . traditional desirable social features or to replace them by an adequate substitute," he was equally short on suggestions of how to achieve sustainable improvements which are both locally desired *and capable of realistic long-term financing*, much less how to go about conserving built-in social features of traditional systems extolled in the abstract.

Moreover, most critiques of past development attempts fail to consider other important goals than meat production (often for export). Even recent works which convincingly document the rationality of many traditional African pastoral practices (Behnke et al., 1993), which propose "to build upon pastoral husbandry practices and incorporate them into formal development programmes," offer few guidelines for practically and affordably proceeding. These are limited largely to recognizing a need for monitoring rain (Sollod, 1991), grassland conditions, erosion, livestock production (Bartels et al., 1993) and the like, but rarely suggest how such proposals might be realized beyond costly remote sensing from satellites or *separate* on-the-ground monitoring systems for each class of variables.

We should now consider, therefore, past efforts which have produced more positive results from pastoralists' perspectives.

### Development Efforts Which Do Enjoy Pastoralist Support

The first author is convinced that his own Dinka people would appreciate properly addressed assistance in the following areas: education, veterinary services, human health services, water resources, crop production, pasture improvement, fish production and cooperatives. But there have been only two types of development programs commonly undertaken thus far with pastoralists' *own desires* at all in mind: local water projects and veterinary programs. There have been major differences between them that bear emphasis.

*Local Water Projects.* Although many local water projects have met with popular approval by pastoralists, their initiation has often been based on the assumption (and the intent) that providing convenient water points would remove the reason these peoples migrate and, ipso facto, would cause them to settle down. Water projects have been, for the most part, one-dimensional one-time efforts, there has been little coordination among donors (S. Sandford, 1983: 63) and maintenance of these new, usually unconventional, water sources (e.g., wells with hand pumps) has been absent or minimal. That is, past water supply efforts have frequently not been sustainable.[6] It is increasingly clear to close observers that "any extension of water supply points [within pastoral Africa] should be strictly carried out in conjunction with an assessment of range conditions," something heretofore rarely done (Janzen et al., 1993). We shall return to this point in Chapter 7 in connection with proposals for local intersectoral actions.


*Veterinary Services.* The other main social service which has been directed to pastoralists themselves where they actually live and which has reached them far more extensively and continuously than have such water projects are veterinary services.[7] We shall simply note that fact here because more effective future utilization of veterinary services *in intersectoral development efforts* will form one of our key proposals for local actions. As a consequence, veterinary services, their past record, present potential and future improvement will form much of the substances of Chapters 6 through 9.

**Other Basic Needs Almost Totally Neglected--Notably Human Health Services**

Most other efforts toward provision of basic amenities to pastoralists have never reached beyond the small populations of their few principal towns. One of the most important areas of neglect is human health, which has high priority among all peoples. Unfortunately, government health services still concentrate overwhelmingly upon treating individuals already ill and in most of the Third World have emphazized building and staffing of hospitals. Bringing this curative approach closer to rural people generally has been an aim of the Primary Health Care (PHC) program of the World Health Organization (WHO).

Prevention-focused portions of that effort have been its Expanded Programme of Immunization (EPI) directed against six readily preventable infections in children and an Oral Rehydration Project for malnourished infants. An example of virtually no success in extending even these to pastoralists is provided by the southern Sudan. Its few urban centers, which contain only 4% of the population, possess 85% of physicians, 100% of pharmacists and 37% overall of health personnel (AMREF, 1984).[8] Moreover, only 20% of this workforce could be characterized as being involved in *any* aspect of primary health care (AMREF 1984: 18, 23). Southern Sudanese medical services make no attempt to reach pastoral people where they actually live and without such mobile capacities they cannot possibly achieve even the objectives of these most crucial WHO/UNICEF-supported efforts. That is, most of the largely pastoral population of the southern Sudan remains unserved by current efforts.

Under comparatively few circumstances elsewhere in Africa have public health/medical services reached pastoral communities. In one instance two mobile teams endeavored to immunize nomadic children in the 615,000-square-kilometer Agadez region of northeastern Niger. But less than 10% of immunization achieved was through that mobile effort, which nonetheless consumed 24% of the public health budget (Aliou, 1992). Aliou attributed failure partly to lack of communication with nomadic groups, the *single intervention* offered and lack of repeat visits. However, even poorer immunization coverage was realized through fixed rural dispensaries and medical posts and only on market days was there any more effective outreach to nomadic patients, who had to walk as far as 30 kilometers to be seen. For the future, Aliou advocated more intensive mobile efforts not so limited in health services offered. No cost estimates were provided for such an augmented *independent effort by medical services alone.*

Is it reasonable to believe that sufficient resources will ever exist for veterinary services, water services, human health services, range improvement services, emergency drought response services (and various other needed services) to *each* create and maintain financially completely independent mobile capacities to reach out to pastoralists within their own scattered camps? We are certain they would not. Then what could be done? We believe the only answer to this basic conundrum must come from locally instituted intersectoral cooperation. Each service must finally realize it cannot possibly afford to "go it alone" in pastoral areas if anything meaningful and sustainable is going to be achieved.

## PUTTING SOME IDEAS TOGETHER

In our opinion, many pieces of a workable pastoral development approach have been suggested by a variety of workers in different disciplines which need to be sifted through, amalgamated where appropriate and field-tested. Working from very different backgrounds and approaches, some have begun to think or conclude similarly about pastoral situations, including ones specifically in Africa. One set of ideas arises from political scientists who draw upon the theories of New Institutional Economics (NIE) (Williamson, 1991) in apropos ways. Ostrom (1990: 25) has joined its strategy of "institutional analyses" to empirical methodologies of field biologists like ourselves to counter beliefs in the inevitability of a "tragedy of the commons." She shows through a series of local accounts that, within some pastoral and other commons situations, indigenous management mechanisms have indeed arisen, sometimes as combinations of public and private approaches. Some economists see such institutional analyses primarily as a way to identify a range of *local factors* that favor sustainable development efforts and other factors that may act as constraints to such efforts. Practical objectives become understanding the reasons behind such factors and, through this information, identifying positive aspects of existing institutions which could be built upon and constraining aspects which might possibly be modified or neutralized. For example, C.L. Schwabe and Schwartz (1992) identified requisites for financial sustainability of EPI efforts among children in Kenya and the Philippines. Leonard (1987,

1993) and his students have extensively applied NIE theory and institutional analyses to veterinary services delivery systems in Africa, principally within sedentary smallholder situations.

From different backgrounds and perspectives, some development and range ecologists (e.g., Coughenour et al., 1985; Behnke et al., 1993) and anthropologists (e.g., Schneider, 1957; Dyson-Hudson and Dyson-Hudson, 1969) carried out complementary studies which provided evidence that African pastoralists are not irrational peoples wantonly degrading their environments or lacking in effective management strategies.  In fact, through opportunistic strategies of response and varying degrees of individual versus collective decision-making and actions pastoral peoples often achieve a level of productivity under marginal range conditions comparable to that under similar conditions in the North (Pritchard et al., 1992: 23). A lesson from such findings was that each situation be studied locally. From such lines of evidence, Behnke and Scoones (1993) suggested more "limited but focused interventions . . . [with respect to range and livestock management, with] less rather than more centralized regulation."

Fewer workers began to creatively link different combinations of findings from varied sources to different aspects of development (e.g., anthropology and veterinary services delivery, Cunnison, 1960; social sciences and pastoral development, Dahl and Hjort, 1976).  Through a multidisciplinary approach among Sahelian nomads, a group headed by veterinarian Albert Sollod (1990, 1991) proposed "drought insurance" in the form of an early warning system for monitoring climatic danger signs, ideas arising from studies of principal survival strategies pastoralists employed (Sollod et al., 1984) and attempts to improve the quality of veterinary services outreach to these dispersed communities (Sollod and Stem, 1991).  Others joined to veterinary service initiatives quantitative epidemiological and anthropological methodologies (Schwabe, 1980, 1982, 1987, 1991a, 1993a, 1996; Schwabe and Kuojok, 1981), econometric and epidemiological methodologies (Zessin, 1991; Zessin and Carpenter, 1985; Zessin and Schwartz, 1993; Zessin and Farah, 1993; Zessin et al., 1985, 1993) or cooperative medical and veterinary efforts in the interests of human health, including under African conditions (Schwabe, 1974, 1978a, 1981, 1984b, 1991b, 1993a; Schwabe and Schwabe, 1990).  The cumulative effect of such suggestions has been growing realization of the value of integrated approaches--one form of which is intersectoral cooperation[9]--both to understanding *and assisting* pastoralists.  We sense that almost all the pieces are now in place for realizing some affordable development among Africa's pastoralists.

Therefore, we would note further at this point that, while economists have been concerned most directly with *fiscal* aspects of development program sustainability, institutions sometimes are analyzed for other aspects of sustainability.  For example, the Veterinary Public Health Unit of the World Health Organization initiated under the direction of Konrad Bögel and D.D. Joshi, first in Nepal, national analyses concentrating on technical, infrastructural and public support factors to identify what is necessary in different situations to develop and sustain practical intersectoral cooperation on zoonotic diseases control between public health and veterinary services (WHO, 1989; and see Chapters 4 and 6 of this book). But at this point, let us consider further the special need to ascertain within each African pastoral situation the presence or absence of institutions which help govern the commons.

## DINKA INSTITUTIONS FOR GOVERNING THE COMMONS

Of the examples Ostrom (1990) chose to illustrate some commons solutions, two directly address the a priori conclusions of Hardin about pastoralists. One was an account (Netting, 1981) of centuries old procedures for communal management of alpine meadows for grazing cattle within the Swiss Canton of Valais. The second author has lived in Switzerland and would add from his own observations that similar grazing commons' governance appears to apply throughout that country and is only one part of a *whole network of evolved ideas to retain the basically rural village-pastoral character of a country of difficult terrain* and maintain the contentedness of this large segment of the Swiss population with their traditional way of life (while providing them also most important benefits of "modernization").

Given the background of one of us, a reasonable question to consider at this point is "What do Dinka do in way of pastoral governance?" We have already indicated in Chapter 2 how they make decisions collectively with respect to moving the "communal transhumant herd" to new grazing sites and in Chapter 3 how the extended family reaches decisions collectively that exchange cattle for persons (both through marriage and settlements for homicide). Let us now consider further the Dinka institutions which mediate decisions on grazing locales, cattle movements, increases and decreases in individual families' cattle numbers and the like.

Some Northern observers have characterized Dinka society as an unusually egalitarian one, while others, failing to see any system of governance at all, believe they comprise an "acephalous" or "uncentralized" society living under a state of near anarchy. While there is some truth to both perceptions, we would agree with Okeny (1986: 33-53) that the Dinka system can better be described as a "decentralized democracy" which employs a "town meeting," Quaker-like consensus-based method for decision-making. That approach is also used to select individuals for judicial (mediating) offices from the level of the smallest cattle camp to principal subtribal divisions. Oral tradition suggests that the two most local offices among these evolved naturally from paramount concerns for exploitation and defense of particular pastures, that is, for managing the commons.

Traditional leadership at the most local level has centered upon an elected *bany wut*, a person who has demonstrated strength, endurance, bravery, hospitality, fairness in settling disputes, readiness to help persons in need and the like. Day-to-day problems concern things such as local moving of cattle and the *sharing* of grazing areas and water points. Broader traditional leadership at the clan level resides in *spiritual* and juridical guidance provided by a *bany bith* "priest" (or a similar person among certain subtribes) who not only settles disputes between contending parties by mediation and persuasion but helps make such major group decisions as when, for example, to move cattle to or from the *toich*. He mediates between the people and the divine not only in such matters, but with respect to external threats, occurence of rain and other questions of considerable community moment. His reputation depends on how successful his forecasts, sacrifices and mediations are.

While those offices receive no governmental stipends, persons occupying higher (government-created) ranks do receive salaries from local authorities. Thus the government is able to influence those individuals. They are: (1) "chief" of a section of a clan (*bany bai* or *magaak*), (2) "chief" of the clan (*bany alaama*), (3) "chief" of the appeals court (*bany rier*) and (4) "paramount chief" or court president of the subtribe (*bany seif*). Election as *bany bai* is also by consensus and *bany wut* and *bany bith* may be among the nominees. *Bany bai* deal with problems arising within the transhumant home base (*bai/dom*) and local cattle camp problems referred by individual *bany wut*. Most of these are disputes over cattle. However, the *bany bai*'s principal duty from the government's standpoint is collection of the poll tax, from which he receives a bonus.

The *bany alaama* is "the watchdog of the clan." New *bany alaama* are nominated from existing *bany wut* and *bany bai*, members of the previous *bany alaama*'s family or other qualified elders. Selection takes place by censussus at an assembly of clan elders after much discussion of each nominee's merits and demerits. Bulls are sacrificed in commemoration of his selection. As the highest clan authority, the *bany alaama* is responsible for watching out for its welfare and for settling disputes between sections of the clan. This would include disagreements over grazing areas or other major cattle issues which threaten violence between families.

*Bany rier* (chiefs of the appeals court) are selected by the *bany seif* of different subtribes within a district from serving *bany alaama* and this process is mediated by a government official. If a consensus cannot be reached, there is a show of hands. The *bany rier*'s dispute-resolving duties, other than referrals to his jurisdiction, are chiefly at the level of those between clans over ownership/use of particular dry season grazing rights. Similar disputes between subtribes are handled by a council of the *bany rier* presided over by the most senior among them. Its decisions are final (from the standpoint of Dinka society), although further appeal can be made to the government and settled outside their domain. The top subtribal position of *bany seif* was created by the British to provide one individual to deal with at the district level. Candidates are often *bany alaama* or *bany rier* or sons or brothers of a previous paramount subtribal chief. He is responsible on the government's behalf to introduce to his subtribe governmental policies or decisions.

Overall, the Dinka are a fairly peaceful, cooperating people and this system has worked quite well. For enforcement, *Bany seif* (and *bany alaama*) each have attached to them unofficial police, who may seize cattle as directed and hand them over to whom the court has ruled in favor. If warfare erupts between two clans (or subtribes) the *bany seif* must report this to governmental authorities, who then can order official police to separate the parties and make arrests. In case of deaths, the *bany seif* convenes emergency courts to assess a blood price in cattle. Beyond such means, Dinka fear the power of *jok* which reside in *bany bith* and their other spiritual leaders and are unwilling to defy their judgments.

Despite his considerable prestige and power to influence, it should be noted that the spiritual leader, the *bany bith*, is not part of this recognized hierarchy of governance, unless he also holds one of those other positions. He must sanction such important things as movements to or from the *toich* or through areas of high risk to man and beast (flooded areas, etc.), plus all matters dealing with epidemics among cattle and people or other potential threats to their wellbeing as a community. Therefore, he is intimately involved in Dinka's traditional management of the commons and his views and functions bear closely upon the mandates (and successes) of some of the most important official governmental services (veterinary, medical and water).

Through extended family cooperation and these adjudicating institutions, several methods are employed in practice to prevent overgrazing's consequences (including beliefs that certain diseases are more prevalent when cattle must graze very closely): (1) cattle are moved to other locations whenever grazing becomes poor (almost every Dinka possesses a large fund of knowledge about vegetation types and animal uses of it); (2) within a general grazing area, designated portions are grazed successively (it is known that leaving an area fallow permits regrowth; in fact, rotation is practiced even if grazing is luxurious because Dinka believe cattle profit from changes in grass types and quality); and (3) old grass is burned annually to encourage regrowth, a collective practice undertaken at the beginning of the dry season.

As Ostrom (1990: 6) points out, "at the heart of [the tragedy of the commons model and its variants] . . . is the free-rider problem. Whenever one person cannot be excluded from the benefits that others provide, each person is motivated [according to that theory] not to contribute to the joint effort, but to free-ride on the efforts of others." Do the Dinka recognize and cope with free-riders? Their resort to discussion and consensus in decisions about grazing and water management--with community enforcement of results--provides considerable protection against free-riding. In Chapter 4, for example, we mentioned in passing one specific situation indicative of such "rules." That is, when Dinka recognize contagious bovine pleuropneumonia in a family's cattle, the community excludes that family from their common grazing areas. This is an instance of enforced quarantine to make safe for all a common resource threatened by an individual livestock owner. That person could well have been a free-rider who did not have his cattle vaccinated, but the community prevented his free-riding any further. For similar reasons of reducing or spreading the risk, Dinka and other pastoral peoples deliberately divide their herds into subgroups which graze in different areas, that is, not share only a single commons. Although Turkana, for example, operate more as individual agents, other traditional mechanisms may accomplish the same among them, as illustrated in their cooperative creation and use of watering points. But these are precisely the kinds of information that must be ascertained in *each* local situation and never simply generalized as has been a propensity in the past.

One other point to note is that there is little or no real congruence or formal interdigitation between Dinka tribal institutions and those at different official levels of government (i.e., local administrative districts, provinces, regions, state) in that, even in most local districts in the southern Sudan, more than one ethnic tribe resides. In fact, as among some pastoral peoples elsewhere, there is one public system of governance, that of the state (and its subdivisions) in which groups of pastoralists may find themselves now imperfectly superimposed upon another, the traditional.  Moreover, in some *fused social systems* (see Table 1.1) distinctions between governmental and private aspects of society become readily blunted over time and their different origins or jurisdictions may not be fully comprehended by some members of the community.  Apropos of that, Ostrom (1990: 14) points out that evolved systems for managing commons resources "are rarely private or public--the 'market' or 'the state.' Many successful . . . [common pool resources] are rich mixtures of 'private-like' and 'public-like' institutions defying classification in a sterile dichotomy.  By 'successful'," she added, "I mean institutions that enable individuals to achieve productive outcomes in situations where temptations to free-ride and shirk are ever present."  The veterinary vehicle we propose for delivery of an extended range of basic social services to pastoralists is one which itself constitutes a mix of private and public goods.

Since it is not our view (nor that of many Northern-educated pastoral elites) that Africa's pastoralists should simply be ignored in the future by the rest of the world (except when Northern "interests" are affected) or preserved in various stages of cultural disruption as "anthropological exhibits" for Northern tourists to marvel at, it goes without saying that pastoralists should be introduced to new possibilities that are realistic and then given the time and incentives to envisage ways to assimilate those changes *they desire* within their existing orders.

Beyond most economists' interests generally in "efficiency" in the Pareto sense, many have been concerned in economic analyses with questions of equity, of fairness. But within societies as alien to most Northerners as those of Africa's pastoralists, other far less familiar nonmonetary and nonmaterial aspects of "quality of life" (including different humane and esthetic perceptions and alternative senses of satisfaction) may matter greatly to particular peoples and represent things they will strive to achieve above all else. We have attempted to illustrate some of this for the Dinka. However, a tendency among free-market economists has been to lump even much more familiar variables which are outside of their discipline (but which may impinge upon market transactions and economic decisions or vice versa) under the very unfortunate term "externalities." While most economists recognize that many of these, as defined by their discipline, are "not determined by the real world but by abstractions from it, . . . after the abstractions are made, there is a strong tendency not to notice what has been abstracted from. . . . [Then] when something is noticed that does not fit the system built on abstractions, . . . either the abstractions will be changed or the new phenomenon will be viewed as an 'externality' deserving only separate and peripheral attention" (Daly and Cobb, 1989: 53). Daly and Cobb "believe that a model that would internalize . . . the interconnections among things [in the real world] . . . into the basic economic theory would be a better response" and urge such a paradigm shift. Although economists like Daly (now with the World Bank) propose such thinking, and some donor agencies encourage this among members of staff, our conclusions as noneconomists are that, vis-à-vis Africa, such individuals must not be within the "decision-making loop." For, even when various nonmonetary values are considered within the bodies of particular studies, within their executive summaries and "bottom lines"--in their translations into policy (political actions)--most simply disappear. Because our backgrounds are otherwise, the proposals we make skirt these and other issues of social science theory and practice which surely need tending to. What we propose is a local approach to development within constraints which are apparent (and susceptible to manipulation) at that level.

## CONCLUSIONS

While "animal agriculture projects, having a lower success rate than crop projects, have often disappointed governments and external sponsors in sub-Saharan Africa . . . [and] those to improve nomadic pastoralism have been the least successful" (Zessin and Farah, 1993), we concur that "there are two key reasons for these failures. Firstly, attempts to replace traditional systems with new production forms underestimated the efficiency of the traditional range-livestock systems. In the second place, the complexity of the systems was also underestimated and information was lacking on indigenous pastoralism as a system, particularly with regard to interactions and interdependencies of eco-climatic factors, rangeland conditions, husbandry practices and the biological performance of herds and how they adjust to changes in external factors such as drought" (Zessin and Schwartz, 1993).

In this chapter we have considered examples of development failures. From these and other attempts, we would conclude that many of their designs and/or goals were fatally flawed from the start. Whether their goals were to benefit pastoralists (as frequently stated) or a country's urban elites (the sometimes hidden agenda) or even some third party (as for a canal bypassing the Sudan's *Sudd*), virtually no livestock development project among pastoralists in Africa has been judged a real success.

What else should have been learned from these experiences over a considerable period of years that could increase chances of success in the future? While we believe each of the four most applied rural development avenues in sedentary agricultural situations all have their own strengths, we doubt any offers practical possibilities to improve the situation of most of Africa's pastoralists within current financial constraints. *Parallel* ministry-by-ministry extension-type and/or skill-providing services with mobile outreach capacities would be absolutely unaffordable and otherwise fail to maximally use scarce personnel and other rare resources. Medical services extension/skill provision suffers the additional constraints for pastoral Africa of being so hospital-based and cure-oriented. "Community development," as applied in village-based rural situations, demands too much of "local generalists," frequently lacks effective links to higher expertise and skills (existing branches of conventional government services and their professional/disciplinary resources) and sometimes ends up creating a separate competing governmental branch.

"Umbrella" development authorities could, but often do not, achieve better intersectoral cooperation partially because they often attempt to ignore, supplant or do "end runs" around existing and long precedented profession- or discipline-based government ministries. Furthermore, such mechanisms tend to inflexibility and to move too fast, to introduce changes far too abruptly for highly opportunistic, risk-minimizing pastoral communities to accommodate. Beyond these problems, grand schemes would usually be too expensive to implement to any sustainable degree within pastoral Africa given current global financial realities/priorities. Finally, they assume prior existence of sufficient information to implement broadly an "ideal solution."

Some external NGOs, while having better track records for complementing existing development channels, greater operational flexibility and abilities to act quickly and interact intensively with local people, have, until now, been involved in pastoral Africa too exclusively in emergency relief situations. However, we strongly favor the greater involvement of the more effective of these across the board, particularly when they can intermesh their efforts with those of other existing channels.

Cooperatives have the greatest potential for certain purposes in our opinion, particularly if they build upon existing traditional frameworks or mechanisms. They would then have abilities to affect good balance points between tradition and "modernization." As one tested form of compromise between global political camps, cooperatives have never fit comfortably within either and probably, therefore, will not feature importantly *until* pastoral development becomes less driven by ideological givens.

We conclude overall that the most prevalent types of past failures in African pastoral development are due primarily to insufficient knowledge on the parts of outsiders involved of specific pastoral societies and their local bases in man-animal-land relationships. This is one of the principal reasons pastoralists themselves must be just as involved in the identification of needs and formulation of development plans as in their day-to-day local implementation. A less-appreciated reason is that pastoralists are members of "fused" societies (see Table 1.1) in which different areas of life and knowledge are not practically and conceptually compartmentalized artificially into the academic disciplines and the like in which "diffracted" disciplinarians from the North are so totally accustomed to conceiving them. That is, pastoralists themselves tend to view life and the world about them holistically (*as they really are*) and do not suffer from the "fallacy of misplaced concreteness" that economist Herman Daly and theologian John Cobb urge economists (and other disciplinarians) to attempt to liberate themselves from in maximizing the common good for a sustainable future.

It is long overdue for logical questions to be asked and answers sought about this record of failure. We started to write this book because we believed very strongly that it is vital to change development strategies and tactics in pastoral Africa. Moreover, we think evidence for this is in hand and ways to proceed are apparent. It is not among the aims of this book to attempt decisions about what all of the specific elements of African pastoral development should be (something for which we are not prepared). While we think that much of pastoral development in Africa has simply chased its own tail, that need not be so, and there are practical ways to proceed *if* elegant theories, some other precious disciplinary "givens" and professional turf wars are not allowed to totally dominate and determine the possible. Our proposals are intended to help develop and implement strategies for sustainable local actions that can begin to affect locally desired changes within the constraints of existing (or reasonably anticipated) resources.

Finally, we believe that, while this past record validates generally S. Sandford's conclusion over a decade ago (1983: 7) that "there are few, if any, universally valid prescriptions which can be applied to all pastoral situations," at least four do seem germane thoughout pastoral Africa at this point: (1) the need for outsiders involved to understand traditional pastoral institutions and practices, (2) active pastoralist participation at all stages of development efforts, (3) locally based actions and, finally, (4) a veterinary services *facilitating* vehicle.

We have outlined the bases for the first two prescriptions, and already widely accepted bases for the third (decentralization) will be considered later in this specific context. But, because the logic underlying our fourth has occurred to far fewer persons, it is vital that economists, political scientists, public health authorities, range ecology specialists, water resource developers and other non-veterinarians concerned with pastoral development in Africa become just as familiar with it.

## NOTES

1. While some recipient countries of external aid virtually "classify" such reports, (amazingly) employees of some donor countries of development aid also are bound by their own country's "official secrets acts" and cannot legally divulge data or reports they generate.

2. This did happen during the rainy season of 1982.

3. Nevertheless, they still use cattle for payment of bride price *(lobola)* at an average of four cattle per wife. They also sell their relatively few cattle not only for payment of school fees, but for buying radios, bicycles, Northern-style clothing and the like.

4. Many Northern governments and businesses have competitively courted Third World rulers as buyers for their modern arms (Sivard, 1990-1994).

5. For example, enormous TV coverage in Somalia during 1993 UN efforts there was almost entirely restricted to the capital city of Mogadishu and the close-at-hand "safe areas" along the Shebelle River. Thus reporters, who two years before may have had difficulty finding Somalia on a map, conveyed the misleading impression on TV night after night that civil problems had much to do with widespread *crop* failures because of internecine fighting among clans. They and their viewers had the impression that Somalia was largely a country of crop cultivators, though crop raising there is virtually restricted to narrow bands along Somalia's *only two rivers*, one of which correspondents saw and considered typical of the country. But Somalia is almost entirely a country of extensive pastoralism.

6. S. Sandford (1983: 63) noted that in the Sudanese province of Southern Darfur northwest of Dinkaland, of 145 boreholes drilled in one area, 44 had never functioned and 28 others were broken or malfunctioning at the time a survey was made. In the area of northeastern Kenya grazed by Somali pastoralists, only 25% of boreholes drilled between 1969 and 1976 were still functioning at the end of that period.

7. Most of the original water projects in pastoral Africa were undertaken by the colonial veterinary services.

8. One of us was involved in the training at the American University of Beirut of 30 of a total of only 32 Ethiopian physicians resident in that country in 1964. Unfortunately, everyone of them located within the capital city.

9. One NIE concept especially relevant here is that of "bounded rationality" (Furubotin and Richter, 1991). It means that although individuals alone or associated with an array of institutions may *intend* to behave rationally, none of them (neither African pastoralist nor Northern agents of development) are "hyperrational"--that is, the rationality of all individuals is bounded by limited ability to acquire and process

information.  Although Africa's pastoralists actually meet many hazards reasonably well *through highly developed opportunism,* in Chapter 8 we will consider how bounds of their rationality might be extended to the benefits of long-term policy formulation and practical applications.

# 6

---

# VETERINARY SCIENCE AS A PASTORAL DEVELOPMENT VEHICLE

With few exceptions government services for pastoral peoples are
not well developed and are usually confined to animal health.

W.R. Pritchard et al., 1992

[In the southern Sudan it is] animals rather than humans who benefit
most from any scientific medical treatment.  Herders who have . . .
never visited a government dressing station, still less a hospital
bring their cattle for inoculation.

Jean Buxton, 1973

[The] prosperity and indeed habitability of enormous areas [of
Africa] hangs upon [the veterinarian's] success or failure in research
. . . along the broadest biological and medical lines.

Julian Huxley, 1931

We believe bases for practical pastoral development within constraints of
existing resources are beginning to suggest themselves.  If past efforts have met
with little success and, if animals and their welfare are so central to every other
aspect of African pastoral life, important questions need be addressed, the first
being "Are there institutions which now endeavor to provide for these needs?"
The answer, quite obviously, is "Yes, governmental veterinary services do."

Moreover, virtual absence of human health outreach to pastoralists (see Chapters 4, 5 and 7), and even cursory knowledge of African pastoral circumstances more generally, indicates that veterinary services are the only governmental branch which has even attempted seriously to interact with pastoralists.

Further questions to address then become "Do veterinary services possess the ability and will to act as facilitators of, or vehicles for, a broader range of pastoral services?" and "Are there precedents for such catalytic roles on the part of veterinary services?" This chapter's overall intent will be to show how the nature and experiences of veterinary science identify a unique situation to build upon for pastoral development. That is, beyond the primary necessity we have illustrated of developers possessing sufficiently detailed local information on people-animal-environment relationships, we turn now to the very difficult question of providing to these mobile populations affordable basic amenities which define most conceptions of human dignity. The practical key will lie, we are convinced, in innovative locally manifested intersectoral cooperation based upon realistic overviews of each current situation and its possibilities. It is also our conviction that the realities of pastoral Africa are such that, to achieve this, some previously accepted beliefs (or professional preferences), whether of academic professors of public administration, economists, international bankers, the medical establishment and the agricultural establishment (including veterinarians, range managers and others), must give way to logical development possibilities that could prove effective and affordable. Toward those ends, we consider first some characteristics of the veterinary field and profession.

## WHAT IS VETERINARY SCIENCE?

Veterinary *science* originally meant, and in most countries continues to mean, all scientific activities which relate disease control, health maintenance, production, care and well-being of animals (WHO/FAO, 1975). However, a pattern of veterinary *medicine* per se and some other aspects of domestic animal science going more or less separate ways developed in a few Northern countries early in this century, in the United States particularly where acceptable standards of veterinary education and establishment of a veterinary branch of the federal government lagged a century behind Europe. In that situation, most persons concerned especially with animal nutrition and genetics followed agricultural rather than veterinary curricula and, ever since, these two groups of scientists often have been more competitive and antagonistic to one another than cooperative. To a lesser extent that rupture occurred also in Britain, but not originally in its colonies.[1]

During the last few decades that schism has led to a postindependence battle in anglophone Africa especially, in which advisors from a few countries attempted to change the previously existing service pattern and the results have been unhappy ones, to say the least. Largely an issue among expatriate advisors initially, this dispute, not evident in francophone Africa, broadened as more and more Africans were trained abroad, particularly in the United States. These divisive influences explain why alternative names like animal health and production services or animal resource services were substituted for formerly called veterinary services in some African countries.[2]

When extended to pastoral areas, such "turf" problems make development unaffordable and impossible to provide, which is precisely what some major donor groups now seem to have concluded. Especially germane, therefore, to any discussions of future development within pastoral Africa is to state that, when colonial veterinary services were first established in parts of Africa at the height of the Microbiological Revolution, they reflected an integrated veterinary *science* perception of responsibilities. Colonial veterinary services initiated, beside some world-class research institutions like Onderstepoort and Kabete, many production-related and extension-type programs. It was well understood then that veterinarians for Africa needed to be biologists as well grounded during their training in care and production of healthy animals as they were in diagnosis and treatment of their ills; to their credit, most African veterinary schools have managed to maintain that dual curricular emphasis despite recent attempts to subordinate or restrict their graduates.   Those preexisting patterns vis-à-vis animal agriculture remain far better suited to continuing African realities than since-argued alternatives (see Chapter 9).

We broach such delicate matters simply because few have faced them publicly and, of all places, African countries can least afford perpetuation of expensive disharmonies introduced from the North. Therefore, our own pastoral development proposals, though growing out of existing realities and not concerned directly with resolution of such macro-level problems, are clearly antithetical to efforts to needlessly multiply already top-heavy bureaucracies and to create ever more new, noncooperating and redundantly costly professional fiefdoms.

In Africa this means relevant curricula (see Chapter 9) must reflect a broad modern definition of livestock health (in terms of production efficiency) and continue to cover all health-associated aspects of animal care, as well as of normal and abnormal animal biology.  Changes from current curricula should be principally toward greater population than individual animal emphases and greater attention to problem diagnosis in all aspects (see Chapters 4 and 8).

A second important point is that veterinary science has always been a multiobjective field. Its key role in food production is widely recognized, much less so that the veterinary field contributes substantually to improvements in human health.  In addition, veterinary research has provided key discoveries about--and has demonstrated practical ways to influence--the reproductive process in people as well as animals (Schwabe, 1984b: 99-104), while other veterinary efforts preserve environmental quality (pp. 501-578) or promote humane values (pp. 632-644).  One result of these multiple orientations is that veterinarians have had intersectoral and interprofessional experiences within

| AGENCY | NUMBER OF VETERINARIANS |
|---|---|
| DEPARTMENT OF AGRICULTURE | 2131 |
| Agricultural Research Service | 75 |
| Animal and Plant Inspection Service | |
| Plant Protection and Quarantine | 11 |
| Veterinary Services | 640 |
| Meat and Poultry Inspection | 1370 |
| Scientific and Technical Services | 33 |
| DEPARTMENT OF HEALTH AND HUMAN SERVICES | 191 |
| U.S. Public Health Service | |
| Food and Drug Administration | 83 |
| Centers for Disease Control | 24 |
| National Institutes of Health | 69 |
| Health Resources and Services Administration | 1 |
| Other | 4 |
| DEPARTMENT OF COMMERCE | |
| Marine Fisheries Service | 5 |
| DEPARTMENT OF INTERIOR | |
| Sports Fisheries and Wildlife | 5 |
| DEPARTMENT OF DEFENSE | 170 |
| DEPARTMENT OF STATE | |
| Agency for International Development | 4 |
| SMITHSONIAN INSTITUTION | |
| National Zoological Park | 4 |
| NASA | 3 |
| ENVIRONMENTAL PROTECTION AGENCY | 19 |
| CONSUMER PRODUCT SAFETY COMMISSION | 1 |
| VETERANS ADMINISTRATION | 15 |
| PANAMA CANAL ZONE | 7 |
| TOTAL | 3154 |

Table 6.1. Numbers of veterinarians employed by agencies of the United States federal government, 1981-1982. (Source: Schwabe, 1984b: 50.)

several service spheres. These have varied from country to country and are reflected, for example, in veterinarians' locations within several different branches of government (see Table 6.1).

Yet, when a feasibility and planning study was carried out in the southern Sudan for furthering new worldwide Primary Health Care (PHC) development goals of WHO/UNICEF, the responsible committee (Lolik et al., 1976) did not take note of such realities. In appraising the great needs and very limited resources available for promotion of human health in that region, they not only failed to mention even in passing the facts that human and animal health services utilize many identical approaches, facilities and types of personnel, but also overlooked the centrality of animals in the lives of the majority of the southern Sudan's people. Instead, its report visualized PHC's mandate as reaching no farther than settled populations, a totally unrealistic approach to a mostly pastoral region's human health needs.[3]

Although growing numbers of Northern city dwellers now think of veterinarians almost exclusively in terms of the welfare of pets, the veterinary profession in almost all countries has been especially associated with rural life. Except in some Northern countries, that still remains much the case. A third point, therefore, is that the veterinary profession represents the longest established, most extensively distributed and largest pool of university-educated manpower within the agricultural sciences, one which traditionally reaches literally to the grassroots. While other university-trained individuals in agriculture are, in many countries, employed largely within academic or research institutions or at higher levels of extension-type services, not only must governmental veterinarians reach *all* livestock owners for key programs, but in some countries their services are complemented by private practitioners.[4] More specifically, a very high proportion of the world's 400,000 or so veterinarians, public and private, comprise a service network in close contact with livestock owners in their local communities. In most rural areas they are the only highly educated individuals likely to cross the thresholds of many farms, ranches or cattle camps and to know well specific groups of livestock owners and their families. That is, theirs is the only branch of government that does not require pastoralists to come often long distances to them, or which offer essentially a one-time input into their lives, like drilling a well. Those are each important facts to consider when it comes to resource utilization for pastoral development in Africa.

## VETERINARIANS AND RURAL LIFE

The first two schools for formal instruction in veterinary science were created in France in the 1760s by a prominent equestrian, encyclopedist of science and lawyer, Claude Bourgelat. Governments were especially keen then to learn the causes of and halt the depredations of rinderpest, foot-and-mouth disease, pleuropneumonia and other epidemic plagues of livestock which were decimating (or otherwise seriously harming) their increasingly dense livestock populations and threatening the basis for most European economies (see Chapter 4).[5] Thus, governments as well as many academicians supported a strong research role for these new institutions and the establishment of governmental services to translate their findings into practical actions. In consequence, a number of the first students of veterinary science already were students, researchers or professors of natural sciences or human medicine (Schwabe, 1978a: 159-187). Among rural peoples in Europe who were accustomed to hearing from their governments only at tax time, or when being conscripted into the military, these veterinary services provided the first demonstration of governmental concern for their welfare beyond that provided intermittently in their defense by a monarch or continuously only in the organized network of activities of a state church.

However, the unusually quick governmental and popular support these innovations received also reflected needs of other major constituencies, each with its own ideas of what professional veterinarians should be, who they should most serve, where prospective veterinary students should mostly be sought, how the graduate profession should be organized, and so on. In some countries, the military, then heavily dependent upon cavalries and animal-powered artillery and services of supply, saw their needs as primary. Others saw the educated veterinarian fulfilling in a much more scientific fashion the roles of traditional, apprentice-trained folk veterinarians or farriers (Lane, 1993). These and others saw rural and urban veterinarians privately practicing their profession on the same fee for services basis as did virtually all physicians. Problems encountered meeting those perceived needs country by country included uncertainty as to whether rural people would be able to pay for these unaccustomed services with sufficient fees to support a formally educated veterinarian in rural practice.

Two general approaches to that problem of income generation and rural acceptance were tried and both were catered to in veterinary curricular revisions. One plan recognized that the people of rural Europe were largely without the services of physicians (who were almost exclusively located in the cities and largest towns). It was urged therefore that either veterinarians be trained also in aspects of human medicine, or that medical students receive training in veterinary practice (Schwabe, 1978b: 159-165). In French veterinary schools instruction was added in emergency aspects of human obstetrics, orthopedics, eye diseases and certification of human deaths.

The second approach, which is especially germane here, proposed that the rural veterinarian also be a general agent for change and improvement in other aspects of rural life (and therefore be partially subsidized locally or nationally in that broader community development role). Some quite unique ideas for supporting this and other forms of rural veterinary practice were tried with varying degrees of success, some of which are especially pertinent to early veterinary experiences with intersectoral cooperation (IC). For example, an IC pattern was devised in Sweden whereby rural veterinary services were "piggy-backed" upon that country's state Lutheran Church (then the only branch of government represented in rural areas).[6]   When the founder of Swedish veterinary science, Peter Hirnquist, a protegé of the famed naturalist Karl von Linné (Linnaeus), and already a doctor of natural sciences, returned to Sweden from pursuing the new veterinary curriculum in France,[7] he had not only to establish Sweden's Royal Veterinary School at Skara, but to face the problem of providing the services his new graduates were prepared to offer to Sweden's unlettered farmers. Learning that pastors of rural parishes were then desperately in need of assistance in the areas of church music and registering vital statistics, he hit upon a brilliant idea. Hirnquist incorporated religious music within the veterinary curriculum and then had his new graduates employed as ministers of music (and vital statisticians) to rural churches! Those duties, which required mostly Sunday and evening labors, earned his new veterinarians' keep while they came to know their farmer parishioners and demonstrate that they could offer animal health services which were worth paying for. The end result of such experiments was that various solutions were found for a significant veterinary role in, and impact upon, rural life in many countries. In a majority of countries today, including most of the Third World, all or a significant portion of this role is provided by governmental veterinary services.[8]

The veterinary profession also has learned the hard way that, although it is usually publicly underfunded and overstretched, public liaison and communications are vital to its programs of outreach to rural people. Elsewhere (Schwabe, 1984b: 456-457) we have given examples of past failures in these respects, sometimes with calamitous results. One outcome of this long period of trial and error was that unusually effective institutions arose in some Northern countries to unite rural service consumers (i.e., livestock owners) with the veterinary profession in commonly achieved efforts (to a far greater extent, for example, than has been the case in human medicine/public health).

Beyond such cooperative mechanisms for effective interactions among government, private veterinarians and livestock producer organizations as the U. S. Animal Health Association, a few individual veterinarians envisaged and promoted the logic of veterinary services assuming greater leadership roles in rural development. One example was in Australia, where realities in the thinly populated pastoral Outback[9] caused a creative veterinary academician to propose post-World War II that veterinary schools were the most logical institutions in which to train individuals as general rural development specialists cum veterinarians. Ironically, lack of acceptance of that idea by the Australian veterinary profession caused him to establish within one university a totally new type of rural service faculty, a settled pastoralist-oriented School of Rural Science. Such more general relationships of veterinary science to rural life have not passed unnoticed by rural people themselves and sometimes have been translated into active political lives for local veterinarians (Schwabe, 1976b). For example, in three Swiss cantons veterinarians have been cantonal presidents and up to seven have served simultaneously in the Swiss federal parliament. Similarly, Norwegian national elections in 1972 propelled two veterinarians from rural parties into national cabinet positions. General leadership roles have also been prominent in Third World countries like pastoral Mongolia. In Africa, veterinarian Walter Odede replaced Jomo Kenyatta as leader of the Kenya African Union when the latter was arrested by Kenya's last colonial government, and of two veterinarians to become newly independent nations' initial vice presidents, one was Uganda's Kabwimukya Babiiha. When asked to explain how he, also a veterinarian, had become the father of his country, its first prime minister then president Sir Daoud Kairaba Jawara of Gambia was quoted in the international press: "I know every cow in Gambia and every Gambian owns a cow."

From such general considerations, let us review some other aspects of the historic evolution of veterinary services at the population level which are relevant to rural development.

## EVOLUTION OF VETERINARY SERVICES

The veterinary profession in toto has been far more oriented to population-wide, preventive and environmental types of action programs than have others of the health professions.[10]  But it was the Microbiological Revolution which ushered in a new historic phase of veterinary science (see Table 6.2) in which highly organized activities began to be undertaken at the population level, often at that of the "national herd."  These initiatives are important to understand today, for they resulted in an extremely successful era of veterinary activity from the early 1880s to the late 1960s when beginnings of a new phase of population-level veterinary science began to emerge.

To understand the revolutionary changes occasioned by the discoveries of infectious etiological agents of many diseases in the late 19th century, ways in which veterinary science pioneered in combatting diseases at the population level, is to understand some principal differences in veterinary versus human medical practice. The first important divergence in the two subfields (after they clinically divided) was early recognition within veterinary science of the etiological principle of contagion.[11] With that, the first two rational intervention tactics against diseases at a population (herd) level were applied, namely quarantine and deliberate slaughter of an ill minority of animals to protect a well majority (Tables 6.2 and 6.3). Three additional tactics were introduced following the establishment of governmental veterinary services during the latter part of the 18th and early 19th centuries.  But it was not until the experiments in 1860 on microscopic "filaments" observed in the blood of animals with anthrax by H.M. Delafond, director of France's second veterinary school and further epochal work by Louis Pasteur, J. B. A. Chauveau, Robert Koch, Henri Toussaint, Edmond Nocard, Friedrich Loeffler, Paul Frosch, Daniel E. Salmon, Sir Arnold Theiler and others[12] that a full understanding of contagion resulted. With these breakthroughs came a new strategy for livestock disease management.  It depended upon a new infrastructural basis for veterinary services pioneered by Daniel Elmer Salmon in the United States in 1883, organized largely along specific campaign lines, with still valuable portions of preexisting sanitary police, military and local actions infrastructures continuing in parallel. Governmental action programs initiated from then on on a geographically extensive population basis characterized that highly productive phase of disease control efforts.  Supporting those new mass actions were newly developed laboratory backup (diagnostic) facilities manned by veterinarians trained in the emerging etiological disciplines and, with this, came the first provisions in vet-

| PHASE | PARADIGMS: THEORY OF DISEASE CAUSALITY | PARADIGMS: INTERVEN-TION TACTICS | ANOMALIES | RESULTANT CRISES | CONSEQUENT SCIENTIFIC REVOLUTION (& EFFECT) |
|---|---|---|---|---|---|
| Healing Magic | Supernatural Factors (e.g. Evil Spirits) | Prayer, Exorcism, Divination, Sacrifice | Draft Oxen Died | Civilization Required More Than Subsistence Food Production | Agrarian Revolution (Emergence of Veterinary Healers) |
| Compara-tive Medicine & Local Actions (3000-200 BC) | Natural Envir-onmental Factors (e.g. Cold, Wind, Miasmas) | 1)Recognition & $R_x$ of Signs & Few Dis-eases (Including Manual $R_x$ Skills) | Military Horses Died | Large States Required Swift & Healthy Animals for Transport, War & Communi-ations | Clinical Revolution (Human & Veterinary Medicine Split; Formation of Military Veterinary Services) |
| Equine Medicine & Military (Herd) Actions (200 BC-1762) | Above Plus Poisons & Contagions | 2)Clinical $D_x$ & $R_x$ Many Diseases, 3)Quarantine, 4)Slaughter of Ill Minority to Protect Well Majority | Civilian Multipurpose Animals Died (Rinderpest Invaded Europe) | Livestock Plagues Threatened Economy as Human & Animal Population Densities Increased | Great Sanitary Awakening (Formation of Veterinary Schools, Civilian Veterinary Services) |
| Veterinary Sanitary Police (1762-1883) | Contagion Plus Decay & Man-made Filth | 5)Farm Hygiene, 6)Slaughter Controls, 7)Animal $R_x$ Centers | Failures of *Cordon Sanitaire* | Above in America & Europe; Threat to American Trade | Microbiological Revolution (Formation of $D_x$ Laboratory Services) |
| Cam-paigns or Mass Actions (1883-1966) | Specific Living & Nonliving Etiological Agents | 8)Mass Testing, 9)Lab $D_x$,10) Vector Control, 11) Mass Immuni-zation, 12) Mass $R_x$, 13) Applied Ecology, 14) Education | Multiple Defects in Koch's Postulates (e.g. Predisposing Causes, Latency, Carriers, Opportunistic Pathogens, Obviously Multicausal Diseases) | "Problem Herds," Cost-Benefit Demands of Management Economists, Service Delivery Needs in Intensive Livestock Production Units, Discontinuities in Veterinary Service Deliveries | Epidemiological Revolution (Formation of Epidemiological Services) |
| Surveil-lance & Selective Actions (1966- | Multiple Interacting Etiological Determinants (Agent, Host, Environmental and Management Factors) | 15) Epidemiol-ogic $D_x$: i) Epidemiologic Intelligence- a) Surveillance, b) Intensive Follow-up, ii) Analysis- a) Epidemiologic, b) Economic | | | |

**Table 6.2. Historical evolution of veterinary practice.** (Revised from Schwabe, 1984b, using concepts and terminology of Kuhn, 1970.)

| COMPARATIVE CLINICAL MEDICINE | Until c.200 BC when first distinctions arose between *iatros* and *hippiatros*; Heraclides of Tarentum last important comparative healer, 1st C BC |
|---|---|
| COMPARATIVE ANATOMY | Basis for understanding human internal structure from early Egypt until human dissections by De Luzzi in 14th C and Vesalius in 16th C |
| COMPARATIVE PHYSIOLOGY | Basis for understanding human internal functions from early Egypt to present day |
| COMPARATIVE PATHOLOGY (INVESTI-GATIVE MEDICINE) | Results from animal necropsies recorded in Hippocratic Corpus & works of Apsyrtos of Nicomedia (4th C AD); first human necropsy by Da Varigna in 14th C; major advances following establishment of veterinary colleges in mid-18th C and through the Microbiological Revolution; relative stagnation until significant rebirth following World War II with creation of field of laboratory animal biology and medicine & associated events |
| COMPARATIVE POPULATION MEDICINE (VETERINARY PUBLIC HEALTH) | Concept of contagion of animal diseases & initiation of quarantine (& slaughter of ill minority to protect well majority) in 1st C Rome (comparable concepts in human medicine with Fracastoro in 16th C); meat hygiene as a founding cornerstone of public health; relative stagnation in relations between World Wars I & II, then accelerated resumption with major veterinary inputs into epidemiology, control of zoonoses & generally |

**Table 6.3. Historical interactions between veterinary and human medicine.** (Adapted from Schwabe, 1991b.)

erinary science for postgraduate specialization. Six new and highly effective tactics for disease prevention and control were introduced then. During this phase major diseases of livestock, which had once thwarted development or sustainability of viable animal industries in Europe, North America, Australia and elsewhere (affecting production of foods of plant as well as animal origin, plus major sources of power for transport and other purposes), were brought under control or completely eradicated nationally or continentally. An important result was the possibility for creating the large scale, intensive production systems for foods of animal origin which increasingly characterize Northern animal agriculture (see Figure 1.1). Veterinary services in Africa, which now face similar problems of economically disruptive livestock diseases, are organized and function according to this mass actions/campaigns model.

At this point we should note that veterinary science also has had considerable experience with the main avenues that rural development overall has followed in the North.

## PAST VETERINARY EXPERIENCES WITH USUAL AVENUES FOR RURAL DEVELOPMENT

Agricultural extension originated in connection with the historically unique American system of land-grant universities and most American veterinary schools were closely associated with these pioneering efforts. This can be illustrated by the activities of Charles Cary, a veterinary leader in the American South under economic conditions highly relevant to present-day Africa. Immediately upon appointment in 1892 as the first Professor of Veterinary Science in the then Alabama College of Agriculture and Mechanic Arts (now Auburn University), Cary began to acquaint rural people of his state with consequences to them of rapidly unfolding advances in microbiology.

He set up what he called Farmers' Institutes, which took him to every corner of Alabama. These were partly about rural health matters and partly efforts to enlist farmers in an unprecedented effort to eradicate from the U.S. Deep South the tick-transmitted blood parasite responsible for the area's most economically disruptive cattle plague, Texas fever (babesiosis, piroplasmosis). Although it was not until 1914 that the U.S. Congress passed the Smith-Lever Act formally establishing a nationwide system of federal-state cooperation for agricultural extension, Cary's Farmers' Institutes pioneered this idea within the U.S. South. Texas fever eradication was among the first and most concrete results of such early American efforts to organize, and demonstrate the effectiveness of, agricultural extension plus cooperative action programs involving rural people and the institutions of government working together. Its success removed the major impediment to interregional trade in cattle within the United States and made possible development of the South's cattle industry as a key contributor to prosperity. That is, veterinary science was significantly involved in agricultural extension from inception of the idea and the Winrock Committee on the future of animal agriculture in Africa (Pritchard et al., 1992: 111-115) noted that veterinary personnel provide an *already existing* cadre for more effective general agricultural extension efforts there.

In some countries, veterinary services to farmers have been provided through farmer-owned cooperatives or unions. In New Zealand a novel veterinary club system was organized whereby local dairy farmer cooperatives built, often with partial government subsidy, a clinical facility and guaranteed a minimum income to a veterinarian who would use it. That system was coordinated by a veterinary service council representative of the profession, the livestock industries and governmental veterinary services. In some other countries veterinary services are provided through insurance plans. In the Canadian province of Quebec a government insurance program subsidizes private veterinary services for farm animals by (1) reducing the private veterinarian's charge to the farmer to a uniform fee per visit regardless of the distance, (2) standardizing fees for treatment and (3) reducing farmers' payments for drugs through their centralized distribution by a governmentally administered agency.

Private veterinarians submit an invoice to the government for each call and fees paid by the farmer then are augmented, depending upon distance traveled and the like. That system also feeds into a governmental livestock disease surveillance program. An insurance-based practice scheme also exists in Israel where veterinarians are employed by a livestock insurance instrument of the Israeli Federation of Labor to which farmers can subscribe.

## VETERINARY SCIENCE AND INTERSECTORAL COOPERATION

The multiple objectives of veterinary science identify several situations in which the veterinary sector cooperates with other sectors of government or in which individual veterinarians participate (see Table 6.1). The largest and most important is human health (see Table 6.3; Schwabe 1984b, 1993b). In Chapter 4 we illustrated some of the ways animal diseases impinge upon human health. IC is mandatory here because many of the means to protect people from hazards of animal-transmitted diseases are veterinary. The first broad relationship concerns research, both basic bench-type research and field-based epidemiological research (the dual contexts of Julian Huxley's quotation at the beginning of this chapter).

### Veterinary Research's Broader Consequences

Few kinds of invasive biomedical research can be carried out directly on people, including initial evaluations for efficacy and safety of newly proposed forms of treatment, but depend, of necessity, upon studies in "animal models." Not only does such *comparative* medical research (see Table 6.3) comprise, by definition, a part of the *field* of veterinary science, but veterinary professionals have always been significant partners in that process to research physicians and other biomedical scientists (Schwabe, 1978a; 1984b: 181-294). This historic importance of animal studies to the episodic progress of human medicine overall is not well understood by the Northern public, but that subject lies beyond our concerns here.

*Zoonoses Investigation and Control.* The major aspect of research which more directly addresses questions relevant to African pastoral development involves understanding and control of infectious diseases. As noted in Chapter 4, at least four-fifths of all infectious agents causing diseases in people also naturally infect other species of vertebrate animals. These more than 250 infections are called zoonoses. For many--rabies, brucellosis, trichinosis, anthrax, as examples--people are never infected from other people but only directly or indirectly from an infected animal. The complex epidemiologies of many such diseases for which veterinary control measures are mandatory were illustrated in Chapter 4 for hydatid disease, a global plague of pastoralists. For only a few zoonoses, chiefly trypanosomiasis and rabies, have significant control efforts within Africa yet been widely attempted. For some the African situation is unique. But even the existence in Africa of many other zoonoses remains unknown or largely uninvestigated. From experience elsewhere it is safe to conclude that some of these are diagnosed today as "fevers of unknown origin" or masquerade as "malaria." For Africa's pastoralists with their most intense man-animal contacts, zoonoses investigation is a specially high priority area for medical-veterinary IC. Progress in that area would develop naturally from any other efforts that stimulate veterinary and human health services to cooperate.

How closely intertwined and consequential such intersectoral efforts can be is illustrated by the history of tuberculosis (TB), a very important disease in Africa. Most human pulmonary TB is caused by a mycobacterium transmitted directly from person to person, but a closely related organism causing bovine TB also is readily communicable to people, especially via infected milk. This bovine bacillus uncommonly involves the lungs, but it is responsible for virtually all other human TB. Linkages between combatting cattle TB and ability to combat all human TB are multiple and go back relatively far. The first major step toward understanding the nature of tuberculosis was recognition in 1790 by J. B. Huzard, one of France's first veterinary graduates and leading proponent of rural health services for France, that this common chronic, debilitating and generally fatal disease in people closely resembled an important disease of confined dairy cattle. Noting that the cattle disease frequently involved multiple animals in a herd, Huzard theorized that it was contagious and went on to suggest that the cause of the human and bovine diseases might be the same and that people and cattle might transmit it to one another. Sixty-eight years later another French veterinary professor, J. B. A. Chauveau, demonstrated natural transmission of bovine TB and induced it experimentally in cattle with material from human patients. Later, German physician Robert Koch isolated the bovine bacillus; Theobald Smith, a physician with the U. S. federal veterinary service distinguished biologically between the bovine and human organisms; and Edmond Nocard, a veterinarian from the Pasteur Institute, identified a third tuberculosis bacterium.

Then, in 1891, the Danish veterinary microbiologist Bernard Bang showed that metabolic products of the in vitro cultivation of tubercle bacilli, when injected subcutaneously in infected cattle, produced a local reaction diagnostic of tuberculosis. His "tuberculin test" was soon applied on a mass scale to millions of cattle in Europe and North America and provided the backbone for launching national campaigns against the bovine disease, an effort with major economic and human health repercussions. Eradication of bovine TB from many areas eliminated human nonpulmonary TB as well, an achievement chronicled by physician epidemiologist J. A. Myers (1940) in *Man's Greatest Victory Over Tuberculosis*. In 1907 French physician Clement Pirquet introduced this test to human medicine and most human tests since have been with a purified antigen (PPD) developed in U.S. federal veterinary laboratories.

Besides tuberculin testing, another cornerstone of the WHO-coordinated campaign against human TB has been the vaccine BCG (bacillus of L. C. A. Calmette and Alphonse Guérin, the Pasteur Institute physician-veterinarian team who developed it).    Ironically, BCG proved of no value for its intended purpose of immunizing cattle, but has been widely used in people.    Beyond such, an at least temporary *coup de grace* to human pulmonary TB in much of the Northern world was rendered post-World War II by the advent of specific therapy (to replace passive sanitorium rest or radical surgery, both frequently unsuccessful). Research leading to the first successful treatments (with streptomycin) was carried out by veterinarian William Feldman, Professor of Experimental Pathology in the Mayo Clinic, an advance ultimately permitting most tubercular patients to be treated successfully at home.

We would note next that veterinary efforts not only to control zoonoses like tuberculosis, but some other purely animal diseases, have not only accomplished those goals, but also demonstated new strategies, tactics (see Table 6.2) or specific weapons with which to combat diseases solely of people.

*Identifying New Approaches to Human Disease Control.*   In addition to the new strategy of *eradicating* an infectious microorganism from a large geographical area, major disease-control tactics like quarantine, mass testing of populations for specific diseases, mass immunization and vector control[13] were first demonstrated by veterinary science, as were some of the earliest applications of mass preventive therapy.   Such led the Surgeon General of the U. S. Public Health Service to note that "we in the public health profession . . . owe to veterinarians wholly or in generous measure, a number of basic ideas upon which our profession is built" (Terry, 1963).   As to specific weapons against important human infections, consider only vaccines being used against major diseases of childhood which form the basis for WHO/UNICEF's worldwide Expanded Programme of Immunization.   As already indicated, tuberculosis vaccine was discovered by a physician-veterinarian team.   Diphtheria and tetanus both are prevented by another type of vaccine called a toxoid, the underlying principle of which, and those specific vaccines, were contributions of Gaston Ramon, another Pasteur Institute veterinarian.   Against whooping cough, a still different type of vaccine called a killed bacterin is used.   Its principle was the discovery of Daniel Salmon and Theobald Smith, a veterinarian-physician team in the American federal veterinary service.[14]

*Other Human Health By-products of Animal Diseases Research.*   A third avenue for veterinary research inputs into human health aspects of development is through totally unanticipated benefits to people's health from studies undertaken with purely veterinary objectives on diseases that are not zoonoses or otherwise affect people directly.   As important examples, we would know very much less, if anything, today about viruses or mycoplasmas had those major classes of etiological agents not been discovered and investigated for important livestock diseases--in the first instance for foot-and-mouth disease of cattle and, in the second, contagious bovine pleuropneumonia.  Thus, in a sense, all diseases of animals provide a "natural laboratory" for first identifying and elucidating totally new biomedical phenomena of the most varied types.

For example, probably nothing less excited the human medical community than an epidemic during the winter of 1921-1922 of a highly fatal hemorrhagic disease of cattle in the Canadian and U. S. Middle West, yet its occurrence had major human health repercussions.  Although it was believed by many veterinarians to be infectious, and diagnosed as anthrax, hemorrhagic septicemia or blackleg, Frank Schofield, Professor of Pathology in Canada's Ontario Veterinary College, showed that it was not typical of those and was, in fact, a completely new disease.

Schofield was especially struck by his observation that rations of affected cattle contained sweet clover, since depredations of the corn borer had caused substitutions that year of sweet clover silage for corn silage in feeding wintered cattle in the North American Midwest.  He noted that sweet clover contained a little known chemical called coumarin and that in all outbreaks investigated, clover was moldy. Finding that prolonged blood coagulation time was a consistent disease feature, he concluded that was due to an absence of thrombin, or an inhibition of thrombin.  He also noted that certain protein split-products can stimulate the liver to produce antithrombin and considered it possible that such are formed in moldy clover and were responsibe for altered clotting time of blood.  He and L. Roderick, veterinary pathologist in the North Dakota Agricultural Experiment Station, each noted that liver damage was a constant feature of the disease and the latter established next that the clotting loss actually resulted from prothrombin deficiency.  Subsequently, H. A. Campbell and K. P. Link at the University of Wisconsin isolated from damaged sweet clover the responsible chemical, dicoumerol, a breakdown product of coumarin noted by Schofield.

The rest of this story is relatively well known.  Schofield's work on Moldy Sweet Clover disease of cattle soon led directly to discovery of the nutritional function of vitamin K and other important aspects of the mechanism of blood clotting and to demonstration of dicoumerol's usefulness not only as a potent rodenticide Warfarin® (a discovery of global importance since rodents maintain diseases like plague and typhus and destroy vast quantities of foodstuffs), but also of its use as the first effective treatment and preventive of embolisms and coronary and other thromboses in people, saving countless human lives since.[15]  Had there not been strong veterinary services in North America, with their associated research capabilities, dicoumerol and its unique properties would remain to be discovered and applied.

Thus, in these and other ways, much of veterinary science's intersectoral experience in the past resulted from its being simultaneously a health field and an agricultural field, necessitating that it must function within both of those spheres.[16]  These relationships become even stronger as a new information-based veterinary delivery system replaces older systems, a development we shall advocate as a high priority for Africa in Chapter 8. The most important point to recognize here is that some of these agricultural-health and other aspects of IC have been practically experienced by publicly and privately provided veterinary services since the late 18th century and have similar African relevance today.

## WHO Veterinary Public Health IC--Analyses of Top-Down Efforts

More than four decades of concerted efforts by WHO's Veterinary Public Health Unit to promote IC at national levels between medical and veterinary services (i.e., veterinary public health, VPH) worldwide, especially for control of human rabies, brucellosis, tuberculosis, hydatid disease, food-borne infections and a number of other important zoonoses (as well as in other spheres, see Figure 7.1), showed that cooperation patterns that worked extremely well in some countries were not adopted by other countries, or did not succeed there (despite often positive lip service from national authorities with overall responsibility in both ministries). Because those have been largely top-down attempts at cross-sectoral cooperation, an obvious reason for some successes and failures was the quality of the director chosen to develop and oversee efforts.

Other reasons have not been so immediately obvious. Some general categories of constraints were identified in 1975 by the Joint WHO/FAO Expert Committee on Veterinary Public Health and "key person" considerations appeared less critical the closer one approached local action situations in which people from different service sectors were actually called upon to work together. Beyond such, it gradually became clear that successes both among countries and within different areas of the same country were being favored, or constrained, by highly individual circumstances, some also involving specific personnel involved, but others apparently reflecting such things as special resources, traditional rural institutions, differing people-animal relationships, different ethnic and religious beliefs and practices, and the like. As the result, the WHO VPH Unit, directed then by Konrad Bögel, commenced in the late 1980s what was to be a series of "national analyses" designed specifically to ascertain the governmental and non-governmental structures and practices, customs, beliefs, popular practices and ideas, precedents and the like which would favor or constrain national VPH IC.

Nepal was chosen for the prototype analysis because it already had achieved some remarkable zoonoses control successes under very difficult circumstances. Their director had been D.D. Joshi, a veterinary epidemiologist who served originally within Nepal's veterinary service, but later as Chief of Epidemiology within its national Ministry of Health. This analysis was carried out by a multidisciplinary WHO team including biomedical and social scientists. WHO then convened a broadly based consultancy under the chairmanship of Joshi to consider the methodology employed and to recommend guidelines for further national analyses in quite different countries or as requested by member governments (WHO, 1989). The second author was asked by WHO to explore the suitability of Somalia for the prototype analysis under African pastoral conditions. An important point to note is that this veterinary initiative vis-à-vis important IC activities had some of the same objectives of identifying positive influences and constraints to the successful functioning of institutions/programs as does the New Institutional Economics (NIE) "institutional analysis" approach of political scientists like David Leonard (who are interested in livestock situations and veterinary services delivery in Africa; see Chapter 4). These research currents could be associated profitably in the future.

### Emergency Planning and Services

Another aspect of veterinary-associated IC relative to human health has had to do with plans for coping with natural and man-made disasters. Normal pastoral existence in Africa bears enough resemblance to major disaster situations in Northern countries to make such plans especially germane to our discussion of veterinary precedents for broader initiatives. Both require, in our view, IC efforts, and the same type of unconventional vision unobstructed by "the cataract of accepted beliefs." The first stage of such emergency planning has been to consider as objectively as possible what can be done with inadequate conventional resources. As a key example, what medical and other health-related services can persons other than physicians provide in situations where demands clearly exceed the capacities of the usual health services (thus reserving physicians for things no one else can do at all or reasonably adequately)? These are emergency activities that are undertaken under special directives and decrees which suspend and supercede all usual procedures, safeguards and legal liability considerations.

Because we believe a similarly open mentality is required for undertaking pastoral development in Africa, let us illustrate this idea more specifically by listing the types of things the American veterinary profession would do under an emergency plan devised for the U.S. federal government in 1957 by the American Medical Association's Commission on National Emergency Medical Care. First, that Commission surveyed all other health and paramedical personnel besides physicians and arranged them into five groups in order of what was considered their overall usefulness for disaster relief tasks. As surprising as this ordering might seem on first consideration to some members of the Northern public, these were: Group I, veterinarians; Group II, dentists; Group III, nurses; Group IV, technicians, therapists and pharmacists; Group V, medical social workers, dieticians, clinical psychologists, and so on. The range of emergency medical services recommended for veterinarians to perform on people included: (1) first aid, including but not limited to artificial respiration, emergency treatment of open chest wounds, relief of pain, treatment of shock and preparation of casualties for movement; (2) control of hemorrhage; (3) attainment and maintenance of patent airway, and intratracheal catheterization, including tracheotomy; (4) proper and adequate cleansing and treatment of wounds; (5) bandaging and splinting; (6) administration of anesthetics under medical supervision; (7) assisting in surgical procedures; (8) insertion of nasogastric tubes and lavage and gavage as directed; (9) administration of whole blood and intravenous solutions, as directed; (10) administration of parenteral medications, as directed; (11) catheterization of males and females; (12) administration of immunizing agents, as directed; (13) sanitation, to include waste disposal; examination of water sources, methods of sterilization and distribution; and inspection of foods, to include detection of radioactive contamination.   Some Northern veterinary schools offer some instruction especially directed to professional organization for such emergency tasks.

Much of that idea is strikingly reminiscent of the normal 18th-century situation vis-à-vis available human health care in rural France (Hannaway, 1977) that caused French veterinary curricula to include instruction in human obstetrics and emergency medicine and in the fact that, in 1843, veterinarians as well as physicians and pharmacists were appointed to a new network of rural health councils in France.   What all of this more than suggests is that very unconventional things that offer more positives than negatives must be tried within pastoral Africa since the ideal, or anything approaching it, cannot be afforded or otherwise provided under any forseeable circumstances.   That members of the veterinary profession frequently have had to face similar situations of improvization individually, simply to practice animal medicine, is reflected in an apt quotation in Chapter 8 from Professor Walter Gibbons about the impossibility of $100 operations on $25 dollar cows.  This is an important point to note, namely that affordable veterinary practice often necessitates using something less than the scientifically most effective procedure.  This mentality needs to become more commonplace among providers of all services in poor parts of the world.  The unacceptable alternative for Africa, as we see it, is to do among pastoral peoples in the future what has been done in the past--that is, almost nothing beneficial.

Let us mention now one important precedent for broader veterinary services development initiatives in Africa.

## A PREVIOUS VETERINARY DEVELOPMENT INITIATIVE IN AFRICA

One of the world's first regional organizations to promote cooperation in technical and other development questions of common interest was the colonial period Commission for Technical Cooperation in Africa South of the Sahara (CCTA), in those respects a forerunner of the postindependence Organization of African Unity (OAU).   Although CCTA eventually involved itself in activities as diverse as plant agriculture, health, nutrition, geology, education, roads, hydrology, labor and social sciences, its genesis was largely veterinary. Conferences held in 1948 led to establishment first of an Inter-African Bureau for Epizootic Diseases and, second, an Inter-African Bureau for Tsetse and Trypanosomiasis. Appropriately, CCTA's founding president was P.J. du Toit, director of South Africa's famed veterinary research institute at Onderstepoort. Moreover, since the Bureau for Tsetse and Trypanosomiasis' efforts were directed against a disease complex both of livestock and people (see Chapter 4), it was intersectoral by design. Therefore, that tsetse and trypanosomiasis effort was doubly germane to the proposals we shall make that veterinary services are well situated to act as the "stem" program throughout pastoral Africa onto which other development programs and social services might be "grafted." We turn now to how, and how well, veterinary services function currently in Africa.


## CURRENT VETERINARY SERVICES DELIVERY IN AFRICA

We might begin with an assessment by a 10-member advisory committee to Winrock International (Pritchard et al., 1992: 119):

> The effectiveness of animal health services in sub-Saharan Africa [overall] has seriously declined over the last two decades. . . . As a result, disease surveillance, vaccine production and epidemic disease control measures are inadequate, curative services are poor or nonexistent, and public health and extension are weak. . . . Only the recent donor-assisted rinderpest campaign [PARC, see below] can be said to be functioning properly. Indeed the recent rinderpest epidemic has been directly attributed to failure of veterinary services to maintain adequate vaccination cover and to detect early outbreaks of the disease. . . . Even though the human resources component of veterinary services has improved dramatically, the services have not gained in effectiveness because there is little money for operations.

While we concur generally in that assessment (especially in its last statement), we think it somewhat disingenuous to compare these two periods of African history so directly. All those who observed veterinary service in much of Africa 30 years ago know that, in countries with white minorities, the colonial veterinary services then served that small community's needs almost exclusively, or, there and elsewhere, were geared to the far more limited exigencies of an export livestock trade. Unless the African livestock owner's own problems impinged upon the fulfillment of those priorities, little or no attention was given by the veterinary services to them--and especially was that so of African pastoralists and their animals. That is, the present constituencies and social priorities for African governments bear little resemblance to those under the largely artificial situations of the colonial and immediately post-colonial transitional periods. We say that not in way of excuse for any present inadequacies of veterinary (and other) services but in the interests of a less gratuitous assigning of blame.

Moreover, such implied criticisms of persons now often working under unbelievably difficult conditions fail also to consider the effectiveness of those particular sectors being criticized in comparison with those provided by other sectors of government, something especially relevant to our concentration upon the development situation pertaining to pastoralists. We shall make some very concrete suggestions for remedies to these current veterinary inadequacies in Chapters 8 and 9 but, with respect to pastoralists and their current well-being, these inadequacies (and those of the livestock sector overall) simply strengthen the logic and practicality of our own unorthodox suggestions. Such efforts could substantially correct within arid and semiarid areas some of these voiced criticisms of veterinary services, while at the same time help bring other basic amenities to pastoral peoples.

The largest and highest priority veterinary programs in sub-Saharan Africa are multicountry vaccination campaigns against a few economically disruptive livestock diseases. Those steps culminated in the mammoth multidonor-assisted JP-15 (Joint Project of OAU) rinderpest campaign in an area eventually extending from Dakar to Mogadishu (Lepissier and Mac-Farlane, 1966; MacFarlane, 1973). In absence of reported cases, some countries claimed to have eradicated rinderpest. Resulting euphoria proved short-lived, however, as it was diagnosed again in East Africa in 1979 (Rossiter et al, 1983) and West Africa in 1980 (Provost, 1981). Explanations advanced included failure of governments to increase budgets for veterinary services sufficiently to maintain vaccination cover, especially inability to meet the cost of increased numbers of personnel without seriously limiting expenditures for adequate quarantine measures, slaughter of infected animals where feasible, maintaining efficient reporting, diagnostic and laboratory services. In other words, when external assistance ceased or was substantially reduced, existing veterinary infrastructures in many countries were insufficient to sustain the program as intended. Additionally, it was clear that in certain countries, the Sudan included, mass vaccination coverage had never been nearly achieved and little knowledge existed there of the actual distribution of rinderpest (see Chapter 4).

Following an emergency vaccination campaign in West Africa in 1983, demands increased to mount a second continental effort. Justification for what was to be called the Pan African Rinderpest Campaign (PARC) emphasized that lessons learned from JP-15 would this time assure eradication of the disease. Specific conditions to be met included (1) nearly 100% vaccination coverage of all cattle in the primary effort, (2) vaccination of all calves for two to three years after the main campaign, (3) vaccination of trade cattle and (4) *monitoring of the "epizootiological situation" in countries in which the disease was presumably eliminated.*

Inadequate understanding of recent advances in the design and operation of epidemiological surveillance systems and their roles in campaigns, reflected in these revised plans, amplified the importance of recognition within some Northern veterinary circles, beginning in the mid-1960s, that such isolated campaigns as the organizational basis for veterinary services delivery were unnecessarily costly and inefficient.  Some epidemiologists questioned therefore whether lessons ostensibly learned from JP-15 were being taken into sufficient account in planning PARC.  Those were reasonable questions in that veterinarians specifically trained "to monitor the 'epizootiological' situation" (that is, in disease intelligence systems and analytical epidemiology) were absent from the postmortems of JP-15 and the design of its replacement.  More drastic changes were urgently required within national veterinary services and this remains the case.

Leonard (1993) has identified for much of Africa some of the constraints hampering veterinary services delivery generally.  It therefore is germane at this point to consider in greater detail what veterinary services are like within pastoral areas of Africa.  We shall attempt especially to identify some of the problems they often face in pursuing even their currently too limited missions.  In this, we shall, again, be focusing upon our principal model situation, the southern Sudan, an area in which, unlike South Africa, Kenya and Zimbabwe, Northerners had not come with intent to permanently settle and, therefore, did much less in creating viable infrastructures during the colonial period.

**The Southern Sudan**

The Sudan as a whole possesses neither the strongest nor the weakest existing veterinary services in Africa. An Animal Disease Act was promulgated in 1901 under the Anglo-Egyptian Condominium when the colonial administration became concerned with the health of horses and riding and baggage camels upon which mobility and communications of the British military depended (Jack, 1961).  A change from military to civilian concerns took place gradually.  Protection of Sudanese cattle against CBPP was recognized as important in 1914 as demand for meat by British military forces in Egypt increased and large-scale vaccination was undertaken then in Kordofan province.  Between 1925 and 1939 a veterinary department of permanent civilian officials was strengthened to resemble that which forms today's organization.  A Livestock and Veterinary Policy Committee was formed in 1946 (Khalil, 1960).  One of its recommendations was that mass immunization against economically disruptive diseases should be initiated.  That was also the beginning in the Sudan of thinking about a more than subsistence basis for livestock production.  British administrators in need of political support reasoned that "if the livestock increase, the Baggara [cattle-keeping Arabs] will be contented and quiet" (Gillespie, 1966).  From then on use of antirinderpest serum was gradually extended to pastoral areas of the western Sudan. Baggara did not enthusiastically receive these measures at first because of lingering distrust of colonial personnel, but, after introduction of rinderpest tissue culture vaccine in 1935, and its demonstrated success, they began to accept these new services with some enthusiasm. A veterinary faculty was established in 1938 in what eventually became the University of Khartoum. While these developments took place in the northern Sudan, the south remained an essentially "closed district" and virtually no veterinary interventions or other aspects of development were attempted.

After independence, a separate Ministry of Animal Resources (comprising animal health services, animal production, range management, game and fisheries) existed until May 1969, when the military regime of Jaafar Nimeiry, under the influence of American advisors, combined it with plant agriculture as a single Ministry of Agriculture and Natural Resources (MANR). Resulting subordination of the livestock sector, so important from the standpoints of employment and subsistence, was regarded by many Sudanese as a retrograde step. Therefore, when civilian government was restored, Animal Resources was reconstituted as a separate ministry. Control of epidemic diseases of cattle like rinderpest and CBPP by mass measures remained the principal concerns of the governmental livestock sector, activities carried out through a provincial and district veterinary network. Veterinary personnel succeeded in reaching a variable proportion of pastoralists' herds during annual vaccination campaigns.

Such efforts in the southern Sudan appear to have begun in 1949 and were funded internally. Outside support became available following Sudan's participation in JP-15 and JP-28. Although a quite low 60% coverage of the national herd was targeted intitially for JP-15 vaccinations, even that was not nearly achieved and efforts in the south ceased in the 1960s as a result of the civil war. After reestablishment of peace in 1972, annual mass immunization campaigns resumed. Other functions attempted whenever feasible included meat inspection in principal towns plus treatment of individual animals in district veterinary clinics, more local dispensaries and, during annual vaccination campaigns, in the cattle camps. Highly appreciated aspects of these latter were bloodless castrations of cattle and treatment of trypanosomiasis.

The first author was privileged to serve then within the Sudanese veterinary services at almost every level from District Veterinary Officer (DVO) to Director of Veterinary Services for the Southern Region. It is from those experiences, both good and bad, that the following account of veterinary services delivery within the southern Sudan is drawn. We believe, as do social scientists influenced by the New Institutional Economics school that, within a development context, identifying for key institutions favorable and unfavorable influences upon successful fulfillment of goals is vital.

The establishment of veterinary services in the southern Sudan as a regional entity dates from 1972. Because the southern Sudan had been left only one secondary school by the colonial regime, a situation continuing for some time after independence, and partly because the importance of an educated veterinary profession for pastoral communities was not appreciated either by the government or pastoralists themselves, there were only six veterinarians originating from the south available then for a cattle population of about 5.5 million (MANR, 1976). Apart from southern veterinarians taking over administrative and technical responsibilities, which was a gradual process, organization and policy continued to follow those of the central government. Animal health and related animal/veterinary science disciplines were within a Department of Veterinary Services headed by a Deputy Director of the Regional Ministry of Agriculture and Natural Resources. National ministerial reorganization resulted in this department being upgraded to a Directorate in June 1978. It consisted of departments of animal health services, animal production (dairy and poultry mainly), planning and epizootics and range management. Deputy directors headed each.

Under policy objectives defined by the Six Year Plan of Economic and Social Development for the fiscal years 1976/77 to 1982/83, veterinary services headed the list of developmental priorities within the agriculture sector. Their first task was to control major epidemic diseases through augmentation of annual mass immunization efforts. The south then had no capability to produce vaccines, requiring their purchase in Khartoum or Nairobi, transport by air to Juba with ultimate distribution overland to the districts (all under refrigeration). Extreme budgetary limitations acted as a major constraint upon vaccine availability. The acute shortage of veterinarians made it impossible initially to post even one Veterinary Officer (VO) to some main cattle districts. Therefore, initial staffing in many districts was solely by veterinary assistants (VAs), and stockmen. These paravets had received formal training at diploma (VAs) or certificate levels, or were individuals trained on the job.

Regional veterinary services received some external financial and technical assistance after 1974. This was largely through a bilateral agreement whereby the German Agency for Technical Cooperation (GTZ) undertook efforts to augment mass cattle vaccinations. The targeted goal of 80% vaccination coverage was not nearly reached, however, resulting in a change of policy objectives whereby GTZ staff withdrew from that program and, instead, carried out disease intelligence among the cattle population of Bahr al Ghazal province. As backup for that effort, the German government built and equipped a subregional laboratory within the provincial veterinary compound in Wau. This initiation for the first time in the Sudan of comprehensive field surveys marked a dramatic change from previously haphazard disease intelligence. The animal health component of another project funded through a World Bank loan (the Southern Regional Agriculture Project, SRAP) was to conduct similar multidisease surveys in the other two provinces. Suggestions were made about new implementing measures and where such initiatives might logically lead (Schwabe, 1980). This Bahr al Ghazal survey was completed and portions of the data analyzed (Baumann, 1983, Zessin et al., 1985, Majok et al., 1991, 1993; also see Chapter 4). Unfortunately, those new surveillance efforts, key to a more rational approach to veterinary services delivery (see Chapter 8) were terminated in 1983 by resumption of civil war. SRAP also provided for the construction and equipping of a central regional laboratory at Juba (CVL) and a subregional laboratory in the provincial town of Malakal. Both the Juba and Wau laboratories were completed as planned and began to function. The initial activities of CVL were to be diagnosis, research, production of CBPP vaccine and training of laboratory technicians. Later other vaccines (particularly against blackleg, hemorrhagic septicemia and anthrax) were to be produced. With those functions, the Juba laboratory was to provide technical support for field efforts throughout the southern region.

Such moves toward decentralization of efforts marked a significant departure from past programs in which every move had been directed from much more remote Khartoum and through which almost nothing permanent had been achieved in the southern Sudan.

*Seasonal Veterinary Activities.* Because of patterns of rainfall and transhumant migrations (se Chapter 2), veterinary activities in the southern Sudan necessarily vary with the season. The wet season is when most activities requiring land travel are suspended. Then vaccination is necessarily confined to herds around district towns in Upper Nile, Jonglei, Lakes and Bahr al Ghazal provinces, and to accessible herds in Eastern Equatoria province. Thus, the wet season is an annual slack period in which staff morale slumps. Main activities are conduct of routine clinics at or near the district office, meat inspection, issuance of health certificates and permits for trade cattle being trekked to other areas and routine office administration, including writing of reports, orders for drugs, vaccines, equipment and supplies.

During the relatively short period between the end of the rainy season and commencement of the dry season, DVOs seek information about the expected condition of grazing areas and the exact *toich* locations to which particular groups will take their herds. They also obtain information about grazing and water conditions in the high and intermediate lands and assess the most probable time migrations will start. DVOs also continue to stock vaccines, particularly CBPP vaccine which has a short storage life, and other supplies: kerosene to run field refrigerators, diesel oil and petrol for the vehicles and syringes and needles. Vehicles are repaired to extents possible. The dry season is the most active period of the year. Almost the sole activity is cattle vaccination by mobile teams in 4-wheel-drive vehicles which travel long distances overland through roadless savannas to reach individual cattle camps. Some clinical work in the field is also done, especially on urgent demand.

*Theory and Practice: Major Constraints.* While all of this is the current program in theory, in practice there are numerous constraints or breakdowns and the results have rarely approached "state of the art" for a campaigns/mass actions-type effort. These constraints and effects of very uneven utilization of all resources throughout the year--alternating from frenetic time-limited efforts to periods in which the dominant scene in a district veterinary office is of boredom and frustration--warrant far more innovative attention than has been given them. We direct special attention to this in Chapter 8. But here we identify major constraints to current veterinary services delivery in the southern Sudan, most of which are wholly or partially external to veterinary services per se. These include (1) almost total absence of any transport infrastructure (roads, rails, water and air), (2) limited and unmaintained buildings, (3) too few professional staff especially and (4) chronic shortfalls of money to pay field staff salaries and/or per diem, plus costs of capital goods and operating expenses. Together they cause service delivery failures, including inability to make diagnoses which require field follow-up.

Taking a closer look at these constraints, the Sudan has an area of about 2.5 million square km, of which about one-quarter are in the south. The larger dimensions of the transport problem in its southern region, solution to which will be dependent upon major investments, are beyond our proposals' concerns and, as with other matters, we accept without enthusiasm this present situation. However, a more manageable dimension of this transport problem involves maintenance of minimally dependable ground links between the several district towns (i.e., the pastoral outreach centers for veterinary services delivery). As no roads are paved, their condition after the rainy season ends causes frequent vehicle breakdowns with the life of a 4-wheel-drive vehicle rarely more than three years. A reasonable short-term local priority, therefore, would be for the regional Department of Roads and Bridges, in consultation with veterinary services, to undertake annual grading of roads leading into main cattle areas early in the dry season so that veterinary teams can reach more herds before they are driven to less accessible sites. An even more crucial local problem is that district veterinary services, in theory, are provided transport to reach pastoralists from the Provincial Commissioner's pool of vehicles and donor-assisted projects. After 1972, the Regional Government became a third source of transport. Of these, only donor-assisted projects have proven dependable and those vehicles became less available after the JP-15 rinderpest campaign and the GTZ project ended in 1976 and 1981, respectively. The Provincial Commissioner's source not only failed to meet ongoing needs, but, instead, existing veterinary services vehicles were requisitioned by government for other functions (such as political programs of the former Sudanese Socialist Union).

Maintenance facilities for available vehicles also have been totally inadequate since donor-assisted projects ended. Two vehicle repair shops were previously available, a GTZ shop in Wau and a Project Development Unit (PDU) shop in Juba. However, repair facilities never existed in any other districts and that meant all vehicles needing maintenance had to be taken to either Wau or Juba. That was often impossible and, even when possible, considerable time was wasted during the short period when vaccination teams had to accomplish their tasks. Currently, even these remote repair facilities are unavailable and minor problems (which disable vehicles) are complicated seriously by lack of spare parts.

Permanent buildings represent another serious constraint. Many physical structures previously available to veterinary services were destroyed during the civil war from 1955 to 1972 and others left unscathed, like the Malakal stockmen's school and DVOs' houses in some of the districts, were occupied by military personnel. Some of these were never returned, others were taken over by local government, while in the three provincial towns, creation of a new regional administration further increased demand for existing facilities. A typical district facility today consists of one small building with two rooms. One is the DVO's office, which he may share. It, in most cases, also houses cold-chain equipment and the limited range of available drugs. The second room accommodates supporting staff and, possibly, additional drug and supply storage. Maintenance of buildings, ostensibly the responsibility of local government, is poor. That problem, coupled with inadequate storage facilities and sometimes inadequate security, has required some DVOs to use their housing for storage. Kerosene and petrol are especially scarce and need to be protected from theft.

A key factor affecting all aspects of veterinary services delivery is insufficient operating funds. For example, most district-level vaccination equipment was provided in the mid-1960s under the JP-15 rinderpest campaign. Much of this equipment is now unusable and has not been replaced. More routine supplies are replaced only with great difficulty.[17] Drug supplies, though limited in range and inadequate in amounts, have always been available to some extent, especially drugs for which pastoralists are willing to pay. There is also the acute problem of delays in payments of salaries, overtime and travel allowances to field staff. This partly results from the system of budgeting at two levels--a provincial council budget and the regional government budget. The former ostensibly provides directly for all personnel needs. From it, and in competition with all other demands (including those of the more politically important, therefore much favored, townspeople), are met all veterinary salaries. Here a whole province resembles more a town or other local government in the Northern world, with the Provincial Commissioner playing the role of "mayor" to whom many persons have fairly easy access, each pleading his own special case. On the other hand, the regional budget is supposed to meet the costs of capital goods. However, allocations for such purposes have always remained very small compared to pastoralists' demands and officials' projected needs. The result has been that veterinary services usually have depended almost exclusively for their actual operations on external funding--for example, JP-15, GTZ and the World Bank.

Personnel shortages are also acute. At their inception regional veterinary services had only one veterinarian in the headquarters of the regional ministry, five in provincial towns and none in the districts. By 1981/82 there were still only 32 governmental veterinarians (see Table 6.4). In addition, there were 14

| | HQR | Bahr el Ghazal | Lakes | Upper Nile | Jonglei | Eastern Equatoria | Western Equatoria | Total |
|---|---|---|---|---|---|---|---|---|
| Veterinarians | 4 | 4 | 4 | 9 | 3 | 6 | 2 | 32 |
| Veterinary Assistants | | 15 | 6 | 13 | 5 | 18 | 2 | 59 |
| Stockmen | | 60 | 41 | 50 | 104 | 34 | 11 | 300 |
| Total | 4 | 79 | 51 | 72 | 112 | 58 | 15 | 391 |

**Table 6.4. Southern Sudan veterinary establishment 1981/82.** (Source: Directorate of Animal Resources, Regional Ministry of Agriculture and Natural Resources, Southern Region, Juba, 1981/82 annual reports.)

expatriates, most of whom were involved in specific livestock projects. Considering a cattle population then of about 7 million, and the vast difficult-to-reach territory, this force was far too small to achieve any lasting success with resources at its disposal.

Having considered generally the record of veterinary services as agents of development in rural areas, then more specifically in Africa with respect to the needs and general well-being of its pastoralists, we focused most intensely, through our primary case example of the southern Sudan, upon how and how well veterinary services meet their major commitments. And, where in places like the southern Sudan, they do not succeed well enough, we have identified reasons why. From having been, in this last instance, so specific, we think that, before stating our overall conclusions to this point, we should indicate one other variable in the pastoral development equation relative to veterinary services' possibly assuming a broader catalytic or facilitating role.

## INTERNATIONAL DIMENSIONS OF VETERINARY SCIENCE

The veterinary profession--to a much greater extent than most other agents of pastoral development (professions, disciplines) like range management--already has available some types of especially relevant outside resources and support which reflect the state of international organization of veterinary science as a long-established and globally valuable field. As examples, besides a sizable cadre of veterinarians within the UN Food and Agricultural Organization, veterinary-staffed programs exist within the World Health Organization, with lesser numbers within the International Office of Epizootics, UNICEF, UNESCO, the World Bank and other international bodies. Significant veterinary representation occurs too within a range of unofficial international scientific, medical, social service, animal conservation/welfare and other organizations. Additionally, a number of internationally organized specialty groups exist within particular subspheres of veterinary science itself, and veterinary professional associations per se exist from local through international levels. Some of these relationships either do not exist or are much less effectively developed for other agricultural disciplines, a point noted by S. Sandford (1983: 196) when, in commenting upon pastoral development, remarked from more negative than positive assumptions that "the international solidarity of the veterinary profession . . . makes it difficult for non-veterinarians to be recognized as the heads of national livestock services." We believe he missed the point: namely, that these multiple organizational linkages and vehicles for communication and concerted actions stimulate a higher degree of  professionalism within veterinary science than found elsewhere within agriculture. They thus provide mechanisms for internal policing of standards of performance, including a partial guard against temptations toward corruption which are strong for public servants under many present African conditions.  Leonard (1987, 1991) much better understood the merits of this international bulwarking of veterinary professionalism in advocating its regional, national and local strenghthening in Africa as an aid to development within the livestock sector.

Some such linkages already exist, but largely at national levels and above. We have cited the veterinary initiatives for development cooperation represented by the late colonial era's Commission for Technical Cooperation in Africa South of the Sahara and its successor programs. Colonial period understanding of the relative importance of veterinary science was reflected also in very early establishment of some veterinary research resources of absolutely first quality and broad influence.  Premier among these was the Onderstepoort Institute for Veterinary Research developed outside of Pretoria by Sir Arnold Theiler.[18]   Another was the Kenya Veterinary Research Laboratory at Kabete, which also contributed importantly to global knowledge of infectious diseases and their control.  Further instances of special note include some of the Pasteur Institutes (particularly Algiers) which pioneered in an intersectoral sense in that they were consciously developed with joint medical-veterinary research and service orientations.  Similarly important for the same reasons became the West African (later Nigerian) Institute for Trypanosomiasis Research at Vom and Kaduna.  Of more recent origin is the International Laboratory for Research on Animal Diseases (ILRAD), located on the former site of the tsetse and trypanosomiasis program of the Kenya Veterinary Research Laboratory. It began operations in 1974 under an agreement between the Rockefeller Foundation[19] and the government of Kenya. In a sense, ILRAD was a replacement on a continental scale for regional research organizations (as part of an intended but unrealized East African Community).

An International Centre for Livestock in Africa (ILCA) began operations in Addis Ababa in 1974 through an agreement with the government of Ethiopia.  Its main emphases have been meat and milk production from cattle and small ruminants, plus promotion and improvement of animal traction.  Its overall program has been broader and more applied than that of ILRAD but, thus far, its animal health facets and other direct veterinary inputs have been negligible (e.g., in cooperation with ILRAD establishment of an African Trypanotolerant Livestock Network).  It is our strong belief that ILRAD and

ILCA must become much more effectively related in the future, as parts of which ILRAD broadens its very narrow focus and ILCA's animal health programs (especially for epidemiological surveillance and veterinary services delivery) are considerably augmented and interdigitated with not only other production-related aspects of its program but also with a broadened basic sciences mission of ILRAD.[20] More recently, a West African regional Centre International de Recherches et Développement sur l'Elevage en Zone Sub-humide (CIRDES) evolved from a prior trypanosomiasis research center in Burkina Faso and will eventually serve all francophone countries in Africa. An International Trypanotolerance Centre is located in Gambia.   Although basically concerned with another agroecological zone than those within which most pastoralists are located, some of their programs are also germane to pastoralists' needs.[21]


## CONCLUSIONS

The subject we are concerned with is the overall development of large communities practicing extensive pastoralism over wide areas, mostly arid or semiarid, of the African continent.   That is, our *initial* interest is in helping these peoples progress in ways that are not culturally harmful.  This approach may be different from those of some international funding and executing organizations involved in agricultural or overall development in Africa.  Their interests vis-à-vis pastoralism have been primarily in economic productivity (in Northern terms) of the land occupied by pastoral peoples, or of development of "animal industries."  Sometimes, objectives of those approaches coincide, but otherwise past efforts have tended to put the cart before the horse.

We have now laid the essential groundwork for elaborating practical proposals for modest but sustainable locally initiated beginnings to a process of pastoral development in Africa. Let us recapitulate the main points we have attempted to make in these first six chapters.

1.  Particularly as pastoralists become more and more confined to lands of limited potential economically and marginal ecologically, attention in each situation must be given to defining the ecosystems of which they are parts and identifying the strategies and tactics each people uses to maintain its niche, and realize its subsistence needs within it.

2.  Requiring equal investigation are man-animal interactions in each situation and how these may be inextricably intermeshed with important social and cultural issues, including pastoralist cosmologies.

3.  For these purposes and others, pastoralists must be fully consulted at all stages of efforts which will involve or influence them.  This will require exploration in each situation of their traditional methods of decision-making,

governance of commons and adjudication and how to gain access to their views and cooperation through indigenous offices and institutions.

4. Recognition is required, therefore, that the multiple roles livestock play in the lives of Africa's pastoralists alone would make veterinary services--from the standpoints of the peoples concerned--uniquely important governmental interventions. This has been illustrated in greatest detail for the more than 2 million Dinka. The fact that the most important thing Dinka desire is the safety of their cattle, in particular their freedom from disease, underscores this pivotal veterinary position. African veterinary services have had varying degrees of success in achieving their highest priority goals of controlling economically disruptive and development-thwarting diseases. The experience of the southern Sudan provides one of the poorer records, if not a nearly worst case scenario. Yet, veterinary services are the only service which has endeavored to (and succeeded often) in reaching pastoralists. The central significance of their activities, and their full acceptance by pastoralists, is forcefully indicated by the fact that, since the resumption in the early 1980s of civil war in the southern Sudan, the only governmental officials permitted to (in fact encouraged to) enter areas under control of the Sudanese Peoples' Liberation Army (SPLA) have been veterinary personnel.

5. Although we visualize ways the livestock sector in pastoral Africa can help earn capital for its own pastoral development purposes, being pragmatists we see little hope that, while such longer term more general changes are taking place, veterinary services *entirely on their own allotted resources* can necessarily overcome the array of constraints upon their programs which now arise with such frequency. Even less, for the same reasons, can we imagine that any other service branch of government will be able to afford to set up parallel avenues of access to pastoralists and thus provide them with other amenities vital to their development. Some alternative notions must be forthcoming at the local level or these peoples will continue to be as neglected in national planning and in promotion of human betterment as they have been until now.

6. We think we also have established that veterinary services are the one branch of government in Africa whose priority programs *demand* that they reach pastoralists where they normally are. Furthermore, as we shall illustrate, even under some of the least satisfactory conditions (as within the southern Sudan) these existing outreach mechanisms can be shared with others who would reach pastoralists with additional things/services they can use (see Chapter 7). And they can be substantially strengthened for such multiple purposes (see Chapters 8 and 9).

7. Although our proposals start with the inefficiencies and other realities of existing situations and will offer practical suggestions for initial progress despite these, we believe that further improvements will be possible with some judicious external inputs. Since it has been mostly among certain NGOs assisting in this poorly coordinated development process that our own local

aims and their achievement have been reflected at all in the past, we believe that NGO inputs must be more encouraged officially. These could lead to new or strengthened indigenous institutions basic to a more modern civil society and facilitate their integration with government efforts.

8.   Finally, we believe that resources *currently exist* to improve pastoralists' lives under many local circumstances *if* mechanisms for their intersectoral use are encouraged.   We see particularly important needs for donors to strengthen all existing mechanisms which would facilitate IC directed toward pastoral outreach.   Ultimately, much of the funding for achieving optimal balance states between tradition and modernization must be generated by pastoralists themselves--and no doubt through their livestock.   However, many donor attempts in the past to generate development capital within pastoral areas have been excessively driven by ulterior (political, ideological, economic and disciplinary) motives which usually do not spring from, much less represent, or achieve the support of pastoral peoples.

## NOTES

1. Such a history, where it occurred, often reflected disease situations that seriously thwarted development or maintenance of viable animal industries.   Thus, meeting those primary needs of keeping food, fiber, draft and communications animals alive and functioning reasonably well--which alone severely strained the limited resources of many veterinary institutions for many years--necessarily set their priorities (which now are undergoing major reordering). Not commonly enough recalled today is that successes in those high-priority areas rapidly created a situation wherein, until the end of World War I, two meat-packing (and exporting) companies ranked among the five largest companies in the United States! Later, this more restricted view of their field rendered even more grave within such countries a severe "midlife crisis," with consequent loss of confidence and momentum, experienced by the veterinary profession globally as the result of a  "one-two punch" dealt it during the 1920s and 1930s. Those blows were (1) very rapid replacement of horse-ox power in the North by the internal combustion engine and (2) the global economic depression and its devasting effects upon all of agriculture (for fuller discussion see Schwabe, 1984b).

2. Not only have there been moves by some donors to subordinate the African continent's longer established livestock-related services to general agricultural services, but to so restrictively define veterinary science as to confine veterinarians' purview entirely to animal diseases (as veterinary *medicine* very narrowly perceived), with all other production and reproduction-related aspects of domestic animal/veterinary science the purviews of agriculturalists who lack veterinary qualifications.   Integrated plant-animal services may make good sense in countries where mostly sedentary farmers produce both plants and animals or where animals may be major power sources for plant agriculture. However, animal resources no doubt fully justifies a separate ministry in countries where it is a major contributor to the rural or national economy.

As an example of moves to restrictively define veterinary services, Leonard (1991: 159-160) recounted how in 1969 the animal extension services of Kenya were removed from the prior jurisdiction of veterinary services and placed under a separate Animal Husbandry Division within the Department of Agriculture "where it was a neglected stepchild." Then, following Kalinjin pastoralist Daniel arap Moi's succession to the Kenyan presidency in 1978, the Animal Husbandry and Range Management divisions of the Department of Agriculture were combined with the Department of Veterinary Services as a separate Ministry of Livestock Development under the former director of veterinary services. Leonard (1991: 178) noted that "the new ministry did not do well, however. . . . [Among other things] no one could get the cooperation from Animal Husbandry that was necessary to create a meaningful extension program and so an opportunity for major donor support in this area was lost." Some of these same problems have been alluded to also by S. Sandford (1983: 195-196).

3. There have been less direct hints that a central veterinary role is at least partially perceived within governmental circles in some pastoral areas of Africa. As examples in the southern Sudan, a veterinarian was founding dean of the University of Juba's College of Natural Resources and Environmental Studies and another served later as that university's Vice-Chancellor (overall academic head, in the British sense).

4. Veterinary science thus has represented globally a fairly equitable historical balance between advantages realizable from centrally planned government-sponsored efforts and others which respond on a fee-for-services basis to demands of the marketplace.

5. European rural power then and urban as well as rural transport were almost totally dependent on animals.

6. Many Christian and Islamic missions throughout Africa are currently involved in development-related activities, especially in health and food areas, and some are willing to interdigitate those with other aspects of IC.

7. Hirnquist was one of the foreign students sponsored by nine different governments to attend the two original French veterinary schools in their first few years.

8. Even in capitalist countries like the United States, about 20% of veterinarians work full-time under some branch of government, national, state or local.

9. The sparse Northern Territory of Australia was once governed by one of Australasia's outstanding veterinary pioneers, John Gilruth (also cofounding director of New Zealand's national public health service).

10. The situation provoking creation of separate schools of public health, a movement encouraged globally and supported initially principally by the Rockefeller Foundation (and necessitated by worldwide neglect of preventive, population and environmental aspects of medicine by existing medical faculties), has never existed within faculties of veterinary science.

11. In contrast, the prevailing theory of disease causality in human medicine became internal imbalances of the "humors." Contagion began to be recognized in human medicine and quarantines were instituted in the 15th and 16th centuries.

12. While these and other pioneers in creating the Microbiological Revolution were physicians, veterinarians and other scientists (e.g., Pasteur), their research arena-- in so far as basic discoveries were concerned--was largely the subfield of veterinary medicine (Schwabe, 1978a, 1984b).

13. The concept that certain infectious microorganisms can be transmitted by arthropods (one of the major breakthroughs of the Microbiological Revolution) was first enunciated and demonstrated within the fledgling federal veterinary service of the United States for tick transmission of bovine piroplasmosis (Texas fever).

14. Beside whooping cough, other killed bacterins have been used to prevent typhoid fever, cholera and plague.

15. Nicely, Schofield's own life was saved by dicoumerol when he suffered a heart attack in San Francisco.

16. While principal governmental veterinary services are usually attached to agriculture, others are independent branches of government and, in some countries, all veterinary services are located in the Health Ministry, less often in the Ministry of Interior. Moreover, a number of countries also have an independent veterinary corps within the military and veterinarians commonly serve within organizations concerned with environmental quality (Schwabe, 1984b: 501-608).

17. These problems have been so critical that we know of instances of a Provincial Commissioner having to personally request and then himself physically transport needles and syringes from Khartoum when he was in the national capital on other business. Allotments of petrol for each provincial department's use were sometimes made *daily* by the Provincial Commissioner (Governor) himself or his Executive Deputy.

18. It and the veterinary laboratories of the U.S. Bureau of Animal Industry, established by Salmon, can be said to have been the only non-European institutions to have participated broadly and germinally in genesis of the Microbiological Revolution. It was many years before South Africa had any human medical research counterpart of Onderstepoort.

19. In 1961 the Rockefeller Foundation also began a program of coordinated assistance to the veterinary faculty of the University of Nairobi (which was then still part of Uganda's Makerere University College), also adjacent to ILRAD, which involved cooperation of several other veterinary faculties in Europe and the United States.

20. As this book was being completed, plans were in the offing to better coordinate the work of ILRAD and ILCA.

21. In the agricultural research sphere overall is the Special Program for African Agricultural Research (SPAAR) based at the World Bank but including representatives of 22 other donor organizations to agricultural aspects of development in sub-Saharan Africa. This linkage was established in 1985. An older coordinating body is the Consultative Group for International Agricultural Research (CGIAR) concerned with management and funding of 16 international agricultural research centers including ILCA and ILRAD. Its sphere is, of course, broader than Africa. It grew out of the Rockefeller Foundation-inspired "Green Revolution" and international grain research

centers associated with the Foundation. Today CGIAR includes representatives from about 40 countries, foundations and international agencies. A newer organization which brings together some donor groups, progressive national leadership and others is the Global Coalition for Africa.

# 7

---

# IMPLEMENTING INTERSECTORAL COOPERATION FOR LOCAL ACTIONS

Necessity is the mother of invention.

R. Franck North, 1694

It is time to rethink animal health delivery to nomadic and transhumant livestock populations . . . to make programs sustainable by building on multiple local initiatives.

Albert Sollod and Chip Stem, 1991

Traditional pastoral societies and their organizations are often . . . multipurpose.

Stephen Sandford, 1983

The proposals for local actions we outline now are intended to provide some basic amenities to Africa's more than 30 million *unusually hard-to-reach* pastoralists within prevailing budgetary and other constraints. That italicized phrase identifies, in our minds, the most vital element of thinking required with respect to pastoral development in contrast to development among rural sedentary peoples--namely, that the hardest and most expensive thing to do is simply to reach pastoralists for any purpose at all. Financial plus general and local transport constraints, so prominent in much of Africa, become monumental when it comes to serving pastoral communities. Therefore, let us state more concisely reasons pastoral communities in Africa have suffered major neglect in provision of public services. One has been their lack of political empowerment, reflecting in part greater ethnic affinity of politicians with sedentary peoples, plus a general prourban educational bias. Another has been the influence of "tragedy of the commons" beliefs among Northern development agents and national leaderships they influence. The third, which we pursue mostly now, has been cost. Service provision to pastoral communities implies much greater start-up or indirect costs than to sedentary communities, the major component of which is transportation.[1] When public funds are scarce, politicians get a much higher return from investments in sedentary communities where indirect costs are relatively low and thus marginal investments are more likely to yield tangible benefits to constituents.

We are convinced, however, that that need not mean these peoples continue to be deprived of basic amenities. What it does mean is that, *when pastoral families can be reached, absolutely maximum use must be made of each visit.* This is what we propose in the form of local intersectoral cooperation. We believe that bringing not only high-priority veterinary services to pastoralists--but also making available to them some rudimentary human health benefits and other very basic amenities like water--are goals which would not prove impossible under many present African conditions (barring wars). But to achieve them *on a sustainable basis* will definitely require doing things that are rarely tried because of a variety of professional and disciplinary "turf" considerations and other vested interests or precedents, including unnecessary rigidity in matters of local budgetary controls and sharing of scarce resources. New thinking is required in all regards. For success under such near-emergency circumstances as are the norm in much of pastoral Africa, portions of Northern administrative theory must give way to more flexibly implemented and opportunistic efforts. The aim should be to eliminate *locally* all avoidable redundancies in existing agencies' functions (not just those of governmental agencies, but of NGOs as well), with active sharing to the extents practical of all potentially multiuse facilities, personnel and routines. Achieving this will require ad hoc efforts that cannot be generalized but must be approached locally by persons alert to their possibilities (*and encouraged to take advantage of them*). We shall supply examples. Although particular needs will vary from place to place and time to time, successes will reflect in considerable measure the qualities and capabilties of individual persons within particular local situations. For, what succeeds here may not succeed there, and what will not work now, may work later on. The main point of our proposals is to remain flexible, keep an eye on the prize--and try. Of considerable importance is that this opportunistic approach is precisely that to which pastoralists are accustomed.

Our ideas for local actions are quite simple ones with just four principal components. The first is to use, for actually reaching pastoralists where they are, the currently most successful and logical vehicle, namely veterinary services.  The second is to similarly stretch the maximum results out of all other existing resources through informedly instituted intersectoral cooperation (IC). To facilitate both of these we suggest means to merge time/place information available only locally with professionally provided information available only from the outside (see Chapter 8).  The third essential component is to make public service provision better reflect local preferences (i.e., demand for public goods).  The fourth is to actively encourage recipients of these services *to suggest what and how they are prepared to contribute to realizing them.*

While what we shall refer to in the first instance is the sharing of local publicly provided resources, we would see this philosophy and practice extending also to the resources of external NGOs, with the whole process working more and more through traditional pastoral institutions where these exist or other appropriately augmented and integrated institutions of civil society.[2] Envisaging smooth interfaces between these diverse components in particular circumstances will involve not only "bridging inputs" from educated pastoral elites and enlistment of traditional local pastoral leadership, but also indicates a need for sensitive inputs by public administration advisors and other outsiders prepared to accept this challenge.

Under such constrained circumstances as exist within pastoralist Africa, we believe that decentralization of many responsibilities within the several public sectors is a vital concomitant.  We will discuss in Chapter 8 areas for decentralization within our services delivery vehicle per se.

## ACCESS AND ACCEPTANCE: UNIQUE VETERINARY KEYS TO IMPLEMENTING INTERSECTORAL INTERVENTIONS

Underlying our proposals is the too-little-considered fact elaborated in Chapter 6 that veterinary services are currently the branch of government in Africa which reaches out to pastoralists most dependably (and, in many circumstances, is the only service which even attempts to).  To provide enough detail about how what we propose might function in practice, we have taken note in Chapter 6 that, as elsewhere, veterinary services in Africa are organized as *rural* service networks which, in most countries, have permanent physical bases at the district level for *mobile grassroots contacts with individual livestock owners, including migratory families, where they and their animals actually live.*  Those district-based services are now usually staffed by at least one university graduate in veterinary science, plus various paraveterinary auxiliaries.  For current vaccination campaigns and future veterinary programs to succeed, they *must* remain in periodic contact with a high proportion of the livestock populations at risk.  Veterinary services have already invested heavily in those indirect inputs as essential components of their highest priority efforts. By their cooperating intersectorally (i.e., sharing these resources), it would become feasible (cost-beneficial) to provide other services to pastoralists.

Such facts provide the first of the three compelling arguments for "piggy-backing" other services upon this existing veterinary outreach vehicle. The second argument is the basic relevance of veterinary services to pastoral peoples (Chapters 4 and 6) and the fact that it is undoubtedly their number one felt need or demand.[3]   Therefore, bypassing veterinary services or attempting to force pastoralists to accept other services first (Chapter 5) could be a sure prescription for continued failures in development efforts. The third argument is that veterinary services already enjoy the confidence of pastoral peoples.  As a result, local populations are more likely to communicate their preferences to veterinary personnel than to other outsiders, thus increasing the probability of sustaining particular service efforts.

As we also have pointed out, in some places like the southern Sudan even the highest priority veterinary objectives have not yet been realized.  Where such relative failures have occurred in the past, however, it has usually not been from lack of technical know-how but a pathetic compounding of the old English nursery rhyme's "for want of a horseshoe nail . . . the kingdom was lost." In large part, such frustrating impediments to local success--like essential 4-wheel-drive vehicles in need of minor repairs--reflect general infrastructural failures at that level, including the present necessity that veterinary services, *like every other service sector,* now are much too often put almost entirely on their own resources for absolutely everything. Our proposals aim to help remedy that major problem at the local level.  The most relevant point to grasp from this is that veterinary services in most pastoral areas of Africa, *totally on their own,* with only financing currently available from national and more local sources, have often not been able to sustainably realize even these primary aims so important to pastoralists, and the nation, to say nothing of extending to pastoralists other of the valuable services of which veterinary science is technically capable.  So veterinary services themselves need help to succeed in their national and continental objectives in Africa.  A corollary to this is that, *because* veterinary services now have uniquely important things to offer to pastoral development efforts overall, they should expect to gain in return from human health, water resources, land resources, educational and other governmental sectors some of the help they need to succeed with their own programs. We shall provide illustrations of ways that might work with an end result that, at relatively small marginal cost, other previously nonexistent services might be made available to pastoral peoples.

In an economic sense, we are making essentially a natural monopoly argument for an existing (though imperfect) veterinary outreach vehicle to very-hard-to-reach pastoralists in Africa.  But, rather than there being a large capital outlay to launch various service operations (as would be the case in building a railroad or highway), the high access costs to reach pastoralists locally would decrease as the scope of service production dependent upon it increases.  In economic terms, this implies that marginal costs will decrease also--that is, that it will become relatively less expensive to "produce an extra unit" of services as their overall scope increases.  Some existing public-sector rigidities (conventions) are deterrents to such efficiency-enhancing intersectoral cooperation.

## REACHING PASTORALISTS WITH SERVICES

S. Sandford (1983: 52) suggested that a main development option in pastoral areas is whether organizations should be multipurpose or specialized. While he regards such as either/or propositions, rightly associates the former with existing discipline- or profession-based sectors of government (i.e., ministries) and believes that government departments have little incentive to assist in efforts within other departments, we think the latter need not necessarily be so.  What we advocate here is a flexible alternative strategy.  We propose a compromise to those possibilities whereby *already existing* (and highly precedented) specialist structures (governmental) and other nonspecialist structures (NGOs) are all built upon and enhanced through local IC--efforts which will tend to realize multipurpose results from service sectors that still remain customarily specialized. We propose not limiting that to the key initiative of a veterinary services delivery vehicle, but two-way IC *wherever* prospects exist.  To us, expecting that discipline- or profession-based departments of government can be induced to implement broader development goals under such minimalist circumstances as African pastoralism is a more realistic and affordable expectation than are Sandford's alternatives for pastoral development as either/or propositions.

In taking such actions, it is important to note that pastoralists already fully understand the logic and economies of multipurpose approaches and flexibly implemented opportunism *as a principal strategy.*  However, most veterinary outreach efforts--visits to pastoralists' cattle camps--until now have been largely single purpose. This is despite the fact that veterinary authorities elsewhere have had relevant experience in other contexts with stretching maximum use out of similarly difficult or expensive initiatives. For example, when it becomes necessary to determine some disease's prevalence in a wildlife population (a difficult, expensive and sometimes a species-threatening procedure), it is common practice, sometimes mandated, that not only as few animals as really needed are sampled, but that *as many additional or subsidiary projects/objects be joined to that primary project/object as possible* (and that, in any event, all body fluids and tissues harvested be shared and/or preserved for possible future research needs).  It is similar multipurpose objectives we propose here not only for veterinary services themselves, but for other forms of outreach they can facilitate.

Moreover, IC is no more a new concept within development circles than it is to veterinary science.  Intuitively attractive to planners, funding agencies, public administrators and legislators alike, IC strategies among existing governmental sectors have been urged often as the most cost effective ways to maximize returns from human, physical, logistical or other expensive and/or scarce resources. Especially has such an approach been visualized as a means to spread substantial capital costs for major physical facilities and to defray recurrent costs involved in supporting and supervising different outreach programs. Less often it has been seen as a way to provide scarce specialist personnel needed by more than one branch of government. Yet, for all its apparent appeal, these possibilities for IC have seldom been achieved with respect to our subject interests beyond serendipitous realization in a few situations of complementary results of independent efforts. In some instances what might appear at first as IC actually results in creating a *new* community development or rangelands sector, which henceforth competes for its *own* share of the pie.

Some of the main reasons that past IC has often not succeeded as intended include (1) no true *quid pro quo*, (2) lack of mutual trust among the specialists involved, (3) lack of ironclad guarantees that none of the cooperating programs would suffer unfairly, (4) unwillingness to give up some conveniences in exchange for advantages, (5) fears or actual instances of unfair distributions of credit or rewards for successes, (6) lack of adequate mechanisms to assure accountability and, most important we feel, (7) *their own situations did not appear to all parties involved as sufficiently dire so that they had no real chances for success unless they did cooperate.* We think this last criterion is fully met in the situation of African pastoral development and must be understood. Another problem is that, in our experience, cooperation across sectors has usually been visualized by outside planners or "generalist administrators" as something to be initiated and developed from the top down. We know of that succeeding, but only when a "key person" is in the right place at the right time (Schwabe, 1984b: 312). On the other hand, we believe that if the potential for practical *locally instituted* IC is to be realized, it must enjoy the support and encouragement of higher echelons in the involved sectors or, at the minimum, not be thwarted by them.

To reduce the negative influences of jealousies at higher levels of government, we believe that each facility or other resource that is to be shared locally should remain formally attached to the one sector already possessing it, or, in the cases of new resources provided by governments or donors, each should go to the most capable (or logical or convenient or precedented) technical/service sector, with IC proceeding from there. This assures that different sectors each have something useful to share *quid pro quo*. And, as in the case of our disbelief in the probabilities for success in pastoral Africa of large umbrella-type development authorities in place of established ministries or services, it is our belief that creation of totally separate common-pool facilities (whereby, for example, a *new* governmental sector is created to control all vehicles and drivers, etc.) rarely works locally as intended and may interfere with the smooth functioning of technical service programs at that level more than facilitate them. We personally have had very frustrating experiences with such separate agencies struggling to assert their own priorities for existence and support. In our view, such multiplication of sectors is far too formal and inflexible an approach for successful functioning under the kinds of minimal and exceedingly difficult circumstances faced by those who actually work "on the ground" in attempts to serve pastoral communities in Africa.

Though many of these constraints to implementing practical IC are manifest regardless of economic context, they may be more acute in areas experiencing poverty, which often are areas where different profession- or discipline-oriented ministries are fiercely competing with one another for the extremely limited funds available for all tasks. Yet we have evidence that, *at local levels*, this too may be surmountable. That is, if the spirit of development is permitted sufficient rein to occasionally triumph over bureaucratic letter, innovative *local* program directors can readily see opportunities for--and sometimes have succeeded in getting away with--practical informal assistance to one another. In our opinion, they should be commended and rewarded for doing that, for putting the achieving of results first.

As we illustrated for the southern Sudan in Chapters 5 and 6, this urgency of giving IC encouragement is underlined by realities of chronic money shortfalls. Most available revenues are being channeled to meet *existing* salary demands in such places, leaving little scope for funding an expanded labor force (however badly needed) or, far too commonly, even for implementation of the most basic programs that that specific branch of government is supposed to be carrying out. The recent Pritchard Committee report (1992: 112), in commenting upon the inadequacy of professional salaries in many African governmental services, mentioned in passing the desirability of exploring other incentives for public service and suggested that savings in personnel might be realized "if systems are streamlined and more pluralistic approaches are taken." Pluralistic approaches are precisely what we propose.

While our initial focus is upon quickly extending some basic civil amenities to the grassroots level of pastoral communities, we are aware that these measures could have broader implications ultimately. For, among these peoples who remain cutoff otherwise from outside influences and are virtually nonparticipatory in most aspects of national life, providing such a multipurpose development vehicle could be the key to their beginning integration within the mainstream of national life. Veterinary services, by already providing a "nose-in-the-tent" so to speak, could in the future facilitate overall attempts to engage these peoples, with their considerable human and other potential resources, within the affairs of the broader economy and nation. That will involve a second plan of actions introduced in Chapters 8 and 9.

Combatting zoonoses and food safety have been commented upon already as globally precedented routes for medical-veterinary IC. These provide two of the main foundations for modern veterinary public health (see Figure 7.1) and major need exists to extend these possibilities to Africa's pastoralists. Because the more immediate results we envisage will also require medical-veterinary cooperation, it is valuable to note that a type of *one-way* IC with respect to securing the services of useful professional personnel other than physicians is not new to the field of public health. Largely through the efforts of the Rockefeller Foundation (which funded the beginnings of schools of public health throughout the world during the first half of this century), the notion of a "public health team" came into prominence within governmental branches of medicine in some countries, and many governmental physicians in the Third World have been exposed to such ideas (at least in theory) over the last four or so decades. That is, although it was understood by everyone that overall public health efforts would ordinarily be led by physicians, other talents and know-ledge not usually possessed by physicians were also required for many measures aimed at protection of *populations* against specific disease risks. As we indicated in Chapter 6, veterinarians were from the start one such nonphysician group. However, one characteristic of most medically initiated IC, as in health education efforts, is that they are *one-way efforts*--that is, other sectors are asked to help the medical/public health sector reach *its* goals. There has been little *quid pro quo*, yet in our opinion that is clearly the key to successful local IC. It cannot all flow one way or turf or cost considerations will become prominent and people will not cooperate.

Those things being said, let us turn to some specific prospects for inter-sectoral sharing and cooperation intended to improve conditions of life within Africa's pastoral communities.

## INTERSECTORAL COOPERATION WITHIN THE SOUTHERN SUDAN

A WHO/UNICEF mission to evaluate progress of the primary health care (PHC) program in the Sudan noted that it has been "undertaken in a narrow way in which PHC was seen as a special programme within the health sector. . . [and for which there was] *little effective involvement of [other] health related sectors*" (WHO/UNICEF, 1982, italics added). As mentioned in Chapter 5, a planning document on PHC for the southern Sudan specifically (Lolik et al., 1976) failed to mention the programs and resources of veterinary services or even the preponderant importance there of man-animal relations.

The cornerstone program of that overall WHO/UNICEF PHC initiative is an attempt to immunize all children against six readily preventable infectious diseases. Yet, although a majority of southern Sudanese are transhumant pastoralists, outreach to them from sedentary health units in the several district

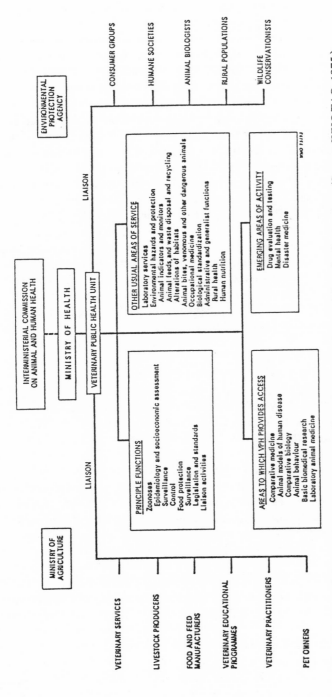

**Figure 7.1. Intersectoral linkages among veterinary science, public health and other sectors.** (Source: WHO/FAO, 1975.)

towns has not even been considered. In fact, just reaching a reasonable proportion of the southern region's townspeople has represented an heroic effort (because, for one thing, it took a major educational campaign to convince many urbanites that vaccination was a good thing[4]). Recent health manpower projections for the southern region's Bahr el Ghazal province alone (AMREF 1984: 31) warn of severe shortages in primary health care personnel (including a deficit of over 400 community health workers and 500 midwives) *if* the provincial medical department should continue to attempt to provide such most basic frontline services wholly on its own. Under forseeable circumstances, assuming settlement of the civil war, it would be impossible to visualize such an expenditure increase for health services.

However, a major educational effort about the merits of vaccination has *already* been accomplished among pastoralists, a situation referred to by anthropologist Jean Buxton (1973) in her study of health beliefs and practices among Sudanese pastoralists--namely, that "herders who have themselves never visited a government dressing station, still less a hospital bring their cattle for inoculation." That substantial accomplishment could be capitalized upon readily by public health officials if the veterinary sector could be induced to share its acceptance and rapport with pastoralists, and cooperate with human immunization efforts. That is an IC initiative that literally cries out for implementation throughout all of pastoral Africa.

### Joint Medical-Veterinary Vaccination Programs

Thus, although WHO's Expanded Programme of Immunization (EPI) was launched by the 27th World Health Assembly in 1974, virtually no note has been taken since then by public health authorities anywhere in pastoral Africa that considerably older veterinary immunization programs have aimed to protect Africa's enormous cattle wealth from similarly avoidable risks *by identical means.* And, beyond EPI's laudable goal of protecting many *individual* children, veterinary programs have the more far-reaching goal of actually eradicating certain cattle diseases. How, in addition to this promotional help about the value of vaccination per se, could medical/veterinary IC assist both of these important vaccination programs to succeed?

*Cold Chains.* One of the greatest technical difficulties in establishing and maintaining vaccination programs involves properly functioning cold chains, which are systems to keep heat-labile vaccines under adequate refrigeration from their points of manufacture to their administration in the field. That this is a major problem in Africa even under urban and settled rural conditions was clearly indicated in Ghanaian experiences that EPI "vaccination was not being achieved on a wide scale because of failings in the cold chain at most of the stations" (Agadzi and Obuobi, 1986). Yet veterinary cold chains have had to incorporate *additional mobile capabilities* to reach far beyond such population centers. For someone not experienced with pastoral conditions in much of Africa, it is impossible to imagine difficulties involved in this task. It includes laboriously making small quantities of ice in kerosene-powered or small diesel electric generator-powered deep freezers, and transporting chilled vaccines in portable ice chests (or battery-operated refrigerators) from district veterinary cold depots overland for many miles of completely roadless terrain to individual cattle camps, where they are administered to cattle which must be individually caught and restrained. Moreover, the kerosene or diesel fuel for these freezers (and for vehicles) must itself be transported to these district-level cold depots in drums over primitive roads which may be seasonally impassable even by 4-wheel-drive trucks or Land Rover-type vehicles.

Partially because of the cost of developing such cold chains for vaccination programs, and these difficulties in maintaining them, the WHO/FAO Expert Committee on Bacterial and Viral Zoonoses (1982) recommended (Schwabe, 1981) that *joint* operation by health and veterinary services of cold chains to rural areas be considered by many countries. But, to our knowledge, the first deliberate efforts to initiate this new form of development IC have taken place under the near emergency conditions of the pastoral southern Sudan.

Beginning in 1984 an existing provincial veterinary cold depot in Wau, capital town of Bahr el Ghazal province, began to be shared with the provincial medical department. From that foundation of locally instigated voluntary one-directional IC, a UNICEF team negotiated an agreement to make this cooperation permanent and to broadly extend it. The key to that agreement was that *equally* valuable benefits would accrue to both departments' programs. In return for veterinary cooperation in maintaining viable vaccines, the EPI program would offer reciprocal assistance to the less-well-financed veterinary services at little additional cost to itself: (1) use of a regular UNICEF plane service for transport of veterinary vaccines from Khartoum to Wau, (2) maintenance services for laid-up veterinary 4-wheel-drive vehicles in another UNICEF-supported repair shop and (3) repairs and assistance in maintenance of veterinary department district-level kerosene deep freezers (which would also be shared by EPI thenceforth). EPI-supplied equipment, including generators, would back-up existing veterinary cold-chain equipment at all levels. In each instance this proffered reciprocity helped the veterinary department beyond some impasses to the successful conclusion of its own program--for example, that it had just before that lost 35,000 doses of rinderpest vaccine for lack of a replacement wick for the kerosene-powered deep freeze in a district veterinary office. This was typical of the kind of "for want of a nail" situations far too frequently encountered in pastoral Africa.

This initiative is worth considering in greater detail because it illustrates well the practicality of our proposals.[5] By the summer of 1984 substantial progress had been made by UNICEF in developing public support for, and initiating EPI (and oral rehydration) programs for children within the southern Sudanese regional capital of Juba.  In addition, UNICEF supported some rural outreach among sedentary agricultural populations by NGOs such as Norwegian Church Aid, German Medical Team and another NGO called ACROSS.  However, another matter altogether was any seeming prospect of reaching the vast bulk of southern Sudanese children, those of transhumant pastoralists who made up almost the entire populations in five of the six large provinces of the region.   Therefore, discussions were undertaken with UNICEF country staff about possibilities for implementation of recommendations of the Joint WHO/FAO Expert Committee on Bacterial and Viral Zoonoses (WHO/FAO, 1982) that IC between veterinary and medical services be extended beyond traditional areas like food safety and rabies control to such costly and difficult to provide facilities as cold chains and diagnostic laboratories.  To that end a two-person UNICEF team[6] undertook an exploratory visit to Wau, ostensibly to assess recent efforts to launch EPI within the town itself, but actually to "test the waters" concerning possibilities for provincial IC.

Totally unexpectedly, the team found that such IC *had already been partially implemented* by *local* officials in response to an emergency situation (unbeknownst to UNICEF or these services' own higher authorities).  Moreover, that action was taken without knowledge on the part of local officials of the WHO/FAO Expert Committee's 1982 recommendation *or* the discussions that had just been held within UNICEF.  To explain further, Wau, population and administrative center for the southwestern Sudan, had been without electric power for the previous three weeks.  Moreover, a backup diesel generator just installed by UNICEF in the new provincial cold depot (in a house owned by the medical department) failed and, in any event, the medical department had not stockpiled diesel fuel for its use.

However, all recently supplied EPI vaccines had been saved by immediately transferring them, upon the provincial Veterinary Services' approval, to its own well-established provincial cold depot. That serendipitous event during an emergency situation dramatically indicates some of the possibilities *normally available* locally for meaningful IC, a striking instance of necessity proving the mother of invention, *if* local officials are resourceful and nothing gets in their way.[7]  The UNICEF team soon learned that this veterinary cold depot was still functioning because it had a working standby diesel generator and veterinary services had stockpiled diesel fuel for such commonly encountered emergencies.  The team also observed that this veterinary facility was by far the superior of the two.  It occupied two air conditioned rooms of a modern diagnostic laboratory block which had been constructed and operated initially by the German GTZ veterinary disease survey. At the time of the UNICEF team's visit it was also storing, besides the salvaged EPI vaccines for children, 350,000 doses of rinderpest vaccine intended for that year's annual cattle vaccination effort.

In fact, the UNICEF team learned that a precedent for this veterinary assistance to the provincial directorate of health services *already existed* prior to the introduction of EPI. That is, the medical department's only vaccine use before then had been human postexposure rabies treatment (the Pasteur treatment).[8] Since the medical department lacked deep freeze facilities then, rabies vaccines for human use had always been stored by the veterinary service. Moreover, the veterinary depot was logging in and out these human vaccines just as they did their own. Thus, *one-way* IC between the human and veterinary health services was already ongoing *at the local level* in Bahr el Ghazal, but one that was not recognized, much less fostered, by the initial planners of EPI in the southern Sudan, nor by the two concerned national or regional ministries.

Next, it was ascertained by the UNICEF team, through exploratory visits with the directors of both provincial services, that (1) this current and past veterinary services assistance was much appreciated by the provincial health director (who was of Dinka origin) and (2) the latter and his associates would be most interested in exploring augmented longer-term cooperation in EPI with the provincial veterinary director.   For his part, the veterinary director reported that (1) his department's efforts against bovine rinderpest and pleuropneumonia *were themselves being thwarted seriously* by interruptions of transport links to Khartoum and (2) there was a lack of spare parts (or service personnel) for the veterinary department's *district-level* kerosene deep freezers. Moreover, some veterinary vaccination teams had been unable to get out into the field at all during that current dry season because a number of their 4-wheel-drive vehicles required repairs and the veterinary service, since the termination of foreign assistance, lacked access to repair facilities. Therefore, the provincial veterinary director was amenable to expanded veterinary cold chain and other assistance to EPI *if* future cooperation could become *two-way*, that is, that IC henceforth be mutually beneficial to the programs of both services.  He sought assurance that the interests of the better-financed human health efforts would in no way overwhelm or prejudice the veterinary programs themselves. Eagerness of both directors to cooperate along those lines was expressed in the report of a joint meeting between them (plus other key persons in each service) and the visiting UNICEF team. The following areas of cooperation were explored and authorized for implementation:

1. The provincial veterinary cold depot would remain veterinary property but would henceforth serve as the common main veterinary-EPI depot for the province. The existing EPI generator would be repaired by EPI and transferred there as an additional backup, together with EPI's own freezers, refrigerators, spare parts and accessories, to all of which EPI would retain title. Two points should be especially noted.  The first reflects the trade-off EPI was willing to make to gain an added measure of assurance that vaccine potency would be safeguarded by storage in an established cold room, through accepting the relative loss of convenience in not having a separate cold depot located on its

own compound.  The second reflects the trade-off the veterinary services were willing to make to gain enhanced confidence that, under EPI supervision, their own vaccines also would not spoil, by relinquishing sole control over their own vaccine storage facility and vaccine handling.  Both directorates recognized that the EPI cold-chain officer, who had received WHO-supported training in monitoring vaccine storage, should henceforth have overall maintenance responsibility for both lots of vaccines, human and cattle.  Thus it became evident that day-to-day management of the jointly used cold-chain facility would require the establishment of a new regimen that provided for efficient operations while ensuring adequate safety and accountability.

2. As an immediate gesture of its encouragement of these proposals, UNICEF agreed to assist thenceforth in the delivery of the veterinary department's vaccines from Khartoum to Wau via weekly intra-Sudan flights of the UNICEF aircraft.

While these initial steps for cooperation were being implemented, several medium- to longer-term areas for additional cooperation were also explored and reported favorably by the two directors.  These included: (a) Identification of suitable personnel from *both* departments to undergo training in refrigeration maintenance under UNICEF sponsorship and equipping these persons with the necessary tools and spare parts; (b) Extension of this cooperation *to the district level* through repair, replacement or backup by EPI of several of the veterinary department's seven kerosene freezers; (c) Exploration of future possibilities for EPI teams (community health workers and, possibly, traditional birth attendants) *to accompany existing veterinary vaccination teams into remote pastoral home bases and cattle camps--that is, to undertake single joint visits to vaccinate people and their cattle.*  The future ideal of forming versatile multipurpose teams capable of administering vaccinations to *both* children and cattle, and certain clinical functions, was also discussed.

Information on this intersectoral cold-chain and vaccination initiative in Bahr el Ghazal was disseminated within the Sudan and when extension of the renewed Sudanese civil war to the area around Wau late in 1984 interrupted temporarily almost all services delivery there, implementation of vaccination IC was attempted elsewhere.

*Further Applications During the Mandari Emergency.*  As a result, ACCOMPLISH (Action Committee for the Promotion of Local Initiative in Self-Help), a local NGO in Terekeka District of Eastern Equatoria province, adopted this approach. ACCOMPLISH had been established initially as a community-based paravet program to facilitate animal health care in the province's Mandari area (Almond, 1991).  Its activities included vaccination of cattle against rinderpest, hemorrhagic septicemia and CBPP. This local response underscored the continuing desire for veterinary services among pastoralists even under conditions of wartime extremis. Rebel groups fighting in the area allowed these paravet teams to carry out this job (as they also did for governmental veterinary teams elsewhere in the South, though access was denied all other representatives of the government).

Thus, the ground had been prepared for an IC vaccination initiative by ACCOMPLISH. Its immediate impetus was simultaneous outbreaks in late 1986 of measles and rinderpest in Terekeka District. This joint medical-veterinary effort, with assistance from UNICEF and OXFAM, succeeded in containing both epidemics and, thus, demonstrated dramatically to Mandari that *human* vaccination was as desirable as bovine vaccination. Again, extension of the civil war temporarily interrupted continuation and broadening of this joint program, though plans were formulated to do that when conditions permitted. But, in the meantime, similar IC efforts were possible among Mandari displaced by fighting to Jebel Kujur and three cattle camps outside of Juba.

An on-the-spot evaluation of that latter effort was undertaken by UNICEF health economist C. L. Schwabe in the summer of 1989 (during an emergency mission primarily to establish Project Lifeline, a program of survival assistance to the southern Sudan's then much-suffering population). To summarize sections of Schwabe's unpublished report on ACCOMPLISH's first 11 months of IC vaccination efforts, that program (using locally trained preliterate pastoralist women to vaccinate children and paravets to vaccinate cattle), fully immunized over 50% of pastoral children, considerably exceeding the Sudanese national average coverage during the *lifetime* of the EPI program. At the same time, approximately 58% of Mandari cattle were immunized against both rinderpest and CBPP, again considerably exceeding the veterinary department's average level of coverage until then for the southern Sudan.

It was also envisaged (during and following the initial Wau discussions in 1984) that joint medical-veterinary vaccination team members serving pastoral populations might in the future receive basic training as health educators with the view to extending meaningful and unprecedented human health extension functions on a more general level to these otherwise inaccessible populations. Such an endeavor would reinforce and complement existing veterinary extension efforts and could aim at some jointly pursued high priority improvements in general environmental sanitation, human and livestock nutrition and recognition and reduction of zoonoses risks.

To recapitulate this local IC initiative as already demonstrated and/or envisioned within the southern Sudan, agreement between veterinary and human health services derived in the first instance from spontaneous efforts in facing an emergency, which was extended through UNICEF's encouragement, and development of a sense of mutual trust between veterinary and health personnel. This was realized through built-in assurances that the interests of neither party would suffer and both would share fully in the benefits of two-way cooperation. Such efforts illustrate not only how economically and scientifically attractive local IC could be in specific aspects of development, but that IC is readily implemented among officials familiar with local possibilities and constraints (and personally acquainted with one another). Under such conditions it is relatively easy to establish local linkages with counterparts in other governmental agencies.[9]    Official encouragement, facilitation and rewards should emanate from higher levels to all such efforts to break down barriers to individual program and overall development goals.

Deciding how to initiate the broadest-based IC possible in *any* national (and especially in any local) situation requires, first of all, a completely open mind about possibilities for cooperation (and about the potentials of individuals or groups) that are unfettered by turf considerations.  The eye must be kept constantly on the prize, which is provision in any ways possible of things that pastoral people most need, and, if not in the "preferred ways" perhaps, in ways that will still make them better off than they would be without such efforts, and affordably so.

In addition to possibilities throughout all of pastoral Africa for zoonoses control and joint immunization campaigns aimed at people and livestock, there are other important areas for potential medical-veterinary IC in support of pastoral development.  One of the most obvious, especially within such severely constrained situations financially, is to establish joint medical-veterinary diagnostic laboratories, as also recommended generally by the WHO/FAO Expert Committee on Bacterial and Viral Zoonoses (Schwabe, 1981; WHO/FAO, 1982). That most attractive idea has also been little considered *officially* within Africa (other than in some few countries with respect to trypanosomiasis control). Diagnostic laboratories are the essential but very expensive backup facilities required for almost all successful programs in human or veterinary medicine, both to provide confirmations to clinical diagnoses, and in support of most disease intelligence activities within populations (Chapters 4 and 8).

### Shared Diagnostic Laboratories

Over 30 years ago the WHO Expert Committee on Health Laboratory Services (WHO, 1962), in noting that "many infectious diseases . . . affect both man and animals, and . . . [that] the disciplines, particularly in the laboratory, of medicine and veterinary science are similar," concluded that "it is obviously of great importance from the purely health and economical point of view that close collaboration and coordination should be fostered between the health laboratory and veterinary laboratory services." Therefore, one of its recommendations--*for implementation everywhere*--was for selected laboratories of veterinary services to be attached to, or, when indicated, integrated with health laboratories. It is long past time to begin to implement throughout Africa such recommendations reiterated by the 1982 WHO/FAO Expert Committee and also made earlier by other expert bodies (WHO/ILO, 1962; WHO/FAO, 1975). Of special relevance to pastoral Africa, these suggestions for combining often redundant support services for human and veterinary medicine have been made in the interests both of economy *and of improved services.*

In contrast to mobile program access to pastoralists considered in connection with vaccination efforts, this sharing of diagnostic laboratory buildings, equipment and personnel between health and veterinary services *can, of course, proceed in either or both directions, depending upon local circumstances.* At the time of the UNICEF team's visit to Wau in 1984, the provincial health services hospital there had no trained technicians and rarely performed even the simplest examinations for parasites. In contrast, the Wau veterinary laboratory possessed bacteriological and parasitological capabilities and specialist services of a southern Sudanese veterinarian with a British graduate degree in microbiology.

What would be the purely scientific merits of such recommendations? In Chapter 4 we considered how difficult it often is to make a correct diagnosis in veterinary medicine and how this may not be possible without laboratory/pathological and/or epidemiological backup. This is equally true of human medicine. Such laboratory and epidemiological backups depend upon qualified professional and technical personnel who are scarce everywhere. Yet, unless medical and veterinary efforts are based upon accurate diagnoses, *much of curative or preventive (human or veterinary) medicine is of absolutely no avail and a total waste of money.* Unfortunately, that is a too common situation within both fields, one often unrecognized by many generalist planners or development funding agencies. National authorities in Africa have often failed to recognize, moreover, that few ordinary medical or veterinary graduates anywhere are qualified currently to perform more than the most routine laboratory procedures and therefore cannot be assigned at random to such laboratory tasks (see Chapter 9). Politically appointed administrators in the Third World also have been prone to not use effectively scarce laboratory personnel they already possess, sometimes by not recognizing the very high skills these individuals have gained through great expenditures of time, money and personal effort. Alternatively, bureaucrats prematurely promote such badly needed individuals into purely administrative positions, thus removing them from their areas of scientific expertise and critical need.[10] The "Peter Principle" (people tend to rise to their level of incompetence) thus runs rampant at enormous cost.

We and others (see Chapters 8 and 9; Pritchard et al., 1992) regard improved diagnostic capabilities, especially at the field level, to be the most vital element for improving veterinary services per se. This is particularly so if they are to serve the functions that precedents elsewhere show they can and, additionally, act as a vehicle or facilitator for other aspects of development. Yet, despite all that recommends them, in only a few instances known to us have joint medical-veterinary laboratories been deliberately established locally anywhere in the Third World. One was created in Ensenada, Mexico (Panico, 1986), and others were stated by WHO/FAO (1982: 38) to exist in San Rafael, Mexico, and Dumaguete City, Philippines. It is especially ironic that this sensible idea has yet to see formal implementation in many local or regional diagnostic laboratories[11] in the Third World, although some of the world's *premier national diagnostic referral and research laboratories* in the North--like the Pasteur Institute of Paris and the U.S. Centers for Disease Control and Prevention (CDC) in Atlanta--have always been staffed by veterinarians (see Table 6.1) as well as physicians and other biomedical scientists.

However, here again, as with cold-chain IC in Wau, even our own limited experiences indicate that *one-way* diagnostic laboratory IC *already* is being implemented locally and without higher authority in some places. Thus, in Juba the central veterinary laboratory not only provides diagnostic assistance to the University of Juba's Student Health Service, but performs urinalyses and bacteriological isolations for the Regional Hospital for the southern Sudan. In Central Somalia also, at the administrative center of Beletweyne, a GTZ veterinary team provided laboratory services to the area hospital which lacked any such facilities (K.-H. Zessin, personal communication). What is needed, of course, is to encourage and facilitate such sharing routinely throughout pastoral Africa *and make it generally two-way.* Let us now consider other IC possibilities outside of the human health sphere.

### Water Resources Maintenance

During the 1984 meetings in Wau between the UNICEF exploratory team and the provincial medical and veterinary directors, possibilities were discussed that a well-drilling project being implemented by the provincial Rural Water Department could also benefit from local IC. Specifically, it was felt that veterinary field teams might facilitate its poor hand-pump maintenance effort by, at the least, reporting from pastoralists to Rural Water about pump breakdowns and similar water-point problems. Beyond that, it was considered that veterinary vaccination teams might undertake some basic pump maintenance themselves. To be recalled in that connection is that surveys have shown that while boreholes are being drilled in pastoral Africa by many different governmental, NGO and private business agencies, most of this one-time effort has no follow-up and high proportions of water points created at considerable effort and expense soon cease to function. It was believed that Rural Water could also benefit from medical-veterinary IC in the development of its sanitation education component. In return, cattle immunization programs could benefit from access to Rural Water's existing but underused vehicle maintenance facility. A further possibility would be shared use of the water department's one-time mobile outreach into some pastoral areas for borehole drilling. Joint medical-veterinary teams might ride to these waterpoint sites in Rural Water's trucks as well as their own vehicles. In some cases it was felt that one visit might accomplish all three sectors' objectives.

Additionally, within some pastoral areas of Africa, vats for dipping cattle in acaricides (to kill ticks) have been located at watering points where pastoralists normally congregate. Under future circumstances where local IC was being generally encouraged and supported, such water points could become even more multipurpose foci for pastoralist/service-sector interactions, including screening for diseases, treating human and animal patients, as well as for extension-type demonstrations over these and a further range of subject areas in which pastoralists have interests or needs--range management, water sources and the like.

### Environmental, Economic and Other Monitoring

Some workers concerned with aspects of range and livestock development (Behnke et al., 1993) have urged long-term monitoring not only of rainfall and grass conditions, but soil erosion, livestock demographics and other important variables.  Implementation is largely conceived as *new* single-sector activities even in the absence of any existing field cadre or, in some instances, *any* governmental infrastructure.  But in Sollod's (1990, 1991) proposals for Early Drought Warning Systems (see Chapter 2), it was visualized that rainfall and pasture monitoring be carried out together with veterinary outreach efforts, as well as with investigations of local coping strategies of pastoral communities. Zessin (1991) indicated other advantages of linking epidemiological surveillance and analysis, an increasingly common basis for veterinary services delivery (see Chapter 8), and other data collection for econometric analyses of animal health and production, with such monitoring tasks.  Moreover, as suggested for veterinary diagnostic laboratories in Africa by Kenyon and Nour (1991), "because of the[ir] provincial distributions . . . and their involvement in data collection and disease reporting, it is also appropriate that they serve as data centers for [other] livestock . . . *[as well as] environmental resource information in the regions they serve*" (italics added).  Thus, various ideas are coming together, suggesting that IC in pastoral areas could not only facilitate intelligence for both veterinary and public health sectors, but also incorporate various aspects of environmental and economic monitoring of value to other sectors' programs.  While we shall consider practical implementation of *two-directional* pastoral information systems for those purposes and others in Chapter 8, we make preliminary mention of a portion of that here because these are activities that also might readily be "piggybacked" on the existing veterinary mobile outreach vehicle.

These several IC prospects surely do not exhaust ones that might be envisaged under particular local conditions, depending upon the expressed needs of pastoralists and more national priorities. For example, although a more remote two-way IC possibility, note should be taken of the increasing popularity of formal education among various groups of African pastoralists, and the difficult, surely inconvenient and costly necessity it entails for young people to be boarding students even in primary school, often at great distances from their families. Yet, among some pastoralists, ownership of less and less expensive battery-operated radios is increasingly observed.   Educational innovations among sedentary but isolated pastoral families using radio, as in the Australian Outback, may have similar possibilities for implementation among pastoral Africans, not only as means for reaching the young for formal educational programming, but of implementing veterinary, public health and other avenues of extension to adults, including as means to inform pastoralists of visits by veterinary or augmented veterinary-cum-other services teams to cattle camps, certain water points, cattle dipping vats or other central locations. It would not be hard to visualize reciprocal benefits of educational IC.

Thus, within this pastoral context of pervasive need and seemingly overwhelming constraints, there clearly exist a range of opportunities for ventures capable of benefitting from the economies and efficiencies generated through local intersectoral linkages.  We shall now attempt to answer another of the questions posed at the beginning of Chapter 6: would veterinary services in pastoral Africa be prepared to render such IC to other service sectors?

## WOULD VETERINARY SERVICES BE WILLING TO SERVE SUCH A FACILITATING ROLE?

Although "in development programs [in Africa], veterinary medicine has often been a prima donna" (Sollod et al., 1984), in our view the main key to veterinary service's willingness to lend its existing access to pastoralists to other governmental or NGO services (and to share its resources otherwise) is real *quid pro quo*. It will also depend upon establishing a sense of trust, especially assurances that veterinary interests will not suffer.  Mutual trust can be fostered by (1) the establishment of practical local intersectoral management structures for shared resources that provide necessary degrees of accountability while assuring enough independence for uninterrupted implementation of each sector's aims; (2) greater sharing of knowledge about each other's programs (their goals, methods of operation and constraints); (3) open-mindedness about the full range of cooperation possibilities which, as in the cases outlined, entails identifying areas of service delivery where different branches of government (and/or NGOs) are using identical, similar or complementary methods, have needs for similar resources or are pursuing parallel or complementary aims; and (4) relaxation of rigid notions of professional "territorial sovereignty" and other barriers to cross-professional and other cross-sectoral consultation and sharing.

As to accountability of officials under circumstances of local sharing of resources, we would hope that it would provide a challenge to public administrators interested in Third World development and that appropriately flexible guidelines could be envisaged which are no more encouraging of corruption and other irregularities than are operating procedures with which public administrators are more accustomed.

## NONGOVERNMENTAL AGENCIES AS INSTIGATORS OR FACILITATORS OF PASTORAL IC

Relationships among NGOs working in Africa, national agencies and bilateral and multilateral programs have sometimes been nonexistent and frequently poorly coordinated.  A uniquely valuable role of some NGOs has been recognized, however, especially with respect to trying unconventional approaches (Pritchard et al., 1992: 126), including those crossing sectoral lines. We have directed attention to creative IC roles in the southern Sudan of an NGO called ACCOMPLISH.

Our personal experiences with another NGO-based IC effort among the Turkana provide a second specific example of possibilities.  This involved a control program for the major plague of pastoralists globally, the parasitic zoonosis hydatid disease (see Chapter 4).  The history of disclosure of the world's highest rate of human hydatid cyst infection among the northern Turkana indicates how a very serious medical problem may afflict pastoralists for many years yet escape scientific disclosure because such people live largely beyond the reach of qualified medical observers. An NGO, the African Medical and Research Foundation (AMREF), became involved because, for many years, hydatid disease could be combatted only in individual patients by radical abdominal, thoracic or other surgery.  Most initial treatment efforts among Turkana were at a Catholic mission hospital established post-independence at the isolated administrative outpost of Lodwar.  Surgery was performed by physicians of the Nairobi-based Flying Doctor Service, the original branch of AMREF, which provided some emergency clinical services to isolated peoples throughout Kenya and neighboring countries. Surgical treatment was often unsuccessful, however, and, in any event, did nothing to decrease the risk of future infections in the afflicted population.  Eventually, AMREF also began a public health effort to *prevent* human infections. This was based upon an IC medical-veterinary approach originating in New Zealand and modified in Tasmania and Cyprus.[12]

This effort resulted almost entirely from the dogged determination of Igor Mann, a veterinary officer from the former colonial veterinary service who assumed Kenyan citizenship following independence.  Mann had distinguished himself during colonial times by being one of relatively few European veterinary officers devoted to the well-being of indigenous Kenyans.  Having established schools for African veterinary/livestock assistants and helped African livestock owners improve and market their products commercially, Mann insisted against most expert opinion that sufficient hydatid disease control to make an effort worthwhile would be forthcoming from a Turkana campaign employing lessons of prior initiatives among settled pastoralists.

That campaign (and an associated program of field research) has been carried out since 1983 by an international AMREF team based at the trading post of Lokichokio in extreme northwestern Kenya. Scientific cooperation was forthcoming from several outside groups. Control measures over an 9,000-square-km area were largely an intensive educational program with technical efforts directed toward dog registration, surveys for infected dogs, dog treatment and dog population reduction (Macpherson et al., 1984, 1986). This *single-purpose* attempt at service to Turkana pastoralists was possible because of substantial privately raised funding from the North, particularly from Germany. Nevertheless, it showed the potential for NGOs to play key development roles and also illustrated a type of IC zoonoses control program that could readily be grafted, more sustainably, and at considerably less cost, upon the multipurpose pastoral outreach mechanisms proposed here.

To this point we have outlined some possibilities for implementing the fourth point of our pastoral development proposals, its more unique facilitating aspect. We return now to its second key point, involvement of pastoralists.

## ASSURING PASTORALIST PARTICIPATION

Since Garrett Hardin's (1968) "tragedy of the commons" paper became required reading in some Northern social science curricula, the cascade of theoretical literature it and its variants provoked should have urgently recommended that commons management become one *field* research topic to explore in every instance of intended pastoral development. But Hardin's theory apparently proved so compelling on its face that the general truth of his pastoral situation argument remained essentially unchallenged until recently by field research or even case studies drawn from existing literature (Ostrom, 1990). As biologists, we are somewhat nonplussed. More conversant personally with some of the main currents of research and theory in sociobiology, we are aware that some of its students explore questions related to natural selection among animal species which display social characteristics, and some infer from these gene bases for such acquisitive behavior in people as free-riding.

Social scientists and sociobiologists who acknowledge higher levels of voluntary sharing or altruism than the family see it mostly as of two special cases: reciprocal altruism (including expectation of a payback in the future) or religious altruism (expectation of a payback in heaven, Marx's opiate of the masses). One way of looking upon the process of intersectoral cooperation we advocate is, of course, as reciprocal altruism. Margolis (1984) has postulated theoretical bases for linkages between these two quite different approaches to altruism and self-interest, particularly in their coming to terms with principal assumptions of classical economic theory. In considering these and related questions of the "common good," economist Herman Daly and theologian John Cobb (1989) proposd a "paradigm shift" within economics to internalize many variables which, while they do not fit well within the abstractions of economic theory, reflect important qualities of the real world. Ours also is a perception of development possibilities which does not perceive cost or benefit solely in materialistic terms, nor does it assume that "Northern motives" in these or any other regards are universal.  Sources of satisfaction differ substantially among different peoples.  Such questions are of interest here with respect to the functioning of traditional institutions of particular pastoral peoples and those peoples' underlying perceptions, both of which need to be ascertained in each situation and built upon in considering remedies to pastoral nondevelopment.

In that connection, S. Sandford (1983: 52, 131) argued that governments have been unwilling to accept kinship (e.g., pastoral clans) as institutional bases for pastoral development. He rightly noted that this arises from difficulties nonpastoralists have in understanding the structure and rationale of traditional pastoral institutions. Kinship- or clan-based organizations are characterized as "primitive" and "not suited for the modern world." However, as Sandford observed, kinship-based institutions have persisted among pastoralists no matter what and it is foolish to ignore them. That is, changes among pastoralists occur carefully and slowly, for they must have learned long ago that, under their precarious conditions of life, haste may indeed make irretrievable waste. We believe that, if meaningful results are to be realized from future development efforts, the ways these traditional social organizations (e.g., clans) and decision-making mechanisms function must be built upon constructively in preference to attempts, almost always failures, to replace or parallel them with ones more felicitous to donors of assistance. Through such channels it then becomes necessary in each instance to determine how pastoralists' own expressed needs--and significant objectives of the overall nation--can be accommodated with minimal cultural trauma and maximum use not only of these institutions but of externally provided services that *already* are most accepted, experienced and successful.

Working when possible through this existing social order and value system does not mean, however, that this current status quo represents an optimal situation. Thus, as Sandford (1983: 131) also noted, "it makes little sense [for outside developers] to try to freeze pastoral institutions, which have continuously adapted themselves to changes in the past, into the particular shape in which they happen to find themselves at the onset of a development program, on the grounds that this shape is 'traditional.'" In addition to indigenous institutions for reaching collective decisions, equally vital to explore and understand vis-à-vis development are indigenous animal management practices; ideas about causes, prevention and treatment of diseases and the like. In urging attention to these latter, the Tufts University group in West Africa believed it "may require innovative education of both herders and governmental veterinary agents in order to develop a dialogue between the two groups," with the aim of enlisting pastoralists in animal health extension systems (Sollod et al., 1984). We will enlarge upon such suggestions in Chapter 8.

Such outsider problems in understanding very different systems are compounded by commonly held beliefs that pastoral societies in Africa are not prepared to change. We think this is not a fair assessment because, while Africa's pastoralists may be basically content with their core institutions and beliefs, they have shown remarkable resilience over time through abilities to reduce risks, *to adapt to changing circumstances*. We have provided specific instances, as with changes in species emphases in facing crises. Others are increasingly positive views of externally provided education and nontraditional veterinary expertise.

### Studying Pastoralists' Governance Institutions

In Chapter 8 we will consider balances between centralized and decentralized models for African veterinary services that we believe would best enable them to act as facilitators of development among pastoral peoples. However, we would make two preliminary statements here before commencing a brief illustration of what it is necessary to learn in each instance about pastoralists' institutions, and how. As we shall use the term, decentralization applies both to decentralized governmental efforts *and* to privatization efforts, including integration of institutions of both types. *Fused* societies (see Table 1.1) rarely distinguish between "public" and "private" institutions. Among Northern social scientists, "both centralization advocates and privatization advocates [have] accept[ed] as a central tenet," in Elinor Ostrom's (1990: 14) words, "that institutional change must come from outside and be imposed on the individuals affected." Like Ostrom, we disagree and would argue that, to the contrary, any practical approach to development among pastoral peoples must explore first their own institutions. For it is Ostrom's view that "that many solutions exist to cope with many different problems. Instead of presuming that optimal institutional solutions can be designed easily and imposed at low cost by external authorities," she continued, "'getting the institutions right' is a difficult, time-consuming, conflict-involving process. It is a process that requires reliable information about time and place variables as well as a broad repertoire of culturally acceptable rules."

Very rare are books or articles by persons of African pastoralist origins about their institutions for governance and ajudication. Such source gaps partially motivate this book. Francis Mading Deng (1971, 1972, 1978, 1980, 1985), a Northern-trained lawyer and one of the highest ranking southern pastoralists within the Sudanese government, considered from a comparative jurisprudence perspective especially the Dinka in terms of prospects for creating a viable unitary nation-state in the Sudan. Our interests in traditional governance are focused somewhat differently in that our objective is to suggest ways in which many pastoral peoples might cooperate with government to improve their present state, and to more meaningfully interact in national life.

### Ascertaining Pastoralists' Needs and Desires

It is imperative, therefore, that outsiders know how to approach each different pastoral community, not only to assess their needs and desires, but to secure their cooperation, including their own suggestions as to how desired developments can be financed.  For example, obtaining an informed opinion among the Dinka is not a problem with proper approach through their traditional leadership, their hierarchy of judicial authorities.  At local levels, the point of contact would be the cattle camp chief.  He would call together elders he thinks could contribute to discussing the questions brought to them. Dinka take considerable pride in being quoted as having said this or that during such group discussions. Their only reluctance to share information or present their own ideas would be with respect to direct questions about the numbers of cattle an individual owns, or issues of a spiritual nature (see Chapter 3).  If this consultative group within the cattle camp thought that the issue was beyond their competence, they would refer it to the *bany bai* (*magaak*) for discussion at the level of the larger transhumant home base (*dom/bai*, village). Similarly, but less precedented, entire sectionwide or clanwide approaches for ideas or cooperation could involve an assembly of *bany bai* (or *bany bai* plus invited *bany wut* and other elders whose opinions were especially valued).

The other highly respected office among the Dinka is the traditional *bany bith* authority on spiritual matters (or similar persons in some subtribes). Although it would probably be difficult, if not impossible, for most outsiders to deal directly with many *bany bith* on development matters, these would assuredly be individuals whom this other leadership would consult for advice (as well as to seek their blessing).  Within that latter function lies the special importance of *bany bith* to any substantive development initiatives.  That is because they are believed by Dinka to speak not from their own resources alone but to reflect the authority of local clan spirits and of paramount "Spiritual Force."  Therefore, *if* a *bany bith* could be convinced of the wisdom of a new idea proposed for the Dinka, his support would carry great authority within his domain.  Other valuable nontraditional intermediaries within Dinka society would be members of their relatively small highly educated elite, especially those who do not have their own personal political axes to grind.

## QUESTIONS OF DEVELOPMENT PROGRAM SUSTAINABILITY

Initiatives proposed in this chapter are motivated by beliefs that they are primarily means to acomplish desirable things despite severe financial constraints, in effect to achieve the maximum "bang" with inadequate "bucks." Any consideration of fiscal sustainability of development initiatives beyond these must be prefaced by acknowledgement of the enormous debt many African countries have accumulated with relatively little concern until recently on the parts of national leaders (or of lenders).  Currently, 10 of the 26 most severely indebted low-income countries (SILICs) are African countries in which extensive pastoralism is important (SIDA, 1992). Tanzania, for example, has a debt/GNP ratio of 216% and Uganda a debt/export ratio of 1,533%. SIDA (1992) has calculated that the total cost to creditor countries of writing off completely the bilateral debts of *all* 26 countries would be only U.S.$30 billion. Conversion of all SILICs' additional multilateral debt to the International Bank for Reconstruction and Development (IBRD) to more favorable terms of the International Development Association (IDA)[13] would cost only an additional U.S.$538 million per year. Thus, in global financial terms, the debts of poor African countries, while totally overwhelming and crippling to themselves and their citizens (and a stimulus to the most destructive future responses), are but a drop in the international financial bucket.[14] Common sense would urge wiping clean these past mistakes. So that they not be repeated, greater self-reliance needs to be encouraged in all ways conceivable. The full potential even of local development IC and, assuredly, any steps beyond require not only exploration of all local cost-recovery possibilities, but longer-term local capital generation.

We believe that reasonable contributions to fiscal sustainability of pastoral development, in addition to currently unrealized economies inherent in IC, must eventually come from pastoralists themselves. Not only do people seem to value more highly things they have actually worked to help achieve, but we believe all peoples should contribute what they are able to their own betterment. We do not subscribe, however, to the view that all segments of society must necessarily pay their own way--or be neglected, shunted aside.  Resource differentials are enormous in different areas of Africa, as therefore are abilities of different peoples to pay for basic amenities generally regarded as consistent with human dignity.  And that should be the absolute bottom line of all development.

Most pastoral communities now inhabit marginal territories with few realizable options available to them beyond maximizing returns from their livestock wealth.  Once major epidemic livestock diseases have been brought under effective control, this will depend upon (1) improving the productivity of local animals, (2) obtaining maximum use from these animals within the communities themselves and (3) export/sale of animals and animal products.  In most of their communities, realization of some of those steps will necessitate changes in pastoralists' outlook and behavior.  It will also urgently require regularization (legalization) of their ownership of the lands they traditionally use.

Let us consider now what we know from southern Sudanese experiences about pastoralists' indicated willingness to pay for nontraditional services, for cost-recovery by government.

### Sudanese Pastoralists' Willingness to Pay for Veterinary Services

Beyond all efforts (1) to increase and make more dependable governmental financial support and (2) to achieve maximum use of scarce resources through IC, it should be possible (3) to involve cattle owners in the financing process by asking them to pay for services they value most. The latter has already been tried for veterinary services to some extent. Throughout the southern Sudan, all treatments of *individual* animals offered within government clinics and dispensaries are paid for by livestock owners. However, such stationary facilities reach an infinitesimally small portion of livestock in need of care and that will always be the case. Therefore, beginning in the early 1970s, the southern Regional Government, in recognition of extreme transport difficulties making it impossible for veterinary services to reach transhumant herds at all times of need, relaxed regulations on drug control. As an interim measure, private individuals who would come in contact with pastoralists were sold drugs by the veterinary department. Although the problem persisted of inadequate supplies of most desired drugs, through such means pastoralists have been paying for trypanocides, some anthelmintics and some antibiotics.[15] Therefore, the only significant services now offered free in the south are vaccinations against rinderpest, CBPP, anthrax, hemorrhagic septicemia, black quarter and rabies (in the north, only those against rinderpest and CBPP).

Beyond such, in 1982, groups of Dinka cattle camp leaders paid collectively for kerosene to run the deep freezers for vaccine storage in Yirol town (Lakes province). Furthermore, under civil war emergency conditions in 1989, it was ascertained by UNICEF that Mandari herders were willing to pay a sufficient price for having their cattle vaccinated against rinderpest alone to underwrite the entire combined cattle vaccination/children's vaccination program carried out among them (C.L. Schwabe, 1989). These examples all suggest that cattle owners in the southern Sudan would pay considerably for whatever services they can be convinced are crucial to the well-being of their cattle. One problem in this gradual involvement of pastoralists in the financing of certain types of veterinary services is that, in places like the southern Sudan, money accruing from sales of drugs and other services has not been available to the veterinary department, either because it enters illegal private channels or it goes into the treasury as general revenue. Matters of a policy nature such as these could be resolved partially were district and provincial veterinary departments granted fuller financial authority to budget for and use locally generated revenues according to their own priorities. A special drug fund account could be established and operated on a revolving basis, an approach GTZ applied in Somalia in 1985 and which showed signs of success (Baumann, 1990).

Other problems can arise with some types of cost-recovery mechanisms which are not due to cost-recovery per se. Among them are the accuracy of diagnoses under circumstances of drug sales in the absence of direct contacts between pastoralists and veterinary service officials, including encouragement of drug-resistant microorganisms and pesticide-resistant disease vectors which arise from improper drug dosages or promiscuous use.


### Capital Generation from Livestock

Pastoral peoples are not averse to new ideas if these are presented well and convince them that resulting changes will not be disruptive of traditional life and will improve their lot in ways they themselves understand. Sollod et al. (1984) ascertained, for example, that, among Fulbe (Fulani) pastoralists in Niger, "most herders would say that the veterinarian's medicine is more effective [than traditional remedies] and much easier to use. . . . Thus, there is an underlying desire by pastoralists to incorporate new technology into their production systems as long as this offers substantial improvements over traditional methods."

In some areas of pastoral Africa subjected to long-term outside influences, as from Islam, traditional systems have been modified to varying extents and an increasing number of pastoralists, such as the Somalis and Hausa, already have become money-earning livestock merchants (Gros, 1993a; Zessin, 1991). Even among the Dinka, beginning in the early 1970s numbers of young men began to be involved in some cattle trading in monetary terms (Majok, 1989). This desire for money remained complementary to the traditional desire for more cattle and was stimulated partially from wanting to buy more desirable types of cattle, but also as the means to acquire other newly "essential" items such as clothing. But until that situation begins to accelerate and money becomes more highly valued generally, is there nothing that can be done to entice pastoralists to generate monetary capital *indirectly* from their cattle wealth?

It is likely that, over time, many African pastoralists will see greater advantages to a monetary exchange system for some purposes than they do now. Confidence that that might happen is increased by knowledge of prior historical trends in other parts of the world. With respect to capital generation, much has been made of the importance of cattle numbers to most African pastoralists and this is understandable in terms of their common regard of cattle as wealth. However, in Chapter 3 we discussed ways in which cattle numbers owned by individuals are reduced by other than direct monetary sale. One such mechanism involves bride price. The numbers of cattle one man can manage is limited by the number of wives (and their children) he has (i.e., their labor). But, to obtain an additional wife, he must part with a number of cattle. Thus there are better times to consider obtaining an additional wife and poorer times. Dinka are knowledgeable about the flexibility this system permits over the shorter and longer terms. But there has been a tendency among outsiders not to recognize or credit such internal mechanisms. Also, contrary to the assumptions of many Northerners, pastoralists will trade a number of ordinary cattle for ones with specially desired qualities. This represents one traditional mechanism which tends to reduce herd numbers, and some of these could be deliberately used to increase offtake rates. Necessarily, such desired qualities must be ascertained in each local situation. One for the Dinka is milk production in cows. Another is the beauty of particular cattle, in some cases esthetic factors linked to religious or social observances or other important customs. We shall illustrate one important instance.

The vast majority of Dinka cattle are white (see Frontispiece), but certain coat colors, mainly black and white (pied) in various combinations, are valued very much by them, especially for song bulls (see Chapter 3). The most prized patterns are called *majok* and *marial*. For example, a pied song bull of either may be exchanged for up to 10 common white cattle, and young Dinka men are known to travel very long distances in search of such beautiful bulls for marriages or for dedication to a special or general spirit. In fact, their shortage has sometimes caused social tensions and animosities to arise between families when specific functions could not be performed. How might such traditional transactions be encouraged to generate capital? At this point we should note that European (and other) pastoralists produced their own recognized breeds of livestock largely by selecting for just such *apparently superficial characteristics* as Dinka and other African pastoralists cherish today--namely, particular coat colors and patterns, horn size and shape and the like. Thus the Holstein-Friesian breed of cattle reflects northeastern Europeans' similar preferences for black and white coat patterns. Herefords are another example of a breed with both a very distinctive color pattern and an atypical horn shape.

In the southern Sudan a breeding program selecting for these most locally valued color patterns could very well be instituted by the veterinary service using indigenous Dinka cattle. This could help achieve two goals simultaneously: on the one hand, provision of more of these bulls for the pastoralists, and, on the other, local capital-generation directly by the sale of white cattle to buy them. Under purely market circumstances, it could be argued that these pied cattle are valuable to Dinka soley because they are in short supply. This is not necessarily so among pastoralists because of the range of important cultural associations such special bulls enjoy, associations which probably could support a significant increase in their numbers without any commensurate decrease in their local value.[16] European experiences also indicate that such strongly held breed characteristic preferences are not associated with rarity of animals, but for purely esthetic and/or utilitarian reasons. Such a special breeding program that could help insure a regular flow of common white steers to domestic markets might attract support from the European Union (EU) or other potential beef importers (with the possibility of foreign capital input).   Under these circumstances, the southern Sudan would benefit not only from capital generation for locally desired development efforts, but also foreign aid.

Success of such an initiative, in terms of actual production of these most valued color-pattern bulls and the acceptability of the program by the Dinka, could pave the way for other cattle improvement programs aimed at developing certain other locally desired characters like milk production, size of horns, fast-running cattle (animals which can lead others to pastures and water facilities) and early conception.

## CONCLUSIONS

We believe that development among Africa's diverse pastoralists is a necessary undertaking which has to begin with better understanding of their existing circumstances and current aspirations. Beyond that, we believe that individual cultures and traditions must be studied sufficiently by outside agents to insure that proposed changes are fully understood and enjoy informed community support. As Deng (1971, 1978) has emphasized for the Dinka, "the system is essentially conservative and while not resistant to change, is selective and restrained, outside elements are adopted and assimilated to reinforce, rather than to alter, the preexisting system." He emphasized that "modernization," thus, is not an end in itself, it is an attempt at value maximization which, together with tradition, is the key to success without sacrificing human dignity.   Therefore, change must be introduced as a series of "necessary inventions" within the pastoralists' own cosmos and be assimilable within it.

Africa's proud pastoralists have frequently been viewed by outsiders as children who do not know what they are doing or what they are doing is wrong. To get the situation right for meaningful development initiatives in pastoral Africa requires less arrogance and less future reliance upon the type of "safari expertise" on which some development agencies and program financers seem more and more to depend.  Our proposal's first aim involves a plan which in its simplicity, gradualism and limited goals may little excite some agents of development accustomed to thinking in more grandiose terms.  However, it is a plan which, in contrast to almost all attempted previously, is practically achievable, could establish ongoing cooperation between pastoralists and outside institutions and thus give a big boost to other longer-term and more far-reaching objectives.

In this chapter, we have attempted to identify and propose certain steps/actions which pastoralists would perceive as "good" and that they themselves appreciate as necessary for the betterment of their lives. Essentially, what we have suggested and illustrated is that A, B, C etc. may very well be possible in light not only of *already existing resources*, but also of insider knowledge one of us possesses about his own pastoral people. Thus, in our discussion of

Dinka institutions of governance, we have indicated how to solicit ideas through different levels of traditional authority. Those interested in the realization of meaningful development among other pastoral peoples must similarly identify their institutions of traditional authority and decision-taking, the means through which new ideas may be introduced and the pastoralists' own ideas and cooperation elicited. That is, Africa's pastoral peoples must not only be recipients of efforts but should participate fully in the planning and implementation of all development initiatives contemplated within their areas. Ample experience (largely failures) has shown how vital that would be to public sustainability. Here the role of educated "elites" will become of greater importance.

Our proposals also aim at refocusing strategies in planning and implementation of development efforts upon those spheres where success is a real possibility. Therefore the roles of cattle (or for some pastoralists other animal species like camels) in their everyday lives have been stressed. This man-animal interdependency, so difficult for outsiders to fully comprehend, provides the core element to all realistic thinking about development in pastoral areas of Africa. Hence we strongly emphasize the need for promotion in the first instances of livestock-related programs. We have provided varied evidence that veterinary services are the only service branch of African governments that have succeeded so far in bringing to pastoral peoples things they really desire. We propose, therefore, that veterinary science should become the vehicle for reaching pastoral peoples with other much needed amenities as well, and that these initiatives provide the foundation for a broader reaching, locally instigated and practically realizable intersectoral approach to pastoral development. This mechanism has been illustrated in certain particulars for the southern Sudan. We believe it provides a model that would work equally well in other pastoral areas of Africa.

## NOTES

1. We are in agreement with Leonard (1987) that a single outreach avenue is the only forseeable possibility. In his view, local transport "is the Achilles heel . . . [and] woefully underfinanced. . . . Sedentary treasury officials simply cannot grasp how intensive livestock work is in its use of transport; they are convinced that [involved] officers must be making huge personal use of their vehicles, and treat transport as one of the first items to cut in any budgetary stringency." He noted that in 1982 Kenya was providing Ministry of Livestock Development staff only 352 km of travel funds per week, versus the requirement of 1,000 km per week for *each* of many individual veterinary service routes.

2. We believe that establishment of totally new institutions is far more difficult within diffuse pastoral communities than elsewhere and therefore new initiatives should be based whenever possible upon existing institutions.

3. For, as summarized by David Leonard (1993), a political scientist concerned with development administration in Africa, "I have not selected veterinary medicine randomly from among the professions. It is also an important and . . . particularly interesting case in its own right. Animal health, obviously, is one of several inputs to a livestock production system. As such it attracts only modest attention in most developed economies. The picture in Sub-Saharan Africa is quite different. First of all, agriculture makes a significant contribution to most African economies and is the major employer of most of its labour force, on average about 70 per cent. Second, within agriculture livestock represent about half of the value of production, particularly if we include the contribution of animal traction. Livestock has the kind of critical importance for African economies that steel might have for an industrialized one. Third, animal health services are the most important *purchased* input in most African livestock systems. Labour generally comes from family members, feeds come from the farm or range and, as yet, little investment is being made in the improvement of grazing. Animal health services thus loom large within a sector that is itself of great importance within the economy of Africa."

4. In its "State of the World's Children" for 1984, UNICEF (1985: 12) especially singled out the relative success of these southern Sudanese efforts under very difficult conditions.

5. Portions of this Sudanese material were contained originally in an unpublished report to UNICEF by C. L. Schwabe, C.W. Schwabe and S.S. Basta (1984), and a published summary by C.W. Schwabe and C.L. Schwabe (1990).

6. The second author's son (C.L. Schwabe, who was then UNICEF program officer for health in the southern Sudan) and himself.

7. Similar reliance of a regional hospital in central Somalia upon a veterinary cold depot was made known to us by K.-H. Zessin (personal communication).

8. Rabies is a zoonosis endemic among some wildlife species and dogs in much of Africa, outbreaks of which within rural and urban areas cause high numbers of human deaths from an untreatable condition annually. Rabies control based largely upon dog control and dog immunization is one of the most important veterinary public health programs worldwide.

9. In remote areas like the southern Sudan, *local* level may include the provincial as well as the district. Thus both of us have been in situations in the southern Sudan where, almost every evening, practically all of the chiefs of services (the mayor, the bank manager, the provincial veterinary officer, the chief of police, etc.) gathered informally for a shared supper and conviviality on the porch or under a tree outside one of their houses. In such isolated places, such small social subcommunities almost always emerge.

10. Part of the latter problem being that such training is usually paid for and arranged by donor agencies at no cost to national governments themselves. In the southern Sudan and elsewhere, we know of instances where the *very* few veterinarians trained abroad at considerable expense and effort in diagnostic laboratory disciplines such as microbiology are being used instead for the same more generalist jobs they did

before their specialist training. These types of stupidities have major impact upon the staff morale problem mentioned in Chapter 6.

Moreover, such newly acquired skills need constant upgrading and can soon become rusty if not properly exercised.   Most experienced persons could cite horror stories of all types in these regards--for example, that carefully selected laboratory personnel, while abroad for the specialized training they require, are replaced in their jobs at home by political appointees totally unqualified for such highly technical tasks while they themselves return after training to unspecialized functions any graduate could perform.

11. During the mid-1960s when one of us (C.W.S.) was involved in establishing a WHO-sponsored Master of Public Health degree course in veterinary public health for India and southeast Asia, he found that medical and veterinary services in India *each* attempted to maintain special diagnostic laboratories for rabies, a major health problem resulting in hundreds of human deaths annually.  Not only did both of those networks of laboratories have *exactly the same scientific requirements* (equipment, types of personnel, tests to be performed, etc.), but because of inadequate funding *none* of them in either service were well enough equipped or staffed to perform the full range of modern diagnostic procedures. Yet, if there is one disease other than AIDS whose diagnosis is *always* a question of life or death, and where the very best diagnostic possibilities should be available, it is rabies.

The ease with which human cases of other common zoonoses can and do remain undetected is reflected in the fact that "Fort Bragg Fever," which occurred epidemically among American soldiers in the U.S. South post-World War II, was wrongly ascribed many etiologies before the Veterinary Laboratory in the Walter Reed Army Institute for Medical Research in Washington, D.C. was furnished human specimens and determined that Fort Bragg fever was, in fact, leptospirosis.

Late in the colonial period the second author personally witnessed human diagnostic sera being almost routinely forwarded by air from Nairobi to South Africa because of technical difficulties encountered by the Kenya medical services laboratories in running complement fixation tests.  Needless to say, test results were often received too late to be useful.  Completely unknown to these medical officials was that the serological expertise to readily solve their problem was available only 10 miles away at the Kenya Veterinary Laboratory in Kabete.

Commonplace lack of expert laboratory confirmation of diagnoses is why almost every instance of febrile illness in people in the Sudan is diagnosed clinically and treated today as malaria.  These common inabilities to identify diseases correctly has masked the presence in parts of Africa, sometimes to alarming extents, of other relatively common infections, some of them serious ones (which, of course, will not respond to unneccessary malaria therapy) and it can also delay for years initial recognition of very serious "new" human diseases like Ebola and Lassa fevers--and, perhaps, even of AIDS, for which there is some evidence for a simian origin in Africa.

12.  The first successful control of hydatid disease was in Iceland where in the last century one in six of its largely pastoral (and fishing) population had become infected

from pastoralists' dogs. That program depended upon drastic measures and informed community cooperation not duplicable in most other pastoral countries. A control program under more typical sedentary pastoral conditions was pioneered in New Zealand through initiatives of a practicing surgeon and a veterinary expert on hydatid disease named Michael Gemmell. The technical control measures identified were IC efforts largely within the province of veterinary science. In 1960 the second author organized a hydatid disease research and control program within WHO which spread information about that New Zealand approach to other countries. An initial effort was in the newly independent nation of Cyprus (Schwabe, 1986). Soon after, similar initiatives were promoted by WHO in pastoral regions elsewhere.

13. IBRD and IDA together comprise the World Bank.

14. Among 20 developing countries with the largest foreign debt, arms imports (1976-80) were the equivalent of 20% of the debt increase for that period (Sivard, 1983) and these proportions have risen since. From another perspective, the cost to a Northern nation of *one* nuclear submarine equals the *combined* annual education budgets of 26 developing countries with 160 million school-age children!

15. Some Dinka purchase trypanocides, antibiotics, deworming agents and acaricides not only through legal channels, but from the black market at very high prices. On rare occasions vaccines also have been bought illicitly through such channels. Thus, in late 1982, cattle owners around Wau paid £S10 per dose for rinderpest tissue culture vaccine to a trader who had obtained the vaccine through unofficial means and smuggled it into Wau.

In a 1983 survey in the Maasai's Kajiado district of Kenya, Leonard (1987) found that a strong demand among pastoralists existed for curative veterinary services which, for the most part, were still nonexistent there despite the fact that Kenya's veterinary service is one of the most extensively organized in Africa. Open market drug purchases by owners, with self-diagnosis and treatment, commonly existed. The very isolated Turkana in Kenya are buying certain drugs for their animals from veterinary assistants or stockmen provided licenses by the Kenya veterinary services administration. Kenyan Maasai of Narok district also indicated they buy drugs, but would not disclose the source (suggesting it is probably an illicit one).

Some Somali pastoralists are paying for drugs provided under the Nomadic Animal Health Auxiliary (NAHA) program launched there by the German Agency for Technical Cooperation (GTZ) (Baumann, 1990). An important point is that all such nontraditional needs depend upon cash, and to obtain it, pastoralists are further encouraged to sell cattle and enter the monetary economy. Commonly, veterinarians and auxiliaries accept unofficial compensation in gifts of livestock (practices indigenous to many pastoral groups and therefore not necessarily negative).

16. Thus, this high value among the Dinka is not for any rare color or pattern, but only for these several black and white patterns. These particular patterns provide prominent reference points for many aspects of Dinka life, including a type of classification system. For example, many other things are routinely identified with these bulls' patterns like *marial* (in which black and white patches are dispersed all over

the animal's body).  As examples, Dinka "classify" as *marial* the white heavenly bodies distributed over the black night sky, the interspersed ground pattern of light and shadow cast by the foliage of a tree in sunlight, or a pattern of sun reflected off the metal roofs of modern buildings scattered among the dark background of dense tree foliage within a district town.

# 8

---

# TWO-WAY COMMUNICATIONS AND MONITORING

> What has not been fully appreciated . . . is that [African] pastoralism is information intensive . . . the decision-making process of nomadic families operates continuously. Pastoral management probably requires more bits of information per unit time than any other agricultural pursuit.
>
> A.E. Sollod, 1991

> The protection of pastoralist herds requires that the veterinary services have an effective mechanism for disease surveillance and monitoring of livestock movements.
>
> S.J. Kenyon and S.M. Kenyon, 1991

One of the main bases for our development proposals is recognition of the central importance of veterinary services to pastoral peoples (Chapter 6), including the high degree of acceptance among African pastoralists their outreach efforts enjoy. They have a unique ability to share this access and rapport (Chapter 7) that would offer possibilities for general development applications. Therefore, efforts by veterinary services to assure their mobile capacities should receive the support of other service sectors. A main advantage of IC would be that the "unit of service" cost of visits to pastoralists would be reduced by making them multipurpose.

To improve this system for multipurpose outreach, some infrastructural changes are desirable within the veterinary sector and probably in other service sectors also. One important question involves communciations. Referring to the urgency generally within Africa to more effectively transmit to "farmers" the knowledge possessed in specialized areas of agriculture, the Pritchard Winrock committee (1992: 111) noted that although "there are more [university graduates all the time], . . . there has been little change in the[ir] organization and methods of communication. . . ." They recommended "improved communications techniques."

Like transportation, communication with pastoralists is a far more difficult problem than that faced more generally in rural areas. However, with increasing availability of cheap battery-operated radios, and wider acquaintance of pastoralists with them, that is one means to establish better links. For this and purely operational reasons, key equipment for district-level veterinary facilities, with their mobile field teams, should be 2-way radios. In fact, one of the first support facilities almost all NGOs and bilateral or multilateral aid programs set up in countries like the Sudan is their own radio communications system.[1] With these and other outreach objectives in mind, we shall consider here a current of reform in delivery of veterinary services which has to do with rapid advances of the last several decades in disease intelligence aspects of epidemiology. Epidemiology's inherently holistic and integrative qualities, in part through overlaps with fields like ecology, anthropology, economics and data management ("informatics"), make these globally initiated reforms especially relevant to development within pastoral Africa.

Currently, veterinary contacts with pastoralists are mostly to route skills and other services, plus extension-type information from the center to the field. However, what we shall explore now is to assure that they also assume a more substantial *monitoring* function (Chapter 2), a communicating function in the reverse direction. This would be not only for livestock diseases, but animal movements, grazing conditions, rainfall, erosion and other things seen increasingly as key elements for timely and effective responses to disease circumstances and drought conditions, as well as for realizing longer-term rangelands and animal productivity improvements. That is, the information a modern epidemiological intelligence system could provide about pastoralists, their practices and environments would also be valuable to other service sectors.

These reforms embrace a global change in the population dimension of veterinary science whereby its very successful hundred-year Phase of Campaigns or Mass Actions began to be replaced in the 1970s by a new Phase of Surveillance and Selective Actions (see Table 6.2). Those initiatives followed conceptualization of modern ideas of disease surveillance within the U.S. National Centers for Disease Control and Prevention, efforts in which numbers of public health veterinarians were centrally involved. Its impetus within veterinary schools was through creation, beginning in the mid-1960s, of post-graduate programs in quantitative epidemiology, animal health economics and related disciplines (Schwabe, 1970, 1984b, 1991b). At that time, some Northern veterinarians recognized that four practice crises in veterinary science (Table 6.2) all had elements in common and that remedies for each depended upon abilities to better monitor and quantify disease occurrence. Possibilities thus arose to identify and investigate the importance of *multiple*, directly or indirectly causal determinants constituting for each disease its "web of causation" (that is, to perform an epidemiological diagnosis; Schwabe, 1982, 1993a). An associated advance was acceptance as a definition of "health" among farm animals not simply the absence of overt disease, but an optimal level of productivity (resulting in stimulus of so-called production medicine). The result was progressive emergence in the North during the latter part of the 20th century of a new and more efficient veterinary infrastructural pattern. We believe that nonveterinarians concerned with pastoral development in Africa must possess a basic understanding of why this matrix shift within veterinary science began and of what it consists.

## CHANGING BASES FOR VETERINARY SERVICES DELIVERY

Some constraints to veterinary services delivery in pastoral Africa have been internal ones. One has been undue reliance upon campaigns directed against *single* diseases (or, at most, two at the same time). Such efforts tend to be *discontinuous*, to consist of spurts of great activity as in a series of military operations.[2] They are the population-level analog of the historical "fire engine" bugaboo of private veterinary food animal practice (to which we will turn later in this chapter in discussing privatization). In a number of African countries, *mass* vaccination campaigns against rinderpest and CBPP alone have virtually commanded, often exceeded, the total resources continually available to their veterinary sectors.

The biggest objection to that late-19th-century approach is when such campaigns define the primary organizational basis for veterinary services delivery, they compartmentalize veterinary efforts which might otherwise share resources--that is, they *fail to realize maximum advantages from visits to livestock owners*, especially under pastoral conditions where these are so difficult and costly. A campaigns-type infrastructure also reduces many veterinary field assignments to boring routines that fail not only to constructively utilize knowledge and skills acquired through a veterinary education, but create needless problems of staff morale. Any qualified person who has closely observed day-to-day operations of campaigns recognizes not only how frequently they become frustrated by petty constraints, but also *how inefficiently used is much of the most skilled veterinary talent.*

Because under that system budgetary allocations tend to become specific campaign line items, it unduly ties a director's hands, leaving him little administrative flexibility to meet emergencies, in discretionary funding of cross-program activities and for experimenting through pilot schemes with new disease management approaches. It is, thus, the antithesis of our development proposals, because interprogram resource sharing (for multiple veterinary purpose visits to livestock owners, a "within sector" analog of intersectoral cooperation) is discouraged. A more modern intelligence-based organization would eliminate service discontinuities and personnel inefficiencies by making intelligence activities *the continuous core program for overall veterinary services delivery* onto which specific time-limited and other programs are grafted, including rapid responses to newly arising or newly recognized problems and situations.

However, the principal rationale globally for an information-gathering core for the veterinary sector is not simply to replace a compartmentalized and discontinuous service infrastructure, but to obviate the need under many circumstances for *mass* interventions. Those have increasingly recognized weaknesses: (1) they usually presume, in the absence of more precise disease intelligence, a *general* risk of particular diseases across large populations; (2) veterinary services may attempt therefore to protect many animals *not at actual risk;* and (3) money and time are wasted (even if the mass campaign eventually achieves its stated goals, as in many Northern experiences). Better information could permit substituting for that blanket approach something more focused and less costly. An epidemiological intelligence system also aims to obtain sufficient information about a *range of diseases and their populations at risk* (1) to make rational decisions for each about the desirability of interventions, (2) to compare alternative intervention strategies for benefits/costs, (3) to select the most appropriate combination of intervention tactics, (4) to monitor program progress and (5) to promptly alter tactics or emphases if intelligence findings demonstrate local or general problems in progress. A mass action *may* remain the preferred intervention approach in some instances, but, for the most part, we have not known whether that were so. More selective alternatives developed in the North (see Table 6.2) have been little considered within pastoral Africa (Schwabe, 1980) because most are dependent upon a better diagnostic intelligence capability than is now prevalent there.

Greater selectivity can realize savings large enough to spell differences between failure and success. For example, in a selective rather than a mass immunization approach, with the same aims of achieving an infection's eradication,[3] only animals considered to be at risk are vaccinated. Such selective efforts directed only at identified populations have had a number of prior regional successes within veterinary science. While that approach requires greater knowledge about distributions of the disease in question than does a mass approach, it has particularly high benefit-cost advantages (Schwabe and Ruppanner, 1972; Zessin and Carpenter, 1985).[4]

To summarize the consequences of this operating largely in the dark vis-à-vis livestock diseases, as is currently the case in Africa, not only may a few types of disease management tactics tend to be overemphasized as panaceas, but, even more important, those tactics must often be applied on a mass basis, or if the tactic is one applied to the environment, as a saturation procedure over sometimes unnecessary environments. Absence of sufficient information for more selective actions also requires obtaining cooperation of many more animal owners than might otherwise be necessary, may seriously prolong the duration and increase costs of overall efforts and, most important under many prevailing African conditions, especially within pastoral areas, may so overstrain resources available as to preclude getting the job done at all. This was the case with the first ambitious continentwide campaign (JP-15) to eradicate rinderpest from Africa.

Since veterinary science has accreted a number of different population-wide disease management tactics (Table 6.2), we are arguing here that *rationally chosen* centrally coordinated technical efforts, essential to many types of veterinary programs, require information adequate to make such choices and that decentralized program outreach initiatives, which are basic to our local IC development proposals, *provide the means to meet that information requirement at the grassroots level.* It is important to note, therefore, that, while central authority strategies have been most promoted within governments organized on the former Soviet pattern, they also have characterized to excessive degrees not only veterinary delivery systems of many capitalist governments, but have been favored approaches in the past to development overall--or specific aspects like range management--within pastoral Africa (see Chapter 5). Some of the local development approaches we advocate, as well as the requirements of sufficient epidemiological intelligence, depend upon a far greater measure of decentralization in decision-making and logistic particulars. Therefore, part of our overall rationale is that there are critical differences between centralization where necessary and imposed "central authority solutions."[5] Moreover, as Elinor Ostrom (1990: 17) has emphasized, both assume that responsible agencies possess sufficient information to make the decisions and take the actions they do. According to her, experience shows that they often do not, as accumulating experience within pastoral Africa surely bears out (Baumann et al., 1993; Behnke et al., 1993). Thus, reforms we advocate vis-à-vis veterinary programs should also suggest internal reforms within other sectors.

So how, more specifically, could this more modern system be implemented in pastoral Africa?

## AN INFORMATION-GENERATING INFRASTRUCTURE

Epidemiological diagnosis involves two main levels of activity, *intelligence* and *analysis.* In its intelligence dimension, it employs two complementary field procedures, surveillance and intensive follow-up (see Figure 8.1). These exist in a cyclical, mutual feedback relationship to one another. These diagnostic approaches not only complement clinical and pathological/laboratory diagnosis (see Table 4.1), but the latter two continually feed information into the former. Results of such "information-for-action" efforts become immediately useful.

Epidemiological analysis is a technical subject which will mostly occupy the attention of a small group of specialists within a country's central veterinary facility and/or its university veterinary faculty. The important thing to note here is that the data employed are not solely from monitoring mortality (e.g., cause specific death rates) and morbidity (incidence and prevalence rates) for different diseases (and/or of progress in their control), but *also* variables which may act as determinants of high or low rates or particular disease patterns. These include not only variations in a responsible *agent* (e.g., strain of a virus) and in composition of herds or characteristics of individual animals (e.g., age, sex, breed, physiological state, concurrent diseases), but also of *environment* and *animal management practices*. Among such variables are weather, soil types, vegetation types, waterways and water sources, distributions of populations of reservoirs or vectors of particular infections, husbandry practices and characteristics of livestock raisers (e.g., demographic, ethnic, religious, economic status differences). Thus, what needs to be ascertained for veterinary diagnostic purposes includes (1) types of information which range managers and disaster planners also now recommend monitoring (see Chapter 2), (2) much of what epidemiologists concerned with human diseases among pastoralists could also use (see Chapter 4) and (3) some of what needs to be known for economic analyses within particular pastoral situations.

A rudimentary vehicle for communicating from the field to the center already exists within African veterinary services *for the primary purpose of communication of knowledge (extension) and skills/interventions from the center to the field*. It requires improvements in both directions for purely veterinary reasons. However, our main point is that no other even rudimentary information-gathering network is already in place or is likely to be affordable by any other sector acting independently. Here we see practical possibilities for realization of the monitoring objectives being advocated as parts of pastoral development initiatives. Only such ongoing mobile capacities will enable veterinary services to forestall, abort or quickly combat the kinds of new disease emergencies or recrudescences that will inevitably arise in the future and, at the same time, redirect their prime efforts to improving productivity of pastoralists' livestock, to encourage greater pastoralist participation in the national economy.

Many experienced veterinarians see strengthening of diagnostic capabilities in Africa as the highest priority internal need of veterinary services. In its population dimensions, this is not something to be added to existing veterinary infrastructures as a frill, but to become *the* essential core program for veterinary services delivery. Veterinary information-for-action suggestions similar in particulars to ones we advocate have already been employed on pilot scales

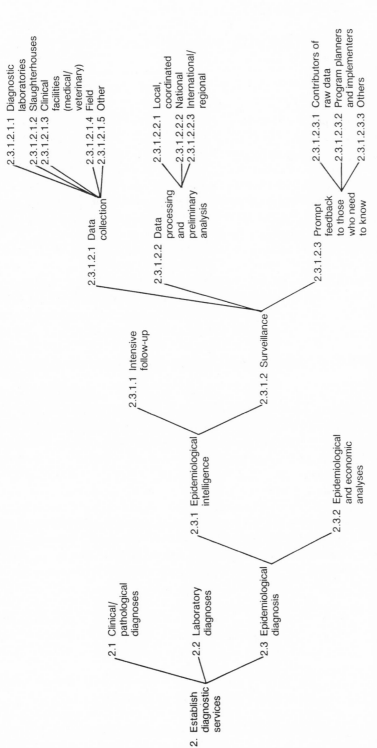

**Figure 8.1. An epidemiological surveillance program and some of its principal components.** (Modified from Dr. Konrad Bögel and WHO/FAO, 1982.)

among Tuareg in Niger (Sollod and Stem, 1991) and among Somalis (Zessin, 1991: 1-26; Baumann et al., 1993). Baseline intelligence-gathering activities upon which those two quite different programs were founded emphasized--in addition to intelligence about livestock diseases, reproduction and production-- ecological and anthropological data collection in the case of the Niger effort and quantitative epidemiological *and economic* analyses of resulting data in the case of the Somali effort. In our view, *all* those features should be fully integrat- ed into any optimally operational veterinary program in pastoral Africa.

Beyond information-gathering mechanisms, the other essential parts of modern epidemiological intelligence systems are their capacities to continually cumulate, collate, analyze, express in the most usable forms and disseminate rapidly all potentially valuable information. The genius of such systems is that *they can begin with any resources and at any level of sophistication.* Their main objective is to describe the state of nature concerning diseases within a population, to yield better and better approximations of the health status of their "patient population." They thus comprise a continuing system of *applied field research* which stimulates and taxes the imagination and the creativity of parti- cipants.

### Pastoral Information Sources and Their Improvement

Epidemiological surveillance makes use of *all* relevant data already being collected. In pastoral areas, such preexisting data will usually be rare and direct data-collecting mechanisms must be created. However, some potential data sources are already under veterinary control and these can constantly be improved. They include reports from field personnel, local veterinary clinics and dispensaries, plus slaughterhouses or slaughter slabs. In the southern Sudan, valuable disease surveillance data could be obtained from these sitees with comparatively little effort and especially such activities could be intensi- fied during the rainy season when annual mass vaccinations of cattle largely stop because of flooding. These activities, involving animal sampling with laboratory follow-up to extents possible, could go a long way toward better year-round utilization of personnel and improvements in staff morale. Other valuable surveillance data sources are diagnostic laboratories and field surveys.

*Diagnostic Laboratories.* Where they exist, veterinary diagnostic laboratories could be very valuable sources of surveillance data. Although current acquisitions give biased indications of disease incidence (since most specimens now submitted originate from obviously sick or dead animals), such provide excellent means to first detect presence of a particular disease or flag situations that require intensive follow-up by a field team. *With attention to sampling methods*, monthly and yearly data cumulations from laboratories could also permit estimates of *relative* incidence and/or prevalence of diseases over time within areas they serve.   However, few diagnostic laboratories in pastoral Africa currently fullfil such potentially valuable functions and their staffs have not been so trained.

Kenyon and Nour (1991) have been among the few veterinarians to discuss problems encountered in countries like the Sudan in operating laboratories.   Their unpublished report deserves broader dissemination.   They note that "laboratory projects provide an attractive technical assistance package for donors, since they are limited in scope, of high visability and fill an apparent need. . . . [Among] compelling reasons for selecting [them] as a vehicle for development assistance . . . [are that] they are discrete, clearly defined and represent the opportunity to transfer specific technology and technical skills. [Moreover, a] large percentage of the funds required for such a project are spent in the donor country on equipment, reagents and transportation.   Because of the long history of this type of assistance an experienced cadre of expatriate personnel for these projects are often on the donor agency's books, and additional personnel are relatively easy to find on secondment from [laboratories] in the industrialized countries. [However, in] many cases these projects . . . have contributed little to the improvement of animal health or human welfare in the developing country."[6]

Another assessment of laboratory operation by Sollod et al. (1984) is even more pointed in its implications for development efforts. In their view, "because it is [so] out of context, research undertaken in laboratories on samples delivered from the field usually gives scant, and often misleading, information on the actual economic and social impact of diseases from the pastoralists' point of view. . . . [Veterinary] diagnostic laboratories [also] are operated with little integration with non-veterinary activities and without measurable impact on pastoral production."   Kenyon and Nour (1991) add that "unless these [laboratories] take into account local circumstances and locally defined needs their success is bound to be limited. . . .   It is essential that the process be driven by the needs of the recipient rather than by the preferences of the donor."   These, of course, are precisely the types of problems our local development proposals address. As part of a solution, A.E. Sollod and coworkers (1984) particularly urge "a better balance between field work and [these] more costly laboratory activities."

Not only can valuable disease occurrence data based upon clinical and pathological diagnoses feed in from such existing veterinary service activities, but deliberate disease surveys may be carried out, almost always with laboratory backups.

*Surveys.* Because of a similarity of words, epidemiological surveillance has been confounded by some with just one of its parts--surveys--and some veterinarians, as well as others, believe that surveys constitute surveillance systems.   Although that is not the case, the single most valuable sources of surveillance data are deliberate field surveys, one-time or repeated, especially surveys conducted with an intent to quantify occurence of *multiple* diseases in a defined population. Thus, as pointed out by Kenyon and Nour (1991) with respect to defects in the present operation of many diagnostic laboratories: "the study of productivity and disease effects in a defined population of animals offers many advantages over the ad hoc collection of disease data from [convenience] samples submitted [haphazardly to laboratories as now with no resort to random sampling methods] by field officers or owners. . . . One of the effects of this type of [periodic] study [of the same herds] . . . is that health problems are identified which do not usually come to the attention of the animal health services." Beyond such, epidemiological surveys collect relatable data on candidate disease determinants. Properly planned and implemented,[7] they are the most *systematic* source of baseline information for setting priorities, planning specific interventions and having a basis to measure their progress. However, their cost and difficulty recommend not only their most efficient execution and analysis, but also their more ongoing supplementation by other less costly, systematic or reliable means.

While the unusual 1979-1981 multidisease baseline survey under normal (nonoutbreak) conditions in the southern Sudan (see Chapter 4) was not designed with epidemiological analysis[8] in mind, analyses undertaken post hoc yielded valuable results and demonstrated the need to devise better sampling methods among migratory herds, to consider herds as well as individual animals as sampling units, and to include other types of information likely to be epidemiologically valuable.[9] Multidisease, production, reproduction, environmental, economic and other data obtained subsequently by this same team in central Somalia (Zessin, 1991; Baumann et al., 1993) met those needs in large part and provided an improved model for pastoral area surveys in the future.

Besides information collection, epidemiological surveillance requires that information obtained be expressed in most usable forms, sometimes subjected to comparisons and/or some level of analysis and made available to fieldworkers and others in timely fashion.


### Data Expression and Geographic Information Systems

Current applications of computer technology for data handling and analysis, with possibilities for easy transfer of information within and between different applications, have proven a boon to epidemiological intelligence. Originally dependent upon expensive mainframe hardware, the current availability of low-cost, high-capacity personal computers--including portable computers, plus hand-held data-entering and position-identifying (navigational) devices that can be battery-operated in the field--has revolutionized prospects for effective surveillance even under the most isolated of African circumstances. Like 2-way radio communications and properly integrated laboratories, this technology is no frill inappropriate to such constrained situations, but provides vital support to intervention efforts, *particularly* within pastoral areas where all fieldwork is so difficult and maximum advantage must be taken of every herd contact.

Discussions of data collating, handling and expression methods may be found in some epidemiology texts.   Here we mention only one approach, geographic information systems (GIS), since they have especially benefitted from modern computer technology.

Medical geography has always been a vital component of epidemiology. Standard techniques include spot maps, grid maps, isodemic maps, isopleth maps and transparent overlay maps.   Some of these are combined as in a temporal series of spot maps of cases overlain to disclose the progress of an outbreak.   Transparent overlays placed on top of one another on a light box may also permit rapid associations between geographic distributions of a new disease and, say, particular vegetation zones, weather conditions or the like. The main difference between older methods and modern GIS are that the latter substitute electronic techniques for mechanical ones in integrating maps of different variables for the same geographical area (Carlton, 1991a, 1991b). Relevant to such approaches in our context is that the first continentwide effort anywhere to incorporate a geographic epidemiological information system within a service/action program was that by the colonial-period Commission on Technical Cooperation in Africa South of the Sahara (CCTA).   Its Inter-African Bureau for Epizootic Diseases endeavored to collect case/outbreak data for major livestock infections from all African countries/colonies by 1 degree coordinates and to disseminate resulting maps to the veterinary services of member governments and to publish some in the *Bulletin of Epizootic Diseases in Africa*.

Most operating GIS employ mainframe computers and some have used data generated by remote sensors from satellites in space. Such costly, high-technology systems are being undertaken by a few internationally funded groups and are in their developmental stages. An early veterinary application to the epidemiology of tick-borne East Coast fever in Africa is being carried out collaboratively by ILRAD (Lessard et al., 1990).[10]  Other potential uses vis-à-vis issues considered here would be, for example, to periodically map rainfall and pastoral vegetation/grazing conditions as aids to pastoralists' planning seasonal migrations and to veterinary and other services wishing to reach and assist them (Behnke et al., 1993).  Available resolution of some satellite-generated maps would permit locations of individual cattle camps, obviating major problems now faced in randomly sampling camps as part of ongoing surveillance efforts.  While this is not currently a technology which could be applied locally to practical development efforts within pastoralist Africa, some of its potential might become available in the future were it to receive international support.  Much more currently practical, in terms of our proposals, would be personal computer (PC)-based systems which, with relatively little cost, could be incorporated today at national or regional levels in all countries within pastoral areas of Africa. Such a system is being used in tandem with other analytical tools for analyses of bovine trypanosomiasis data from the GTZ multidisease surveys in the southern Sudan (Carlton, 1991a, 1991b, 1992).

The third vital component of modern epidemiological intelligence is prompt feedback of processed data and related information of value to those who supplied them and others who can use them.

Thus, modern epidemiological intelligence, effectively interdigitated with laboratory backup facilities plus mobile access to the field, can provide the quality of information which is required to more rationally mandate centralized veterinary actions. We would advocate a gradual buildup of intelligence systems, allowing time for results to more or less keep pace with investment. For example, modest facilities at a selected district in each province on a pilot basis might be the initial policy objective. This gradualist approach has been inherent to surveillance everywhere.

## BROADER DEVELOPMENT IMPLICATIONS

If veterinary services are to provide a delivery vehicle for broader development possibilities, the key importance of epidemiology's special information-gathering and processing capacities becomes even more apparent. This is in part because it is an integrative discipline using data also of interest to other sectors (and disciplines). Relationships especially relevant to our proposals include those with ecology, anthropology and economics.

### Epidemiology and Ecology

Epidemiology's evolution represented a merger of three streams of activity, of which medical ecology was one. Another was disease intelligence, the aspect with which this chapter is concerned. The most recent was quantitative analysis (see Schwabe et al., 1977 for more complete discussion). Perpective and methods contributed by the medical ecology stream derived from studies of biologically complex infectious diseases, especially of transmission mechanisms and patterns of occurrence *across a range of host species*. That approach was prominent in studies of zoonoses and other diseases transmitted among vertebrate animals (including man) by invertebrate vectors (like insects, ticks, mites and snails) and in infections caused by animal parasites, which often have very complicated life cycles. A medical ecology approach (i.e., a *qualitative* analytic approach) led, as examples, to identification of anomalies in fulfillment of Koch's postulates (latent infections, the carrier state, opportunistic pathogens, etc., see Table 6.2) and to the notions of multicausal diseases and complex webs of disease causality.

Pritchard et al. (1992: 66) have urged that a "monitoring system to better inform users where grazing is abundant or scarce would help pastoralists to . . .

promptly take steps to mitigate the potential impact of drought." Since the "impact of drought" is malnutrition, sometimes death, in livestock and pastoralists, what we are talking about practically are drought's *medical* outcomes. Not surprisingly, therefore, it was a veterinarian *cum* parasitologist, Albert Sollod (1990, 1991), who argued the desirability of integrating development of an Early Warning System for droughts in Africa with delivery of veterinary services to pastoralists. In fact, consequences not only of such environmental problems, but human food supply and population growth problems are all taken seriously by the general public and many political leaders *only* when they do assume the proportions of medical problems.

A corollary follows. Forewarnings of such medically consequential disasters in the future--or simply to plan for more manageable ecological variability--will depend upon creation of *intelligence systems* (Behnke et al., 1993). Thus, a modern infrastructure for delivery of veterinary services not only *uses* various types of environmental data, but readily lends itself to data collection *for broader development purposes.* Therefore, reforms this chapter advocates would increase considerably already existing capabilities of governmental veterinary services to act as vehicles for and facilitators of other aspects of development, including those related to disaster preparation and range improvement.

### Epidemiology and Anthropology

Epidemiological studies on human diseases consider with respect to risk such variables as age, sex, occupation, religion, kinship and ethnic group. These also are of concern to veterinarians, especially in the epidemiology of zoonoses and, in studies of purely livestock diseases, for identifying and/or characterizing animal uses, alternative systems of animal management and care, beliefs about animals and their diseases, traditional medical/veterinary practices and man-animal relationships in other particulars.

Therefore, it was with good reason that Julian Huxley, writing about Africa's development potential over 60 years ago, identified the key role veterinary science must play and opined that "to be a good veterinary officer [in Africa] . . . you must be a first-class biologist and you must be a knowledgable and sympathetic anthropologist as well" (Huxley, 1931). Thirty years later an anthropologist working among Baggara pastoralists of the Sudan pointed out to a veterinary audience that, while "the anthropologist may not be very strong on . . . veterinary techniques, . . . he has perhaps a wider view of their social consequences" (Cunnison, 1960), and broader attention was directed subsequently to such notions (Schwabe, 1964: 26). However, except in the work of a few veterinarians like Igor Mann in Kenya (see Chapter 7), too little attention was paid to such needs before the 1980s. Since then some coordinated anthropological-veterinary-ecological studies were undertaken, as by Sollod and his co-workers in Niger (1984), and it was suggested that traditional healers might provide an already existing grassroots-level disease intelligence resource (Schwabe, 1980; Schwabe and Kuojok, 1981).

While, in the view of a husband-wife veterinarian-social scientist team experienced of pastoral Africa: "veterinary anthropologist[s] are going to be rare birds indeed [and t]he discipline will be carried by those who are able to collaborate across disciplines" (Kenyon and Kenyon, 1991), all veterinarians in Africa can be oriented meaningfully to such possibilities and their importance (see Chapter 9). To which Kenyon and Nour (1991) add in the same vein as this chapter, "the skills of the social scientist and the epidemiologist must [both] complement those of the [clinical or laboratory type] diagnostician." Thus, while an optimal melding of anthropology and veterinary science has yet to be realized, all the pieces are available to be integrated and applied more generally. Epidemiology provides the key linkage.

### Epidemiology and Economics

There are several overlaps between economics and veterinary epidemiology. The first concerns a broadly shared methodology for quantitative studies, econometrics and analytical epidemiology employing similar methods of study design, data handling and analysis.

Beyond such are overlaps between veterinary *practice* and economics. Some reflect ancient wealth relationships between livestock (especially cattle) and man (see Chapter 3), including origins within the livestock sector of basic vocabulary (and associated concepts) of economics and finance. The first school of veterinary science, founded in France in 1762, was initially called the school of rural veterinary economy. The veterinary profession remains acutely conscious of the economic basis of most veterinary practice (at both the individual animal and animal population levels) in terms not only of animals' value to families and society, but to related monetary constraints on its procedures and programs and how these can be reduced or managed. Walter Gibbons, a leading American professor of food animal medicine, drilled into his students during the middle decades of this century that "a veterinarian needs to know not only the best, most modern procedure to apply in any instance, but also the cheapest, reasonably satisfactory procedure. You absolutely cannot," he would add, "do your great $100 operation on a $25 cow").[11]

Note was taken in Table 6.2 that one of the four crises faced in the delivery of food animal veterinary services post-World War II was an unprecedented demand by economists newly in positions of power within some governments that budget requests from various sectors be bulwarked by appropriate benefit-cost justifications. That challenge to previously sufficing "professional judgement" or "experience-generated expertise," though not especially welcomed by governmental veterinarians, was responded to initially in the United States by several veterinarians being sent to pursue master's degrees in economics, during which they carried out benefit-cost studies on disease control campaigns then in progress. More organized veterinary responses were forthcoming from the mid-1960s to this crisis and a second veterinary economic crisis prompted by development of the first large-scale intensive production units for livestock and how private veterinary practitioners could relate to them. Roger Morris at the University of Melbourne (the first veterinarian to earn a Ph.D. degree in economics), with Douglas Blood, a leading food animal clinical professor, organized a postgraduate program specifically in animal health economics. Soon after, a postgraduate option in animal health economics was added to M.P.V.M.[12] and Ph.D. programs in quantitative epidemiology within the University of California at Davis, and both veterinarians and economists thenceforth could pursue that new cross-disciplinary field.

At about the same time a few economists became interested in animal health problems (Schwabe and Ruppanner, 1972). In 1976 those currents were more broadly joined through convening an International Symposium on Veterinary Epidemiology and Economics (with formation of an international association bridging the two disciplines). Its successor symposia[13] have not only attracted larger and larger audiences, but have yielded a Proceedings reflecting an ever broader range of methodological applications of these two approaches (often together) to an array of problems. A journal, *Preventive Veterinary Medicine*, also reflecting these developments, especially in quantitative methodologies, appeared in 1982 under the editorship of Hans Riemann of the University of California.

Besides those early contributions, including ones by H.E. Jahnke, Lovell Jarvis and a University of Reading group headed by veterinarian Peter Ellis, one of the first linkages in Africa of epidemiologic and economic methodologies to veterinary services delivery was a benefit-cost study on alternative approaches to contagious bovine pleuropneumonia (CBPP) control in the southern Sudan (Zessin and Carpenter, 1985). More African economic applications were forthcoming in Ph.D. research by Zessin (1991) upon findings of the GTZ veterinary component of the large rangelands development project in the Central Region of Somalia (Baumann et al., 1993 and see our Chapter 10).

Citing his personal reasons for deciding to concentrate on problems of veterinary services delivery in Africa, political scientist David Leonard (1993) opined in relation to development overall that "if we can succeed in developing a theory [of development incorporating insights of New Institutional Economics, of collective action, rational choice theories of politics and refinements in organizational theory] for animal health [in Africa], we will have made a major step toward developing one for other professional services--not only for human medicine, which is quite similar in science and organizational structure, but also for areas such as education and agriculture." In *pastoral* Africa we believe such conclusions are especially germane and we stress the potential to pastoral development of deliberately linking through IC mechanisms not only these relationships of economics to epidemiology, but of both also to anthropology and range ecology. In this, we see key roles for concerned political scientists/public administrators.

At the crux of these infrastructural reforms and related interdisciplinary initiatives are not only local intelligence capabilities, but local decisions and actions which reflect a considerably more decentralized veterinary delivery system administratively than is now the case in Africa. We have already addressed portions of this. Let us now consider decentralization in terms of the infrastructural sustainability of pastoral development efforts.

## DECENTRALIZATION OF DEVELOPMENT INITIATIVES

Our proposals' success requires *local* initiatives, both decisions and actions, and therefore strongly supports decentralization of authority wherever it makes good sense to do so. This is not only for reasons of efficiency in fulfilling tasks, but also of economy and public support. At the same time, we recognize that major parts of veterinary services constitute public goods, many of which not only fully justify public provision, but require in part centralized efforts for reasons of the total population coverage which is needed, consistency/uniformity of procedures which must be followed and ongoing nationwide monitoring, evaluation and similar functions which must be built into them.[14] Experiences elsewhere illustrate very well how sufficient locally acquired information is vital to the success of mandatory aspects of veterinary programs *and* how, in turn, only a centralized component has the affordable ability to put this information into forms that are most useful to persons working at the local level. Thus, the cyclical reenforcing nature of the intelligence systems which comprise the core activity for a modern veterinary services infrastructure.

Leonard (1984) noted that overconcentration of administrative authority in Africa not only stifles development because, in addition to delaying actions, it favors corruption; it also creates irrational and inefficient management practices whose costs developing countries cannot afford. Similar views are now widely held, including that administrative decentralization is a precondition for economic growth (Rondinelli, 1981). On the other hand, results of attempted decentralization in some African situations (Maddick, 1963) have not been encouraging. Thus, Kenya's decentralization of planning to the district level in 1979-1983 achieved few of the desired goals because of ineffective implementation mechanisms in the face of limited resources (Migot-Adholla, 1984: 199-232). Failures there and elsewhere were described by Leonard and Marshall (1982).

Many important veterinary programs involve measures that require for their success participation of *all* livestock owners, not just those who may choose to participate. "Free-riders" are eliminated by enforceable penalties.

Thus, rather paradoxically, while most veterinarians as individuals have traditionally reflected the political conservatism *cum* personal individualism of the rural communities from which they came, their delivery systems, even in avowedly capitalist countries, have reflected overall a highly socialized pattern of professional organization and operation. We eschew any ideological political bias in our suggestions about an optimal veterinary infrastructure in interests of pastoral development. Our proposals involve an opportunistic approach to real situations. That is also the only approach consistent with the outlook (mindset) of pastoralists themselves.

### Applications in the Southern Sudan

In the Sudan, the concept of decentralization came to the fore during the military rule of Jaafar Mohammed Nimeiry (1969-1985). Leaders of the Sudan Socialist Union, the country's only political party then, considered some degree of decentralization (regionalization) as a precondition for political stability (foremost, the end of the first civil war)--thus the granting in 1972 of semiautonomous rule to the three southern provinces (thence divided into six provinces) within a united Sudan. Although that experiment failed politically and retained an inefficient and corrupt civil service at the center of power, it did identify as a continuing problem the lack of sufficient *financial* autonomy with authority to plan, budget and implement projects at the regional level. Decentralization was an appropriate development policy choice for the southern Sudan, but lack of political will, coupled with the lack of capacity to facilitate implementation of its prescriptions fully, frustrated efforts.

Hence, for almost all externally financed projects, the southern region depended on plans and programs proposed by foreign nationals, many of whom were short-term visitors ill-informed about local situations. As a result many programs lacked necessary social and cultural orientation or citizen acquiescence, much less enthusiasm. As an overall result, regional officials did not explore alternative means of maximizing use of scarce resources through, for instance, IC at provincial and/or district levels, even in those spheres where possibilities should have been obvious.

From the first author's perspective at several levels of that regional government, other sources of decentalization failure were heterogeneous forms of "clientilism," reflecting competition among various ethnic and religious groups, political parties and other movements within the Sudan. This suggested that decentralization to only regional levels was insufficient, but that more appropriate would be further devolution, where possible, to provincial and district levels. Remedies will also require recognition that the Sudan falls within the category of "soft" or "weak" states (Azarya, 1988). These have limited jurisdiction over some societies within their bounds and therefore are incapable of implementing programs effectively and of achieving stated goals (Rothchild and Curry, 1978; Rothchild, 1988). Lack of citizen participation characterizes such states and inequitable allocations and/or distributions of national resources usually result. A vicious cycle may result when severity of societal disengagement and disenfranchisement promotes citizen responses ranging from organized protests (such as riots and strikes) to adoption of unofficial means of trade like black marketeering (Rothchild, 1988). The extreme case of societal protest is a civil war, such as occurred in the Sudan from 1955 to 1972, and again beginning in 1983. We believe that true decentralization indicates the only way out of the present state of nondevelopment (economic and political chaos) in the southern Sudan. Most needed will be ways to promote appropriate organization and insure full participation of the largest target group, the region's totally neglected pastoralists.

We shall now address the problem of strengthening ongoing grassroots-level liaison in light of our proposals.

### Ongoing Grassroots Linkages

With S. Sandford (1983: 150), we believe that under many circumstances, grassroots level outreach to pastoralists is more logically based upon social groupings of pastoralists than upon a specific territory. One main reason would be the continuity of contacts with particular families and their herds that this would favor. Another reason in some countries is that the pastoral population is not linguistically homogeneous. In the southern Sudan, for example, a large number of mutually unintelligible languages are spoken and this complicates enormously the delivery of any services.

The GTZ group in Somali has had success in making repeat visits to the same pastoralist herds by ascertaining from their owners (a possibility in Somalia) where they intended to move next within a particular *degaan* and approximately when. This may also be a possibility (which needs to be investigated) in other places, and some of these grazing sites may be accessible to 4-wheel-drive vehicles. But clearly the type of regular route for traveling veterinary personnel, which may well suffice for sedentary livestock owners (Leonard, 1993), could not be applied under most extensive pastoral circumstances.

*Paraveterinary Auxiliaries.* All African veterinary services, recognizing that manual skills needed to carry out certain veterinary disease or injury *treatment* interventions could be adequately taught to persons with much less education than veterinarians possess, have employed various kinds of paraveterinary personnel (with different levels of formal education). Pritchard estimated in 1988 that there were then over 40,000 such veterinary auxiliaries in all categories on the African continent. Some of them have traveled with specific pastoral peoples (Baumann, 1990). In the early years of independence, some of these grassroots forms of outreach were weakened or abandoned in the belief that sufficient fully trained veterinarians would soon become available to serve Africa's entire animal-owning public (as in the North), and/or that more highly trained auxiliaries based at district and provincial administrative centers could perform all necessary services.  Sandford (1983: 182) noted that senior veterinary officials in Kenya saw no need to train nomadic/transhumant animal health auxiliaries.  The "epidemiological revolution" (see Table 6.2) had not yet begun in earnest, and very limited uses could be made then of intelligence information, as compared to today.

Most paraveterinary auxiliaries now working in Africa have had at least primary school educations, many in languages (e.g., in the Sudan, English or Arabic) not native to themselves or the livestock owners they serve. These exposures to outside influences have distanced those of pastoral origins from their roots and the way of life of their own peoples.  The result is that official veterinary personnel seldom live in the pastoral environment or in the traditional manner.

Thus, sources of animal health auxiliaries and the functions different types were asked to perform, the types of training required and so on were often more varied in the past.  We believe it is time to reexamine those past efforts, identifying ones that were more successful and less successful and why.  That is, newer epidemiological and intervention technology, as well as national aspirations vastly different from those of the colonial period or immediately thereafter, now create new circumstances and needs. We shall emphasize only a few critical points which have particular pertinence to our development proposals.  In our opinions, and as is commonly the case now, one type of paraveterinary individual should be based within district veterinary offices and, together with at least some of the fully trained veterinarians based there, staff the mobile teams that (1) conduct well-designed sample surveys of pastoralist herds for baseline and other major purposes at intervals which would vary for specific diseases, (2) follow with a more frequent schedule of visits *particular* "geographic sentinel herds" to satisfy other information monitoring needs, including of area grass conditions, intended movement patterns, herd demographics, production, etc., and (3) promptly follow up more intensively in the field all especially important findings identified through (1) and (2) and other facets of the epidemiologic intelligence system.  Some of these or other district-based auxiliaries would also help with field interventions, slaughterhouse operation and other veterinary public health functions, as well as serve as laboratory assistants and the like.

A second type of veterinary auxiliary within pastoral areas would be less formally attached to the veterinary services establishment, would be a pastoralist himself (with his own herds) and would travel with segments of the pastoral community rendering a variety of services (some of which would be supported in key ways by the formal veterinary establishment).

We propose that intelligent but otherwise unschooled or minimally schooled pastoralists who can reach other pastoralists' herds with useful equipment and drugs (which they know how to use), communicate with them and enjoy local respect for their disease knowledge and/or veterinary skills be more or less formally linked to the veterinary establishment. Persons of these types could be taught additional skills *in their vernacular*. Beyond such, they might collect specimens such as feces and blood smears which may not require special handling, as well as disease, management and environmental information. That is, beside rendering direct curative services, they would provide vital links in an epidemiological intelligence system.

Problems encountered in colonial-period efforts to have veterinary auxiliaries travel with pastoralists included (1) having government officials select the individuals (some of whom were not closely enough associated with the particular community served), (2) selecting only individuals with prior formal schooling, (3) selecting individuals who did not already enjoy reputations within their communities for their animal-related knowledge or sufficient prestige otherwise and (4) problems with compensation and definition of relationships to the remainder of the veterinary establishment. Some recent revivals of interest in the idea of grassroots traveling auxiliaries (D. Sandford, 1981; Halpin, 1981a, 1981b; Schwabe, 1980, 1996; Schwabe and Kuojok, 1981; Almond, 1991; Baumann, 1990; Sollod and Stem, 1991) propose meeting some of these past problems by different combinations of the following: (1) having the specific pastoral community select the individual; (2) omitting a requirement of formal schooling and offering necessary instruction in the vernacular; (3) setting up such auxiliaries in forms of private practice rather than as government employees; (4) having their practice kit restricted to a few items which are easy to store and use; (5) requiring pastoralists to pay full price for all drugs and vaccines; (6) seeing that auxiliaries interact with pastoralist institutions, so demands for drugs, vaccines and such can be effectively transferred from herders to auxiliaries thence to the official veterinary services; (7) making continuing support for such assisted private practices and official linkages to the government veterinary establishment contingent upon periodic assessments of satisfactory performance; (8) enlisting cooperation when possible of non-governmental organizations; and (9) attempting the co-option of certain types of existing traditional healers for such service. Programs incorporating some of these features were initiated in Ethiopia (D. Sandford, 1981), Niger (Sollod et al., 1984) and the Central Region of Somalia (Zessin, 1991; Baumann, 1990; Baumann et al., 1993).

We believe that such a system of private pastoralist practitioners would be as vital to the monitoring/intelligence needs outlined above as to more effective provisions of preventive and curative services. While they would have official recognition, advice, access to supplies and various nonsalary rewards, in our version of this initiative they would also be participating pastoralists with their own herds of animals.

*Co-opting Traditional Healers as Traveling Auxiliaries.* Traditional healers of several types exist within most African societies[15] and, generally, no distinction is made between veterinary and human applications (Schwabe, 1978a: 8-14, 40-49). Some provide mental and/or physical relief from illness and trauma, including conditions regarded as having supernatural origins (Dunlop, 1975). Other techniques include manual skills like surgery, especially operations to alleviate pain, as well as employment of herbal remedies (Roles, 1967). While Nchinda (1976) and others group such traditional healers into surgeon,[16] herbalist,[17] and psychiatrist (or diviner) categories, all share one characteristic in common: they function within the psychological framework of their clients' beliefs, cultures and expectations. Therefore, pastoralists and others have faith in such healers. WHO has given serious consideration during recent decades to what traditional healers might offer beyond what they already do and how such traditional skills might be maximally exploited within primary health care systems. Veterinary authorities have done far less along those lines but the pastoral situation is the one of greatest urgency today and the traditional healer model proposed here is a logical starting point. Let us pursue these possibilities under circumstances prevailing in the southern Sudan.

Some individuals among the Dinka possess special skills which enable them to perform a range of health-related functions for cattle and people. In the psychiatrist/diviner category are itinerants called *tiet*, as well as respected traditional spiritual leaders like the *bany bith*. There are also herbalists called *ran wal*, some of whose remedies for conditions like snakebite and scorpion stings enjoy wide repute. Also among the Dinka is a manual healer called an *atet*[18] (see Figure 8.4; Schwabe, 1984b: 172ff, 1996; Schwabe and Kuojok, 1981). These individuals are skilled in mechanical arts such as wound and abscess surgery, bonesetting, obstetrics and castration (the latter two for animals only). *It is only individuals like* atet *who we believe should qualify for co-opting as grassroots veterinary auxiliaries.* These traditional veterinary healers (TVHs) are herd owners themselves, and often very successful ones. Thus, their presence in migratory cattle camps and at transhumant home bases makes them easily available to pastoralists. Not all are equally accomplished, but some are known over very wide areas and are in special demand.

Dinka TVHs are not only informed about mammalian anatomy, but they have some reasonable ideas about physiology and recognize a number of cattle (and human) diseases which they diagnose and sometimes attempt to treat (Chapter 4). Although drug therapy is not now a primary function of most Dinka TVHs, pastoralists generally in the southern Sudan have become increasingly acquainted with uses of syringes and needles for injecting locally valued therapeutic agents like antibiotics and trypanocides, as well as with use of deworming agents and acaricides, and some, including many *atet*, are skillful in their administration. There can be little doubt that selected *atet* could improve delivery of individual animal treatments, including bloodless

**Figure 8.2. A traditional Dinka "veterinarian-physician"** *atet* **(third from left). Skilled in bovine obstetrics and bovine and human orthopedics and wound surgery, he discusses a problem with a government veterinary assistant (second from left) and the cattle camp chief (***bany wut***, second from right), while other cattle owners look on.**

castrations. They could also help governmental veterinary personnel in immunization efforts and serve as an important source of primary data for development-related monitoring tasks identified above. TVHs could provide this and otherwise difficult-to-obtain information *if* a plan for data acquisition (contacts, reporting forms, etc.) were properly designed and executed. The Tufts University group working in the Sahel devised a series of reporting forms for preliterate pastoralists using simple line drawings (of animals, anatomy, lesions, other pathological findings, specimens, etc.) which require only checks or counting strokes by the reporter (Sollod and Stem, 1991). Another important advantage of co-opting TVHs is that they are currently in competition with governmental personnel. Such co-option would make competitors into collaborators.

Where skilled manual TVHs do not exist (nor another class of possibly suitable traditional healers), as in central Somalia (Karl-Hans Zessin, personal communication), the next best source of persons to serve as this most grassroots arm of veterinary services would be other pastoralists who enjoy the respect of their communities. That approach was followed by the GTZ Somalia team with their Nomadic Animal Health Assistants (NAHAs). Trained NAHAs' surveillance functions were monitored by a veterinarian's visit every two months during which (1) records were collected, (2) each was subjected to a standard interview about these and other qualitative and quantitative information and (3) their drug supplies were replenished after accounting (Zessin et al., 1993; Baumann, 1990).

Important observations made by such pastoralist auxiliaries would be subjected to intensive follow-up by more highly trained personnel. However, certain cautions in co-opting traditional healers or other pastoralists must continually be observed, especially about possible noncongruence of traditional and scientific diagnoses (Sollod et al., 1984). Even under routine conditions, more formally educated personnel would need to periodically complement these ongoing, less reliable efforts in order to confirm their field diagnoses and prevalence estimates.

*Fully qualified veterinarians must more commonly lead many more such field efforts than is currently the practice in much of Africa.* Therefore, a vitally important consideration is how best to use scarce and expensive fully qualified veterinarians in both purely veterinary and pastoral development contexts.

### Uses of Veterinarians

Lack of veterinarians has been mentioned frequently as a serious hindrance to program development and implementation. In Botswana, Chimbombi (1988) indicated that some district-level veterinary services were run by official paravets alone without professional supervision. This was found also to be generally true in central Somalia by the GTZ group working there. Ratios in Ethiopia of 1 veterinarian per 361,904 livestock units (LU) (Haile Yesus, 1988) and in the southern Sudan of 1 veterinarian per 417,667 LU in 1981/82 rendered disease control practically nonexistent over wide areas. This problem in some other areas may be as much one of *priorities in assignments* of veterinarians, of obtaining something closer to optimal use of these highly educated personnel, as of absolute shortages. Some relative economies of personnel must be attempted at the upper levels of veterinary administration in places where the best-trained professionals prematurely gravitate to desk jobs. But even more important is that locally serving veterinarians must be used with the greatest effectiveness possible throughout the entire year.

Examples of what only a few veterinarians *in the field* in remote pastoral areas can do are the substantial accomplishments of a single three veterinarian GTZ team in the southern Sudan and, later, in central Somalia. All local district veterinarians could accomplish these same types of extremely valuable diagnostic/intelligence functions *if* they too spent reasonable portions of their own time taking mobile diagnostic capabilities to the field and backing these up with laboratory and epidemiological analyses. To optimize those would require major veterinary educational reforms in Africa (see Chapter 9). To stimulate such more generally is, in part, to encourage local initiatives, and to reward successes and valuable innovations, if not through augmented salaries exclusively, by merit systems that offer other well-received recognitions or benefits. These could include opportunities for professional meeting attendance, publication opportunities, publicized scientific and service awards and *merit* promotions to leadership roles. Leonard (1993) and Gros (1993c, 1993d) both stressed possibilities to monitor and reward  good performance which draw more intentionally upon a highly developed sense of veterinary professionalism internationally.

### Future Privatization of Veterinary Services in Africa

Partly from frustrations of past failures to recognize sufficiently that efforts to improve livestock production in Africa cannot possibly succeed until highly disruptive diseases are effectively controlled or eliminated--failures characterized by efforts to put the cart before the horse in livestock develop-ment schemes (mostly among sedentary farmers)--some donors of development funds for Africa have recently sought alternative solutions. Privatization of at least some tasks currently the sole responsibility of governmental veterinary services in the majority of African states has been urged by some donors (Haan and Nissen, 1985; Cheneau, 1985) in the belief that by transferring many vet-erinary tasks to the private sector, veterinary service delivery in Africa can be improved and more reasonably financed.  We believe that some of those pro-posals are totally unrealistic under most African circumstances, although, as already indicated, we believe that "private practice" by selected pastoralists co-opted on a nonsalaried basis by government veterinary services offers a partial solution to extending veterinary services more effectively in pastoral areas. Other suggestions to overcome liabilities of insufficient funds to succeed in-clude (1) increasing cost recovery for services rendered and inputs provided; and (2) a freeze on new recruitment and, if necessary, a staff reduction to increase the share of nonpersonnel recurrent funds in budgets (Haan and Nissen, 1985).  We have already addressed some prospects for cost-recovery in pastoral areas.

While public and private veterinary practices coexist, unusually comple-mentarily, in many economically developed countries, it is incorrect to con-clude that successes achieved under those circumstances are likely to be dupli-catable anytime soon, if ever, within pastoral Africa.  For one thing, it needs to be clearly understood that *private food animal veterinary practice almost everywhere has always been either indirectly or directly subsidized* by varied devices. Moreover, the stage of food-related veterinary services delivery now reached in economically developed countries is principally one of participation in the intensification of animal production, activities free from the constraints of the primary problems still plaguing Africa.

Despite recent and prominent changes in the bases for veterinary efforts in the North, nonveterinarians must understand that private veterinary practice in rural areas everywhere has depended almost exclusively until very recently

(Schwabe, 1993a) upon unpredictable farmer-identified medical emergencies (illnesses or injuries in individual animals) resulting, by analogy with the work of firemen, in an essentially discontinuous "fire engine type" practice of ad hoc responses to problems which are often at considerable distances. Thus, family farm practice everywhere is, and will remain, almost entirely on an outpatient (and ambulatory response) basis, which is very uneconomical of the veterinarian's time, especially considering what most farmers have been able or willing to pay to save an individual animal.

Mention was made in Chapter 6 of the unique form of "State Lutheran Church subsidization" of new veterinary practitioners in the early years of veterinary science in Sweden and, ever since, a variety of other direct or *indirect* props to private food animal practice have been employed. Until the 1960s, private food animal practices of American veterinarians, for example, were supported economically largely by (1) performance of large numbers of routine annual vaccinations against costly livestock diseases like hog cholera for which no official eradication/control programs then existed; (2) part-time contract employment of up to 50% of all privately practicing American veterinarians for routine testing of livestock (e.g., tuberculosis, brucellosis, etc.) and inspections of farms (e.g., garbage-feeding of swine) as part of official governmental disease control/eradication programs;[19] and/or (3) development of pet animal practice (mostly among the nonfarming population). The first of these approaches to a more dependable income (a not very exciting bread-and-butter activity), was facilitated in the United States until the 1960s by the fact that veterinarians themselves had founded and owned a large number of vaccine and serum laboratories, almost all of which restricted their sales to graduate veterinarians.[20]

When these first two main private practice props were lost or seriously eroded from about 1960 on, almost the entire response by America's veterinarians was the only remaining assurance *under relatively affluent American conditions* of pet animal practice (including horses and more unusual species). Consequently, by 1980, of 25,357 members of the American Veterinary Medical Association (AVMA) engaged in any form of private practice, about 12,000 were already *exclusively* pet animal practitioners, as compared to 6,922 veterinarians in mixed practices with a 50% or higher large animal component (which included pet horses for a sizable amount) and about 4,000 others who did some large animal practice (again, including pet horses). That is, by then only 1,050 American veterinarians engaged *entirely* in private mixed large animal practice (including pet horses), while only 262 had exclusively cattle practices and 30 exclusively swine.[21] A nadir was reached in California, for example (which then had livestock industries worth more than those of all but six *countries* in the world), when, of 128 veterinary graduates in 1972, only two entered *any* aspect of food animal practice!

Other props were provided in some countries by farmer-subsidized practices, as through veterinary clubs in New Zealand (see Chapter 6) and livestock producers' cooperatives. In some other countries, most rural veterinary practitioners are virtually full-time employees of pharmaceutical/feed manufacturers (as in parts of Latin America and within the poultry industry in the United States and elsewhere) and/or livestock insurance schemes, as in Israel. In some places, direct subsidies are paid to private veterinarians (to equalize and reduce costs to farmers), as in Canada's province of Quebec. But beyond such deliberate direct subsidization of rural veterinary practice are other "invisible subsidies" in most countries of milk price supports, other commodity supports and the like to farmers (giving them the dependable incomes to, among other things, engage privately provided veterinary assistance).

Therefore, it is unrealistic to speak of *private* veterinary food animal practice, for except under special circumstances (usually not involving typical farmers) it has not been a really free market proposition. Nor should it be expected to be, because much of what private food animal veterinarians provide are vital public goods (Leonard, 1993). Although veterinary science has achieved a better balance historically between the two ideological extremes of all planned/state-supplied or all marketplace-determined/private enterprise systems than has either human medicine or other agricultural sciences, those relationships are not as simple or straightforward as they might at first appear.

Our ideas for enlisting and utilizing TVHs within a system of pastoral veterinary services delivery envisages a largely private practice approach *at that level*, but not one which could possibly sustain fully qualified veterinarians. In the dual-level public/private system which we suggest for pastoral conditions, the "private practitioner" does not travel by Land Rover, but on foot, or by animal, like other pastoralists do.

Such facts notwithstanding,

in the wake of the "Great Third World Depression" of the 1980s and 1990s and the consequent fiscal collapse of most sub-Saharan African states, international donors have sponsored a massive attempt to restructure African economies. Led by the World Bank, donors have sought to move services wherever possible from the public to the private sectors. . . . The Bank's staff certainly believe that it is more important to privatize economic enterprises than social services. Beyond that, however, to judge by the Bank's actual practice, the theory appears to be that any form of privatization or fee recovery to which African political leaders will consent is economically and socially desirable. This . . . "theory" alerts us to danger, for it really is no more than an assumption and a poorly grounded one at that. . . . The current argument for privatization [of veterinary services in Africa] . . . depends on the theory that the market can outperform the state in virtually any circumstance and that privatization is therefore desirable no matter what form it takes" (Leonard, 1993).

More specifically, Leonard argues, "World Bank attempts to promote privatization [of veterinary services] in Africa suggest an oversight or willingness to ignore the issue of regulation under imperfect market conditions." We think it additionally ignores veterinary history. Where privatization has been virtually forced by external donors, as in Cameroon, these new entrepreneurs have necessarily retreated to the cities and pet animal practice (Gros, 1993a, 1993c), a luxury Africa can scarcely afford.

## A CENTRALIZED-DECENTRALIZED MODEL FOR VETERINARY SERVICES DELIVERY

As do we, the FAO (1981) has suggested that implementation of development programs in agriculture in general depends upon establishment or strengthening of that level of administration which can act as a link between a network of all local-level organizations--that is, of both governmental grass-roots-level field services and people-rooted institutions (e.g., pastoralists' traditional groupings, other NGOs) and an upper level represented by national (and, in the case of very large countries like the Sudan, regional) government. In a situation of an extreme lack of resources, as in the southern Sudan, pro-vincial and district levels are currently most appropriate for such people linkages and, therefore, provincial and district personnel must be given sufficient authority to budget for, and implement independently, services under their charge. Their demonstrated abilities to do that if unimpeded by regu-lations and red tape were illustrated for local veterinary-facilitated IC efforts in Chapter 7. We shall discuss here only two aspects of central level activities that appear to us to be most pertinant to our overall proposals.

### A Central Diagnostic Laboratory and Epidemiological Investigation Facility

A Central Diagnostic Laboratory and Epidemiological Investigation Facility would provide the highest level of veterinary diagnostic support available in a country. Most countries now make an attempt to provide (in a technical sense) the laboratory half of this required facility, and such efforts have been generously supported by external donors. This central facility would concentrate upon solutions of difficult problems referred from lower levels or disclosed by its own investigations. The less-precedented epidemiological investigation half of such a facility should be staffed with individuals trained to the Ph.D. level in quantitative epidemiology, biostatistics, animal health economics and computer science. A special feature would be its Epidemiolog-ical Intelligence Service (EIS). Besides planning and coordinating the nation-wide surveillance program and of analyzing surveillance information for the design, monitoring and evaluation of national animal health and production programs (see Figure 8.1), it would be able to dispatch skilled experts upon short notice to any part of the country where intensive follow-up of animal health problems of special importance or complexity required efforts beyond those ordinarily available through district (field) offices (e.g., major outbreaks, suspected exotic pathogen invaders, special problem herds encountered during large-scale interventions).   EIS staff would also carry out with assistance of district personnel a periodic series of baseline and follow-up sample surveys in different geographical areas for a selected range of livestock diseases.   This service would determine, in consultation with field personnel, the kinds of data to be collected by them and devise effective monitoring systems for thoroughness of compliance with these local functions.   It would also conduct studies on the economic costs of diseases and cost-benefits of alternative approaches to interventions in particular situations.   As suggested by Kenyon and Nour (1991), it could also process data usable by other sectors sharing the veterinary-facilitated collection possibilities outlined.

### Technical/Technological Sustainability of Programs

Related to these centralized aspects of services delivery is the technical/technological sustainability of total efforts and their principal components. We discussed in Chapter 7 fiscal and public support sustainability of IC programs and earlier in this chapter their infrastructural sustainability.  The questions of technical/technological sustainability we address now are peculiarly neglected ones that apply to *delivery of the most essential veterinary (and other social) servic*es to pastoralists.  We agree especially with Kenyon and Nour (1991) that "in the design and implementation of many laboratory projects in developing countries there has been a disinclination to deal with the sustainability of veterinary laboratory services.  In some instances there has been a 'technology race' between donors which has been abetted and encouraged by veterinary managers in the recipient government, particularly those that have trained overseas to higher degree level.  Bench methods [labor-intensive diagnostic and other laboratory methods in common use in the North until a few decades ago] may be more time consuming, but are likely to survive in a resource poor environment long after a high capacity auto-analyzer [complex automated apparatus] has been side-lined for lack of parts or reagents."  Labor costs are not usually the most limiting factors in African countries. That is, despite the fact that veterinarians have been generally sensitive to the economic lability of their efforts throughout history, Kenyon and Nour are totally correct regarding the last few decades in Africa that "this concept of [cheapest technically acceptable methods] is quite at odds with the 'state of the art' philosophy aspired to by veterinary scientists in developing countries and promoted by most development agencies."

## CONCLUSIONS

What we have been concerned with mostly in this chapter is providing a modern information-based infrastructure for delivery of mobile veterinary services to migratory pastoralists. While this process can be initiated immediately, epidemiological surveillance (the basis for this new infrastructure) is by nature a continually improving activity and that improvement could be markedly expedited by favorable decisions of government and judicious short-term infusions of money.

Past failures in parts of Africa to eliminate disruptive economic burdens of several major livestock diseases have resulted less from absence of suitable technical procedures and weapons than from insufficient ongoing epidemiological intelligence to better pinpoint use of severely limited resources. Moreover, there has been insufficient ability, even in some of the more initially successful efforts, to promptly detect reintroductions or recrudescences of these same or other destructive diseases, and mobile capacities have often been inadequate to respond promptly to situations identified. From the purely veterinary standpoint, considerably enhanced intelligence capacities will also facilitate initial recognitions (and subsequent determinations of the distributions and importance) of other less dramatic diseases. From experiences elsewhere in the world we can reasonably expect their importance as productivity limiters. History indicates further that, partially because of its diverse and relatively dense populations of mammalian, avian and reptilian wildlife, a number of new infections of livestock and/or people will continue to make their first appearances in Africa, some with not only major consequences there (trypanosomiases, Rift Valley fever, Ebola and Lassa fevers as examples), but to wider areas of the world in cases where such previously unknown infections have escaped the African continent. Major examples from the past include not only Rift Valley fever but African swine fever, bluetongue and African horsesickness. That is, there are not only global veterinary but also public health reasons for veterinary institution-building in Africa with regard to more effective information-gathering and analysis.

Such mechanisms could also be core activities for other needed social responses within pastoral areas. For, besides services to livestock and human health and other possibilities, such as water source maintenance, which an improved veterinary-based mobile system could provide (see Chapter 7), we noted in Chapter 2 the conclusions of increasing numbers of persons in other fields concerned with pastoral development that effective monitoring for variables such as rainfall, grazing conditions, soil erosion, animal movements, animal productivity and pastoralists' practices will prove vital in the future if meaningful progress in drought response and range management, as key examples, are also to be forthcoming. Clearly each of those sectors for potential activity of value to pastoralists and/or the improvement of territories they inhabit cannot *alone* provide the mobile, information-gathering and processing capacities they require. Such would be utterly unaffordable.

A modern veterinary infrastructure urged here as a very-high-priority development goal would possess the study design and analytical capabilities to serve the information needs not only of its own sector but also, in at least its mobile component, other governmental branches. Thus, what has been laid out in this chapter would strengthen and make more sustainable the kinds of key local IC initiatives illustrated in Chapter 7 *and provide a whole new intelligence-monitoring-communications dimension of development IC which could have much broader national implications than locally instituted pastoral services per se.* This multipurpose pastoral communications system would be two-directional. From the outside to the pastoralists it would transmit badly needed skills and direct technical aid (e.g., veterinary and medical disease prevention and treatment capacities), plus new information (extension efforts in animal husbandry, sanitation, human health, nutrition, range management, water resources management, etc.). And from the pastoralists and their environments to outside agencies it would transmit locally collected information critically valuable to emergency responses, priority setting among various needs and other aspects of planning and program implementation and evaluation.

For these two-way communications *cum* service processes to succeed, greater decentralization of activities will be required for some sectors and, for the veterinary/livestock sector, a new composite decentralized/centralized model will arise. Some privatization possibilities at the literally grassroots level are readily visualizable as a component of such an overall veterinary services delivery system among difficult-to-reach peoples but, practically speaking, these will be limited to services of certain pastoral auxiliaries, rather than of veterinarians themselves.

Finally, little attention, if any, is yet paid in Africa to those diseases which impair productivity of individual animals. The surveillance-type veterinary infrastructure advocated here, unlike the campaigns/mass actions infrastructure of the past, recognizes that--since (1) more time- and money-efficient campaigns can be realized through the better pin-pointing of disease occurrence and (2) that most of the cost of a campaign is in reaching scattered livestock populations--attempts to derive *multiple* benefits ("killing more than one bird with one stone") from as many program activities as possible is vital. Thus, expensive visits to migratory cattle camps and transhumant home bases should never be *solely* to vaccinate cattle against single diseases, but also to collect essential disease, demographic and husbandry intelligence vital to efficiently combatting these and other diseases *and* improving productivity (plus information of similar value to other cooperating sectors).

## NOTES

1. Government personnel have usually been very quick to appreciate and borrow these radio connections. Mobile radio-telephones were rapidly adopted by Northern vet-

erinary practitioners following their availability to reduce a costly, time-consuming service delivery problem (so-called fire engine practice).

2. Analogies between veterinary and military actions (organization and teminology) were first drawn by Maurice Hall (1936); a summary can be found in Schwabe (1984b: 296).

3. Veterinary science pioneered a "public goods approach" to disease management.

4. That more refined strategy has had one *global* success so far for a widely distributed pathogen, the WHO-coordinated effort which has eradicated smallpox, whereas a prior *mass* immunization campaign approach lacked sufficient resources for success in many Third World countries. (Apparent global eradication was achieved earlier in the case of more restrictively distributed vesicular exanthema of swine.) Interestingly, the last two countries to eradicate smallpox were in Africa (Ethiopia and Somalia) with virtually no countrywide public health infrastructures and many hard-to-reach populations of pastoralists. The matter of locating and ring-vaccinating around these last cases of smallpox was a very costly one-time intelligence (search and find) effort with major international inputs, but was more than justified by the permanent global implications of its successful outcome. Were the veterinary intelligence system advocated here in place at that time (and the philosophy of local IC accepted), such heroic efforts in Somalia and Ethiopia could have been much more cheaply accomplished.

5. These are not to be equated, as some ideologues would insist. During the 1960s the second author had unusual opportunities within WHO to interact with Soviet public health authorities and to observe the operation and results of undeviating "central authority solutions" in the field. When methods being used (diagnostic, intervention and otherwise) were state-of-the-art, the consistency of their applications--for data collection and expression and the like, as well as for interventions--was truly enviable in terms of what he had observed anywhere else. But methods and approaches adopted and applied in the Soviet Union were not uniformly state-of-the-art by any means. Resultant stifling of local intitiatives (including any experimenting with alternative methods) prevented self-improvement feedback from the field and generally depressed morale in personnel remote from the top.

6. Specific problems identified include (1) too few samples are received, (2) samples are inappropriate for the disease suspected, (3) samples are not accompanied by adequate history or clinical details, (4) samples are improperly preserved, (5) malfunctioning equipment can not be repaired without returning to the country of origin, (6) recurrent funds are not allocated for vehicle and equipment maintenance, reagent purchase and other running costs to maintain activity, (7) there is frequent replacement or reassignment of staff without apparent regard for the nature of their skills. "In the case of assistance to veterinary field services . . . [the current veterinary diagnostic laboratory] may simply be seen as a bottomless pit [absorbing all major donor-provided resources]" (Kenyon and Nour, 1991).

7. While active population surveys for pathognomic signs of disease, specific etiologic agents of disease, immunodiagnostic reactors and the like have been carried

out frequently for over a century within veterinary science, more often than not they have been for single diseases (or a few closely related diseases). Moreover, most often they have been prompted in the past by local outbreaks or more extensive epidemics within an area (a characteristic of most surveys in Africa) and therefore may poorly reflect the experiences of animal populations under more normal (interepidemic or endemic) conditions.

8. Epidemiological analysis is considered in some detail in Schwabe et al. (1977), Martin et al. (1987) and, with specific African emphases, in Putt et al. (1987).

9. Farver (1987) has described two-stage sampling designs for situations where variability in prevalence among herds is larger than the within-herd variability, a condition generally prevailing in pastoral areas. Cluster sampling is useful in transhumant situations where cattle in multiple herds are kept in specially organized patterns like cattle camps and when a frame that lists all the population elements is not available, or when travel costs from population unit to population unit are considerable. Camps would be considered clusters and the family herds within each of them would be the elements. McDermott et al. (1987) followed such a procedure to estimate prevalence, and age, sex and breed associations for brucellosis and CBPP in one Dinka area.

On the other hand, systematic sampling is appropriate for nomadic herds for which the only suitable ordering of herds occurs at watering points where family herds are watered in turns. A starting point (herd) would be selected randomly and then every kth element (herd) thereafter sampled. The main advantage of systematic sampling is that the population size need not be known/estimated before the survey starts. Thus, there may be a saving on the overall survey cost. Other combinations of sampling designs may fit other circumstances.

Difficulties in random sampling within Dinka herds, as would be the case when data collection involved activities like bleeding, could be overcome in substantial part by first stratifying cattle by age, sex or horn size or other stratification criteria appropriate in terms of cattle owners' beliefs. For example, many owners consider bleeding risky to cattle. But, while Dinka would thus protect animals with long horns, milk cows, stud bulls and name bulls, ordinary steers or animals with short horns could be bled. Such sampling designs require either "insider information" or sufficient expertise in veterinary anthropology.

10. An annotated bibliography (Carlton, 1992) describes systems already developed in Africa.

11. Individual veterinarians have extrapolated such basic animal health economics to areas seemingly removed from usual circumstances of veterinary practice. Thus, early in this century Nathan Sinai, son of a California rancher, after obtaining his veterinary degree and a stint in private practice, became chief of environmental health in the city health department of Stockton, California (environmental health began with meat, milk and water hygiene and veterinarians commonly held such city health department positions). Promoted subsequently to director of the Stockton city health department, Sinai enlarged its jurisdiction to create the first combined city-county health department in the United States (governments then offered no health services to

rural people and Sinai reasoned that if rural livestock could have governmental health services provided so should rural people).

Moving on to the University of Michigan, Sinai eventually became the world's first professor of public health economics, an important American founder of that field and of programmed health care, plus a long-term advisor in such matters to WHO. In addressing the second author's veterinary students within the University of California years later, Sinai made the direct linkage from his beginnings in veterinary practice--the kinds of constant thinking about practical compromises between costs and affordable levels of care--and his seminal applications of those same ways of looking at realities and making difficult choices to conceptually similar problems of human health.

12. Of 554 graduates through 1993 of the Master of Preventive Veterinary Medicine (M.P.V.M.) epidemiology program in the University of California, 72 have been from 16 African countries.

13. In 1994 the 7th Symposium was held in Nairobi.

14. Veterinary services in African countries either *must* reach pastoral communities who own enormous numbers of ruminant animals or sacrifice their highest national mandates and current justifications for Northern support. Key veterinary interventions cannot omit migratory pastoralists because it is inconvenient gaining access to them and simply concentrate upon the sedentary livestock-owning public.

15. Mathias-Mundy and McCorkle (1989) published an annotated global bibliography of traditional veterinary practices. McCorkle et al. (1996) have edited a book entitled *Ethnoveterinary Research and Development*. McCorkle and Mathias-Mundy (1992) and Bizimana (1994) have also published reviews of what is known of traditional forms of veterinary practice and practitioners in Africa. One of the earliest and fullest accounts of traditional healing (veterinary and human) within sub-Saharan Africa was provided by Merker (1910) from among the Maasai in then German-administered Tanzania. Among other early accounts was that for the Bunyoro of Uganda, in which Roscoe (1915: 18ff) mentioned that sons of chiefs were trained to heal cattle.

16. We would add other forms of manual healing (bone setting, obstetrics, etc.) Hot iron cautery is another manual technique used, for example, among Turkana (many hydatid patients we have seen have been thus treated already and have scar patterns from burns over the cyst site).

17. WHO has especially recommended studies of the traditional remedies of this herbalist class in-as-much as a very large number of drugs within the current global scientific pharmacopeia orginated in such empirical ways.

18. *Atet* simply means "specialist" in Dinka. Thus a spearmaker or any other person with skills ordinary herdsmen do not possess is called *atet*.

19. Similarly, some private veterinarians worked on a part-time basis carrying out antemortem and postmortem inspections of animals in local slaughterhouses.

20. Since then virtually all of these biologicals manufacturers (some of them quite large companies) have been quietly bought up by huge multinational pharmaceutical firms which no longer restrict most of their products to veterinarians, but market directly to farmers.

21. By 1993, of 41,228 AVMA members in the United States in all forms of private practice, 23,571 were exclusively small pet animal practitioners, as compared to 1,511 exclusively large animal (including pet horses), 514 exclusively cattle, 90 exclusively swine and 142 exclusively poultry practitioners (AVMA, 1994: 22). In contrast, of approximately 23,000 Japanese veterinarians in 1980, only 5,201 were in private practice (2,171 on food animals) (Sugiyama, 1980).

# 9

---

# EDUCATIONAL REFORMS
# SUPPORTIVE OF DEVELOPMENT

The dual importance of veterinary work in human health and
nutrition and in agricultural economy . . . explains the interest of
both WHO and FAO in veterinary education.

WHO/FAO, 1963

African veterinary schools need not, and perhaps should not, follow
the same curricular formats used elsewhere in the world. . . . The
dominant skills required . . . [in Africa are] of preventive medicine
as applied to populations of animals. . . .

W.R. Pritchard, 1988

This chapter will be concerned with preparing key personnel for pastoral
development in Africa. We do not consider educational reforms for the full
spectrum of sectors that should serve pastoralists, because we do not have the
expertise to do so nor is it necessary for purposes of our proposals. What we
address is how veterinarians, as the *already existing pastoral outreach cadre,*
could be more optimally prepared to act as development catalysts and
facilitators of intersectoral cooperation, as well as anchor effective communications between pastoral communities, their environments and the outside. However, much of this will have relevance to preparing other specialists, particularly those within the human health sector.

We have suggested that broadening the roles of existing local-level
personnel may be desirable in connection with multipurpose visits to pastoral-

ists' camps. We also see a need for one or more persons near the top in each, sector, who would combine a deep knowledge of problems and their solutions *in that sector* with a broad view of how such efforts relate to other needs and the priorities that may exist from place to place and time to time in apportioning limited resources. We believe that, while *both* specialists and at least some true generalists are required to fully realize the potentials of our proposals, the latter should arise among especially competent members of the former[1] and, we think, there are affordable ways to facilitate that broadening of specialists' concerns and competencies, especially during their university educations. We consider these questions first through an appraisal of programs initiated previously within the southern Sudan's fledgling University of Juba.

## EDUCATION FOR DEVELOPMENT: THE UNIVERSITY OF JUBA EXPERIENCE

The idea of a university for the southern Sudan was conceived in 1965 during the Round Table Conference to discuss the "problem of the southern Sudan," political issues that led to the civil war then in progress and how to end that war. The Conference resolved that, at the conclusion of hostilities, a university should be established in the south. The Establishment Act provided for two colleges, Social and Economic Studies and Natural Resources and Environmental Studies, plus a University Council. The latter promptly approved creation of two additional colleges, Education and Adult Education and Training. The objectives of the new university, which opened in 1977, were "to train manpower for the developmental needs of the southern Sudan."

In our view, there was from the beginning a sense of unreality in this venture which, other than in its response to acute needs for teachers, seemed to take relatively little into account the actual conditions in the Sudanese south, especially the existence of extensive pastoralism as its preponderant occupation and the felt needs of that community for particular services, in the first instances, for improvements in animal and human health. Rather, even the names of the first two colleges give the impression they were conceived within a Northern donor's boardroom far away where "social and environmental studies" had both become decidedly more voguish than more conventional studies in agriculture, medicine/public health and veterinary science. One of these obviously highest priority areas of need was partially faced when the University Council authorized, in 1978, a fifth college, Medicine.

The Natural Resources/Environmental college's stated objectives were (1) to train "natural resources managers,"[2] (2) to undertake research on natural resources in order to determine rational methods for their exploitation, (3) to inculcate "environmental awareness" in the Sudanese people and (4) to participate in the development of rural people through outreach programs. All students enrolled in that college for the B.Sc. degree program in Natural

Resources took the same courses during their first two years. After that, they followed one of five curricular tracks for three years: plant agriculture, forestry, animal science, fisheries or wildlife management.

Plant agriculture, a major subsistence activity not only of many of the southern Sudan's pastoralists, but also the primary life support for its sedentary populations in the far south and southwest, fared poorly. Its initial graduates numbered only 17, while even that college's forestry curriculum, a much lesser area for regional concern, graduated 21! Of the quite small number of Natural Resources graduates overall, many were not even from the southern Sudan; for example, in the first two classes in the animal science curriculum, only two-thirds were southerners (University of Juba, 1984).

Almost unbelievably, no veterinary science college was established[3] and the curriculum in animal science graduated initially only 15 students, although the majority of southern Sudanese are livestock owners. Things were seriously out of academic kilter from the start. The stated aim of this animal science curriculum, in which the first author taught, was to train the essential cadre for the livestock sector. Students electing this specialization were to be trained to become "animal production officers" capable of handling animal production problems and, also, given "an adequate background . . . in animal health and hygiene." That is, broadly based veterinary science, as already developed throughout much of Africa (see Chapter 6), was not reflected in this academic plan and, in its place, the intent was to train a *new* cadre of nonveterinary animal husbandry graduates for which there was no existing outreach mechanism outside of the veterinary services. That plan was in face of livestock sector realities, in which even the highest priority need of the majority of southern Sudanese (i.e., control of economically and socially disruptive livestock diseases) was not yet being met and some important livestock districts lacked a single veterinary service officer. In fact, the University calendar stated explicitly: "graduates of this specialization are expected to play an important role in livestock production *through filling the gap in production that is not adequately covered by training in the veterinary sciences*" (Univerity of Juba, 1984: 154, italics added). The student pool apparently failed to recognize the career potential of such training in that other animal resources curricula of far less importance to the South's peoples, fisheries and wildlife management, together graduated more students than did domestic animal science (University of Juba, 1984).

This new academic departure, which clearly intended to parallel or re-place the only existing mechanism for services delivery and other rural outreach, reflected a development battle being waged in Africa by some Northern advisors within animal agriculture more than actual circumstances in the region or an alternative historic outreach record to pastoralists anywhere (see Chapter 6). An evaluation of employment experiences of its initial graduates (Majok, 1988) indicated that major difficulties occurred in assigning them field functions. By 1988 the national Ministry of Animal Resources, the largest employer in the Sudanese public sector, had not hired one of these graduates for any purpose. Other potential employers like the Animal Production Corporation and the Livestock and Meat Marketing Corporation (government parastatals) also failed to employ any. Their training did not meet priority needs within pastoral districts. With only 122 contact hours of work in animal health, they were not able to substitute for veterinary officers (still in totally inadequate supply), or even effectively augment cadres of lower level veterinary auxiliaries. It was more logical and economical to employ someone within limited numbers of employment slots who could be flexibly assigned than to employ an equally costly person who could not.

Not only was the stated justification for this new animal science program in terms of an alleged "gap" in Sudanese veterinarians' animal husbandry and production training undocumented by outside advisors influencing that aspect of the university's academic plan, but it was also untrue. The 612 contact hours that University of Juba animal science students pursued in livestock care and production courses per se was no different than the 636 hours in those same subjects taken by students in the veterinary college of the University of Khartoum. Thus, despite the positive legacy within African animal agriculture of colonial policies, in which veterinary medicine *and* animal husbandry were taught jointly as veterinary science, the academic plan for the University of Juba reflected retrograde influences of dubious appropriateness to the Sudan, to say the least. In deliberately attempting to divorce these previously linked activities through the educational process, overlooked entirely were the very hard-learned temporal order of priorities essential within any developing livestock-based economy among efforts directed toward disease control, nutritional improvements and genetic upgrading of livestock.

## ARE NORTHERN VETERINARY CURRICULA APPROPRIATE FOR PASTORAL DEVELOPMENT?

Of 28 veterinary schools located within Africa in 1987, 18 were south of the Sahara (Pritchard, 1988). The University of Pretoria's school at Onderstepoort, founded in 1920, is the oldest. The language of instruction in most schools is English, followed by French. Of about 21,300 African veterinarians in 1985, some 12,500 were in Egypt, another 1,500 in South Africa, leaving only 7,300 for the remainder of the continent. According to Pritchard, the total number of graduates in 1987 was only about 1,100.

Among principal conclusions reached by African veterinarians enrolled in the University of California's Colloquium on Veterinary Aspects of Development in Africa in the late 1980s about curricula they had followed, most agreed that not only were improved programs of services delivery required, but that a drastic overhaul of curricula was urgent.

Considering the needs of Africa, the most essential competencies of *most* veterinarians working there *today* must be investigation, prevention and control at the population level of major economically and socially disruptive livestock diseases.    Wherever control of such major plagues has been reasonably achieved, however, equally important veterinary science roles become efforts to improve animal productivity and efficiency of animal production systems.  A third role, one which also requires much more effective implementation right now, is the safeguarding of human health in the several ways that animals and veterinary science influence it (see Chapters 4 and 6; WHO/FAO, 1975; Schwabe, 1984b).

Persons with competence in each of these three main areas are or will be required. In particular countries other more local needs for lesser numbers of graduates exist with respect to terrestrial wildlife and/or fisheries.  The lowest priority veterinary science role throughout Africa today should be to treat illnesses in *individual* animals *except* where plant agriculture is animal powered or a commercial dairy industry does or should exist. Even then instruction should concentrate exclusively upon *economically* important animal species.[4] In our view, these same priorities apply equally under most African conditions of sedentary agriculture.  However, within most present African veterinary curricula the respective emphases given to individual animal therapeutic medicine versus population-level medicine remain to some extent reversed.  That is, African veterinary schools follow far too closely European and North American curricular models.  A major part of efforts to correct this situation depends upon much more emphasis upon *all* aspects of diagnosis, including surveillance and analytical capabilities in epidemiology, and to the full present range of alternative approaches to prevention and control of diseases (see Table 6.2). The student contact hours to realize such curricular emphases must be achieved through commensurate downgrading of attention to treatment of individual sick animals (especially to the teaching of subjects like surgery and in the amount of time many African veterinary curricula devote to teaching about diseases of little or no present consequence in Africa, including diseases of animal species which have no current importance there).  Such concerns have been voiced repeatedly in international FAO/WHO meetings and Expert Consultations on veterinary education held since the 1960s which have stressed high-priority local needs for provision of effective services.  But, despite such repeated calls, most consultative bodies have not been specific in remedies and few concrete results are apparent in moving African curricula toward more appropriate models.

Two nonpedagogical forces tend to define veterinary curricula everywhere and have done so since creation of the first veterinary schools in the mid-18th century.  One of these continues to be social needs, the kinds of largely public goods that persons knowledgeable about normal and abnormal animal biology would be most expected to provide. The second force is that of the "marketplace"--how easily will *most* graduates of a particular school find gainful employment?  That force *may* reflect primary needs of society as a whole, or represent services for which certain more privileged persons within a society are prepared to pay.

Purely marketplace considerations have been responsible for assumptions by many Northern veterinary faculties that the vast majority of graduates will (and should?) obtain employment as private practitioners of individual animal curative medicine. Such private goods provision through a fee-for-services system surely has been possible and desirable in countries where the market (i.e., the animal-owning public) values its *individual* animals highly enough, and considers the veterinary services offered valuable enough, to pay sufficiently for them, to assure veterinarians a reasonable living. But, especially where veterinarians are scarce, and people materially poor, such avenues may not prove the best uses for most veterinarians' talents. Moreover, as discussed in Chapter 8, direct or indirect subsidies have usually been required to support veterinary services to rural people everywhere.

Northern and especially American veterinary curricular models have often followed quite passively little-explored or -evaluated market forces (Schwabe, 1967). However, if veterinary schools are to be responsive germinal centers alert to new and multiple social needs that veterinarians can help meet *within each society*, another major choice must be faced in curricular design. *If* all veterinary students within any school pursue exactly the same curriculum (are afforded the same *faculty-mandated choice*), there will be either constant pressure to extend the length of the curriculum or to remain nonresponsive to significant needs. There are practical limits to extending the time required to become a member of any profession. Several approaches to that problem have been experimented with during the past few decades to better prepare graduates for a range of careers for which veterinary training is apt within the shortest period of time. These include: (1) some limited free elective course choice, (2) alternative series of related elective courses pursued together as blocks, (3) selection by each student among two or more career-focused curricular "tracks" following a common core-block of subject matter and (4) dual degree programs.

These possibilities are based upon recognition that a professional curriculum can accommodate varying degrees of specialization and that there is no need for students to be exposed, often intensively, to material they will never make use of in their intended careers. However, the common "core" curriculum all students do pursue must include that body of knowledge and skills necessary to reasonably characterize every graduate as a veterinary biologist within the diversely employed global profession. Two innovative situations we shall consider are among the more refreshing in terms of development needs in Africa. Since both attempted to use limited resources in imaginative ways, it is not for their specifics, as much as this spirit and alertness to local needs and veterinary potential that these illustrations are apt.

One of the better examples of a veterinary school which attempted to balance its country's current needs for veterinary inputs against limited resources has been the relatively new faculty of Tufts University in the United

States. One of only a few American veterinary schools situated within a private rather than a state university, Tufts has had available less in the way of intramural funding than have had most other American schools. Nevertheless, under Dean Franklin Loew, it assumed a leadership role in curricular design, resource acquisition and management and cooperative arrangements with other institutions toward multiple ends.

The first two veterinary years of study constitute a common program at Tufts (which build upon prior university preveterinary courses, including one year of organic chemistry, one semester of biochemistry and one semester of genetics). In their third year students begin a series of elective courses followed by individualized career options in their fourth year. While some options are related to clinical practice, including management and health of different farm animal species, less usual ones include international veterinary medicine (tropical herd health and livestock production), wildlife biology and medicine, biotechnology, ethics and values in veterinary science and veterinary ethology-- the latter two administered through Tufts' Center for Animals and Public Policy. As examples, recent projects in International Veterinary Medicine have included an epidemiological and ethnoveterinary study of rinderpest eradication in the Horn of Africa, a study of bovine rabies in Israel, an oral rabies vaccine trial in Nepal, a comparison of traditional and modern methods for tick control in cattle in Cameroon, organization of an animal health training program for Afghani nomads and farmers and cattle vaccination in the southern Sudan.

Additional possibilities exist at Tufts for selected students to pursue dual professional/postgraduate degrees. Beside more usual combined Doctor of Veterinary Medicine (D.V.M.)-Ph.D. programs in biomedical sciences, these include a unique combined D.V.M.-M.A. program offered jointly with Tufts' Fletcher School of Law and Diplomacy. That effort, related closely to the option in international veterinary medicine, is designed to prepare graduates for "policy making positions in livestock development, wildlife management, fisheries biology and herd health management." Courses include economics, international food and agricultural policy, the debt crisis of Third World economies, international law and politics. Further examples of cooperative use of resources include a Tuft's laboratory within Massachusetts' famed Marine Biological Laboratory at Woods Hole and services provided by the school's Veterinary Diagnostic Laboratory to almost 1,000 private veterinary practices and biotechnology companies.

The innovative idea of a more formally organized "core and track" curriculum designed to accomodate specialized social needs for veterinarians originated in Teheran University under the leadership of Dean A. Rafyi.[5] It is highly apropos to the situation in the southern Sudan. During the 1960s the faculty of that well-equipped and -staffed school designed and initiated a new six-year curriculum which permitted specialization along socially focused curricular tracks. All students followed an identical core curriculum their first two and a half years and then one of four increasingly divergent tracks during the last three and a half. The tracks were (1) Domestic Animal Medicine (diagnosis, treatment, prevention, control), (2) Livestock Health and Production, (3) Food Safety and (4) Fisheries Biology and Medicine.

Track 1, or Tracks 1 plus 2, were similar to most veterinary curricula elsewhere and enrolled the largest numbers of students. Track 3 concentrated upon the safe production, handling, processing, distribution and use of foods of animal origin, emphasizing areas such as food and environmental microbiology and toxicology; food preservation and sanitation; zoonoses epidemiology, diagnosis and control; food plant management and the like--much of the content of modern veterinary public health.[6] The fisheries Track 4 reflected a significant veterinary career avenue in several countries. In Iran, the sturgeon-caviar industry is, after petroleum, the principal earner of foreign exchange and, besides fish reproduction and medicine, and fish and fish products sanitation and safety specifically, its veterinary profession has provided it general scientific direction.

We move on now to specific remedies for Africa as illustrated through a model appropriate to development needs within the southern Sudan via its predominant resource sector. The following is a bare outline of some key portions of a general academic plan for the University of Juba which would capitalize on lessons learned from earlier efforts which became victim of renewed civil war over major regional issues--including that of nondevelopment--which remain unresolved. Let us assume for our purposes that a reconstituted University of Juba would comprise six colleges: Education and Training, Social Sciences and Human Resources, Medicine and Public Health,[7] Agriculture and Plant Resources,[8] Veterinary Science and Animal Resources.[9] We will center specific suggestions upon a new College of Veterinary Science and Animal Resources which, with the College of Agriculture and Plant Resources, would replace the University of Juba's initial College of Natural Resources and Environmental Studies.

## A COLLEGE OF VETERINARY SCIENCE AND ANIMAL RESOURCES FOR THE SOUTHERN SUDAN

What can be accommodated within professional veterinary curricula is only a small part of the modern knowledge base of veterinary science. This necessitates hard choices of what is included, what is not. Such is being done by design or default in every country and *there is nothing inherently sacred about the emphases in curricular content which have been chosen elsewhere.* This process is even more difficult under African circumstances, where educational influences of a few Northern countries have remained so uncritically and unrealistically paramount, and the easiest thing to do has been to attempt to imitate such "prestigious" foreign models.

Given that the Sudan is Africa's largest country geographically, that it has the world's largest pastoralist population, that its north and south are quite different in important ways, that a southern Regional Government (with supposedly considerable autonomy) exists and that the lives of a majority of southern Sudanese center completely upon their livestock, it is difficult to believe that a second Sudanese veterinary science faculty was not one of the highest priority initial developments within the newly established University of Juba. Therefore, we shall suggest here what a socially focused academic program for animal resources development in Africa might be like, most immediately how its graduates could considerably improve the only existing outreach and communications channel to that continent's migratory populations. Only rarely have organizational and curricular models ostensibly addressing important local needs been designed for veterinary schools within developing countries anywhere and almost never have these been published except for very limited distribution. One model was that developed for a planned but never built veterinary faculty for the University of Riyadh in Saudi Arabia (Pritchard et al., 1975; Schwabe, 1984b: 654-657). As to projected cost guidelines for such a program, we envisaged initial resource allocations approximately equal to those devoted to the present veterinary faculty of 44 members within the University of Zimbabwe.

We propose a modification, adapted to the southern Sudan's needs, of the career-track curriculum of the University of Teheran. In recognition of (1) current fiscal realities, (2) initial staffing problems for certain disciplines because of global shortages of specialists and (3) current priority demands for particular kinds of personnel within the southern Sudan, the full curriculum would be implemented in three stages. With its ultimately five curricular tracks (covering the entire area of animal resources appropriate to the southern Sudan at this time), it would produce a service network of highly versatile veterinary biologists who could be flexibly shifted within governmental and other areas of potential employment in order to meet certain highly seasonal service functions for which augmented manpower was temporarily required (or other service emergencies) and whose numbers enrolled within each track could readily be varied over time in response to changing regional needs. To achieve further cost-effectiveness, we also follow the example of Tufts University in taking full advantage of resources potentially available elsewhere within the university, as well as without.

**Emphases Upon Populations, Prevention, Environment, Production**

We began this design process from certain "givens." The first was the actuality of local circumstances in the southern Sudan. The second was that a relevant curriculum should place sole emphases upon animal species which are now of economic importance to the southern Sudan. A third was that it should be strongly oriented to population, preventive, production-economic and environmental aspects of veterinary science and optimal development over time of the region's considerable animal resources.   In keeping with widely held opinion, greater emphasis would be provided *all* aspects of diagnosis (clinical, pathological, laboratory, epidemiological) than in almost all curricula elsewhere, with commensurately less attention given to the medical or surgical treatment of individual sick animals.   An FAO Consultation on Veterinary Education in Africa held at ILRAD in 1984 recommended that *postgraduate* education on the continent concentrate upon epidemiology; other aspects of diagnostic medicine, including pathology; and on reproduction and food safety (FAO, 1984).   We believe strongly, however, that *postgraduate* attention to such skill and knowledge priorities begs the question. Most of those needs must be accommodated *within the professional curriculum itself,* and postgraduate studies in those fields would then build further upon this already substantial base (for selected individuals needed for more specialized posts within governmental service, academia and otherwise).

For these reasons, holistic causal thinking about diseases and health, plus epidemiological principles and methods, are emphasized and reinforced throughout. The aim of the proposed *core* curriculum, to be pursued by all students, is to assure that each graduate, regardless of track, possessed sufficient practical knowledge to (1) participate effectively in epidemiological surveillance and other aspects of disease and production intelligence, especially at the cattle camp and district levels; (2) perform various types of intervention trials; and (3) participate in the full implementation of adopted intervention and production-enhancing programs.

### Integrating Education, Research and Services' Delivery

We concur with recommendations of the Winrock Committee to assess animal agriculture in Africa (Pritchard et al., 1992: 88) that appropriate university faculty members in Africa become much more closely involved with practical developments in animal agriculture.   Interests of economy, as well as education, science and social needs, are served by maximum integration between programs (and personnel) of teaching, research and social service institutions.[10]   For these reasons, some African veterinary schools are located adjacent to major research facilities, as at Onderstepoort in South Africa and Kabete in Kenya. The same applies to proximity to major veterinary service support units such as central diagnostic laboratories and epidemiological investigation facilities.   California provides but one example of many where senior veterinary school professors direct diagnostic units within the State Veterinary Diagnostic Laboratory system.

The Winrock-sponsored committee (Pritchard et al., 1992: 75) noted further that, while "research is required to improve animal health technologies [new vaccines, drugs, tests] . . . more information also is required on the economic consequences of animal diseases and control procedures and the interaction of diseases, management and environment . . . , on development of computer models that integrate economic, production and epidemiological data at regional, national, district and farm levels. Such models should be based in GIS (geographic information systems) technology[11] . . . to provide better information for planning improvements in animal agriculture. . . . There is [also] need for methodological research on the delivery of veterinary services." In our proposals, the former areas of basic research (animal health technologies) would be carried out largely within appropriate university departments or centers. Applications of these basic technologies would also involve the Central Veterinary Diagnostic Laboratory. But less precedented areas of field and service delivery research would involve also not only personnel of other university departments and of the Central Epidemiological Investigation Facility (see Chapter 8), but some research would be carried out, and applied on a pilot scale, within special Field Research and Training Districts.

### Organizational Model

We suggest that the College of Veterinary Science and Animal Resources consist of seven academic departments, most combining areas of basic and applied studies (disciplines to be represented ultimately are indicated in parentheses). Department of Morphology and Pathobiology (anatomists, cytologists, pathologists,[12] surgeons[13]); Department of Physiology and Nutrition (nutritionists, physiologists, biochemists, molecular biologists,[14] toxicologists, pharmacologists); Department of Reproduction and Genetics (geneticists; sperm, ovum and embryo technologists; bovine obstetricians; udder health specialists); Department of Infectious Diseases and Immunology (virologists, bacteriologists/mycologists, parasitologists, vector biologists, immunologists); Department of Epidemiology and Veterinary Economics (epidemiologists, biostatisticians, animal health economists, computer/data management technologists, livestock disease prevention/control specialists); Department of Animal Production (beef production specialists, milk production specialists, small ruminant production specialists, poultry production specialists, wildlife biologists, fisheries biologists); Department of Public Health and Pastoral Development (public health veterinarians, slaughterhouse management specialists, creamery management specialists, extension-education-communications specialists, veterinary administration specialists, anthropologists[15]).

### "Core and Tracks" Curriculum

The Juba curriculum will require six years following secondary school graduation.[16] For economic, regional priority and other reasons, the full curriculum of five tracks would be implemented in three stages. Stage One would see initiation of the core and Track 1 curricula.

Track 1, *Livestock Disease Investigation and Control*, with the largest numbers of students initially, is oriented to population-level medical and related activities among domesticated livestock. At the district level, its graduates would direct and fully participate in all aspects of the epidemiological surveillance core program for veterinary services delivery, carry out intensive follow-ups in the field (outbreak and "new disease" investigations, etc.), would conduct and oversee laboratory diagnoses at the district level, would carry out the preliminary processing and analyses of surveillance data, would oversee and help conduct specific disease-prevention and control interventions for protection of mammalian livestock and engage in therapeutic practice as required. After Track 1 was functioning, Tracks 2 and 3 would be initiated as Stage Two of curriculum development.

Track 2, *Food Safety and Public Health*, would admit a lesser number of students. Besides its biomedical foundations, this track focuses upon safe production, distribution and marketing of foods of animal origin, zoonoses and other human health importance of animals. Graduates would be posted to all district veterinary offices where they would supervise slaughterslabs, slaughterhouses, creameries, milk marketing and (with veterinary fisheries biologists) fish processing plants and fish marketing; carry out epidemiological surveillance within such facilities; cooperate with district medical personnel in carrying out outbreak investigations of suspected food-borne infections or intoxications; engage in surveillance of zoonotic infections; and consult and collaborate with medical personnel with respect to suspected human cases and outbreaks. They would be responsible for canine rabies vaccination and other zoonotic disease control campaigns where required and would have primary responsibilities for all other ongoing IC linkages with medical services (as in joint livestock/human vaccination efforts described in Chapter 7). These veterinarians *would also help staff district-level livestock vaccination and other highly seasonal disease control programs as required.*

The importance of these first two tracks to pastoral economies and well-being of pastoral peoples is well understood and these are both major historic avenues of service for persons trained in veterinary science. However, in some African pastoral areas special conditions exist that suggest other needs that veterinary science has met or helped meet. For instance, despite the fact that pastoral Africa is largely a rain-deficient area, at least seasonally, some pastoral peoples inhabit areas bordering upon significant rivers and large lakes. Thus the Dinka, Nuer, Shilluk and other pastoralists in the southern Sudan live or migrate near the White Nile, its tributaries and flood plain and, as described in Chapter 2, fishing is a major seasonal occupation and source of food. Consequently, one original natural resources curriculum within the University of Juba was fisheries biology.[17]

Track 3, *Fisheries Production*, would admit at first a relatively small number of students. Besides its biomedical foundations, it would train individuals with competence in fish culture, management of fisheries resources, fish diseases and their control and related efforts to protect the aquatic environment. Graduates would be posted to appropriate district veterinary offices and would instruct rural people in fishing techniques, fish preservation methods, safety considerations for fish as food (in cooperation with public health veterinarians) and fish marketing. They would also help set up and advise fish processing cooperatives and other fish processing plants, carry out surveillance and outbreak investigations of zoonoses or livestock diseases with aquatic reservoirs or vectors, design and engage in programs for snail and other aquatic vector control *and, in emergencies, assist in highly seasonal district-level livestock vaccination or other high-priority livestock programs.*

At an appropriate time after the full functioning of these three track programs and when the stage of southern Sudanese development of its primary animal resources is apt, Stage Three of the full curriculum's implementation would be realized with addition of Tracks 4 and 5.

Track 4, *Livestock Production*, besides its biomedical foundations and husbandry and productivity orientations, conveys some additional clinical skills and service competencies including health of individually valuable animals (e.g., bovine obstetrics and udder health). Within the government service, these graduates would eventually be part of district-level staffs and would participate at that and grassroots levels of surveillance (especially with regard to improved demographic, family economic, livestock reproduction and nutritional data); have responsibility for extension-educational functions with respect to husbandry improvements and productivity and marketing enhancements; encourage formation of cooperatives and/or pastoral producers' associations and advise same; carry out poultry disease control efforts; render emergency obstetric and other therapeutic services in the field; handle or oversee any increased needs for individual animal medical services as more intensive production units (or animal-powered crop agriculture) may develop; *and also help staff vaccination and other highly seasonal disease control programs as required.* They would also run the Artificial Insemination (AI) Farms and manage the veterinary faculty's flocks and herds. They would become primarily responsible for all local IC linkages between veterinary/animal resource services and most non-medical branches of government (e.g., water point maintenance, environmental and other required field monitoring, coordinated educational efforts among pastoralists, facilitation of "piggybacked" outreach of such other personnel to pastoralists' camps as required).

Track 5, *Wildlife Biology and Medicine*, would probably admit relatively few students. Besides its biomedical foundations, it prepares veterinary biologists with competence in wildlife management and conservation and wildlife diseases investigation and control.[18] Graduates would be posted to veterinary offices within appropriate districts. They would oversee any government wildlife preserves/parks and develop them as national assets (including developments for generation of foreign exchange through tourism), help facilitate seasonal migrations of wildlife with minimum interference with pastoral husbandry and vice versa, instruct rural people in wildlife conservation and sustainably cropping wildlife for food, participate in surveillance and control of zoonoses or livestock diseases with reservoir hosts in wildlife, participate in other broader ecological studies and efforts to protect the environment, *as well as help staff district-level vaccination and other highly seasonal disease control programs as required.*

In some African countries (Kenya being perhaps the prime example), where conservation of wildlife resources represents a major effort and/or regulated wildlife management and cropping have local food-producing importance or potential, wildlife programs have attracted major external NGO funding support and are often very important earners (in the form of tourism) of foreign exchange. For such reasons, wildlife biology was one of the original curricula in the University of Juba, although in our view that was a very premature effort given the realities of the southern Sudan.

*Core Curriculum.* The suggested core curriculum to be pursued by all professional students in the College of Veterinary Science and Animal Resources would be as follows:

*Year One*: Total Contact Hours= 834. Chemistry (144 contact hours), Biology (168 hours), Mathematics (72 hours), Statistics (36 hours), Scientific English (132 hours), Peoples and Ecology of the Southern Sudan (36 hours), Economy and Resources of the Southern Sudan (36 hours), Veterinary Science and its Roles (24 hours), Livestock Types in the Southern Sudan and Livestock Restraint (24 hours), Veterinary Anthropology: Man-Animal Relationships in the Southern Sudan (36 hours), Computer and Data Management Skills (90 hours), Biomedical Information Sources and Retrieval (36 hours).

*Year Two*\*[19]: Total Contact Hours= 806. Scientific English (36 contact hours), Organic Chemistry (90 hours), Nutritional Biochemistry (90 hours), Organ Systems: Normal Structure, Function, Embryology (450 hours), Animal Genetics (80 hours), Epidemiological Principles and Measurements (60 contact hours).

*Year Three*\* (Core Portion Only= 674 contact hours). General Pathology (80 contact hours), Molecular Biology (36 hours), Immunology (36 hours), Pathogenesis of Infectious Agents (54 hours), Diagnostic Bacteriology and Mycology (96 hours), Diagnostic Virology and Rickettsiology (80 hours), Diagnostic Protozoology (46 hours), Diagnostic Helminthology (53 hours), Forages and Range Management (80 hours), Feeds and Nutritional Diseases (36 hours), Surveillance Systems and Intensive Follow-up Investigations (36 hours), Field Study Design (52 contact hours).

*Year Four*\* (Core Portion Only= 296 contact hours). Pharmacology and Applied Therapeutics (60 contact hours), Toxicology (32 hours), Necropsy Pathology Rotation (24 hours), Invertebrate Vectors of Disease (36 hours),

Analytical Epidemiology (52 hours), Computer and Data Management Skills (90 hours).

*Year Five* (Core Portion Only= 132 contact hours). Veterinary Communications and Extension (36 contact hours), Animal Health Economics (60 hours), Intersectoral Cooperation: Veterinary Science as a Key Pastoral Development Agent (36 hours).

*Year Six* (No core curriculum).

One major strength of this core curriculum is that it prepares all veterinary biologists (even in those areas like wildlife and fisheries for which relatively small numbers of graduates will probably ever be required in the southern Sudan) for broader areas of service vis-à-vis livestock (portions of which have unusual personnel requirements seasonally or under emergency circumstances). Thus, great flexibility is built into the veterinary/animal resource services at minimum cost at the same time as diverse social and economic needs are effectively addressed.  To illustrate track curricula which will complement this core curriculum, those for the tracks in Livestock Disease Investigation and Control and in Fisheries Production are outlined.

*Livestock Disease Investigation and Control Curriculum.*  This content begins in the third year for these track students.

*Year Three* (in addition to 674 contact hours in core, for total contact hours= 810).  Small Ruminant Diseases (100 contact hours), Disease Management Strategies and Tactics (36 hours).

*Year Four* (in addition to 296 contact hours in core, for total contact hours= 790).  Small Ruminant and Camel Diseases (50 contact hours), Cattle Diseases (210 hours), Clinical Pathology (120 hours), Veterinary Medical Genetics (36 hours), Basic Obstetrics and Teratology (54 hours), Udder Health (24 hours).

*Year Five* (in addition to 132 contact hours in core, for total contact hours variable).  Cattle Diseases (90 contact hours), Clinical Skills Practical Proficiency Certifications,[20] Cattle Camp Field Practice Rotations§,[21] District Laboratory Practice Rotations§, Epidemiological Data Processing and Analysis Rotations§.

*Year Six.*  Laboratory Practice Rotation (in Central and Subregional Laboratories); Epidemiological Practice Rotation (in Central Epidemiological Investigation Center); Herd Health, Obstetrics and Management Rotation (in university herds and flocks); Individual Research Project.

*Fisheries Production Curriculum.*  As with other tracks, this begins in the third year.

*Year Three* (in addition to 674 contact hours in core, for total contact hours= 804).  Ecology (50 contact hours), Fish Anatomy and Embryology (80 hours).

*Year Four* (in addition to 296 contact hours in core, for total contact hours= 792).  Fish Ecology (72 contact hours), Fish Physiology (72 hours), Aquatic Population Dynamics and Measurements (72 hours), Fish Nutrition (48 hours), Fish Diseases (100 hours), Limnology (72 hours), Fish-borne Zoonoses and Livestock Diseases: Epidemiology and Control (60 hours).

*Year Five* (in addition to 132 contact hours in core, for total contact hours= 810).  Fish Culture (180 contact hours), Riverine Fisheries (72 hours), Reservoir Fisheries (72 hours), Aquatic Disease Vectors and Control (100 hours), Crafts and Gear (72 hours), Fish Technology: Processing, Preservation and Sanitation (100 hours), Land Use Planning (36 hours), Wildlife Law and Administration (36 hours).

*Year Six.*  Field Research and Training Station Rotations (Fisheries Station), Cattle Camp Field Practice Rotations.

While we shall not consider here the other three tracks of this model curriculum, or all of the total program's more unique contents, we illustrate two high-priority content areas insufficiently emphasized in African veterinary curricula.

*Social and Environmental Foundations.*  This core curricular block defines the physical, biological and human settings in which veterinary biologists within the southern Sudan will serve.  It especially considers man-animal-environmental relations in terms of the diverse peoples of the region.  It addresses historic roles of veterinary-trained biologists in terms of southern Sudanese needs.  It examines alternatives for appropriate and sustainable development in the south (especially with respect to the enlistment of traditional leadership and institutions in these processes and possibilities for local development initiatives through intersectoral efforts based upon existing or reasonably anticipated resources).  Finally, it considers "resting points," intermediate goals of sustainable development that may prove practical under anticipated conditions.

This core block is consistent with similar ideas for university reforms generally in interests of coordinated solutions to major global problems (Daly and Cobb, 1989: 357-360; Schwabe, 1978b).  Specific courses would include: Peoples and Ecology of the Southern Sudan (first year); Economy and Resources of the Southern Sudan (first year); Veterinary Science and its Roles (first year); Veterinary Anthropology: Man-Animal Relationships in the South-ern Sudan (first year) (e.g., pastoralism as a socioecologic system; contrasting man-animal relationships in pastoral, agrarian and industrian societies; man-animal beliefs and practices in Africa, with special reference to the southern Sudan; traditional veterinary medicine in the southern Sudan); Forages and Range Management (third year); Animal Health Economics (fifth year); Intersectoral Cooperation: Veterinary Science as a Key Pastoral Development Agent (fifth year); Veterinary Communications and Extension (fifth year) (e.g., means to communicate and educate, with emphasis upon preliterate peoples; preliterate information recording systems; extension programs; comparative basic and veterinary vocabularies in main pastoral languages).

In keeping with emphases upon diagnostic competence, including at the population level, this curriculum gives considerably more attention to quantitative skills than do Northern veterinary curricula.

*Quantitative Skills.* The surveillance and analytical dimensions of epidemiology are heavily dependent upon a high order of quantitative skills in disciplines such as biostatistics and computer-based data management, including word processing, spreadsheets, graphics and use of analytical/statistical programs like BMDP, SPSSX and SASS. We believe that biostatistics is of such importance to the practice of population medicine that, following an introductory course in the first year, most methods be introduced (and reenforced) *wherever within the curriculum situations arise where these are germane and can be applied.* Considerable advantage comes from opportunities for students to immediately use what they have learned and move beyond cookbook aquaintance with important methods.[22]

### Training in the Field

Considering current needs of the southern Sudan, we recommend ultimately three district-level field facilities for training and research, one main station for livestock disease and production activities to be established first. When it is fully operational, and Stage Two of curricular track implementation is carried out, a second station for fisheries production activities would be created. Finally, for Stage Three of track implementation, there would be a wildlife investigation and conservation activities station. These three specially designated Field Research and Training Districts would be regular administrative districts of the southern Sudanese government's Veterinary Science and Animal Resources Service. Thus, their academically augmented staffs would carry out the same programs as veterinary offices in all other districts, but would additionally possess field facilities (a field station) adequate to support research and training activities within an academic track's working context.

Let us consider what this would imply for the Livestock Disease and Production Station. It would be located in the district town of a major pastoral area, say, Wau. Its research activities would be with respect to new and/or improved approaches of service to livestock owners (including their pilot level trials). The staff of this District Office/Station would include faculty members of the Departments of Animal Production and of Epidemiology and Veterinary Economics. Through it would rotate students within curricular Tracks 1, 2 and 4 for practical clerkships during which they would perform under close supervision all the normal field activities of district veterinary officers with their particular track qualifications. Additionally, the faculty/staff of this Office-Station would organize and run training programs for veterinary field and slaughterslab auxiliaries and certain continuing education courses relevant to the principal avenues of veterinary employment within the country (except for wildlife and fish).

The second and third Field Research and Training Stations would be located, for terrestrial wildlife activities, in the district town of Gemeiza and, for fisheries activities, on the Nile at Malakal. Both would also be attached to those regular district veterinary service offices and would perform similar types of applied research as that identified above (e.g., in the third station on fisheries production, including hatchery management, fish sanitation and fish disease management) and teaching functions within Tracks 3 and 5, respectively, as well as continuing education for veterinary biologists in connection with those two classes of nondomesticated animal resources.

Through interactions with the government Veterinary Science and Animal Resources Service, faculty members would also assist in development and operation of, initially, one AI Farm[23] in each province (with the eventual aim of one or more in each significant livestock district). The college would also maintain as near as possible to the university campus, for both teaching and research, its own herds and flocks of cattle, small ruminants and chickens raised under traditional as well as various continually and practically improved modifications of traditional husbandry systems. Included would be an improved dairy herd as a model for similar development within the proximity of population centers. That is, in our proposals for the southern Sudan, significant portions of the educational experiences of students within the University of Juba's College of Veterinary Science and Animal Resources would be carried out outside of the university.

In summary, the curriculum proposed would prepare state-of-the-art practitioners of population medicine, better diagnosticians overall than do most conventional Northern curricula and veterinary biologists with a broad understanding of their profession and its multiple roles in pastoral development. Moreover, it would provide personnel in appropriate numbers for all principal avenues of veterinary/animal resources service and ones who can flexibly augment emergency and/or highly seasonal efforts of very high priority with minimum numbers of university trained personnel overall.

## REGIONAL COOPERATION IN EDUCATION

Regional cooperation in higher education is not new to veterinary experience. Within the southern United States immediately following World War II, as livestock production increased dramatically in that then-poorest region, increased demands for veterinary services occurred. Although the South then had only two veterinary schools, at Auburn University in Alabama and Texas A. & M. University, the legislature of every other southern state faced strong local demands for creation of a veterinary faculty. However, only Georgia actually did take on that major financial commitment because the veterinary dean at Auburn University, Redding S. Sugg, proposed a novel plan for regional cooperation in postgraduate and professional education. This began with a 13-state compact for *joint support* of the three existing centers of veterinary education. Subsequently, each state without a veterinary faculty had a quota of students to fill in these schools, for which it paid the host institution an agreed-upon fee. That veterinary initiative was soon extended to other fields and the overall approach was copied in other American interstate compacts. Additionally, the states of Virginia and Maryland eventually decided to *jointly* underwrite and support one veterinary college between them. Similar initiatives undertaken in Africa should be expanded at both professional and postgraduate degree levels.

## DEVELOPMENT SPECIALISTS WORKING TOGETHER

In 1970 the second author was the veterinary profession's representative on a WHO advisory panel formed to explore scientific, economic and logistic possibilities and advantages worldwide for cross-professional cooperation in education within the health sciences (WHO, 1972). To the initial surprise of its dental, pharmacy and nursing representatives, the panel's final report illustrated opportunities for more potentially profitable interactions--sharing of faculty members, facilities, courses and aspects of practical instruction--between medical and veterinary schools than between medical schools and those of any others of these more directly *human* health-oriented professions. This WHO group noted that "there are two foci for veterinary participation in multiprofessional activities in health sciences education. The first [is] with respect to parallel subject matter . . . [and a] second focus [is] in delivery of health services at the community level." The first "would include all of the basic medical sciences, general pathology, principles of epidemiology, nutrition, toxicology and pharmacology, as well as some aspects of fields such as radiology, radiobiology, nuclear medicine and infectious diseases. . . . Overlap would also exist in those clinical areas such as surgery, where introductory courses are taught using animals, or ophthalmology, where only minor differences exist between the same organ in different species. . . . Similarly, in fields such as reproductive physiology, the veterinarian and physician enjoy many areas of interest in common."

In the second area of services delivery in the community, the consultative group noted that "the veterinarian is particularly familiar with and concerned about delivery of rural health services, including general epidemiological services, food hygiene, the prevention and control of infections, and environmental monitoring through animal populations of potential . . . hazards to man." Among other possibilities for cooperation stressed by this multiprofession group was "over the broad area of medical research which is dependent upon animal experimentation."

In describing above the duties of food safety/public health veterinarians in settings such as the largely pastoral southern Sudan, we mentioned specific areas in which they and medical services personnel would cooperate locally. In

Chapters 4 and 6 we surveyed briefly some of the other important relationships and historic implications overall of veterinary science to human health. One suggested facet for local IC outlined in Chapter 7 involved additional common-sense possibilities very seldom implemented for sharing scarce diagnostic laboratory expertise and resources between the medical and veterinary sectors. And our key illustration of how other sectors might readily "piggyback" important parts of their own service programs onto the grassroots outreach of veterinary services involved joint medical-veterinary vaccination campaigns and difficult maintenance of the associated cold-chain and transport infrastructures. Preparation for such medical-veterinary IC can be furthered by means for cooperating in educational programs in which students preparing for work in both sectors may take certain instruction in common.

Examples of other IC efforts at the level of graduate training include the M.A. program within Tufts University concentrating on international policy issues vis-à-vis animal agriculture in which students pursue a joint program of the veterinary school and Tufts' Fletcher School of Law and Diplomacy. Thus, in that and many other contexts, departments and individual personnel of a veterinary science/animal resources faculty can fruitfully interact in teaching and research with those in medicine/public health, economics, anthropology, ecology and environmental studies, mathematics, range science, water resources and other fields. Intrauniversity cooperation is similarly required for imaginative teaching inputs throughout other curricula to better prepare all other specialists (physicians, water resource specialists, plant and rangelands agriculturalists and others) for working together at local levels.

## CONCLUSIONS

As considered in Chapter 6, unwillingness to cooperate between livestock specialists with and without veterinary qualifications from some anglophone countries, when transmitted to Africa through donor agency or consultant orientations (and through African students trained in those countries), has surely been the most important "turf barrier" to realizing any improvement in the local situation of pastoralists and their more effective integration within national economies. We propose to erase this relatively new externally instigated deterrent to progress by reinforcing and partially redirecting a broad non-factional veterinary/animal resources cadre.

Significant development of Africa's pastoral *areas* will depend upon educational and associated research initiatives at all levels which are appropriate not only to existing local circumstances and balanced priorities of national governments, but to the most affected peoples' own evolving aspirations and preparedness to contribute. Therefore we have considered here some of the educational thrusts which, in our view, would favor optimal application of local intersectoral development initiatives and help better prepare some of the key personnel. Especially emphasized have been educational formats which would promote among future development principals the *idea* of innovative cross-disciplinary and cross-professional efforts.

This approach will require new thinking on the parts of many international as well as national participants in the process. But, eventually, payoffs should become clearly evident in increased productivity of the livestock sector (which already contributes the most nationally in some countries like Somalia) and, in many other circumstances, the participation of pastoralists in national economies beyond subsistence contributions to themselves. In the first instance, where pastoralists already contribute so much relatively, they must begin to be much more adequately recompensed, and empowered. But in the latter, too, pastoralists must be encouraged to actively help set area priorities, make plans, cooperate in operation of programs and determine how they will help pay for services and amenities which they may desire from the outside.

Required most from outsiders--particularly of Northern outsiders--in our view will be the patience to allow pastoralists to "test the new waters," to assess risks and advantages to their own satisfactions--that is, to employ further the amazingly successful opportunistic strategies that have permitted them over past millennia to inhabit in sizable numbers many areas of the world which most others consider impossible. The alternatives, already too amply attempted, could only perpetuate further disasters.

## NOTES

1. We note at the same time that there is a sometimes arrogant condescension about all such "technicians" (i.e., physicians, agriculturalists, veterinarians, engineers and the like) on the parts of some so-called administrative generalists within particular funding agencies.

2. This terminology is highly evocative of the types of "management-methodology" over technical competence philosophy becoming prominent within Northern business circles (the M.B.A. idea). In fact, the initial organization and philosophy overall of the University of Juba's College of Natural Resources and Environmental Studies closely resembled those adopted about then within American Land Grant universities. Colleges of agriculture were scrambling almost desperately (under vastly different and rapidly changing circumstances) to acquire new names and orientations (e.g., Food and Agriculture, Agricultural and Environmental Studies, Food and Natural Resources). Such changes reflected an increasingly urbanized environment, one in which agriculture's political clout was receding rapidly and where what "agriculture" implied was increasingly perceived by a quite removed public (rightly or wrongly) as being more part of the "problem" than the solution.

3. In 1994, during the renewed civil war, the Sudanese government created on paper another southern university at Wau with intended faculties of education, veterin-

ary science and medicine, choices which more represented priorities as viewed by people of the south.

4. If African urban areas begin to provide opportunities for practice of curative medicine on individual animals (pets), the expense of special education for such limited private goods provisions should be borne by the veterinarian who will benefit from the earnings of such a practice, not by the public. For now, such additional training should be obtained by them on another continent.

5. Iran already possessed one of the best veterinary research institutions among developing countries, the world-class Razi Institute. In 1972 the University of California also adopted a core and track curriculum but in less imaginative fashion than Teheran. Most innovative were tracks in zoological medicine (wildlife medicine) and two dual degree tracks (Ph.D. plus D.V.M., the other for the D.V.M. plus the Master of Preventive Veterinary Medicine [M.P.V.M.] degree).

6. When Dr. Betty Hobbs and the second author were asked to evaluate this third (food safety) curriculum, they considered it as offering most of the conventional content of veterinary education plus the equivalent of an M.Sc. degree in Food Science and Technology within a British or American university.

7. The addition of public health to medicine would imply many reforms in training physicians for the southern Sudan comparable to those we stress here for veterinarians.

8. Including forestry.

9. Including fisheries and wildlife.

10. It is poorly informed individuals who believe that, within universities themselves, teaching and research are largely unrelated activities competing for the time and attention of professors. No university worthy of the name can flourish without major emphasis upon advancement of knowledge on the part of its faculty and advanced students. Universities are *essentially* communities of scholars (i.e., learners, students) at *all levels* from the novice (the undergraduate who requires maximum guidance and programming in the process), the more advanced apprentice (the graduate student who with guidance "pips" the research horizon), the probationary scholar (postdoctoral fellows, assistant professors charged with demonstrating their capacities for scholarly independence) to the independent scholar--that is, a researcher (a tenured associate or full professor) who is fully capable of advancing mankind's knowledge and of associating lower-level scholars with this process of discovery. Research and teaching cannot conceivably be regarded therefore as activities in conflict or competition. Formal classroom teaching is but one way to learn and a way that should become progressively less important as preparation for any professional career progresses. Consequently, as stressed by Pritchard (1988) with specific reference to Africa, "it is . . . essential that governments recognize that veterinary schools are valuable research resources and make provision for funding research in veterinary schools."

11. GIS is an essential part of epidemiological training and practice (see Schwabe et al., 1977: 114ff and Chapter 8 of this volume).

12. Including ultimately a wildlife pathologist.

13. This faculty model envisages no surgical *emphasis* within the curriculum per se. Therefore the faculty would include only a single appointee in surgery (to offer very basic instruction in this discipline to all veterinary students). His research interests would be in reproductive surgery and he might therefore have a cross-appointment in the Department of Animal Reproduction and Genetics.

14. As a logical example, one molecular biologist could have research interests and a cross-appointment in the Department of Animal Reproduction and Genetics; a second (if possible) in the Department of Infectious Diseases and Immunology.

15. An administration specialist, an anthropologist and a communications specialist would be seconded part-time from the College of Social Sciences and Human Resources.

16. In the Sudan, university admission is at British "O" level equivalent, rather than the higher "A" level equivalent. Thus the veterinary studies portion of this program is the same length as the five-year Zimbabwe curriculum and the total veterinary science program is the same length as the University of Juba's curriculum in human medicine.

17. In the southern Sudan, fishing is also an occupation for some settled peoples. In recent years, some Dinka have supplied sun-dried fish to town markets in Juba, Malakal and Bor. Further commercialization of fishing therefore has development potential among pastoral as well as some other peoples. Veterinary interests in fisheries resources in Africa are truly ancient ones, the first reference to fish diseases anywhere appearing in the c. 1800 BC Kahun Veterinary Papyrus, one of the two oldest surviving Egyptian medical papyri. A number of veterinary schools have had fisheries medicine units and courses, as well as courses on fish sanitation, for many years and in major fish-producing and consuming countries, these have provided significant veterinary career avenues. Veterinarians currently serve as directors and staff of major aquariums and oceanaria (Schwabe, 1984b: 510ff), an International Association of Aquatic Animal Medicine was formed in 1969 and there is a Permanent Commission on Diseases of Fish in the Office International des Epizooties (OIE) in Paris. Information on occurrence of fish diseases worldwide is included in the FAO/WHO/OIE *Animal Health Yearbook*.

18. Wildlife biology has long been an area to which veterinarians and veterinary institutions have contributed more prominently in some countries than in others (Schwabe, 1984b: 506ff). A major new impetus, especially since World War II, has come from disclosures that many arbovirus and other significant infections of man and livestock have their reservoirs in wild mammals and birds. Although less explored, important reservoirs of human diseases like some of the salmonelloses have also been disclosed in reptiles. Innovative approaches to some of these have been developed, for example, rabies is currently being combatted in some countries through vaccines orally administered in baits dropped by air to fox and other wild reservoir hosts.

Veterinarians, associated with major zoos since the early 19th century, commonly direct such institutions and wildlife preserves and parks, particularly ones engaged importantly in comparative medical research and/or wildlife conservation efforts. In Africa, Frankfurt's zoo director, Bernard Grzimek, was a major instigator of international interest in the future of East Africa's wildlife, and many other veterinarians are currently involved in varied aspects of wildlife study and conservation in Africa. For example, James Else, who directed Kenya's major primate research center for many years, later became director for biological studies of the National Museums of Kenya. Particularly since development by Frank Hayes within the veterinary school of the University of Georgia of syringe gun technology for immobilizing wild mammals, veterinarians in larger numbers have been associated with conservation efforts in the field in Africa and elsewhere.   Working in both Kenya and South Africa, Anthony Harthoorn pioneered in defining for different wildlife species the most suitable doses and antidotes for immobilizing drugs.

19. During core portions of years marked with an *, biostatistics is integrated into all appropriate courses.

20. Students would need to individually demonstrate proficiency in a variety of clinical skills.

21.  Instruction marked with a § is offered first in a Field Research and Training District/Field Station and then students are each assigned to a regular veterinary services district office for a further clerkship.  There students are part of field teams vaccinating and treating animals, carrying out surveillance activities and intensive follow-up investigations. The students follow their own specimens into the district-level laboratory (for processing, testing and forwarding specimens to higher levels) and their other data for preliminary processing and epidemiological analysis. These students thus also provide an augmented field force for routine and special purposes.

22. As illustrations, suppose in a laboratory exercise in physiology teams of students each carry out a series of measurements of some organ function in individual animals. That very early point in the curriculum is where to introduce measures of central tendency (means, modes, medians) and dispersion (range, variance, standard deviation, etc.) and have students calculate each of these from measurements that day in the laboratory.  Then, say, within clinical pathology later, students would repeat such procedures.  As each other statistical method is learned, its understanding and use is *henceforth assumed* and students are required to repeatedly demonstrate these. For example, in the course on epidemiological surveillance systems, the very important subjects of sampling and properties of diagnostic tests would be thoroughly explored.

23. These AI farms, ultimately in all cattle districts, would be sites to which pastoralists could bring cows to be bred artificially when they come into heat, following the Botswana model.

# 10

---

# SMALL STEPS TOWARD NEW BALANCES

In the minds of many . . . [Northern] development planners, nomadic
pastoralism in subsaharan Africa has been associated for decades
with famine and ecological degradation, a permanent crisis that
ranges from overpopulation and overgrazing through problems of
veterinary health to lack of social control.

K.-H. Zessin and A.D. Farah, 1993

We believe that the above *viewpoint* reflects the tragedy of Africa's pastoral
peoples as much as effects of periodic droughts, even famines compounded by
political strife. Droughts focus world attention momentarily, yet brief spurts of
emergency assistance do little or nothing to improve the circumstances of these
peoples in sustainable ways. This viewpoint also represents the challenge to
outsiders who are, or could be, involved over the longer term in bringing them
some actual "betterment of life." For, if fatalist views of their situation and
destiny remain the norm in Northern eyes, what possibilities are there for
reaching out to these numerous peoples with meaningful assistance, much less
sustainable development prospects for the ecologically marginal areas to which
they are increasingly restricted? That is what this book has been about.

To help permanently dispose of repeatedly unsuccessful courses of action
illustrated in Chapter 5, let us ponder statements from an evaluation by GTZ
(German Agency for Technical Cooperation) staff involved in the large multi-
donor effort initiated in Somalia in 1980 under the title Central Rangelands
Development Project (CRDP) (Baumann et al., 1993). CRDP was conceived as
an action, not a fact-finding, program. What needed doing was already obvious

to its designers. Some 30% of rangelands were to be put under controlled grazing in about 75 guarded reserves, each involving a "detailed and difficult process" of formation and governance (Zessin and Farah, 1993). Covering 20% of the land area of Somalia (149,000 square km with a human population of 544,000, 75% of whom were directly involved in livestock production), CDRP was on an impressive scale by any token. For, of the 80% of Somalia's overall foreign exchange which was earned by livestock, this region's 3.9 million goats, 1.2 million sheep, 1.0 million camels and 0.9 million cattle alone provided a full 40% of goat exports, 20% of sheep and 10-20% of camels and cattle. Major results in *national* terms were contemplated from this program.

From the beginning doubts existed on the parts of some experienced scientists about a plan which "attempted to replace existing nomadic ways. . . . Communication between project components was lacking . . . [and] it became more and more evident that reservations concerning validity of a number of project objectives were justified. . . . Knowledge about the pastoralists' natural and socio-economic environment was either nonexistent or extremely limited" (Zessin and Farah, 1993).

That eventually prompted a reassessment of original objectives and procedures with the result that, *four years after its initiation*, CRDP was scaled-down from 13 to 3 districts and, although "project objectives officially were not changed," at the end of the project's first six-year phase "there still was no proof of the CRDP's working assumption that reserves would improve rangelands . . . and immediately lead to enhanced livestock production." By then, a general feeling existed among participants that considerably more knowledge was required about traditional production systems before such a sweeping approach could be justified.

To quote further from this evaluation after the total effort was terminated by civil war:

A development program [among pastoralists] oriented towards responding to the . . . perception of a general crisis, rather than . . . development planning based on long-term monitoring and research activities, will not consider the pastoral producers as the target beneficiaries. . . . The best development approach seeks to avoid disrupting existing, albeit imperfect ways until it can be demonstrated that new ways are better, low-risk and appropriate. . . . It is wrong to condemn nomads as a negative, ecologically and culturally minor deviation from sedentary lifestyle, whose imperfections must be "fixed" by technical interventions. . . . A mere conservationist approach, which romantically portrays nomadism as the superior way of life of a proud, independent people, who must be kept free from the destructive influences of modern civilization is a-historical. With change inevitable, it is really a question of how change is applied. *It is the mode, speed and control over the direction of change that determines the well-being and fate of pastoralists*. Neither the "'technical fix" nor the "structural fix" schools of thought have so far been able to identify workable and proven development measures. This paucity of alternatives and the sensitive nature of the dessicated lands involved here make clear the need for a cautious, conservative and trial-oriented approach to nomadic rangeland development (Zessin and Farah, 1993, italics added).

Hence the need for less glamorous, but affordable local actions with improved intelligence and communications.

In light of this long series of failures of livestock development programs in Africa to meet the high (and insufficiently informed) expectations of outsiders (see Chapter 5), the Winrock assessment group on animal agriculture (Pritchard et al., 1992: 125) concluded similarly that "any [single] national program [of rangelands management] increases the chances of failure and reduces the likelihood of government agencies being able to render assistance to communities that really have a commitment to reforms." As close outside observers are now much more prone to emphasize, local actions and decisions are essential in all efforts to optimize productivity of African rangelands (Shanmugaratnam et al., 1991; Behnke et al., 1993). These conclusions have taken some Northern funding agencies far too long to realize.

Some of this book's proposals flow naturally from our long-shared agreement with such conclusions. Continued attempts to abolish or seriously manipulate insufficiently studied traditional practices of pastoralists are at least as callous, and will have about as much chance of success as would much less far reaching attempts to get Americans or English to take their annual vacations in February rather than August and to change their date for celebrating Christmas. Would anyone be so arrogant as to even suggest things like these just because he *thinks* they might "increase productivity" or make "them" more like "us" in little-examined ways? More humility needs to be injected into this whole notion of Third World development and, with it, realization that *every* people and nation are underdeveloped in significant ways.

Therein lies the second *tragedy* of Africa's pastoral peoples. Not only their practices but their desires have not been known to many who propose "development" measures among them. Often pastoralists have not been even a part of the development equation. Almost all that people like Kenyan Maasai have experienced of outsiders' ideas during the past century has been loss of large areas of traditional lands. The Jonglei canal, for whatever else it may prove to others, and what good or other bad effects it may "incidentally" have in the southern Sudan, is seen by Dinka as little more than an unwanted access barrier to traditional grazing lands.

To ascertain the wishes and priorities of pastoralists themselves, to gain their support and cooperation--and to get *them* to suggest how *they* will help pay for what they want--require knowledge of how to achieve interactive communications. For this outsiders would be advised to seek help from educated pastoral elites who are increasingly numerous and who often are enthusiastic about development prospects. Elites can advise not only who to talk to, but when and how. For example, Dinka can be reached most easily at their transhumant homesteads just before they migrate to the *toich*. Since that is one of two seasons in which important social or religious activities take place, all those who matter in community decision-making would be available. Similarly valuable would be advice on behavior considered normal or abnormal among particular groups of pastoralists. Small courtesies and sensitivities go far among such peoples. For example, among Dinka learning a local joke or memorizing characteristics of one special pied-color bull with which the outsider would identify *himself* would not only make for well-appreciated fun, but would prompt Dinka to say "this person knows us."

## STEPWISE PROGRESS

In themselves, the involvement of pastoralists and use of the veterinary outreach vehicle for some of the most obvious areas of IC could move some groups of pastoralists from their current state to a considerably improved one. This improvement could be sufficiently apparent to make local IC a priority governmental policy goal and to begin institution-building efforts (Chapters 8 and 9) that could enhance and complement these IC efforts sufficiently to involve pastoral communities more integrally within national economies. For, in eliciting from them their own ideas about ways to contribute to these further inputs, means would begin to be visualized to render these demonstrated benefits sustainable at a level of balance which the pastoral peoples could themselves embrace as "indigenous" and therefore help perpetuate.

For example, as spelled out in Chapter 8, better-targeted external aid could convert the existing veterinary outreach vehicle for action into the means also for grassroots information acquisition and environmental monitoring, suggesting possibilities for small-scale pilot intervention trials of many kinds, as advocated by Zessin and Farah (1993), Behnke et al. (1993), Sollod (1991) and others. The total potential of this step-by-step process of decentralized IC initiatives and local pilot trials will also require imaginative educational reforms. We have given examples of some of the directions this could take.

Beyond stimulation of such a chain of actions, our aim has been principally to provide a more "common meeting ground" for cooperation among public administrators, economists, veterinarians, range specialists and other agriculturalists, educators, public health and primary care providers, anthropologists, and others who are, or should become, interested in development among pastoral peoples in Africa. We have suggested that this opportunistic approach to development requires of these Northern disciplinarians some shedding of their sectoral "tribalisms," some practical retreat from their so-accustomed abstractions and "misplaced concretenesses" (Daly and Cobb, 1989).

## OUTSIDER'S INITIATIVES

Here we more concisely lay out what we believe "outsiders" (national and inter-national) could do in the future:

1. Avoid temptations to create additional parallel or "umbrella sectors" of government expressly for grassroots outreach or for large-scale projects with their own central direction and independent administrative hierarchies.

2. Instead, initiate and promote governmental decentralization in all appropriate areas within each established ministry which is organized down to the district level, especially with respect to setting local priorities and decision-making regarding resource allocations.

3. Promote within each ministry, and government generally, the logic and attractiveness of local IC in the dual interests of economies and improved services (within existing structures and with existing resources) and *reward those who suggest, initiate and successfully carry out such efforts.*

4. Correct through priority budgetary allocations critical *local* transport inadequacies which hinder the ability of the one already existing grassroots outreach sector to dependably perform its crucial "piggybacking" service to other sectors on a continuing basis (if this cannot be accomplished already within local IC arrangements).

5. Provide external assistance to expeditiously convert existing "campaigns-mass actions" veterinary service delivery infrastructures to more time- and cost-effective and scientifically rational "surveillance-selective actions" infrastructures in interests of sufficient ongoing information for meaningful actions beyond initial IC efforts.

6. Provide donor assistance for broader institution-building through creation and on-going support as required of appropriately sited institutions of higher education which are meaningfully oriented to the local needs and circumstances of pastoralists and cost- and results-effective cooperation mechanisms for grassroots delivery of essential services.

For some of that to succeed, interested political scientists, public administrators and economists must propose new workable IC "rules of accountability" that will not become mired at *already overly difficult* local levels in masses of additional red tape. In some of her writings, Ostrom has considered doing this largely within traditional institutions in ways that would make accountability the pastoralists' problem in large measure. In that connection, it is our belief that tightknit communities such as among pastoralist kinship groups may condone negative aspects of nepotism and corruption when they believe individuals who are benefitting are doing so *at the expense of "outsiders."* If, however, they can be convinced (because it is so) that they have a major vested interest in the success of an enterprise (perhaps really own it), and if it is not a success because of corruption or other causes it is *they collectively and individually who will most suffer*, then much of this problem of accountability in a system of informal *quid pro quo* IC may disappear. Through such means, government at higher than local levels may shift more and more to providing technical inputs with the pastoralists themselves through traditional and nontraditional local governments meeting recurrent financing responsibilities (e.g., making decisions about maintaining and replacing vehicles, and how to do it). We believe that many traditional institutions have possibilities for so evolving, if pastoralists are consulted and co-opted at every stage. We have cited an example of where Dinka herders paid for freezer upkeep in a cold chain to deliver vaccinations to their cattle. Clearly they recognized their interest in the success of that venture and were prepared to pay for it.


## SUMMARY

In the past, there have been major conflicts of interest in the pastoral development process. On the one hand, planners often have been interested in a kind of development that serves values alien to pastoralists. In fact, pastoralists' own interests may be at sharp variance with some of those objectives (which they often do not comprehend anyway). Reconciliations of such divergent interests can be achieved only by identifying appropriate, sustainable development initiatives within the traditional subsistence economies themselves--*or as logical outgrowths from them*--which aim toward new balance points for pastoral communities.

We both believe from our common and different experiences that the first new balance point for the Dinka people may resemble in certain material particulars that realized now by many southern Somalis. And, as for what the stage beyond that one might be for the Dinka, we think it too early to venture much, except that, with ever-growing numbers of "educated elites," new things in ways of compromise will undoubtably be tried and first demonstrated by those among them who still feel strong ties to their people's traditions.

In moving toward such new sustainable points of balance throughout pastoral Africa, we believe, to summarize our proposals' main points, that (1) pastoral development in every individual circumstance must result from the full participation at all stages of the pastoralists themselves; (2) it must be much more firmly based upon intimate knowledge and full consideration of the intricacies of the man-animal relationships that exist *locally* in each case, including the customs and institutions these have spawned; (3) decentralization of decision-making and program implementation must be encouraged among all sectors; (4) general recognition must be forthcoming that, among various service sectors, only veterinary services has made a serious effort, and has had any success, in reaching Africa's mobile pastoralists at the literally grassroots level they live; (5) these advantages could be shared through a fairly broad range of cost-attractive intersectoral cooperation efforts and some basic amenities provided to pastoralists by grafting these upon existing veterinary programs; (6) recognition that these new development proposals are as opportunistic and multipurpose as pastoralists' own strategies and institutions; (7) infrastructural changes in veterinary services delivery could create equally practical means for ongoing two-way communications with pastoralists, including for environmental monitoring in the interests of disaster preparedness and range improvement; and, finally (8) under our paradigm, individual ministries or services would not relinquish control of their facilities or programs but simply allow their surplus or potentially surplus capacities to be used by others.

The real challenge to public administrators, planners and development funders is to encourage, facilitate, recognize and reward locally practical IC initiatives. Sufficient economies and scientific advantages should be realized thereby to make modest yet meaningful and sustainable advances within the constraints of existing resources (in the first instance). We can see no other way under such circumstances of multiple shortages as prevail throughout most of pastoral Africa and, surely, past decades of failures to succeed otherwise should have fully established that. If, as Amartya Sen (1981) put it: "At any given time a policy definition reflects a balancing of community capabilities and desires," such defining criteria are badly in need of assessing vis-à-vis most development attempts within pastoral Africa.

Continued pursuit of discredited alternatives to these suggested actions could subject many African pastoralists to the unenviable fates of Japan's Ainu, Australia's aborigines, the Western Hemisphere's native inhabitants and other unempowered peoples. If such hardy and resolute peoples are not to be crushed by temptations and other unrelenting pressures from alien cultures and if nothing more on their behalf can be attempted, their only survival mechanism may be to increasingly become crippled anthropological exhibits for foreign tourists to come and gaze upon, as in some museum. That is already beginning to happen to some more accessible pastoral peoples like Kenya's Maasai.

Or some common sense can begin to cut through the maze of sectoral, professional and disciplinary barriers to creative solutions which surmount the tendencies of each entity to jealously guard its own turf. Here is a wonderful opportunity for social scientists and active academic humanists especially (Schwabe, 1978b) to join hands with custodians of technical knowledge and skills in encouraging and rewarding successful local efforts whose aims are to stretch scarce talents and other resources to their maximums under circumstances of dire necessity.

We began this book with the optical analogy developed by Frederick Riggs in the 1950s through the 1970s (see Table 1.1) to help make clear to other Northern public administrators involved in the new process of "Third World development" the enormous cultural-communications gaps that separated peoples within "fused" (pastoral) societies from those of the "diffracted" (industrian) North--and how to help bridge these. We can do no better than to conclude with another analogy from the realm of optics (*vision*) ascribed to

Arthur Koestler: "Every creative act in science, art or religion involves a new innocence of perception liberated from the cataract of accepted beliefs." For now is surely the moment for political scientists, economists and public administrators concerned with Africa's future to overcome opacities of vision and cast out motes of inappropriate Northern precedents that may still blind them to new or little-tried possibilities. By helping facilitate their success, they will offer promise of a more hopeful future for Africa's proud pastoral millions.

# REFERENCES

Abdullahi, A.M. 1993. Livestock policy in Somalia: past and present status and future prospects. In: Baumann, M.P.O., Janzen, J. and Schwartz, H.J. (eds.), *Pastoral Production in Central Somalia*. Eschborn, Germany: Deutsche Gesellschaft für Technische Zusammenarbeit.

Agadzi, V.K. and Obuobi, A.D. 1986. Repairing the links in Ghana's cold chain. *World Health Forum* 7: 345-347.

Ahamed, A.G.M. 1973. Nomadic competition in the Funj area. *Sudan Notes and Records* 54: 43-56.

Aliou, S. 1992. What health system for nomadic populations? *World Health Forum* 13: 311-314.

Almond, M. 1991. A para-vet programme in south Sudan. In: Oxby, C. (ed.), *Assisting African Livestock Keepers: The Experience of Four Projects*. ODI Agricultural Administration Unit Occasional Paper 12. London: Overseas Development Institute.

AMREF. 1984. *Health Manpower in Southern Sudan: A Study of Health Manpower in the Three Regions of the Southern Sudan, 1984*. Nairobi: African Medical and Research Foundation.

Araujo, F.P., Schwabe, C.W., Sawyer, J.C. and Davis, W.G. 1975. Hydatid disease transmission in California: a study of the Basque connection. *American Journal of Epidemiology* 102: 291-302.

Aronson, D.R. 1980. Must nomads settle? Some notes toward policy on the future of pastoralism. In: Salzman, P.C. (ed.) *When Nomads Settle. Processes of Sedentarization as Adaptation and Response*. New York: Praeger.

Ater, J.M. 1976. *The Dinka Priesthood*. Thesis. Beirut: Near East School of Theology.

AVMA. 1994. *AVMA Directory*. Schaumburg, Illinois: American Veterinary Medical Association.

Azarya, V. 1988. Reordering state-society relations: incorporation and disengagement. In: Rothchild, D.S. and Naomi, C. (eds.), *The Precarious Balance: State and Society in Africa.* Boulder, Colorado: Westview Press.

Barkan, J.D. 1984. *Politics and Public Policy in Kenya and Tanzania.* 2nd ed. New York: Praeger.

Barney, G.O. (study director) 1980. *Global 2000 Report ot the President: Entering the 21st Century.* A Report Prepared by the Council on Environmental Quality and the Department of State. Washington, D.C.: U.S. Government Printing Office.

Bartels, G.B., Norton, B.E. and Perrier, G.K. 1993. An examination of the carrying capacity concept. In: Behnke, R.H., Scoones, I. and Kerven, C. (eds.), *Range Ecology at Disequilibrium.* London: Overseas Development Institute, International Institute for Environment and Development.

Basinski, J.J. 1957. Some problems of agricultural development in the southern provinces of the Sudan. *Sudan Notes and Records* 38: 21-46.

Bates, D.G. and Conant, F.P. 1980. Livestock and livelihood: a handbook for the 1980s. In: *The Future of Pastoral Peoples.* Proceedings of a conference held in Nairobi, Kenya, 4-8 August 1980. Ottawa: International Development Research Center.

Baumann, M.P.O. 1983. *Eine serologische Studie über das Vorkommen der Brucellose bei Rindern und kleinen Wiederkäuern im Südsudan und deren sanitäre Bedeutung.* Inaugural-Dissertation zur Erlangung des Grades eines Doktors der Veterinärmedizin an der Freien Universität Berlin.

Baumann, M.P.O. 1990. *The Nomadic Aninimal Health System (NAHA-sytem) in Pastoral Areas of Central Somalia and its Usefulness in Epidemiological Surveillance.* Master of Preventive Veterinary Medicine thesis. University of California, Davis.

Baumann, M.P.O., Janzen, J. and Schwartz, H.J. (eds.). 1993. *Pastoral Production in Central Somalia.* Eschborn, Germany: Deutsche Gesellschaft für Technische Zusammenarbeit.

Behnke, R.H. 1983. Fenced and open-range ranching: the commercialization of pastoral land and livestock in Africa. In: Simpson, J.R. and Evangelou, P. (eds.), *Livestock Development in Subsaharan Africa.* Boulder, Colorado: Westview Press.

Behnke, R.H. and Scoones, I. 1993. Rethinking range ecology: implications for rangeland management in Africa. In: Behnke, R.H., Scoones, I. and Kerven, C. (eds.), *Range Ecology at Disequilibrium.* London: Overseas Development Institute, International Institute for Environment and Development.

Behnke, R.H., Scoones, I. and Kerven, C. (eds.). 1993. *Range Ecology at Disequilibrium.* London: Overseas Development Institute, International Institute for Environment and Development.

Berntsen, J.L. 1977. *Maasai and Iloikop: Ritual Experts and their Followers.* Occasional Paper no. 9. Madison: University of Wisconsin.

Beshai, A.A. 1976. *Export Performance and Economic Development in the Sudan, 1900-1967.* London: Ithaca Press.

Bizimana, N. 1994. *Traditional Veterinary Practices in Africa.* Schriftenreihe no. 243. Eschborn, Germany: Deutsche Gesellschaft für Technische Zusammenarbeit.

Blaxter, K.L. 1973. Increasing output of animal production: technical measures for improving productivity. In: Recheigl, M. (ed.), *Man, Food and Nutrition: Strategies and Technological Measures for Alleviating the World Food Problem*. Cleveland: CRC Press.

Boulding, E. 1988. *Building a Global Civic Culture*. Syracuse, New York: Syracuse University Press.

Bouzarat, D. Zessin, K.-H., Baumann, M.P.O. and Gautsch, K.D. 1988. Studies on farming systems and small ruminant production in central Somalia. GTZ/CRDP Veterinary Component, Beledweyne, Somalia. Addis Ababa: International Livestock Centre for Africa.

Branagan, D. 1962. The Development of Maasailand. Unpublished report, Department of Veterinary Services, Government of Tanganyika (Original not seen, see Tepilit, 1978.)

Branagan, D. and Hammond, J.A. 1965. Rinderpest in Tanganyika: a review. *Bulletin of Epizootic Diseases in Africa* 13: 225-46.

Brown, L.R. (Project director) et al. 1990-1995. *State of the World*. Annual volume. Washington, D.C.: Worldwatch Institute.

Buringh, P., van Heeemst, H.D.J. and Staring, G.J. 1975. *Computation of the Absolute Maximum Food Production of the World*. Wageningein, the Netherlands: Agricultural University, Department of Soil Science.

Burton, J.W. 1987. *A Nilotic World. The Atuot-speaking Peoples of the Southern Sudan*. New York: Greenwood Press.

Buxton, J. 1973. *Religion and Healing in Mandari*. Oxford: Oxford University Press.

Bywater, A.C. annd Baldwin, R.L. 1980. Alternative strategies in food-animal production. In: Baldwin, R.L. (ed.), *Animals, Feed, Food and People*. American Association for the Advancement of Science Selected Symposium, volume 42. Boulder, Colorado: Westview Press.

Carlton, T.L. 1991a. Desktop geographical mapping--a graphical look at four tools. *Windows and OS* 2: 62-74.

Carlton, T.L. 1991b. *Geographical Analytical Epidemiology of Bovine Trypanosomiasis: Preliminary Results Using Desktop Mapping Software*. Master of Preventive Veterinary Medicine thesis, University of California, Davis.

Carlton, T.L. 1992. Geographical Epidemiology: The Use of Geographical Information Systems (GISs) South of the Sahara, and Geographical Analytical Epidemiology of Bovine Trypanosomiasis in the Southern Sudan. Unpublished Working Document. Davis: University of California, School of Veterinary Medicine, Department of Epidemiology and Preventive Medicine.

Cheneau, Y. 1985. The organization of veterinary services in Africa. *Office International des Epizooties Revue Scientifique et Technique* 5: 107-54.

Chimbombi, M.C. 1988. Technical consultation on animal health and production. Animal Health Section, Botswana. In: *Animal Health Problems in Selected African Countries*. Report of a Technical Consultation in Lusaka, Zambia 23-28 November 1987. Uppsala, Sweden: International Rural Development Center, Swedish University of Agricultural Sciences.

Clutton-Brock, J. 1981. *Domesticated Animals from Early Times.* Austin: University of Texas Press.

Clutton-Brock, J. (ed.). 1989. *The Walking Larder--Patterns of Domestication, Pastoralism and Predation.* London: Unwin Hyman.

Collins, R.O. 1985. The big ditch: the Jonglei Canal scheme. In: Daly, M.W. (ed.), *Modernization in the Sudan.* New York: Lilian Barber Press.

Collins, R.O. 1990. *The Waters of the Nile. Hydropolitics and the Jonglei Canal, 1900-1988.* Oxford: Clarendon Press.

Conrad, J.R. 1957. *The Horn and the Sword--The History of the Bull as Symbol of Power and Fertility.* New York: Dutton.

Coughenour, M.B., Ellis, J.E., Swift, D.M., Coppock, D.L., Galvin, K., McCabe, J.T. and Hart, T.C. 1985. Energy extraction and use in a nomadic pastoral ecosystem. *Science* 230: 619-25.

Cunnison, J. 1960. The social role of cattle. *Sudan Journal of Veterinary Science and Animal Husbandry* 1: 1-18.

Dahl, G. and Hjort, A. 1976. *Having Herds: Pastoral Growth and Household Economy.* Stockholm Series in Social Anthropology, 2. Stockholm: Department of Social Anthropology, University of Stockholm.

Daly, H.E. and Cobb, J.B. 1989. *For the Common Good.* Boston: Beacon Press.

De Leeuw, P.N., Diarra, L. and Hiernaun, P. 1993. An analysis of feed demand and supply for pastoral livestock: the Gourma region of Mali. In: Behnke, R.H., Scoones, I. and Kerven, C. (eds.), *Range Ecology at Disequilibrium.* London: Overseas Development Institute, International Institute for Environment and Development.

Democratic Republic of the Sudan, Southern Region 1977. *The Six-Year Plan of Economic and Social Development 1977/78-1982/83.* Juba, Sudan: Directorate of Planning, Regional Ministry of Finance and Economic Planning.

Deng, F.M. 1971. *Tradition and Modernization: A Challenge for Law Among the Dinka of the Sudan.* New Haven, Connecticut: Yale University Press.

Deng, F.M. 1972. *The Dinka of the Sudan.* New York: Holt, Rinehart and Winston.

Deng, F.M. 1978. *Africans of Two Worlds. The Dinka in Afro-Arab Sudan.* Khartoum: University of Khartoum Press.

Deng, F.M. 1980. *Dinka Cosmology.* London: Ithaca Press.

Deng, F.M. 1985. Development in context. In: Daly, M.W. (ed.), *Modernization in the Sudan.* New York: Lilian Barber Press.

Dodd, J.L. 1994. An assessment of the desertification/degradation issue in sub-Saharan Africa and the role of livestock. *Bioscience* 44: 28-34.

Dodds, E..R. 1960. *Euripides Bacchae.* Oxford: Clarendon Press.

Doran, M.H., Low, A.R.C. and Kemp, R.L. 1979. Cattle as a store of wealth in Swaziland: implications for livestock development and overgrazing in Eastern and Southern Africa. *American Journal of Agricultural Economics* 61: 41-7.

Dorwart, R.A. 1959. Cattle disease (rinderpest?)--prevention and cure in Brandenburg, 1665-1732. *Agricultural History* 33: 79-85.

Duggan, W.R. 1986. *An Economic Analysis of Southern African Agriculture*. New York: Praeger.

Dumont, R. 1975. *Croissance ... de Famine: une Agriculture Repensee*. Paris: Le Seuil.

Duncan, A. 1978. Livestock husbandry and agriculture among the Dinka. Juba, Southern Sudan: Project Development Unit (PDU), Regional Ministry of Agriculture.

Dunlop, D.W. 1975. Alternatives to "modern" health delivery systems in Africa: public policy issues of traditional health systems. *Social Sciences and Medicine* 9: 581-586.

Dyson-Hudson, R. and Dyson-Hudson, N. 1969. Subsistence herding in Uganda. *Scientific American* 220: 76-80.

Dyson-Hudson, R. and McCabe, J.T. 1985. *South Turkana Nomadism: Coping with a Unpredictably Varying Environment*. Human Relations Area Files. New Haven, Connecticut: HRAFlex Books.

Economist Intelligence Unit. 1989. Sudan country report no. 4. London: The Economist Intelligence Unit.

Economist Intelligence Unit. 1990. Sudan country report no. 2. London: The Economist Intelligence Unit.

Ellis, J.E., Coughenour, M.B. and Swift, D.M. 1993. Climate variability, ecosystem stability and the implications for range and livestock development. In: Behnke, R.H., Scoones, I. and Kerven, C. (eds.), *Range Ecology at Disequilibrium*. London: Overseas Development Institute, International Institute for Environment and Development.

Evans-Pritchard, E.E. 1937. Economic life of the Nuer. *Sudan Notes and Records* 20: 209-245.

Evans-Pritchard, E.E. 1940. *The Nuer: A Description of the Modes of Livelihood and Political Institutions of a Nilotic People*. Oxford: Oxford University Press.

Evans-Pritchard, E.E. 1948. *The Divine Kingship of the Shilluk of the Nilotic Sudan*. Cambridge: Cambridge University Press.

Evans-Pritchard, E.E. 1951. *Kinship and Marriage Among the Nuer*. Oxford: Clarendon Press.

Evans-Pritchard, E.E. 1956. *Nuer Religion*. Oxford: Clarendon Press.

FAO. 1967. *Production Yearbook, 1966*. Rome: UN Food and Agricultural Organization.

FAO. 1981. Administering agricultural development for small farmers: issues in decentralization and people's participation. Economic and Social Development paper 20. Rome: UN Food and Agricultural Organization.

FAO. 1984. *Report of the FAO Expert Consultation on Veterinary Education in Africa*. Rome: UN Food and Agricultural Organization.

FAO. 1989. *Production Yearbook, 1988*. Rome: UN Food and Agricultural Organization.

FAO/WHO. 1971. *Report of the Third Meeting of the FAO/WHO Expert Panel on Veterinary Education*, 12-16 July 1971. Rome: UN Food and Agricultural Organization.

Farver, T.B. 1987. Disease prevalence estimation in animal populations using two-stage sampling designs. *Preventive Veterinary Medicine* 5: 1-20.

Felton, M.R. and Ellis, P.R. 1978. Studies on the control of rinderpest in Nigeria. Study no. 23. Reading: University of Reading.

Ford, J. 1971. *The Role of Trypansomiasis in African Ecology*. Oxford: Clarendon Press.

Frankfort, J. 1948. *Kingship and the Gods*. Chicago: University of Chicago Press.

French, C.M. and Nelson, G.S. 1982. Hydatid disease in the Turkana district of Kenya. II. A study in medical geography. *Annals of Tropical Medicine and Parasitology* 76: 439-457.

Furubotin, E.G. and Richter, R. 1991. The New Institutional Economics: an assessment. In: Furubotin and Richter (eds.), *The New Institutional Economics*. College Station: Texas A&M University Press.

Galaty, J.G. 1980. The Maasai group ranch: politics and development in an African pastoral society. In: Salzman, P.C. (ed.), *When Nomads Settle: Processes of Sedentarization as Adaption and Response*. New York: Praeger.

Gibbons, W.J. 1953. Lecture notes, Auburn University, College of Veterinary Medicine.

Gillespie, I.A. 1966. The nomads of the Sudan and their livestock in the 20th century. *Sudan Journal of Veterinary Science and Animal Husbandry* 7: 13-23.

Goldschmidt, W. 1980. The failure of pastoral economic development programs in Africa. In: *The Future of Pastoral Peoples*. Proceedings of a conference held in Nairobi, Kenya 4-8 August 1980. Ottawa: International Development Research Centre Publication.

GOS. 1954. *Natural Resources and Development Potential in the Southern Provinces of the Sudan*. A preliminary report by the Southern Development Investigation Team. London: Government of the Sudan.

Gros, J.-G. 1993a. The New Institutional Economics, market failures and optimal regulation of private livestock services delivery in Cameroon. Unpublished manuscript, Department of Political Science, University of California, Berkeley.

Gros, J.-G. 1993b. The privatization of livestock services in sub-Saharan Africa: neglected issues and prospects. Unpublished manuscript. Department of Political Science, University of California, Berkeley.

Gros, J.-G. 1993c. *The Privatization of Livestock Services in Sub-Saharan Africa: A Study in the Feasibility of State and Market Participation in the Promotion of Structural Economic Reforms*. Ph.D. dissertation, Department of Political Science, University of California, Berkeley.

Gros, J.-G. 1993d. Seminar at the University of California, Davis, February 1993.

Gulliver, P.H. 1955. *The Family Herds. A Study of Two Pastoral Tribes in East Africa. The Jie and Turkana*. London: Routledge and Kegan Paul.

Gulliver, P. and Gulliver, P.H. 1953. *Ethnographic Survey of Africa. East Central Africa Part VII: The Central Nilo-Hamites*. London: International African Institute.

Güsten, R. 1966. *Problems of Economic Growth and Planning: The Sudan Example*. Berlin: Springer-Verlag.

Haan, C. de and Bekure, S. 1989. Animal health services in sub-Saharan Africa: initial experiences with new approaches. Washington, D.C.: World Bank.

Haan, C. de and Nissen, N.J. 1985. Animal health services in sub-Saharan Africa: alternative approaches. World Bank Technical Paper no. 44. Washington, D.C.: World Bank.

Haile Yesus, T. 1988. Animal health in Ethiopia. In: *Animal Health Problems in Selected African Countries*. Report of a Technical Consultation in Lusaka, Zambia, 23-28 November 1987. Uppsala: International Rural Development Center, Swedish University of Agricultural Sciences.

Hall, M.C. 1936. *Control of Animal Parasites: General Principles and their Application*. Evanston, Illinois: North American Veterinarian.

Halpin, B. 1981a. The design and management of pastoral development. Pastoral Network Paper 11. London: Overseas Development Institute, Agricultural Administration Unit.

Halpin, B. 1981b. Vets--barefoot and otherwise. Pastoral Network Paper 11C. London: Overseas Development Institute, Agricultural Administration Unit.

Hannaway, C.C. 1977. Veterinary medicine and rural health care in pre-revolutionary France. *Bulletin of the History of Medicine* 51: 431-47.

Hardin, G. 1968. The tragedy of the commons. *Science* 162: 1243-1248.

Hedlund, H.G.B. 1971. The impact of group ranches on a pastoral society. University of Nairobi, Institute for Development Studies Staff Paper no. 100 (Original not seen, see Behnke, 1983.)

Herskovits, M.J. 1926. The cattle complex of East Africa. *American Anthropologist* 28: 230-72, 361-88, 494-528, 633-64.

Hooper, W. (trans.) 1935. *Marcus Porcius Cato on Agriculture. Marcus Terrentius Varro on Agriculture*. Cambridge, Massachusetts: Harvard University Press.

Hopper, W.D. 1976. The development of agriculture in the developing countries. *Scientific American* 235: 197-205.

Howell, P. 1951. Notes on the Ngok Dinka. *Sudan Notes and Records* 32: 239-93.

Howell, P., Lock, M. and Cobb, S. 1988. *The Jonglei Canal. Impact and Opportunity*. Cambridge: Cambridge University Press.

Huntingford, G.W.B. 1953. *Ethnographic Survey of Africa. East Central Africa Part VI. The Northern Nilo-Hamites*. London: International African Institute.

Huntingford, G.W.B. 1969. *Ethnographic Survey of Africa. East Central Africa Part III. The Southern Nilo-Hamites*. London: International African Institute.

Huxley, J. 1931. *Africa View*. New York: Harper and Brothers.

ILACO. 1982. Pengko Pilot Project Technical Note 21. Animal products. Arnheim, The Netherlands.

ILCA. 1987. *ILCA's Strategy and Long-term Plan*. Addis Ababa: International Livestock Centre for Africa.

Jack, J.D.M. 1961. The Sudan. In: West, G.P. (ed.), *A History of the Overseas Veterinary Services*. Part One. London: British Veterinary Association.

Jahnke, H.E. 1982. *Livestock Production Systems and Livestock Development in Tropical Africa*. Kiel: Lieler Wissenschaftsverlag Vauk.

Janzen, J. 1993. Mobile livestock keeping in Somalia: general situation and prospects of a way of life undergoing fundamental change. In: Baumann, M.P.O., Janzen, J. and Schwartz, H.J. (eds.), *Pastoral Production in Central Somalia*. Eschborn, Germany: Deutsche Gesellschaft für Technische Zusammenarbeit.

Janzen, J. Schwartz, H.J. and Baumann, M.P.O. 1993. Perspectives and recommendations for pastotal development in Somalia. In: Baumann, M.P.O., Janzen, J. and Schwartz, H.J. (eds.), *Pastoral Production in Central Somalia*. Eschborn, Germany: Deutsche Gesellschaft für Technische Zusammenarbeit.

Jarvis, L. and Erickson, R. 1986. Livestock herds, overgrazing and range degradation in Zimbabwe: how and why do the herds keep growing? ALPAN Network Paper no. 9. Addis Ababa: International Livestock Centre for Africa.

Kaplan, I. 1982. The society and its environment. In: *Somalia, a Country Study*. Washington, D.C.: U.S. Government Printing Office.

Kenyon, S.J. and Kenyon, S.M. 1991. The importance of attitudes to animal health and production in development assistance projects. Paper presented at the American Anthropological Association meeting, Chicago, 20 November 1991.

Kenyon, S.J. and Nour, A.V.M. 1991. Animal disease diagnosis laboratories: what are their functions in a less developed country? Paper presented at the Center for African Studies Symposium "Technology, Culture and Development in the Third World: Lessons and Examples from Africa." Ohio State University, Columbus, 23-26 May 1991.

Khalil, I.M. 1960. Developing the animal wealth of the Sudan. *Sudan Notes and Records* 41: 6-20.

Kjekshus, H. 1977. *Ecology Control and Economic Develpment in East African History*. Berkeley: University of California Press.

Kuhn, T.S. 1970. *The Structure of Scientific Revolutions*. 2nd ed. Chicago: University of Chicago Press.

Laitin, D.D. and Samatar, S.S. 1987. *Somalia: Nation in Search of a State*. Boulder, Colorado: Westview Press.

Lako, G.T. 1988. The Jonglei scheme: the contrast between government and Dinka views on development. In: Barnett, T. and Abdel Karim, A. (eds.), *Sudan State, Capital and Transformation*. London: Croom Helm.

Lane, J. 1993. Farriers in Georgian England. In: Mitchell, A.R. (ed.), *History of the Healing Professions: Parallels Between Veterinary and Medical History*. Vol. 3 of the Advancement of Veterinary Science, the Royal Veterinary College Bicentenary Symposium series. London: CAB International.

Lappé, F.M. 1975. *Diet for a Small Planet*. New York: Ballentine Books.

Lees, F.A. and Brooks, H.C. 1977. *The Economic and Political Development of the Sudan*. London: Macmillan.

Lele, U. 1975. *The Design of Rural Development--Lessons from Africa*. Baltimore: Johns Hopkins University Press.

Leonard, D.K. 1984. Class formation and agricultural development. In: Barkan, J.D. (ed.), *Politics and Public Policy in Kenya and Tanzania* 2nd ed. New York: Praeger.

Leonard, D.K. 1987. The supply of veterinary services: Kenyan lessons. *Agricultural Administration and Extension* 26: 219-236.

Leonard, D.K. 1991. *African Successes: Four Public Managers of Kenyan Rural Development*. Berkeley: University of California Press.

Leonard, D.K. 1993. Structural reform of the veterinary profession in Africa and the New Institutional Economics. *Development and Change* 24: 227-267.

Leonard, D.K. and Marshall, D.R. 1982. *Institution of Rural Development for the Poor. Decentralization and Organizational Linkages*. Berkeley: Institute of International Studies, University of California.

Lepissier, H.E. and MacFarlane, I.M. 1966. OAU/STRC joint campaign against rinderpest. Final report of tthe coordination on Phase 1. *Bulletin of Epizootic Diseases in Africa* 14: 194-224.

Lessard, P., L'Esplattenier, R., Norval, R.A.I., Kundert, K., Dolan, T.T., Croze, H., Walker, J.B., Irvin, A.D. and Perry, B.D. 1990. Geographical information systems for studying the epidemiology of cattle diseases caused by *Theileria parva*. *Veterinary Record* 126: 255-62.

Lewis, B.A. 1972. *The Murle: Red Chiefs and Black Commoners*. Oxford: Clarendon Press.

Lewis, I.M. 1969. *Ethnographic Survey of Africa. North Eastern Africa, Part 1. Peoples of the Horn of Africa*. London: International African Institute.

Lienhardt, G. 1961. *Divinity and Experience. The Religion of the Dinka*. Oxford: Oxford University Press.

Lincoln, B. 1981. *Priests, Warriors and Cattle*. Berkeley: University of California Press.

Lolik, P.L. (chrmn) et al. 1976. *Primary Health Programmes, Southern Region, Sudan, 1977/78*. Juba: Democratic Republic of the Sudan.

Loomis, R. 1976. Agricultural systems. *Scientific American* 235: 98-105.

Lugard, F.D. 1893. *The Rise of Our East African Empire*. Vol. 1. Edinburgh: Blackwood.

Luxmore, H.B. 1950. Final Veterinary Report on Equatoria, Sudan Veterinary Service. (Original not seen; see *Natural Resources and Development Potential in the Southern Provinces of the Sudan*. A Preliminary Report by the Southern Development Investigation Team, 1954. London: Government of the Sudan, p. 104.).

MacFarlane, I.M. 1973. Joint campaign against rinderpest in Africa: Joint Project 15 (JP-15). *State Veterinary Journal* 28: 199-207.

Mack, R. 1971. The great African cattle plague epidemic of the 1890s. *Tropical Animal Health and Production* 2: 210-9.

Macpherson, C.N.L., Zeyhle, E. and Romig, T. 1984. An *Echinococcus* pilot control programme for north-west Turkana, Kenya. *Annals of Tropical Medicine and Parrasitology* 78: 188-192.

Macpherson, C.N.L., Wachira, T.M., Zeyhle, E., Romig, T. and Macpherson, C. 1986. Hydatid disease: research and control in Turkana. IV. The pilot control programme. *Transactions of the Royal Society of Tropical Medicine and Hygiene* 80: 196-200.

Macpherson, C.N.L., Craig, P.S., Romig, T. and Watschinger, H. 1989a. Observations on human echinococcosis (hydatidosis) and evaluation of transmission factors in the Maasai of northern Tanzania. *Annals of Tropical Medicine and Parasitology* 83: 489-497.

Macpherson, C.N.L., Spoerry, A., Zeyhle, E., Romig, T. and Gorfe, M. 1989b. Pastoralists and hydatid disease: an ultrasound scanning prevalence survey in East Africa. *Transactions of the Royal Society of Tropical Medicine and Hygiene* 83: 243-47.

Maddick, J. 1963. *Democracy, Decentralization and Development.* New York: Asia Publishing House.

Majok, A.A. 1988. Employment trend for graduates of College of Natural Resources and Environmental Studies (animal science specialization) of the University of Juba. Report to the Vice-Chancellor. Khartoum: University of Juba.

Majok, A.A. 1989. *Analyses of Baseline Survey Data on Rinderpest in Bahr el Ghazal Province, Southern Sudan.* Master of Preventive Veterinary Medicine thesis, University of California, Davis.

Majok, A.A., Zessin, K.-H., Baumann, M.P.O. and Farver, T.B. 1991. Analysis of baseline survey data on rinderpest in Bahr el Ghazal province with proposal of an improved vaccination strategy against rinderpest for southern Sudan. *Tropical Animal Health and Production* 23: 186-196.

Majok, A.A., Zessin, K.-H., Baumann, M.P.O. and Farver, T.B. 1993. Apparent prevalences of selected parasitic infections of cattle in Bahr el Ghazal province, southern Sudan. *Preventive Veterinary Medicine* 15: 25-33.

Malik, S.L. 1979. Comment, p. 845 in Simoons, F. 1979.

MANR. 1976. Resource management and research. In: *Sudan National Livestock Census and Resource Inventory, 1976.* Khartoum: Ministry of Agriculture and Natural Resources.

MAR. 1987. Animal resources economics administration. *Annual Bulletin of Animal Resources Statistics.* no. 7. Khartoum: Ministry of Animal Resources.

Margolis, H. 1984. *Selfishness, Altruism and Rationality.* Chicago: University of Chicago Press.

Martin, S.W., Meek, A.H. and Willeberg, P. 1987. *Veterinary Epidemiology. Principles and Methods.* Ames: Iowa State University Press.

Mascarenhas, A.C. 1977. Resettlement and desertification: the Wagogo of Dodomo District, Tanzania. *Economic Geography* 53: 376-380.

Mathias-Mundy, E. and McCorkle, C.M. 1989. *Ethnoveterinary Medicine: an Annotated Bibliography.* Bibliographies in Technology and Social Change 6. Ames: Iowa State University Research Foundation, Center for Indigenous Knowledge and Agricultural and Rural Development (CIKARD).

McCabe, J.T. 1987. Drought and recovery: livestock dynamics among Ngisonyoka Turkana of Kenya. *Human Ecology* 15: 371-389.

McCorkle, C.M. and Matthias-Mundy, E. 1992. Ethnoveterinary medicine in Africa. *Africa* 62: 59-93.

McCorkle, C.M., Matthias-Mundy, E. and Schillhorn van Veen, T.W. 1996. *Ethnoveterinary Research and Development*. London: ITDG Publications.

McDermott, J.J., Deng, K.A., Jayatileka, T.N. and El Jack, M.A. 1987. A cross-sectional cattle disease study in Kongo Rural Council, southern Sudan. 1. Prevalence estimates and age, sex and breed associations for brucellosis and contagious bovine pleuropneumonia. *Preventive Veterinary Medicine* 5: 111-23.

Mefit-Babtie Srl. 1983. Technical assistance contract for range ecology survey, livestock investigations and water supply. Executive Organ of the National Council for Development of the Jonglei canal area. Draft final report Vol. 8, Effects of the canal. Khartoum: Goverment of the Democratic Republic of the Sudan, Ministry for National Planning.

Mellaart, J. 1967. *Çatal Hüyük*. New York: McGraw-Hill.

Merker, M. 1910. *Die Masai*. Berlin: Dietrich Reimer.

Migot-Adholla, S.E. 1984. Rural development policy and equality. In: Barkan, J.D. (ed.), *Politics and Public Policy in Kenya and Tanzania*, 2nd ed. New York: Praeger.

MLFR/GTZ. 1990 *Somali Livestock Statistics, 1989/90*. Mogodishu: Ministry of Livestock, Forestry and Range/Deutsche Gesellschaft für Technische Zusammenarbeit.

Myers, J.A. 1940. *Man's Greatest Victory Over Tuberculosis*. Springfield, Illinois: Charles C Thomas.

Nair, K. 1961. *Blossoms in the Dust, the Human Element in Indian Development*. London: Gerald Duckworth.

Nchinda, T.C. 1976. Traditional and western medicine in Africa: collaboration or confrontation? *Tropical Doctor* 6: 133-5.

Nelson, H.D. 1983. *Sudan, a Country Study*. Foreign Affairs Studies. Washington, D.C.: American University.

Netting, R.M. 1981. *Balancing on an Alp*. Cambridge: Cambridge University Press.

North, R.F. 1694. Quotation searched and ascribed in the second electronic edition, *Oxford English Dictionary*. Oxford: Oxford University Press.

NRC/NAS. 1975. *Agricultural Production Efficiency*. Washington, D.C.: National Research Council-National Academy of Sciences.

NRC/NAS. 1982. *Specialized Veterinary Manpower Needs Through 1990*. Report of the Committee on Veterinary Medical Sciences. Washington, D.C.: National Research Council- National Academy of Sciences.

Ohta, I. 1984. Symptoms are classified into diagnostic categories: Turkana's view of livestock diseases. *African Study Monographs* 3 (supplementary issue): 71-93.

Okeny, K. 1986. Political structures and institutions in southern Sudan, 1820-1885. In: *The Role of Southern Sudanese People in the Building of the Modern Sudan*. University of Juba First Conference, February 26-28, 1985. Khartoum: Arrow Commercial Printing Press.

O'Leary, P. 1976. A five year review of human hydatid cyst disease in Turkana District, Kenya. *East African Medical Journal* 53: 540-4.

Ostrom, E. 1990. *Governing the Commons, the Evolution of Institutions for Collective Action.* Cambridge: Cambridge University Press.

Panico, L.A. 1986. *Development and Implementation of a Dual-Purpose Teaching and Diagnostic Laboratory for Developing Countries.* Master of Science thesis, School of Veterinary Medicine, University of California, Davis.

Pankhurst, R. 1966. The great Ethiopian famine of 1888-1892: a new assessment. *Journal of the History of Medicine* 21: 95-124, 271-93.

Pappaioanou, M., Schwabe, C.W. and Sard, D.M. 1977. An evolving pattern of human hydatid disease in the United States. *American Journal of Tropical Medicine and Hygiene* 26: 732-742.

Petrie, W.M.F. 1953. *Ceremonial Slate Palettes.* London: British School of Archeology, Egypt.

Prebble, J. 1966. *Glencoe, the Story of the Massacre.* London: Penguin Books.

Pritchard, W.P. 1988. Veterinary education in Africa: past, present and future. *Journal of Veterinary Medical Education* 15: 13-6.

Pritchard, W.P., Rhode, E.A. and Schwabe, C.W. 1975. *Report of a Mission to Advise on the Development of a Faculty of Veterinary Medicine at the University of Riyadh in Saudi Arabia.* Davis: University of California, School of Veterinary Medicine.

Pritchard, W.P., Doyle, J.J., Gitzhugh, H., de Haan, C., Lynam, J., MacGillivray, I., Masiga, W., Peberdy, J., Sawadogo, A. and Tacher, G. 1992. *Assessment of Animal Agriculture in Sub-Saharan Africa.* Morilton, Arkansas: Winrock International Institute for Agricultural Development.

Provost, A. 1981. In: Karstad, L., Nestel, B. and Graham, M. (eds.), *Wildlife Disease Research and Economic Development.* Ottawa: International Development Research Center, September 8-9, 1980.

Putt, S.N.H., Shaw, A.P.M., Woods, A.J., Tyler, L. and James, A.D. 1987. *Veterinary Epidemiology and Economics in Africa. A Manual for Use in the Design and Appraisal of Livestock Health Policy.* Reading: Veterinary Epidemiology and Economics Research Unit, Department of Agriculture, University of Reading.

Regional Ministry of Finance and Economic Affairs. 1984. *Proceedings of the Conference on Development in the Southern Region of the Sudan,* 5-8 April 1983, Juba.

Regional Ministry of Finance and Economic Planning. 1977. *The Democratic Republic of the Sudan, Southern Region. The Six Year Plan of Economic and Social Development 1977-1982/83.* Juba: Directorate of Planning.

Rifkin, J. 1992. *Beyond Beef--The Rise and Fall of the Cattle Culture.* New York: Dutton.

Rigby, P. 1969. *Cattle and Kinship Among the Gogo.* Ithaca, New York: Cornell University Press.

Riggs, F.W. 1957. Industria and agraria--toward the typology of comparative administration. In: Siffin, W.J. (ed.), *Toward the Comparative Study of Public Administration.* Bloomington: Indiana University.

Riggs, F.W. 1973. *Prismatic Society Revisited.* Morristown, New Jersy: General Learning Press.

Robertshaw, P. 1989. The development of pastoralism in East Africa. In: Clutton-Brock, J. (ed.), *The Walking Larder--Patterns of Domestication, Pastoralism and Predation.* London: Unwin Hyman.

Roles, N.C. 1967. Tribal surgery in East Africa during the 19th century. Part 2. Therapeutic surgery. *East African Medical Journal* 44: 17-30.

Rondinelli, D.A. 1981. Administrative decentralization and economic development: the Sudan's experiment with devolution. *The Journal of African Studies* 19: 595-624.

Roscoe, J. 1915. *The Northern Bantu, an Account of Some Central African Tribes of the Uganda Protectorate.* Cambridge: Cambridge University Press.

Rossiter, P.B., Jesset, D.M., Wafula, J.S. Karstad, L., Chema, S., Taylor, W.P., Rowe, L., Nyange, J.C., Otaru, M, Mumbala, M. and Scott, G.R. 1983. Re-emergence of rinderpest as a threat in East Africa since 1979. *Veterinary Record* 113: 459-61.

Rothchild, D. 1988. Hegemony and state softness: some variations in elite responses. In: Errgas, Z. (ed.), *The African State in Transition.* Hampshire: Macmillan.

Rothchild, D. and Curry, R. 1978. *Scarcity, Choice and Public Policy in Middle Africa.* Berkeley: University of California Press.

Salzman, P.C. (ed.). 1980. *When Nomads Settle--Processes of Sedentarization as Adaptation and Response.* New York: Praeger.

Salzman, P.C. (ed.). 1982. *Contemporary Nomadic and Pastoral Peoples: Africa and Latin America.* Studies in Third World Societies Publication no. 17. Williamsburg, Virginia: College of William and Mary, Department of Anthropology.

Sandford, D. 1981. Pastoralists as animal health workers: the range development project in Ethiopia. Pastoral Network Paper 12c. London: Overseas Development Institute.

Sandford, S. 1983. *Management of Pastoral Development in the Third World.* New York: John Wiley and Sons.

Schneider, H.K. 1957. The subsistence role of cattle among the Pakot in East Africa. *American Anthropologist* 59: 278-99.

Scholz, F. 1986. Resourcennutzung und Resourcenerhaltung. In: DSE (ed.), *Interaktion Tier und Umwelt.* Expertengespräch. 11-14 Dez. 1985 in Feldafing: 113-122. (Original not seen; quoted by Janzen, 1993.)

Schwabe, C.L. 1989. The ACCOMPLISH Joint Immunization Project--An Evaluation of Immunization Coverage and Willingness to Pay for Vaccination. Consultant's Report to UNICEF, New York.

Schwabe, C.L. and Schwartz, J.D. 1992. Immunization Sustainabilty: An Institutional Economic Perspective with Special Reference to the Problems of Financial Sustainability in the Philippines and Kenya. Paper presented at the Conference on Consequences on EPI Sustainability in Africa of the New Immunization Goals and of the Evolution of the World Vaccine Market, International Children's Center, Paris, 8-10 December 1992.

Schwabe, C.L., Schwabe, C.W. and Basta, S.S. 1996. Vaccination of Children and Cattle in Pastoralist Africa: Practical Intersectoral Cooperation (in preparation).

Schwabe, C.W. 1964. *Veterinary Medicine and Human Health.* 1st ed. Baltimore: Williams and Wilkins.

Schwabe, C.W. 1967. Are our veterinary schools really equal to their tasks? *Michigan State University Veterinarian* (Fall): 9-15. (Reprinted in PAHO 1969. *Symposium on Education in Veterinary Public Health and Preventive Medicine.* Scientific Publication no. 189. Washington, D.C.: Pan American Health Organization.)

Schwabe, C.W. 1970. Graduate study for regulatory veterinarians. *Proceedings of the 73rd Annual Meeting, United States Animal Health Association*: 18-30.

Schwabe, C.W. 1974. Veterinarians on faculties of human medicine. *Journal of the American Veterinary Medical Association* 165: 183-185.

Schwabe, C.W. 1976a. Mankind's most basic needs--how can the veterinary profession more meaningfully respond? (Reprint of Opening Address for the First World Veterinarians' Day). *Journal of South African Veterinary Association* 47: 159-160.

Schwabe, C.W. 1976b. On treating political animals. *Journal of the American Veterinary Medical Association* 168: 329-334.

Schwabe, C.W. 1978a. *Cattle, Priests and Progress in Medicine.* 4th Spink Lectures on Comparative Medicine. Minneapolis: University of Minnesota Press.

Schwabe, C.W. 1978b. Holy cow--provider or parasite? A problem for humanists. Franklin Lecture on Science and Humanities. *Southern Humanities Review* 13: 251-78.

Schwabe, C.W. 1980. Animal disease control. Part II. Newer methods, with possibility for their application in the Sudan. *Sudan Journal of Veterinary Science and Animal Husbandry* 21: 55-65.

Schwabe, C.W. 1981. Animal diseases and primary health care: intersectoral challenges. *WHO Chronicle* 35: 227-232.

Schwabe, C.W. 1982. The current epidemiological revolution in veterinary medicine. Part I. *Preventive Veterinary Medicine* 1: 5-15.

Schwabe, C.W. 1984a. Drinking cow's milk: the most intense man-animal bond. In: Anderson, R.K., Hart, B.L. and Hart, L.A. (eds.), *The Pet Connection--Its Influence on Our Daily Life and Health.* Minneapolis: University of Minnesota Center to Study Human-Animal Relationships and Environments.

Schwabe, C.W. 1984b *Veterinary Medicine and Human Health.* 3rd ed. Baltimore: Williams and Wilkins.

Schwabe, C.W. 1986. Current status of hydatid disease: a zoonosis of increasing importance. In: Thompson, R.C.A. (ed.), *The Biology of Echinococcus and Hydatid Disease.* London: George Allen and Unwin.

Schwabe, C.W. 1987. Dinka "spirits," cattle and communion. *Journal of Cultural Geography* 7: 117-26.

Schwabe, C.W. 1991a. Helminth zoonoses in African perspective. In: Macpherson, C.N.L. and Craig, P.S. (eds.), *Parasitic Helminths and Zoonoses in Africa.* London: Unwin Hyman.

Schwabe, C.W. 1991b. History of the scientific relationships of veterinary public health. *Office International des Epizooties Revue Scientifique et Technique* 10: 933-949.

Schwabe, C.W. 1993a. The current epidemiological revolution in veterinary medicine. Part II. *Preventive Veterinary Medicine* 18: 3-16.

Schwabe, C.W. 1993b. Interactions between human and veterinary medicine: past, present and future. In: Mitchell, A.R. (ed.), *History of the Healing Professions: Parallels Between Veterinary and Medical History,* vol. 3 of the Advancement of Veterinary Science, the Royal Veterinary College Bicentenary Symposium Series. London: CAB International.

Schwabe, C.W. 1994. Animals in the ancient world. In: Manning, A. and Serpel, J. (eds.), *Animals and Society--Changing Perspectives*. London: Routledge.

Schwabe, C.W. 1996. Ancient and modern veterinary beliefs, practices and practitioners among Nile Valley peoples. In: McCorkle, C.M., Matthias-Mundy, E. and Schillhorn van Veen, T.W. (eds.), *Ethnoveterinary Research and Development*. London: ITDG Publications.

Schwabe, C.W. and Kuojok, I.M. 1981. Practices and beliefs of the traditional Dinka healer in relation to provision of modern medical and veterinary services for the southern Sudan. *Human Organization* 40: 231-8.

Schwabe, C.W. Riemann, H.P. and Franti, C.E. 1977. *Epidemiology in Veterinary Practice*. Philadelphia: Lea and Febiger.

Schwabe, C.W. and Ruppanner, R. 1972. Animal diseases as contributors to human hunger--problems of control. *World Review of Nutrition and Dietetics* 15: 185-224.

Schwabe, C.W. and Schwabe, C.L. 1990. Veterinary cooperation for delivery of primary health care to pastoralists. *Community Health Association of Southern Africa Journal of Comprehensive Health* 1: 116-20.

Scrimshaw, N.S. and Taylor, L. 1980. Food. *Scientific American* 243: 78-88.

Seligman, C.G. 1932. Egyptian influence in Negro Africa. In: *Studies Presented to F.L. Griffith*. London: Egypt Exploration Society.

Seligman, C.G. and Seligman, B.Z. 1932. *Pagan Tribes of the Nilotic Sudan*. London: George Routledge and Sons.

Sen, A. 1981. *Poverty and Famines--An Essay on Entitlement and Deprivation*. Oxford: Clarendon Press.

Shanmugaratnam, N., Vedeldi, T., Mossige, A. and Bovin, M. 1991. Resource management and pastoral institution building in the West African Sahel: Report to the World Bank. Aas, Norway: NORAGRIC.

Shaw, T. and Colville, G. 1950. Colonial Office report of the Nigerian livestock mission. London: H.M. Stationery Office (Original not seen; see Goldschmidt, W. 1980. The failure of pastoral economic development programmes in Africa. In: *The Future of Pastoral Peoples*. Proceedings of a conference held in Nairobi, Kenya 4-8 August 1980. Ottawa: International Development Research Centre).

SIDA. 1992. *A Way Out of the Debt Trap. Proposals to Relieve the Debt of the Poorest and Most Indebted Countries*. Stockholm: Swedish International Development Authority.

Simoons, F. 1970. The traditional limits of milking and milk use in southern Asia. *Anthropos* 65: 547-593.

Simoons, F. 1971. The antiquity of dairying in Asia and Africa. *Geographical Review* 61: 431-439.

Simoons, F. 1979. Questions in the sacred cow controversy. *Current Anthropology* 20: 467-493.

Sinclair, A.R.E. and Fryxell, J.M. 1985. The Sahel of Africa: ecology of a disaster. *Canadian Journal of Zoology* 63: 987-994.

Sivard, R.L. 1990-1994. *World Military and Social Expenditures.* (Annual series). Leesburg, Virginia: World Priorities, Inc.

Sollod, A..E. 1990. Rainfall, biomass and the pastoral economy of Niger: assessing the impact of drought. *Journal of Arid Environments* 18: 97-107.

Sollod, A.E. 1991. Climate-driven development policy for Sahelian pastoralists. In: Stone, J.C. (ed.), *Pastoral Economies in Africa and Long-Term Responses to Drought.* Aberdeen: University of Aberdeen, African Studies Group.

Sollod, A.E. and Stem, C. 1991. Appropriate animal health information systems for nomadic and transhumant livestock populations in Africa. *Office International des Epizooties Revue Scientifique et Technique* 10: 89-101.

Sollod, A.E., Wolfgang, K. and Knight, J.A. 1984. Veterinary anthropology: interdisciplinary methods in pastoral systems research. In: Simpson, J.R. and Evangelou, P. (eds.), *Livestock Development in Subsaharan Africa--Constraints, Prospects, Policy.* Boulder, Colorado: Westview Press.

Sugiyama, F. 1980. The status of the veterinary profession in Japan. *Veterinary Record* 106: 554-6.

Tacher, G., Jahnke, H.E., Rojat, D. and Keil, P. 1988. Livestock development and economic productivity in tsetse-infested Africa. In: *African Trypanotolerant Livestock Network: Livestock Production in Tsetse Affected Areas in Africa.* Nairobi: International Livestock Centre for Africa.

Tepilit, O.S. 1978. A Maasai looks at the ecology of Maasailand. *Munger Africana Library Notes.* Issue no. 42. Pasadena: California Institute of Technology.

Terry, L.L. 1963. A century's progress in public health. *Journal of the American Veterinary Medical Association* 142: 1287-1291.

Titherington, G.W. 1927. The Raik Dinka of Bahr el Ghazal province. *Sudan Notes and Records* 10: 159-209.

Toure, O. 1988. The pastoral environment of northern Senegal. *Review of African Political Economy* 42: 32-8.

UNICEF. 1985. *The State of the World's Children, 1984.* New York: United Nations Childrens Fund.

University of Juba. 1984. *Calender, 1984-1986.* Juba, Sudan: The Catholic Printing Institute.

USDA. 1990. *World Agriculture: Trade and Indicators, 1970-89.* U.S. Department of Agriculture Statistical Bulletin 815.

Van Onselen, C. 1972. Reaction to rinderpest in southern Africa. *Journal of African History* 13: 473-88.

Voll, J.O. and Voll, S.P. 1985. *The Sudan: Unity and Diversity in a Multicultural State.* Boulder, Colorado: Westview Press.

von Lengerken, H. and von Lengerken, E. 1955. *Ur, Hausrind und Mensch*. Berlin: Deutsche Akademie Landwirtschafts Wissenschaften.

Welsh, B.W.W. and Butorin, P. 1990. *Dictionary of Development*. New York: Garland Publishing.

West, G.P. 1961. *A History of the Overseas Veterinary Services*. Part One. London: British Veterinary Association.

Whitehead, A.N. 1925. *Science and the Modern World*. New York: Macmillan.

WHO. 1954. *Expert Committee on Public Health Administration*. Technical Report Series no. 83. Geneva: World Health Organization.

WHO. 1962. *Expert Committee on Health Laboratory Services*. Third Report. Technical Report Series no. 236. Geneva: World Health Organization.

WHO. 1972. Report of Consultation of Multi-Professional Training of Health Personnel, 30 November-4 December 1970. WHO/EDUC/72.153. Geneva: World Health Organization.

WHO. 1989. *Report on Intersectoral Cooperation in Veterinary Public Health*. Geneva: World Health Organization.

WHO/FAO. 1963. *World Directory of Veterinary Schools*. Geneva: World Health Organization.

WHO/FAO. 1975. *The Veterinary Contribution to Public Health Practice*. Report of the WHO/FAO Expert Committee on Veterinary Public Health. Technical Report Series no. 573. Geneva: World Health Organization and Rome: UN Food and Agricultural Organization.

WHO/FAO. 1982. *WHO/FAO Expert Committee on Bacterial and Viral Zoonoses*. Technical Report Series no 682. Geneva: World Health Organization and Rome: UN Food and Agricultural Organization.

WHO/ILO. 1962. *Expert Committee on Occupational Health*. Fourth Report. Geneva: International Labour Organization and World Health Organization.

WHO/UNICEF. 1982. Report of the WHO/UNICEF Mission for Evaluation of the Health Development Programme in the Sudan, 14-29 November 1981. EM/NHS/7, EM/PHC/15.

Wienpahl, J. 1984. Turkana herds under environmental stress. *Nomadic Peoples* 16: 59-87.

Williamson, O. 1991. The economics of governance: framework and implications. In: Furubotin, E. and Richter, R. (eds.), *The New Institutional Economics*. College Station, Texas: Texas A. & M. University Press.

World Veterinary Association. 1991. *World Veterinary Directory*. Madrid: Imprenta Fareso.

Worldwatch Institute. 1990-1995. *Worldwatch Papers* (series). Washington, D.C.: Worldwatch Institute.

Wray, J.R. 1958. Note on human hydatid disease in Kenya. *East African Medical Journal* 35: 37-39.

Yongo-Bure, B. 1983. *Background to the Current Economic Conditions in the Southern Sudan*. Halifax, Canada: Dalhousie University.

Yongo-Bure, B. 1985. The first decade of development in the southern Sudan. Paper presented at the Conference on North-South Relations Since the Addis Ababa Agreement, 6-9 March 1985, Khartoum, Sudan.

Young, F.M. 1979. *The Use of Sacrificial Ideas in Greek Christian Writers from the New Testament to John Chrysostom.* Cambridge, Massachusetts: Philadelphia Patristic Foundation.

Zessin, K.-H. 1991. *Ecology, Production and Health of Small Ruminant Flocks in Somalia.* Ph.D. dissertation, School of Veterinary Medicine, University of California, Davis.

Zessin, K.-H. and Baumann, M.P.O. 1982. *Report on the Livestock Disease Survey, Bahr el Ghazal Province, Sudan.* Berlin: Deutsche Gesellschaft für Technische Zusammenarbeit.

Zessin, K.-H., Baumann, M.P.O., Schwabe, C.W. and Thorburn, M. 1985. Analyses of baseline surveillance data on contagious bovine pleuropneumonia in southern Sudan. *Preventive Veterinary Medicine* 3: 371-89.

Zessin, K.-H. and Carpenter, T.E. 1985. Benefit-cost analysis of an epidemiological approach to provision of veterinary services in the Sudan. *Preventive Veterinary Medicine* 3: 323-37.

Zessin, K.-H. and Farah, D.A. 1993. The Central Rangelands Development Project (CRDP)--an approach for the improvement of rangeland conditions and income generation in a pastoral area. In: Baumann, M.P.O., Janzen, J. and Schwartz, H.J. (eds.)., *Pastoral Production in Central Somalia.* Eschborn, Germany: Deutsche Gesellschaft für Technische Zusammenarbeit.

Zessin, K.-H., Heuer, C. and Schrecke, W. 1993. The Central Rangelands Development Project (CRDP)--veterinary component. In: Baumann, M.P.O., Janzen, J. and Schwartz, H.J. (eds.)., *Pastoral Production in Central Somalia.* Eschborn, Germany: Deutsche Gesellschaft für Technische Zusammenarbeit.

Zessin, K.-H. and Schwartz, H.J. 1993. Simulation models for impact of drought on small ruminant flocks in central Somalia. In: Baumann, M.P.O., Janzen, J. and Schwartz, H.J. (eds.)., *Pastoral Production in Central Somalia.* Eschborn, Germany: Deutsche Gesellschaft für Technische Zusammenarbeit.

# INDEX

## About the Authors

AGGREY AYUEN MAJOK is a Dinka pastoralist from the southern Sudan. With veterinary training in the University of Khartoum and graduate degrees from British and American universities, he pursued dual careers in government service and Academe. Formerly Director of Veterinary Services for the southern region of the Sudan and Senior Lecturer on the Faculty of Natural Resources and Environmental Studies of the University of Juba, he has also worked in several other African countries, most recently as chairman of the Department of Clinical Veterinary Studies in the University of Zimbabwe.

CALVIN W. SCHWABE, Professor of Epidemiology at the University of California, Davis and San Francisco, founded and chaired academic departments in schools of veterinary medicine, public health and medicine in the United States and abroad. An international authority on control of tropical and parasitic diseases, he has played a leading role within the World Health Organization and elsewhere in fostering cooperative efforts between the medical and veterinary professions.

ISBN 0-89789-477-4

EAN

9 780897 894777

90000>

HARDCOVER BAR CODE